Andrew J. DuBrin
Professor of Behavioral Sciences
College of Business
Rochester Institute of Technology
Rochester, New York

Human Relations for Career and Personal Success

Second Edition

Prentice Hall
Englewood Cliffs, New Jersey

Library of Congress Cataloging-in-Publication Data

DuBrin, Andrew
  Human relations for career and personal success.

  Includes bibliographies and indexes.
  1. Success in business. 2. Organizational behavior.
3. Interpersonal relations. 4. Psychology, Industrial.
I. Title.
HF5386.D768 1988   650.1'3   87-29247
ISBN 0-13-445537-1

Editorial/production supervision and
  interior design: Nancy Follender, Fred Dahl
Cover design: Diane Saxe
Manufacturing buyer: Ed O'Dougherty

 © 1988 by Prentice-Hall, Inc.
A Division of Simon & Schuster
Englewood Cliffs, New Jersey 07632

Printed in the United States of America

10 9 8 7 6 5 4 3

ISBN 0-13-445537-1

Prentice-Hall International (UK) Limited, *London*
Prentice-Hall of Australia Pty. Limited, *Sydney*
Prentice-Hall Canada Inc., *Toronto*
Prentice-Hall Hispanoamericana, S.A., *Mexico*
Prentice-Hall of India Private Limited, *New Delhi*
Prentice-Hall of Japan, Inc., *Tokyo*
Prentice-Hall of Southeast Asia Pte. Ltd., *Singapore*
Editora Prentice-Hall do Brasil, Ltda., *Rio de Janeiro*

To Drew, Douglas, Melanie, and Andrew
May you all enjoy career and personal success

Contents

4   Dealing with Stress and Burnout, 77

PART TWO
DEALING EFFECTIVELY WITH OTHER PEOPLE

5   Communicating with People, 109

6   Being Assertive with Others, 143

7   Getting Along with Your Boss, 171

Preface

The purpose of this book remains the same as that of the first edition: to show you how you can become more effective in your work and personal life through knowledge of and skill in human relations. The application of such knowledge is illustrated by numerous case examples.

A major theme of this book is that success in work and success in personal life are related to each other. Success on the job often leads to success in personal life, and success in personal life can lead to job success. You need to deal effectively with yourself and other people in order to progress in your career. Dealing effectively with people is also valuable in personal life. As a result, human relations continues to be an important part of the curriculum in many programs of study including general business, office practices, secretarial studies, computer science, data processing, sales training, and trades programs such as auto service and equipment repair.

One major audience for this book is students who will meet human relations situations in business and in personal life. The text is designed for use in human relations courses taught in colleges, vocational-technical schools, business schools, and other postsecondary schools. Another major audience for this book is managerial, professional, and technical workers who are forging ahead in their careers. (Readers of the first edition proved to be equally split among students and full-time career people.)

Organization of the Book

The text is divided into four parts, reflecting the major issues in human relations. Part I covers four aspects of understanding and managing yourself: Chapter 1 focuses on self-understanding and the interrelationship of career and personal success; Chapter 2 explains how to use goal setting and other methods of self-motivation to improve your chances for success; Chapter 3 explains the basics of solving problems and making decisions with an emphasis on creativity; and Chapter 4 deals with managing stress and burnout.

Part II examines the heart of human relations—dealing effectively with other people. The topics in chapters 5 through 9, respectively, are: communicating with people; being assertive, getting along with your boss, getting along with co-workers, and handling conflict with others.

Part III provides information to help career-oriented persons capitalize on their education, experience, talent, and ambition. The topics of chapters 10 through 13 are: choosing a first or later career, finding a suitable job, developing good work habits, and getting ahead in your career. Chapter 14 is about the related topics of developing self-confidence and becoming a leader.

Part IV, "Managing Your Personal Life," is divided into two chapters. Chapter 15 offers realistic tips on managing personal finances. Chapter 16 offers suggestions for enhancing your personal social and family life, including how to find new friends and keep a personal relationship vibrant.

Human Relations for Career and Personal Success is both a text and a workbook of experiential exercises including role plays and self-examination quizzes related to the text. (An experiential exercise allows for leading by doing, along with guided instruction.) Each chapter contains one or more exercises and ends with a human relations case problem. The experiential exercises can all be completed during a class session. In addition, they emphasize human interaction and thinking and minimize paperwork.

Changes in the Second Edition

The second edition reflects an updating and expansion rather than a reorganization or reorientation of the first edition. New topics include: self-motivation techniques in addition to goal setting, networking, VDT stress, handling yourself in meetings, making constructive use of anger, business manners and etiquette, and getting along with an intolerable boss. One-half of the case examples and case problems are new to the second edition. New features include role plays for every chapter, additional cartoons (in response to audience demand), and thought-provoking questions at various places in the text.

The instructor's manual for this text is substantially enlarged and improved. It contains over 400 test questions, chapter outline and lecture notes, answers to discussion questions and case problems, and comments about the exercises. In addition, the manual includes step-by-step instruction for the use of Computer-Assisted Scenario Analysis (CASA).

CASA is a user-friendly way of using any word processing program with any computer to assist in analyzing cases. The student enters an existing case into the computer, and then analyzes it by answering the case questions in the text. Next, the student makes up a new scenario or twist to the case, and **enters this scenario in bold into the case.** The case questions are reanalyzed in light of this new scenario. Any changes in the answers are **printed in bold.** CASA gives the student experience in a creative application of word processing. Equally important, it helps students develop a "what-if" point of view in solving human relations problems.

ACKNOWLEDGMENTS

A book of this nature cannot be written and published without the cooperation of many people. My thanks go first to my editorial team at Prentice-Hall, Catherine Rossbach, Susan Jacob, and Julianne Eriksen. My outside reviewers, H. Ralph Todd, Jr., of American River College, Ruth V. Kellar of Indiana Vocational Technical College, Pamela Simon of Baker College, and Mary Dean Brewer of the Rochester Institute of Technology, provided many helpful suggestions for improving the manuscript. The helpful comments from instructors who adopted the first edition of this book and from readers were also much appreciated.

Andrew J. DuBrin
Rochester, New York

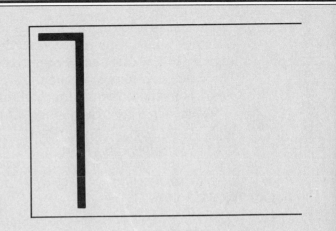

Human Relations and Yourself

Learning Objectives

After studying the information and doing the exercises in this chapter you should be able to:

- Explain the meaning of human relations
- Pinpoint how work and personal life influence each other
- Know specific methods of gaining self-understanding
- Explain how self-acceptance improves the self-concept
- Become aware of your level of self disclosure

Mark, a television camera technician, works effectively with the people in the TV studio. (Effective in this sense means achieving mutually compatible goals with other people, not being overly nice, punitive, or manipulative.) He is quiet, but sincere and hardworking. Mark's job doesn't require much conversation because he is always caught up in his camera work. Off the job, Mark is a loner. He would like to make friends, but he doesn't take the initiative to reach out to people. Mark prefers work to off-hours, largely because he deals with people better in a TV studio than in a social setting.

Linda, a nurse's aide, has difficulty dealing with people in the hospital. She resents the low wages she is making as a nurse's aide and sometimes takes it out on patients, nurses, attendants, and physicians. Linda's supervisor wrote on her last performance report that "Linda is too short with people to last very long with us." Off the job, Linda's personality becomes more positive. She can be mildly sarcastic at times, but her friends realize that Linda's sharp wit is a small price to pay for her worthwhile friendship.

Tony, the manager of a fast food franchise restaurant, is a likable young man who interacts well with people both on and off the job. Tony is only twenty years old while several of the people who work for him are in their mid-twenties. As one of them puts it, "Who cares if Tony is young? The guy is a natural leader." Despite Tony's irregular working hours, he has many friends with whom he shares his free time. His friends include day people and night people. Tony's friends are particularly impressed with his smooth and confident manner and his ability to be a good listener at the same time.

The three people just described tell us something about the meaning of **human relations.** Mark practices a limited type of human relations. He deals effectively with people primarily on the job. Linda is the opposite. She is effective with people primarily in social settings. Tony practices the type of human relations emphasized in this book—he is effective with people in both work and personal settings.

The term human relations has several meanings. In this context human relations is taken to be the art of using systematic knowledge about human behavior to improve your personal and job effectiveness. In other words, you accomplish more in dealing with people—whether in a social or job setting—by relying on guidelines developed by psychologists, counselors, or other human relations specialists.

This book presents a wide variety of suggestions and guidelines for improving your personal relationships both on and off the job. Most of them are based on systematic knowledge about human behavior. Our main concern, however, will be with the tips and guidelines themselves, not the methods by which these ideas were discovered. Most

people reading this book will be doing so to improve their careers. Therefore, the book centers around relationships with people in a job setting. Keep in mind from the outset that human relationships on and off the job have much in common.

HOW WORK AND PERSONAL LIFE INFLUENCE EACH OTHER

If we followed the cases of Mark and Linda over an extended period of time, we would probably discover certain similarities in their relationships with people on and off the job. As Mark continued to develop confidence in his role as a camera technician, he would slowly become more effective in handling people off the job. Impressed with his job skills, a few of his co-workers might begin to invite him to social gatherings. As Linda became increasingly bitter about her job, some of her bitterness would probably spill over into her personal relationships. Her occasional sarcasm might turn into a steady flow of verbal abuse toward others.

Your Job Can Affect Your Physical and Mental Health

In other words, the satisfactions you achieve on the job contribute to your general life satisfactions. Conversely, if you suffer from chronic dissatisfaction on the job, your general satisfaction with life will begin to decline. Disappointments on the job have been shown to cause marital relationships to suffer. Frustrated on the job, many people take to feuding with their spouses. Although the behavior of a spouse beater is not to be condoned, it does indicate that job satisfaction influences mental health. Good feelings about yourself generally contribute to good mental health. Bad feelings about yourself generally contribute to poor mental health.

An unsatisfying job can also affect physical health, primarily through stress (see Chapter 4). Intense job dissatisfaction may even lead to heart disease, ulcers, and skin problems, for example. Research has shown that people who liked their jobs outlived people whose attitude toward their jobs was strongly negative.[1] Thus job satisfaction appears to have the potential of adding years to people's lives.

What bearing does the above information have on relationships with people? Simply, your relationships with people heavily influence whether or not you like your job. Other factors—such as the nature of your work, your wages, and your general physical working conditions—are also important of course. Yet, how well you like (and get along with) other people on the job also influences your level of satisfaction.

The quality of your relationships with people off the job can influence the quality of your relationships with people in the office, plant, laboratory, or mill. If, for example, there is intense conflict in your family, you might be so upset on the job that you will be unable to form good relationships with your co-workers. Similarly, if you have a healthy, rewarding personal life, it will be easier for you to form good working relationships on the job. People you meet on the job will find it pleasant to relate to a seemingly positive and untroubled person.

HUMAN RELATIONS BEGINS WITH SELF-UNDERSTANDING

A widely accepted principle of human behavior is that before you can understand other people, you must understand yourself. Similarly, before you can deal effectively with others, you must learn to deal effectively with yourself. Every reader of this book already knows something about himself or herself. An important starting point in learning more about yourself is self-examination.

Suppose that instead of being about human relations, this book were about roller skating. The reader would obviously need to know what other skaters do right and do wrong. But the basic principles of roller skating cannot be fully grasped unless they are seen in relation to your own style of skating. Seeing a film of your skating, for example, would be helpful. You might also ask other people for comments and suggestions about your skating.

Similarly, to achieve **self-understanding,** you must gather valid information about yourself. Achieving self-understanding and personal improvement is a primary goal of the modern-day human potential movement. One example of this movement's activities is a personal growth group in which the group members, guided by a human relations specialist, receive encouragement and support from each other. Remember that every time you read a self-help book, take a personality quiz, or receive an evaluation of your work from a boss or instructor, you are gaining some self-knowledge.

Here we discuss six types of information that contribute to self-understanding: (1) general information about human behavior, (2) feedback from other people in natural settings, (3) feedback from personal growth groups, (4) feedback from self-examination exercises, (5) feedback from superiors, and (6) insights gathered in psychotherapy and counseling.

General Information about Human Behavior

As you learn about people in general, you should also be gaining knowledge about yourself. Therefore most of the information in this book is presented in a form that should be useful to you personally. Whenever general information is presented, it is your responsibility to relate such information to your particular case. Chapter 9, for example, discusses some causes of conflicts in personal relationships. One such general cause is limited resources; that is, not everyone can have what he or she wants. See how this general principle applies to you:

"That's why I've been so short with Melissa lately. She was the one given the new word processor, while I have to use the same old one."

In relating facts and observations about people in general to yourself, be careful not to misapply the information. Feedback from other people will help you avoid the pitfalls of introspection (looking into oneself).

Feedback from People in Natural Settings

Feedback is information that tells you how well you have performed. An eighteen-year-old man grew one notch in self-confidence when co-workers at the restaurant where he is employed began to call him "Lightning." He was given this nickname because of the rapidity

with which he clears tables. His experience illustrates that a valuable source of information for self-understanding is what the significant people in your life think of you. Although feedback of this type might make you feel uncomfortable, when it is consistent, it accurately reflects how you are perceived by others. Many places of work offer their employees systematic feedback as part of the routine evaluation of job performance.

To supplement the feedback you receive in job performance reviews, ask people their opinion of you. One man enrolled in a human relations course obtained valuable information about himself from a questionnaire he sent to fifteen people. His directions were:

> I am hoping that you can help me with one of the most important assignments of my life. I want to obtain a candid picture of how I am seen by others. What they think are my strengths, weaknesses, good points, and bad points. Any other observations about me as an individual would also be welcome.
>
> Write down your thoughts on the enclosed sheet of paper. The information that you provide me will help me develop a plan for personal improvement that I am writing for a course in human relations. Mail the form back to me in the enclosed envelope. It is not necessary for you to sign the form.

A few skeptics will argue that friends never give you a true picture of yourself, but rather say flattering things about you because they value your friendship. Experience has shown, however, that if you emphasize the importance of their opinions, most people will give you a few constructive suggestions. You also have to appear and be sincere. Since not everyone's comments will be helpful, you may have to sample a number of people.

Feedback from Personal Growth Groups

One method of acquiring self-understanding is to attend a personal growth group (also referred to as an encounter group). A **personal growth group** is a small training group in which participants are encouraged to express their feelings and give each other emotional support. Exhibit 1–1 describes a method that will help you experience what it is like to be part of a growth group. Personal growth groups are conducted by school counseling centers, YMCAs, YWCAs, Jewish Community Centers, and mental health professionals in private practice.

As a starting point in the growth group, you usually receive feedback on how you are perceived by other members of the group. Such perceptions by others have a positive impact on self-understanding. The self-understanding may lead to personal growth, as will the emotional support you receive from others in the group. Feedback can occur at any phase in the life of the personal growth group. A sample of the type of feedback that took place at an early stage of a growth group is presented next.

EXHIBIT 1–1   THE ICE-BREAKER

The class is arranged in one large circle, or two or three small circles. One circle at a time participates while the other class members observe. Proceeding in a clockwise direction starting with the person seated to the left of the instructor, each member tells the group several things:

1. Why I am taking this course
2. What I hope to get out of this course
3. The title of my most recent job
4. My favorite hobby or interest
5. My three strongest points, attributes, or skills
6. What I dislike most

After this brief presentation, the person asks the group, "What question would you like to ask me?"

After everyone has taken a turn, the class will hold a general discussion of their reaction to this exercise. For example, was it worthwhile? What did you learn about people? How did you feel when it was your turn? How did you feel waiting for your turn?

GROUP LEADER: To get things started, everybody will tell everybody else what kind of first impression they have made. We'll do this in a clockwise manner, starting with Jeanne sitting to my left. Everybody, beginning with Jack, will tell Jeanne what he or she thinks of her. Of course, if Jeanne has made absolutely no impression on you, if she is the invisible woman, you can pass (group laughs). Okay, Jack, look Jeanne straight in the eye and tell her what you think.

JACK: My first impression of you, Jeanne, is that you're kind of cool. The type of woman I'd like to know better.

MERYL: Jeanne, I would guess that you have a lot of friends. No doubt you are a nice person. But those eyes of yours give me something to worry about. They look a little shifty. I wouldn't trust you fully until I got to know you better. (Nervous laughter from the group.)

MAGGIE: I think you try to give the impression that you are very casual. But underneath, you have worked very hard to create that impression. I know for sure that your jeans cost about three times as much as the usual type you find in the discount store. I'll bet you worked hours on your hair to achieve that casual look.

GEORGE: Don't take Maggie too seriously. I think you're one fine-looking woman. You also give me the impression of being very intelligent. I like the way you talk. I think you should "go for it" in life. There's nothing stopping you.

TERRY: I can see those good points about you, too. I think the real you, however, is a fun-lover. I can see Jeanne out on a sailboat taking long weekends. I think that underneath you're the party type. Am I wrong?

CAROL: So long as we're being candid, I'll make this comment. You're kind of pushy in a nice way. I noticed it was you who manipulated things so you could be right next to the group leader. You've also got this look about you that you think you're superior to other people. Maybe it's that you're a natural leader.

JEFF: It's tough to be last. All the good comments have been used up. I'll have to go along with the good comments made about Jeanne. She's terrific. I wish I wasn't already engaged. Jeanne would be a lot of fun to go out with.

GROUP LEADER: Jeanne, tell us how you feel about what has just happened to you.

JEANNE: I feel terrific. Thanks for all the compliments. Even your negative comments were helpful. Maybe I do come on a little too strong at times. I like to be on top of situations. This is the first time anything like this has ever happened to me. Thanks again.

How might this session have benefited Jeanne? First, she perceived the tone of the feedback to be positive. This would probably give her at least a temporary boost in self-confidence. Second, the session might give her some ideas for self-improvement, even if they are somewhat superficial. She can't do much about her alleged "shifty eyes," but she might try not to appear stand-offish or pushy *when she does not want to be perceived in this manner*. If Jeanne leaves the session with a boost in self-confidence and one valid suggestion for self-improvement, we can conclude that the session was worthwhile for her.

Feedback from Self-examination Exercises

Many self-help books, including this one, contain questionnaires that you fill out by yourself, for yourself. The information that you pick up from these questionnaires often provides valuable clues to your preferences, values, and personal traits. Such self-examination questionnaires should not be confused with the scientifically researched test you might take in a counseling center or guidance department, or when applying for a job.

The amount of useful information gained from self-examination questionnaires depends on your candor. Since no outside judge is involved in these self-help quizzes, candor is usually not a problem. An exception is that we all have certain blind spots. Most people, for example, believe that they have considerably above-average skills in dealing with people.

You will be asked to complete three self-examination questionnaires in this chapter. The Self-awareness Checklist gives you a number of terms useful for self-description. The Self Disclosure Survey gives you an estimate of whether you are open or closed with others. The Self-Knowledge Questionnaire presented at the end of the chapter is a comprehensive survey of yourself. It provides a sound basis for profiting from much of the information in this book.

Feedback from Superiors

Virtually all employers provide employees with either formal and/or informal feedback on their performance. A formal method of feedback is called a performance appraisal. During a performance appraisal your superior will convey to you what he or she thinks you are doing well and not so well. These observations become a permanent part of your personnel record. Informal feedback occurs when a superior discusses your job performance with you but does not record these observations.

The feedback obtained from superiors in this way can help you learn about yourself. For instance, if two different bosses say that you are a creative problem solver you might conclude that you are creative. If several bosses told you that you are too impatient with other people, you might conclude that you are impatient.

Since work life consumes so much of a working adult's time, it becomes a valuable source of information about the self. Many people, in fact, establish much of their identity from their occupations. Next time you are at a social gathering, ask a person "What do you do?" Most likely, the person will respond in terms of an occupation or a company affiliation. It is rare person in our culture who responds something like, "I sleep, I eat, I watch television, and I talk to friends."

Insights Gathered in Psychotherapy and Counseling

Many people seek self-understanding through discussions with a psychotherapist or other professional counselor. **Psychotherapy** is generally regarded as a method of overcoming emotional problems through discussion with a mental health professional. However, many people enter into psychotherapy with the primary intention of gaining insight into themselves. A representative area of insight would be for the therapist to help the client detect patterns of self-defeating and self-destructive behavior. For example, some people unconsciously do something to ruin a personal relationship or perform poorly on the job just when things are going well. The therapist might point out this self-defeating pattern of behavior. Self-insight of this kind often—but not always—leads to useful changes in behavior.

YOUR SELF-CONCEPT: WHAT YOU THINK OF YOU

Another aspect of self-understanding is your self-concept, or what you think of you and who you think you are. A successful person—one who is achieving his or her goals in work or personal life—usually has a positive self-concept. In contrast, an unsuccessful person often has a negative self-concept. Such differences in self-concept can have a profound influence on your career.[2] If you see yourself as a successful person, you will tend to engage in activities that will help you prove yourself right. Similarly, if you have a limited view of yourself, you will tend to engage in activities that prove yourself right. For example, you may often look for convenient ways to prevent yourself from succeeding.

Self-concepts are based largely on what others have said about us. If enough people tell you that you are "terrific," after a while you will have the self-concept of a "terrific" person. When people tell you that you are not a worthwhile person, after a while your self-concept will become that of a not worthwhile person. People who say, "I'm OK," are expressing a positive self-concept. People who say, "I'm not OK," have a negative self-concept. As Todd recognizes in Exhibit 1–2, it is important to reinforce the positive self-concept.

The Self-concept and Self-confidence

A strong self-concept leads to self-confidence, which is a basic requirement for being successful as a leader (see Chapter 14). Why some people develop strong self-concepts and self-confidence, while others have weak self-concepts and self-confidence is not entirely known. One contributing factor may be inherited talents and abilities. Assume that a person quickly learns how to do key tasks in life such as walking, talking, swimming, running, reading, writing, and driving a car. This person is likely to be more self-confident than a person who struggled to learn these skills.

Another contributing factor to a positive self-concept and self-confidence is lifelong feedback from others (as mentioned above). If, as a youngster, your parents, siblings, and playmates consistently told you that you were competent, you would probably develop a strong self-concept. However, some people might find you to be conceited. Some of the feedback Jeanne received in the personal growth group indicated such a response.

EXHIBIT 1–2   TODD, THE HUMAN RELATIONS PRACTITIONER

Todd received several greeting cards on his birthday. Among the well-wishers were the employees in his department, his wife, Jody, and his daughter, Melissa. Todd's subordinates all signed a card that included the message, "Happy Birthday to a straight-shooting boss." Melissa's contained the inscription, "The best Daddy in town." Jody's card included the message. "Just to let you know I appreciate the way you show your appreciation of me."

In addition to buying Todd a new pair of running shoes for his birthday, Jody threw a party for him. She invited several close friends and Todd's boss, Dave. After dinner, Todd and his boss stood out on the apartment balcony to capture some fresh air. Dave opened the conversation with these words: "I've been wanting to ask you something for a while, Todd. Maybe this is a good opportunity. I can't help noticing how well you get along with your employees. You're no pushover, yet they speak of you in glowing terms. At home it seems to be the same way. Jody and Melissa are crazy about you. Any particular methods you use to get people to like you?"

"Thanks for the compliment," responded Todd. "I simply make good use of human relations in dealing with people at home and on the job."

"I get it," said Dave. "You use a few psychological tricks that you've learned in business courses at school."

"I would hardly call them tricks," said Todd. "Getting along with people is a very complicated topic. Believe me, I'm no expert. But I do use two techniques consistently that no doubt pay dividends. They're so obvious that many people neglect them."

"And what are these techniques?" asked Dave.

"Listening to people and giving them positive reinforcement. I get along with my wife, daughter, and people in the shop because I listen to their problems. It cuts down on misunderstandings and conflicts. At home I listen to any problem Jody or Melissa might want to talk about. It enables me to get close to them. Neither Jody nor Melissa has to feel self-conscious telling me things."

"Tell me how you go about using positive reinforcement," said Dave.

"It's a long story, but I'll give you two recent examples. Melissa is learning to swim. At first she was getting nowhere. Instead of intimidating her by saying that all her friends could swim, or threatening to dump her into the water, I used encouragement. Each time she made a little progress I gave her a big hug. Hugs work better with Melissa than do candy or verbal compliments. She paddles like a puppy just to get a big hug.

"On the job I don't give out hugs for good performance, but I still use positive reinforcement. The rewards I use include handshakes, buying beers for my employees, or putting a nice note in one of their personnel files. Also, I tell people I appreciate their work when they do a good job. But I never give out phony compliments.

"I don't think I have any natural charm with people that makes them want to cooperate with me. I just apply human relations in a sensible manner."

> **Todd is a good example of how using basic human relations techniques (in this case, positive reinforcement and listening) can help you get along better with others on the job and in personal life. By using good human relations techniques in both settings, Todd has more opportunity to practice them. Elsewhere in this book we will present many other positive examples of people who apply human relations principles and techniques at home, on the job, or in both places. You may profit from following their examples.**

Your Body Image as Part of Your Self-concept

Our discussion of the self-concept so far has emphasized mental traits and characteristics. Your **body image,** or your perception of your body, also contributes to your self-concept.[3] The current emphasis on physical fitness stems largely from a desire on the part of people to be physically fit and healthy. It is also apparent that being physically fit contributes to a positive self-concept. Being physically unfit can contribute to a negative self-concept. The relationship between the self-concept and physical fitness also works the other way: If your self-concept is positive it may push you toward physical fitness. Conversely, if you have a negative self-concept you may allow yourself to become physically unfit.

Having a positive body image is obviously important for personal life. Some people, for example, who are dissatisfied with their bodies will not engage in sports or attend activities where too much of their bodies is revealed. Also, having a positive body image helps one be more confident in making new friends.

A positive body image can also be important for work life. Employees who have a positive body image are likely to feel confident performing jobs that require customer contact such as sales work. Many business firms today expect their managers to appear physically fit, and to present a vigorous, healthy appearance. Managers with these qualities would generally have positive body images.

SELF-ACCEPTANCE: THE KEY TO A GOOD SELF-CONCEPT

Although the different ways of discussing the self may seem confusing to the reader, these various approaches to the self strongly influence your life. Self-acceptance plays a particularly important role. When you accept yourself for who you are, when you do not reject yourself, you are able to develop a positive self-concept. People who regard themselves highly also tend to regard others highly. In contrast, the self-rejecting person tends to reject many other people. If your level of self-acceptance is high, you will not find it necessary to put down or discriminate against others.[4]

Effective leaders tend to be high on self-acceptance. Since they are proud of who they are, such people have less need to pull rank on subordinates. People who are self-accepting also enjoy better mental health both on and off the job.

Our attention here is directed toward two plausible methods of improving your self-acceptance: increasing your self disclosure, and taking an inventory of your strengths.[5] Exercises will be presented for using both of these methods.

Self Disclosure and Self-acceptance

One method of increasing your self-acceptance is to engage in the right amount of **self disclosure,** the process of revealing your inner self to others. Self disclosure aids self-acceptance because if you reveal more of yourself, there is more for others to accept. Conversely, if you keep yourself hidden from others there is little opportunity to be accepted by others. Yet you must be careful of excessive self disclosure. Many people feel uneasy if another person is too self-revealing.[6] The overly candid person thus risks rejection. For instance, if you communicate all your negative feelings and doubts to another person, that person may become annoyed.

Figure 1–1 presents a questionnaire to assist you in assessing your level of self disclosure. A person with a high degree of self disclosure is open, while a person with a low degree of self disclosure is closed.

Awareness of Strengths and Self-acceptance

Another method of improving your self-acceptance is to develop an appreciation of your strengths and accomplishments. A good starting

FIGURE 1–1. THE SELF-DISCLOSURE QUESTIONNAIRE

Directions

The following quiz may indicate how much of yourself you reveal to others. Think about the person closest to you, whether he or she is a spouse, parent, or close friend. Using the list of responses provided, review the questions and select the number of the response that best describes you.

1. I have not mentioned anything about this.
2. I have talked about this to some degree.
3. I have confided this to a large degree.
4. I have disclosed practically all there is to know about this.

Quiz

_____ 1. Traits I am ashamed of, such as jealously, daydreaming, and procrastination
_____ 2. Pet peeves or prejudices about others
_____ 3. Facts about my love life, including details about flirting, dating, and sexual activity
_____ 4. Things I have done or said to others that I feel guilty about
_____ 5. What it takes to make me extremely angry
_____ 6. My feelings about my attractiveness and sex appeal, and my insecurities about how my romantic interests perceive me
_____ 7. Aspects of myself I wish I could improve, such as my figure or physique, mental abilities, shyness
_____ 8. What I worry about most, such as illness, job loss, death, etc.
_____ 9. Impulses I fear will get out of control if I "let go," such as drinking, gambling, sex, and anger
_____ 10. My very deepest sensitivities, dreams, and goals

Scoring and Interpretation

To tally your score, add the numbers that correspond with the answers you gave to the quiz questions.

10 to 17 points: You are a closed person. You may feel satisfied with the level of intimacy you have established with others, but it's likely you would benefit from sharing your feelings more openly. Doing so allows others to give you feedback on your feelings and goals, helping you to get a clearer picture of yourself. Begin to change your style by making small disclosures at first. Perhaps it will be easier to start by talking about your goals.

18 to 28 points: You are average on self disclosure and have a good balance between your private self and your openness.

29 to 40 points: You are a very open type of person, but beware. Sometimes indiscriminately revealing too much can be a sign of personal insecurity, guilt, or the need for acceptance by others. If others take advantage of you, look down on you, or feel uncomfortable with you, you may be telling more than the listener wants or cares to handle.

SOURCE: Reprinted with permission from Salvatore Didato, "Self-Disclosure Isn't Easy But It's Necessary to Bring People Together." Copyrighted feature appearing in newspapers, April 1985.

point is to list your strengths and accomplishments on paper. This list is likely to be more impressive than you expected. The list of strengths and accomplishments requested in the Self-Knowledge Questionnaire presented later can be used for building self-acceptance.

An appreciation of your strengths can also be achieved by participating in an exercise used in a personal growth group. Refer back to Exhibit 1–1, and observe statement 5, "My three strongest points, attributes, and skills." After each group member has recorded their three strengths, that person discusses them with the other group members. Each group member then comments on the list. Other group members sometimes add to your list of strengths or reinforce what you have to say. Sometimes you may find disagreement. One man told the group: "I'm handsome, intelligent, reliable, athletic, self-confident, very moral, and I have good sense of humor." A woman in the group retorted, "And I might add that you're unbearably conceited."

A CHECKLIST FOR SELF-AWARENESS

One problem in becoming more aware of yourself is that you may not know enough terms to describe yourself. Think of the first time that you were asked to describe a painting, perhaps for a class in art appreciation. At first, you might have been at a loss for terms, finding yourself limited to words like interesting, colorful, imaginative. Describing yourself requires considerable descriptive skill if it is to lead to greater self-awareness and self-knowledge.

An aid to developing self-awareness is the adjective list shown in Figure 1–2. Read through this list and circle the ten adjectives that you think best describe you. You have now formed a brief self-description composed of ten adjectives—for example, aggressive, ambitious, bold, courageous, extroverted, friendly, greedy, skillful, tenacious, and zestful. Next discuss your list with a friend. Your friend should be encouraged to discuss his or her list with you. This exchange should result in feedback that will help you determine the accuracy of your self-perceptions.

It is helpful to discuss the adjective lists of various people in a group setting. Each group member thus has an opportunity to obtain feedback from a greater number of people.

HOW THIS BOOK WILL HELP YOU

A person who carefully studies the information in this book and incorporates its suggestions into his or her way of doing things should derive

FIGURE 1–2. ADJECTIVE LIST

able	foolish	malicious	proud	simple
accepting	frank	manipulative	questioning	sinful
adaptable	free	materialistic	quite	skillful
aggressive	friendly	maternal	radical	sly
ambitious	genial	mature	rational	sociable
annoying	gentle	merry	rationalizing	spontaneous
anxious	giving	modest	reactionary	stable
authoritative	greedy	mystical	realistic	strained
belligerent	gruff	naive	reasonable	strong
bitter	guilty	narcissistic	reassuring	stubborn
bold	gullible	negative	rebellious	sympathetic
calm	happy	nervous	reflective	taciturn
carefree	hard	neurotic	regretful	tactful
careless	helpful	noisy	rejecting	temperamental
caring	helpless	normal	relaxed	tenacious
certain	honorable	objective	reliable	tender
cheerful	hostile	oblivious	religious	tense
clever	idealistic	observant	remote	thoughtful
cold	imaginative	obsessive	resentful	tough
complex	immature	organized	reserved	trusting
confident	impressionable	original	resolute	trustworthy
conforming	inconsiderate	overburdened	respectful	unassuming
controlled	independent	overconfident	responsible	unaware
courageous	ingenious	overconforming	responsive	uncertain
cranky	innovative	overemotional	retentive	unconcerned
critical	insensitive	overprotecting	rigid	uncontrolled
cynical	insincere	passive	sarcastic	understanding
demanding	intelligent	paternal	satisfied	unpredictable
dependable	introverted	patient	scientific	unreasonable
dependent	intuitive	perceptive	searching	unstructured
derogatory	irresponsible	perfectionist	self-accepting	useful
dignified	irritable	persuasive	self-actualizing	vain
disciplined	jealous	petty	self-assertive	vapid
docile	jovial	playful	self-aware	visionary
dogged	juvenile	pleasant	self-conscious	vulnerable
domineering	kind	pompous	self-effacing	warm
dreamy	knowledgeable	powerful	self-indulgent	willful
dutiful	lazy	pragmatic	selfish	wise
effervescent	learned	precise	self-righteous	wishful
efficient	lewd	pretending	sensible	withdrawn
elusive	liberal	pretentious	sensitive	witty
energetic	lively	principled	sentimental	worried
extroverted	logical	progressive	serious	youthful
fair	loving	protective	silly	zestful
fearful				

SOURCE: Reprinted with permission from David W. Johnson, *Human Relations and Your Career* (Englewood Cliffs, NJ: Prentice-Hall, 1978), p. 230.

the five benefits discussed below. Knowledge itself, however, is not a guarantee of success. Since people differ greatly in learning ability, personality, and life circumstances, some will get more out of this book than others.

You may, for example, be getting along well with co-workers (or peers) so that the chapter on this topic is unnecessary from your viewpoint. Or you may be so shy at this stage of your life that you are at present unable to capitalize on some of the tips for being assertive with people. You might have to work doubly hard to reap benefit from that particular chapter.

The major benefits this book provides are:

1. It should help make you aware of valid information about human relations. To feel comfortable with other people and to make a favorable impression (both on and off the job) one needs to understand how people think and act. This book will provide you with some basic knowledge about interpersonal relationships such as the meaning of emotional security, openness, and nonverbal messages. You will even learn about such things as "violating somebody else's territorial space."

2. It should help you develop skills in dealing with people. Anyone who aspires toward high-level jobs or an enriched social life needs to be able to communicate with others, resolve conflict, and behave in a confident manner. Studying information about such topics in this book, coupled with trying them out in practice, should help you develop such interpersonal skills.

3. This book will help you cope with job problems. Almost everyone who holds a responsible job inevitably runs into human relations problems. Reading about these problems and suggestions for coping with them could save you considerable inner turmoil. Among the job survival skills that you will learn about in the following chapters are how to cope with job stress and how to overcome what seems to be an overwhelming workload.

4. You will learn how to cope with personal problems. We all have problems. An important difference between the effective and ineffective person is that the effective person knows how to manage them. Among the problems this book will help you cope with are shyness, finding a job when you are unemployed, overcoming low self-confidence, and working your way out of debt.

5. You will learn how to capitalize on opportunities. Many readers of this book will someday spend part of their working time taking advantage of opportunities rather than solving daily problems. Every career-minded person needs a few breakthrough experiences in order to make his or her life more rewarding. Toward this end, the book discusses how to get ahead in your career and how to become a leader.

SUMMARY

Human relations is the art of using systematic knowledge about human behavior to improve your personal and job effectiveness. Work life and personal life often influence each other. For instance, a high level of job satisfaction will tend to spill over to your personal life. Conversely, an unsatisfactory personal life could lead to negative job attitudes.

Another close tie between work and personal life is that your job can affect your physical and mental health. Severe negative job conditions may lead to a serious stress disorder, such as heart disease. Thus, people who enjoy their jobs tend to lead healthier and longer lives.

To be effective in human relationships, you must first understand yourself. Six methods of gaining self-understanding are: (1) acquire general information about human behavior and apply it to yourself; (2) obtain feedback from other people in natural settings; (3) obtain feedback from personal growth groups; (4) obtain feedback from self-examination exercises; (5) obtain feedback from superiors; (6) gather insights in psychotherapy and counseling.

An important aspect of self-understanding is your self-concept, or what you think of you and who you think you are. The self-concept is based largely on what others have said about us. A strong self-concept leads to self-confidence, which is a basic requirement for being successful as a leader.

Natural abilities contribute to a person's self-concept and level of self-confidence. Your body image, or your perception of your body, also contributes to your self-concept. A positive body image can help you in both your work and personal life because it enhances your self-confidence.

A high degree of self-acceptance contributes to a positive self-concept. One way to increase self-acceptance is to disclose more of yourself to others. Another is to develop an appreciation of your strengths and accomplishments.

One problem in becoming more aware of yourself is that you may not know enough terms to describe yourself. An aid to developing self-awareness is an adjective checklist presented in this chapter. After you prepare a self-description based on adjectives, you can share this profile with a friend.

QUESTIONS AND ACTIVITIES

1. Why do you think it is difficult to succeed in business if you have poor human relations skills?

2. Some successful career people make very poor vacation companions. What does this tell you about their human relations skills?

3. Many companies and government agencies now provide day care facilities for the children of employees. What does this employment practice tell you about the relationship between work and personal life?

4. Give an example from your own experience of how work life influences personal life and vice versa.

5. What do you think are the negative consequences of being too much involved with self-examination?

6. What do you think are the disadvantages of relying on feedback from your peers as useful information for self-understanding?

7. Of the six sources of information about the self described in this chapter, which one do you think is likely to be the most accurate? Why?

8. How does self disclosure relate to being intimate with others?

9. Suppose you use the Checklist for Self-awareness again ten years from now. What changes in self-perception do you think there will be between now and then?

10. Interview a person whom you perceive to have a successful career. Ask that person to describe his or her self-concept. Be prepared to discuss your findings in class.

A HUMAN RELATIONS SELF-EXAMINATION EXERCISE: THE SELF-KNOWLEDGE QUESTIONNAIRE

Directions: Complete the following questionnaire for your personal use. You might wish to make up a worksheet before putting your comments in final form.

I. Education
   1. How far have I gone in school?
   2. What is my major field of interest?
   3. Which are (or have been) my best subjects?
   4. Which are (or have been) my poorest subjects?
   5. What further educational plans do I have? Why?

     6. What extracurricular activities have I participated in?

     7. Which ones did I enjoy? Why?

II. Work Experience

     8. What jobs have I held since age sixteen?

     9. What aspect of these jobs did I enjoy? Why?

    10. What aspect of these jobs did I dislike? Why?

    11. What were my three biggest accomplishments on the job?

    12. What kind of employee am (was) I?

    13. What compliments did I receive from my bosses or co-workers?

    14. What criticisms or suggestions did I receive?

    15. What would be an ideal job for me?

III. Attitudes Toward People

    16. The kind of people I get along best with are:

    17. The kind of people I clash with are:

    18. How many close friends do I have? What is it I like about each one?

    19. Would I prefer working mostly with men or women? Why?

    20. How much contact with other people do I need?

    21. My arguments with other people are mostly about:

IV. Attitudes Toward Myself

    22. What are my strengths?

    23. What are my weaknesses or areas for improvement?

    24. What do I think of me?

    25. What do I worry about most?

    26. What is my biggest problem?

    27. What things in life do I dislike?

    28. What have I accomplished in life so far?

    29. Has this been enough accomplishment?

    30. So far, what has been the happiest period of my life? Why?

    31. What gives me satisfaction in life?

    32. In what ways do I punish myself?

    33. What motivates me?

V. How Others See Me

    34. What is the best compliment my spouse (or a good friend) has paid me?

    35. In what ways would my spouse (or a good friend) like me to change?

    36. What do my friends like best about me?

    37. What do my friends dislike about me?

VI. Hobbies, Interests, Sports

    38. What activities, hobbies, interests, sports, and so forth do I actively participate in?

39. Which one of these do I really get excited about? Why?

VII. My Future

40. What are my plans for further education and training?
41. What positions would I like to hold within the next five years?
42. What are my career goals beyond five years?
43. Where would I like to be at the peak of my career?
44. What activities and interests would I like to pursue in the future?
45. What goals do I have relating to friends, family, and marriage?

Additional Thoughts

1. What other questions should have been asked of you on the Self-Knowledge Questionnaire?
2. To what use can you put all or part of this information?
3. What impact did completing the Self-Knowledge Questionnaire have on your self-understanding?

A HUMAN RELATIONS ROLE PLAY: SELF DISCLOSURE

In a role play, you assume the role of the person described in a scenario. In this and other role plays presented in this book, it may be your responsibility to add details to the brief sketches provided. Unlike an actor or actress, you will have to improvise beyond the bare essentials of the script presented by the author. Or your instructor may modify the role play to provide you with additional details.

In this role play, two co-workers are having lunch together. One student plays the role of an employee who is eager to disclose as much as possible about his or her inner self. Similarly, this employee would like the luncheon partner to be self disclosing.

Another student plays the role of the second employee. This person is much more closed than open but nevertheless does not necessarily dislike allowing the luncheon companion to open up to him or her.

Those students not in the role play should make observations of the role players, and later use these observations as a basis for class discussion. The class discussion may include comments about the effectiveness of the role players.

REFERENCES

[1] An original study on this topic is E. Palmore, "Predicting Longevity: A Follow-up Controlling for Age," *The Gerontologist,* Winter 1969, pp. 247–250. More recent information on this topic is Thomas I. Chacko, "Job and Life

Satisfactions: A Causal Analysis of Their Relationships," *Academy of Management Journal,* March 1983, pp. 163–169.

[2] David A. Laird and others, *Psychology: Human Relations and Motivation,* 4th ed. (New York: McGraw-Hill, 1975), p. 209.

[3] Thomas F. Cash, Barbara A. Winstead, and Louis H. Janda, "Your Body, Yourself," *Psychology Today,* July 1985, pp. 22–26.

[4] A comprehensive discussion of acceptance of self and others appears in David W. Johnson, *Reaching Out: Interpersonal Effectiveness and Self-Actualization* (Englewood Cliffs, NJ: Prentice-Hall, 1972), pp. 141–157.

[5] Ibid., pp. 142–148.

[6] Ibid., p. 147.

SOME ADDITIONAL READING

DRUCK, KEN. *Secrets Men Keep.* New York: Doubleday, 1985.

FREEMAN, LUCY. *Listening to the Inner Self.* New York: Jason Aronson, 1984.

HANKINS, NORMAN E. *How to Become the Person You Want to Be.* Chicago: Nelson Hall, 1979.

LIFTON, ROBERT JAY. *The Life of the Self: Toward a New Psychology.* New York: Basic Books, 1983.

MARTIN, MIKE W. (Ed.). *Self-deception and Self-understanding. New Essays in Philosophy and Psychology.* Lawrence: University Press of Kansas, 1985.

ORBACH, SUSIE. *Fat is a Feminist Issue.* New York: Berkley Publishing Corp., 1978.

SCHLENKER, BARRY R. (Ed.). *The Self and Social Life.* New York: McGraw-Hill, 1985.

WESTEN, DREW. *Self and Society: Narcissism, Collectivism, and the Development of Morals.* New York: Cambridge University Press, 1985.

YATES, BRIAN T. *Self-Management: The Science and Art of Helping Yourself.* Belmont, CA: Wadsworth, 1985.

Goal Setting and Self-motivation

Learning Objectives

After studying the information and doing the exercises in this chapter, you should be able to:

- Explain why each chapter in this book begins with a list of objectives
- Prepare a useful set of goals to guide you in your career and personal life
- Pinpoint the differences between several types of goals
- Stay alert to the possible drawbacks of being too rigid about pursuing your goals
- Select several techniques for motivating yourself

WHY GOAL SETTING?

A writer about success says, "All truly successful men or women I have met or read about have one thing in common. At some point in their lives, they sat down and wrote out their goals. The first great key to success begins with you, a piece of paper, and a pencil."[1] This statement indicates why goal setting is so important. A **goal** is an event, circumstance, object, or condition a person strives to attain. A goal thus reflects your desire or intention to regulate your actions. Goals are useful for several reasons.

Consistent Direction

When we guide our lives with goals, we tend to focus our efforts in a consistent direction. Without goals, our efforts may become scattered in many directions. We may keep trying but will go nowhere unless we happen to receive more than our share of luck.

Improved Chances for Success

Another value of goal setting is that it increases our chances for success, particularly since success can be defined as the achievement of a goal. The goals we set for accomplishing a task can serve as a standard to indicate when we have done a satisfactory job. A motorcycle sales representative might set a goal of selling $150,000 worth of cycles for the year. By November he might close a deal that places his total sales at $150,500. With a sigh of relief he can then say, "I've done well this year."

Improved Motivation and Satisfaction

Another key value of goals is that they serve as motivators or energizers. People who set goals tend to be motivated because they are confident that their energy is being invested in something worthwhile. Aside from helping you become more motivated and productive, setting goals can help you achieve personal satisfaction. Most people derive a sense of satisfaction from attaining a goal that is meaningful to them. The sales representative mentioned above probably achieved this sense of satisfaction when he surpassed his quota.

In this chapter we look at different types of goals and how to increase your chances of attaining them as well as several other techniques of self-motivation. Goals will be discussed again in Chapter 13, which deals with getting ahead in your career.

WHAT TYPE OF GOALS LEAD TO SUCCESS?

"I'd like to be a big success someday," is a nice thought but not likely to ensure success. A more useful goal would state specifically what you mean by success and when you expect to achieve it. For example, "I want to operate a profitable contracting firm by January 1, 1995." The following paragraphs provide some tips on setting goals that are likely to prove useful.

1. Formulate clear, concise, and unambiguous goals. A useful goal can usually be expressed in a short, punchy statement, much like a headline or a telegram. Such a goal might be: "Decrease the energy leaks in our house whereby our fuel consumption is decreased by 10 percent by December 31 of this year."

2. Describe what you would actually be doing if you reached your goal. A vague goal for a typist would be to "become a better typist." A more useful goal would be to "increase current speed to seventy-five words per minute," or "Increase the average number of pages typed per day." The meaning of "better typist" needs to be narrowed down as much as possible. Similarly, if your goal is to "get into good shape" you need to specify what kinds of behavior signify "good shape." It could mean such things as "weigh between 195 and 203 pounds," "run a mile in less than seven minutes," or "fall asleep at night without the use of alcohol or sleeping pills."

A student once complained to a counselor that people pushed him around and took advantage of him. "I think I'm kind of wishy-washy," he said. The counselor replied that this vague statement conveyed little specific information about the student's behavior or situations he had to face.

"What is your goal?" asked the counselor.

"To stop being wishy-washy, I guess," he replied.

"In very concrete terms, what things would you be doing if you were at your goal?" he was asked by the counselor.

"I would say no when my friends asked to borrow my car. I would be sure people didn't jump ahead of me when I was standing in line. Things like that."[2]

Once the student had specified several behaviors in specific situations, he was able to begin working on one or more of them. His goal was to become more assertive in a variety of situations.

3. Use past performance as a guide. A good starting point in setting goals is to set them based on what you have achieved in the past. Your past behavior gives you some guide as to your capabilities. This information becomes a foundation for defining ordinary and reasonable levels, barring any unforeseen changes or events.[3] For example, your current grade point average is a good basis for setting goals for a future grade point average.

4. *Set interesting and challenging goals whenever possible.* Later we will return to this point. For now it is important to recognize that trivial goals aren't particularly motivational—they don't spring you into action. At the same time, goals that are too far beyond your capa-

bility may lead to frustration and despair because there is a good chance you will fail to reach them. A trivial goal would be to "wear athletic socks every time I go running." A more challenging goal would be to "run six miles without stopping by May 31 of this year."

5. *Specify what is going to be accomplished, who is going to accomplish it, when it is going to be accomplished, and how it is going to be accomplished.* Establishing the "who," "what," "when," and "how" of your goals reduces the chances for misinterpretation. Here is a work

goal that meets these requirements: "The VCR sales manager will increase the number of sales by 40 percent within fifteen months by selling to customers with good credit records. Returns will be subtracted from the total number of sales." Specifying that sales must be made to qualified customers and that returns will not be counted, focuses on the "how." It implies that sales should not be increased by pushing VCRs on unqualified or uninterested buyers who will later return the merchandise.

6. *Review your goals from time to time.* A sophisticated goal setter realizes that all goals are temporary to some extent. In time one particular goal may lose its relevance for you, and therefore may no longer motivate you. At one time in your life you may be committed to earning an income in the top 10 percent of the population. Along the way toward achieving that goal, some other more relevant goal may develop. You might decide that the satisfactions of being self-employed are more important than earning a particular amount of money. You might therefore open an antique store with the simple financial goal of "meeting my expenses."

Psychologist David Campbell expressed the desirability of flexible goal setting in this way:

> Practically all goals tarnish with time if not renewed in some way. A job that is exhilarating during the first year becomes less so after five years; without renewal it becomes an automatic activity after ten years, and a prison after twenty. The same for a marriage. The divorce rate, perhaps the best indication of marriage failure, continues to climb and demonstrates that even relationships of love ("till death do us part") can weaken and change with time if there are no changes.[4]

MAINTENANCE VERSUS CHALLENGING GOALS

An important distinction can be made between goals that keep us in a state of equilibrium and those that stretch our capabilities.[5] Just because a goal helps us maintain our equilibrium or take care of routine tasks, its importance should not be dismissed. Two examples of such status-quo goals are: "Spend no more than 10 percent of my gross income on time payments," and "Maintain a body weight of no less than 105 pounds for the next twenty-four months." If attained, the first goal could contribute to your mental health. Being in too much debt provokes tension. The second goal would contribute to your physical health if your height were five feet or taller.

On-the-job, routine, or maintenance goals are also significant. A large part of most jobs involves a host of daily chores that have to be done even if they do not challenge your special capabilities. Chiefs of state have to attend routine banquets and pass judgment on what some would call minor bills, such as legislation to increase federal funding for combating gypsy moths in economically depressed areas.

People derive the most benefit from goal setting if they establish some challenging goals in addition to those of a maintenance or routine

nature. Such goals help you grow and prosper; they expand your horizons and are personally uplifting. If, for example, you had been skiing for only two seasons, a challenging goal would be to "navigate safely a hill officially labeled very difficult." If you proceeded too swiftly in reaching this goal, you could easily injure yourself (or the person[s] with whom you collided). A challenging work goal for a computer programmer might be to "qualify as a systems analyst by August 31 of this year."

A third category of goal difficulty is "breakthrough." Attaining breakthrough goals brings you recognition and usually represents a major improvement in your work or personal life. One such breakthrough goal is to "win a $10,000 suggestion award within the next five years." Another is to "write a best-selling novel this decade that will include movie rights of at least $250,000." Few people set and attain many breakthrough goals in their lifetimes. Nevertheless, such goals have a place in your life. We will discuss far-reaching goals again toward the end of this chapter.

SET YOUR GOALS FOR DIFFERENT TIME PERIODS

The word goal means different things to different people. A goal may be a general state toward which you strive, like the goal of becoming happy and wealthy. You may set short-range objectives to help you achieve that general goal. Getting an A in your math course, for example, might represent a small step toward becoming happy and wealthy. To avoid confusion over the terms goals and objectives you should categorize goals according to their time frames.

The important message here is that to gain maximum advantage from goal setting you should set goals roughly as follows:[6]

long-range goals
medium-range goals
short-range goals
daily goals
immediate goals

Long-range goals relate to the overall lifestyle that you wish to achieve, including the type of work and family situation you hope to have. Although every person should have a general idea of what lifestyle would bring him or her happiness, long-range goals should be flexible. Too many unanticipated events may take place. You might, for example, plan to stay single until age forty. But while on vacation next summer you might just happen to meet the right partner for you.

Medium-range goals relate to events that will take place in the next five years or so. They concern things such as the type of education or training you plan to undertake and the next step in your career. If your long-range goal was to become a real estate tycoon, a sensible preliminary goal would be to buy a small apartment building within the next four years. You usually have more control over medium- than long-range goals and you can tell how well you are achieving them. If you are falling behind in reaching a medium-range goal, you can adjust your actions accordingly. For instance, if two years had passed and you had not saved any money toward a down payment on that first building, you would have to accelerate your savings program.

Short-range goals cover the period from about one month to one year into the future. Such goals should be set realistically—stretch yourself but do not set yourself up for discouragement. Our future real estate tycoon, for example, might plan to save $2,000 this year by banking all the money he or she makes from moonlighting as a waiter or waitress.

Daily goals relate to what you intend to accomplish today. Most successful people establish daily goals for themselves in the form of a "to do" list. As each goal (or chore) is accomplished, you cross it off your list. Most people feel exhilarated when each item is crossed off. A person's daily goals might include items such as, "Take clothing to the dry cleaner," "Call Phil to discuss my job résumé," "Call the vet about worm medicine for Rex," "Call Mr. Madison about making up statistics test." Chapter 11 offers more comments about the value of list making.

Immediate goals are concerned with the next fifteen minutes to an hour. No one can accomplish long-range, medium-range, short-range, or daily goals without paying attention to immediate goals. So you want to write that term paper this week? Go down to the library right now and find at least one good reference. As the old adage states, "The best way to eat an elephant is one bite at a time."

A successful philosophy of goal setting contends, "The only kind of planning you have direct control over are the modest little goals; the trick of planning a successful life is to stack together these smaller goals in a way that increases your chances of reaching the long-range goals you really care about."[7]

GOAL SETTING ON THE JOB

If you are already well into your work career, you have probably been asked to set goals or objectives on the job. Virtually all modern organizations have come to accept the value of goal setting in producing the results they want to achieve.[8] Executives at the top of the organization are supposed to plan for the future by setting goals such as "Improve profits by 10 percent this fiscal year." Employees at the bottom of the organization are supposed to go along with such broad goals by setting more specific goals: "I will decrease damaged merchandise by 10 percent this fiscal year; I will accomplish this by making sure that our shelving is adequate for our needs."

An interesting aspect of goal-setting programs on the job is that they lead you to pursue goals set both by your employer and yourself. The firm or company establishes certain goals that are absolutely essential to staying in business. A bank, for example, might impose the following goal on the tellers: "Shortages and overages of cash must be kept within 2 percent of transactions each week." The tellers will thus work extra hard to be sure that they do not give customers too much or too little money. Similarly, the top management of a hospital might impose the following goal (or objective) on all ward personnel: "All prescription drugs must be accounted for with 100 percent accuracy."

You participate in the goal-setting process by designing goals to fit into the overall mission of the firm.[9] As a teller in the bank mentioned above, you might set a personal goal of this nature: "During rush periods, and when I feel fatigued, I will count twice all the money that I handle." In some goal-setting programs, employees are requested to set goals that will lead to their personal improvement. One employee working as an auditor for the state set this goal for herself: "Within the next twelve months, I will enroll in and complete a supervisory training course in a local evening college." This woman aspired toward becoming a supervisor.

A sample set of work goals is shown in Figure 2–1. The service and repair shop supervisor who set these objectives took into account the requirements of his boss and the automobile dealership. Even if

FIGURE 2–1. MEMO FORM USED IN AUTOMOBILE DEALERSHIP FOR STATEMENT OF GOALS

Job Title and Brief Job Description

Manager, Service Department: Responsible for supervision of service department of automobile dealership. Responsible for staffing service department with appropriate personnel and for quality of service to customers. Work closely with owner of dealership to discuss unusual customer problems. Handle customer complaints about mechanical problems of cars purchased at dealership.

Objectives for Scott Gilley

1. By December 31 of this year, decrease by 10 percent demands for rework customers.
2. Hire two general mechanics within 45 days.
3. Hire two body specialists within 45 days.
4. Decrease by 30 percent the number of repairs returned by customers for rework.
5. Reduce by 10 percent the discrepancy between estimates and actual bills to customers.

you set goals by yourself, they must still take into account the needs of your employer. As you read through the goals listed in Figure 2–1, see if they conform to the suggestions made in the section "What Types of Goals Lead to Success?" Exhibit 2–3 toward the end of this chapter explains how a business person used goal setting to overcome a serious problem in his computer store.

PERSONAL GOAL SETTING

Personal goals are important in their own right. If you want to lead a rewarding personal life, your chances of doing so increase if you plan your personal life. Personal goals heavily influence the formulation of career goals as well. For this reason it is worthwhile to set personal goals in conjunction with career goals. Ideally, they should be integrated. Some examples are in order.

- One young man may have a strong interest in visiting museums, shopping at retail stores, dancing at rock night clubs, and dining at a variety of restaurants. One personal goal he might formulate is to have enough money for this lifestyle and to live in an area where it would be available. His occupational goals should then include developing job skills that are needed in large cities. The same young man may set a personal goal of dating a large number of women for many years into the future. His career planning might then focus on obtaining employment in a geographic location such as Washington, D.C., where there are many more single women than men.

- A young woman might develop a preference early in life for the outdoors, particularly for hunting, fishing, and camping. She might also be interested in raising a large family. Part of her career planning should include developing skills that are in demand in rural areas where her preferences are easier to satisfy than in a city. When she learns that in recent years many manufacturing facilities have been developed in rural and semirural areas, her career planning might then include the goal of developing job skills that are in demand in a factory or mill. Secretarial skills, of course, are in demand everywhere. Another alternative for her would be to develop technical and professional skills that would enable her to find a manufacturing job. For instance, she might seek a job as a manufacturing technician.

Types of Personal Goals

Personal goals vary more than work goals because personal life is much more complex. Personal goals can be subdivided into those relating to social and family life, hobbies and interests, physical and mental health, and finances. An example or two of each type follows:

SOCIAL AND FAMILY: "By age thirty I would like to have a spouse and two children"; "have my own apartment by age twenty-three."

HOBBIES AND INTERESTS: "Becomes a black belt in karate by age twenty-eight"; "qualify as a rodeo barrel racer by age twenty-one."

PHYSICAL AND MENTAL HEALTH: "Be able to run four miles without stopping or panting for breath by April 15 of next year"; "get my dermatitis under control within six months from now"; "maintain normal blood pressure for the indefinite future."

FINANCIAL: "Within the next four years be earning $30,000 per year, adjusted for inflation"; "build my money market fund account into a total value of at least $15,000 within five years."

The exhibits accompanying this discussion will give you an opportunity to set both work and personal goals. Ideally, reading this chapter and doing the exercises in it will start you on a lifelong process of using goals to help you plan your life. But before you can capitalize on the benefits of goal setting, you need a method for translating goals into action.

EVERY GOAL NEEDS AN ACTION PLAN

An **action plan** describes how you are going to reach your goal. The major reason you need an action plan for most goals is that without a method for achieving what you want, the goal is likely to slip by. Few people ever prepare a road map or plan that will lead them to their goal. Exhibit 2–1 illustrates how to go about this task.

EXHIBIT 2–1   GOAL-SETTING AND ACTION PLAN WORKSHEET

The purpose of this activity is to help you gain some experience in setting both work and personal goals and action plans to accompany them. Before writing down your actual goals, consult both Figure 2–1 and the section, "What Type of Goals Lead to Success?" For each of the following level of goals, set a work goal, personal goal, and a brief action plan for each goal. If you are not currently employed, set up hypothetical goals and action plans for a future job. Or use goals and action plans that would have been appropriate for some job you held in the past.

LONG-RANGE GOALS

Work: _____

Action plan: _____

Personal: _____

    Action plan: _____

Medium-Range Goals

Work: _____

    Action plan: _____

Personal: _____

    Action plan: _____

Short-Range Goals

Work: _____

    Action plan: _____

Personal: _____

    Action plan: _____

Daily Goals

Work: _____

    Action plan: _____

Personal: _____

    Action plan: _____

Immediate Goals

Work: _____

    Action plan: _____

Personal: _____

    Action plan: _____

Many people who would like to write a book have asked me how to go about it. My answer is to begin small. See if you can get a letter to the editor published. Then you might try writing an article for the school newspaper. After you have accomplished that, branch out into articles for magazines. This advice is essentially an action plan for building your competence in writing step-by-step so that you will eventually be able to achieve your long-range goal of writing a book. In the same way, if your goal were to build your own log cabin, part of your action plan would be to learn how to operate a buzz saw, to read a handbook on log-cabin building, to learn how to operate a tractor, and so forth.

Do You Always Need an Action Plan?

Some goals are so difficult to reach that your action plan might encompass hundreds of separate activities. You would then have to develop separate action plans for each step of the way. If your goal is to lead a rewarding and satisfying career, the techniques presented in this book can help you formulate many of your action plans. Among these skill-building techniques are assertiveness, resolving conflict, developing good work habits, and managing your money wisely.

Some immediate goals do not really require an action plan. A mere statement of the goal may point to an obvious action plan. If your immediate goal were to start painting your room, it would not be necessary to draw up a formal action plan such as: "Go to hardware store, purchase paint, brush, and rollers. Borrow ladder and drop cloth from Ken. Put furniture in center of room," and so on. Nor do you need an action plan to begin your running program for today. Simply put on the appropriate attire, and get moving. Don't stop until you've reached your immediate goal of whatever distance you have decided is appropriate for your physical condition.

CAUTION: GOAL SETTING CAN CREATE SOME PROBLEMS

Despite all the wonderful things that have been said about goal setting in this chapter, the process is not without flaws. As one woman expressed it, "I have never taken goal setting too seriously. I like to live my life spontaneously. It's fun never really knowing what the future will bring. Fate is my best friend." Exhibit 2–2 suggests how to avoid some problems in goal setting. Two major criticisms made of goal setting will be discussed next.

EXHIBIT 2–2   GOAL SHARING AND FEEDBACK

Each person selects one work and one personal goal from Exhibit 2–1 that he or she would be willing to share with other members of the class. In turn, every class member presents those two goals to the rest of the class exactly as they are stated on the worksheet. Other class members have the privilege of providing feedback to the person sharing his or her goals. Here are a few types of errors commonly made in goal setting that you should avoid:

1. Is the goal much too lengthy and complicated: Is it really a number of goals, rather than one specific goal?
2. Is the goal so vague that the person will be hard-pressed to know if he or she has reached the goal? (Such as, "I intend to become a good worker.")
3. Is the action plan specific enough to serve as a useful path for reaching that goal?
4. Does the goal sound sincere? (Admittedly a highly subjective judgment on your part.)

Goal Setting May Create Inflexibility

If you set difficult goals on the job, quantity may be given priority over quality. You might, for example, turn out numerous shoddy products just to meet your quota. Meanwhile, in your social life you might set an arbitrary goal of dating six new people over the next three months. In your quest to date six people you might fail to recognize that the fifth person you dated would make an excellent intermediate or long-range companion for you. In short, in addition to setting goals, you should set priorities as to the relative importance of quantity or quality. You should not lose all flexibility because of goal setting.

Goals Sometimes Become Obsessions

In some instances people become so obsessed with reaching particular goals that they cannot react to emergencies, or they fail to grasp real opportunities, as in the example just cited. Many sales representatives neglect to invest time in cultivating a prospective customer simply because of the pressure to achieve a specific sales quota.

Short-range goals sometimes backfire for another reason. Long-term negative consequences are sometimes ignored for the sake of short-range gain. The argument has been advanced, for example, that saving the taxpayer money by cutting back on youth programs could in some cases incur more expense in the long run. Some of the young people no longer enrolled in the youth program might turn to crime. It can cost society as much as $38,000 a year to imprison one convicted criminal.

Goals can become an obsession in another way. Sensing that reaching goals is the only thing the company cares about, an individual might neglect other important aspects of his or her job. Suppose you are a salesperson in a furniture store. You are paid strictly on a commission basis. In order to maximize your pay, you might concentrate on selling fast-moving merchandise (such as inexpensive roll-top desks). In the meantime you might neglect trying to sell slower moving items such as deluxe bedroom sets. Some students find themselves facing a similar situation when taking a course. That is, they might be tempted to concentrate their efforts on the details they think will be on a forthcoming test and neglect to review other aspects of the course.

Goals Can Interfere with Relaxation

Finally, a preoccupation with goals makes it difficult for a person to ever relax. Instead of improving one's life, goals become a source of stress. In the words of one ambitious sales representative, "Ever since I caught on to goal setting as a way of life, I feel like I'm a basketball player racing from one end of the court to another. Even worse, nobody ever calls a time out."

Despite the problems that can arise in goal setting, goals appear to be valuable tools for managing your work and personal life. Used with common sense, according to the ideas presented in this chapter, they could have a major positive impact on your life.

HAVE A NICE FANTASY

Some people find it exciting to add an element of fantasy to their personal goal setting. Such fantasies can bridge the gap between personal and career goal setting. Typically, a fantasy goal is far beyond attainment at your present stage in life, but could someday become a realistic goal. Fantasy goals also reflect your vision of the ideal type of life you would like to lead. They help you dream the impossible dream. Many articles in *Success!* magazine have shown that people born into average circumstances can reach their fantasy goals. Here is a sampling of fantasy goals found in the career reports of young adults.

"I'd like to be a free-lance photographer for major news magazines. My specialty would be shooting civil unrest and border wars."

"I'd like to have a high school named after me in a poor neighborhood."

"Someday I would like to own a stable of horses and have one of them win the Kentucky Derby."

"I'd like to become one of the highest paid fashion models in New York City. At the same time, my face would become one of the most recognized in the country."

Aside from being exciting to pursue, fantasy goals are important for another reason. Research suggests that your fantasy life can help with personal adjustment and overcoming stress. A well-developed fantasy can result in a pleasurable state of physical and mental relaxation. Furthermore, fantasy goals can help you cope with an unpleasant current situation by giving you hope for the future.[10]

EXHIBIT 2–3   TOM TURNS AROUND A BUSINESS PROBLEM*

Tom Valdez owned and operated Computer Discount, a store that sold computer hardware and software. Business grew quickly to the point where Tom and his assistant were unable to handle the volume by themselves. Tom decided to hire a full-time manager. After several months of searching for the right candidate, Tom hired Dave Parsons, a high school computer science teacher.

Tom and Dave agreed upon an incentive plan that would give Dave a starting salary of $600 per month plus 50 percent of the profits in excess of Computer Discount's first-year profits. In addition, Dave would become a part-owner of the business at the end of a summer probationary period.

Both men entered the new relationship with enthusiasm. Tom anticipated an expansion of the company, while Dave looked forward to a career change and a larger income. However, personality differences soon became apparent in their working relationship. Tom was ambitious, optimistic, aggressive, and impulsive. He maintained control over every aspect of the operation from installing computer systems in customer offices, to locking the store doors at night. Dave was much more laid back and methodical.

Tom called upon Dave primarily to cover walk-in customers and handle demonstrations. As Dave's frustrations mounted, he told the assistant, "Tom led me to believe that I was to become a partner in the business, not a glorified store clerk." Tom was also dissatisfied with his working relationship with Dave. Tom told the assistant, "Dave is learning the business too slowly. He has yet to free me up enough to justify his salary."

Valdez called in a consultant, Dr. Eugene Falco, to help him decide how to resolve the problem. To Tom's surprise, Falco's first move was to have him establish clear short- and long-term goals for both himself and the company. Tom said his short-term goal was to increase sales to $600,000 the following year. His long-term goal was to expand the company into franchises. Tom developed detailed action plans to back up these goals.

The consultant told him, "Tom, this plan looks good. You've decided that to reach your goals, you need to bring a manager into the company. Before bringing in such a manager, you must specify how a manager could help you, and what the manager would be responsible for. Since Dave Parsons is already on board, let's bring him into these sessions to get his opinion."

Together Tom and Dave planned how Dave should go about learning each aspect of the company, and how Tom could help Dave learn the business. Falco stressed that Tom and Dave should work together in setting goals for Dave. He said, "In a small-company atmosphere, you need democracy."

Tom and Dave agree to extend their working relationship for a second probationary period with the same terms as the original contract. Dave helped Tom establish goals and action plans for the company, giving them both a better understanding of each other's positions. The company has since expanded to several locations. Dave Parsons now owns the franchise to operate the store he was originally hired to manage.

The turnaround of Computer Discount is a dramatic illustration of the potential value of goal setting. Tom and Dave were floundering before they set goals and action plans. Neither had a clear picture of his responsibilities in the newly formed business relationship. Tom had neglected to translate clearly his goals and ideas in terms of the role Dave would play in the future of Computer Discount. Their personality differences became relatively unimportant once they focused their efforts on mutually agreed-upon goals.

---

* Case researched by Tamara L. Browning, The Rochester Institute of Technology.

ADDITIONAL TECHNIQUES FOR
SELF-MOTIVATION

Many people never achieve satisfying careers and never realize their potential because of low motivation. They believe they could perform better but admit, "I'm just not a go-getter," or "My motivation is low." Goal setting is one of the most important techniques of self-motivation. If you set long-range goals and back them up with a series of smaller goals set for shorter time spans, your motivation will increase.

Assume you knew that once you had passed a real estate broker's licensing exam you would be guaranteed a lucrative job as a commercial real estate broker. You would have two clearly defined goals: attaining the new position, and passing the exam. If the position was important to you, you would be strongly motivated to pass the exam. Your longer-range goal of having a satisfying career would lead you to set shorter-range goals such as, "Study two hours today."

Here we discuss five additional techniques of self-motivation:

1. Identify the needs you are trying to satisfy.
2. Get feedback on your performance.
3. Apply behavior modification to yourself.
4. Improve your skills relevant to your goals.
5. Raise your level of self-expectation.

Identify the Needs You Are Trying to Satisfy

A **need** is a deficit within a person that creates a craving for its satisfaction. Unsatisfied needs are generally strong motivators because the person tries to fulfill them. Dozens of psychological needs have been observed. The best-known category of needs is **Maslow's need hierarchy.** According to psychologist Abraham Maslow, people strive to satisfy the following groups of needs, in step-by-step order:

1. *Physiological needs* refer to bodily needs, such as the requirements for food, water, shelter, and sleep.
2. *Safety needs* refer to actual physical safety and to a feeling of being safe from both physical and emotional injury.
3. *Social needs* are essentially love or belonging needs. Unlike the two previous levels of needs, they center around a person's interaction with other people.
4. *Esteem needs* represent an individual's demands to be seen as a person of worth by others—and to himself or herself.
5. *Self-actualizing* needs are the highest levels of needs, including the need for self-fulfillment and personal development.[11]

Other important needs useful in motivating yourself include achievement, power, and recognition. **Achievement** is the need to accomplish something difficult, to win over others. **Power** is a strong need to control other people and resources, and to want fame. **Recognition** is a need to be noticed by others, usually for a worthwhile accomplishment.

How do these needs relate to self-motivation? First you have to ask yourself, "Which need or needs do I really want to satisfy?" After answering that question honestly, concentrate your efforts in an activity that will most likely satisfy that need. For instance, if you are hungry for power, strive to become a high-level manager or a business owner. If you crave esteem, focus your efforts on work and social activities that are well-regarded by others. The point is that you will put forth substantial effort if you think the goal you attain will satisfy an important need.

Get Feedback on Your Performance

Few people can sustain a high level of motivation without receiving information about how well they are doing. Even if you find your work to be challenging and exciting, you will need feedback. One reason feedback is valuable is that it acts as a reward. If you learn that your efforts achieved a worthwhile purpose, you will feel encouraged. For example, if a graphics display you designed was well received by company officials, you would probably want to prepare another graphics display.

Apply Behavior Modification to Yourself

Behavior modification is a system of motivating people that emphasizes rewarding them for doing the right things and punishing them for doing the wrong things. In recent years, behavior modification has been used by many people to change their own behavior. Specific purposes include overcoming eating disorders, tobacco addiction, nail biting, and procrastination.

To boost your own motivation through behavior modification you would have to first decide what specific motivated actions you want to increase (such as working thirty minutes longer each day). Second, you would have to decide on a suitable set of rewards and punishments. You may choose to use rewards only, since rewards are generally better motivators than punishments.

Getting back to the extra half-hour of work example, you might treat yourself to a six-pack of your favorite beverage each week that you stayed with your new schedule. If you use punishments also, you might donate ten dollars to a political party you dislike each week you deviated from the new schedule.

Improve Your Skills Relevant to Your Goals

The **expectancy theory of motivation** states that people will be motivated if they believe that their efforts will lead to desired outcomes. According to this theory, people hold back effort when they lack confidence that their efforts will lead to accomplishments. For example, many unemployed teenagers appear to be poorly motivated to apply for jobs even when openings exist. According to one employment counselor, these people are only poorly motivated because they lack confidence in their interviewee skills. One way to increase the motivation of these teenagers is to help them develop skill in being interviewed and completing a job application form.

Similarly, you may be able to increase your motivation by developing skills relevant to goals you want to achieve. For example, you might become better motivated to write reports if you develop good report-writing skills.

Raise Your Level of Self Expectation

A final strategy for increasing your level of motivation is to simply expect more from yourself. If you raise your level of self expectation—if you expect more from yourself—you are likely to achieve more.

Often this same phenomenon is called developing a **positive mental attitude,** a conviction that you will succeed. Since you expect to succeed, you do succeed. The net effect is the same as if you had increased your level of motivation.

High self expectations and a positive mental attitude take a long time to develop. However, they are critically important for becoming a well-motivated person in a variety of situations.

SUMMARY

A goal is an event, circumstance, object, or condition a person strives to attain. Goals are valuable because they (1) focus efforts in a consistent direction, (2) improve one's chances for success, and (3) improve motivation and satisfaction.

An effective goal (1) is clear, concise, and unambiguous; (2) describes what you would be doing if you reached your goal; (3) uses past performance as a guide; (4) is interesting and challenging whenever possible; (5) specifies what, who, when, and how; (6) is subject to review from time to time.

Goals can be classified according to whether they are used to maintain the status quo (maintenance goals) or whether they are challenging. Highly challenging goals are referred to as "breakthrough" goals. Goals can also be classified according to the time in which they will be accomplished: long range, medium range, short range, daily, and immediate.

Goal setting is widely used on the job. Goals set by employees at lower levels in an organization are supposed to contribute to goals set at the top. Frequently individual employees are asked to participate in goal setting by contributing ideas of their own.

Goal setting in personal life can contribute to life satisfaction. For maximum advantage personal goals should be integrated with career goals. Areas of life in which personal goals may be set include (1) social and family, (2) hobbies and interests, (3) physical and mental health, and (4) financial.

Action plans are an essential part of goal setting because they indicate how you will reach your goal. Immediate goals do not usually require an action plan, however, because the plan is self-evident.

Goals can create some problems if they are pursued too strictly. For example, in the pursuit of quantity you may neglect quality. Or, you can become so obsessed with your goals that you neglect emergencies or unplanned opportunities that arise.

Fantasy goals have a place in life. They help point you toward an ideal state of events to strive for. In addition, they can help you with personal adjustment and overcoming stress because a fantasy can be physically and mentally relaxing.

Key techniques of self-motivation in addition to goal setting are: (1) identify the needs you are trying to satisfy, (2) get feedback on your performance, (3) apply behavior modification to yourself, (4) improve your skills relevant to your goals, and (5) raise your level of self expectation.

QUESTIONS AND ACTIVITIES

1. So far, how useful has goal setting been to you in your work and personal life?
2. A twenty-two year old man wrote in a career report that his goal was to become President of the United States. His job at the time was floor manager in a department store. If you were his instructor, what comments would you make about his goal?
3. Is a person who sets easy goals necessarily lazy? Explain.
4. Success books have been criticized for encouraging almost everyone to shoot for the top. What is wrong, statistically and psychologically, with everyone shooting for the top?
5. In what way are dreams used as goals?
6. What goals do business firms have in addition to making a profit?
7. In order to improve their motivation, some people listen to tapes with inspirational messages about having a positive mental attitude. How effective do you think these tapes are likely to be?
8. Ask any manager if his or her company uses goal setting. If the answer is affirmative, ask for details about the goal-setting system. Be prepared to discuss your findings in class.
9. How can setting easy goals be used to make you look good?
10. What needs can you satisfy by achieving your career goals?

A HUMAN RELATIONS CASE PROBLEM:
STOP MANIPULATING ME

You are the chief administrator of a foundling home that receives much of its support from the United Way. The United Way decides that every agency receiving support will operate under a system of goal setting called management by objectives (MBO). You spend one week in a training program on MBO and leave with a good understanding of what is required to operate the system. You hold a conference with your staff to announce the MBO program.

As a starting point, you schedule a conference with Irene, the director of placement, who is in charge of placing children in foster homes. You ask Irene to complete a form that focuses on employee goal setting. You also ask her to meet with you again to discuss her goals (or objectives as they are called in MBO).

On the agreed-upon date, you open the meeting with Irene in this manner: "Thanks for being here so promptly, Irene. Could you please tell me what objectives you have established for yourself? She replies, "Stop trying to manipulate me. They are your objectives and you know it. I won't be part of this deception."

Questions

1. In what way does Irene feel she is being manipulated?
2. Do you believe that Irene is being manipulated?
3. How can you change Irene's attitude?
4. What is the nature of the misunderstanding between you and Irene?

A HUMAN RELATIONS ROLE PLAY: THE MANIPULATED GOAL SETTER

Now that you have analyzed the above case problem, it can serve as a useful role play. One person plays the role of the chief administrator of the foundling home. The other person plays the role of Irene, the director of placement. After listening to Irene's complaints of being manipulated, the chief administrator tries to convince her that goal setting can be beneficial to her and the agency. Irene, however, strongly believes that she is being manipulated.

In this and subsequent role plays, follow the general directions about role plays given in the role play for Chapter 1. For example, those students not chosen for this role play should observe the role players and provide feedback to them later.

REFERENCES

[1] "Getting There: 1983 *Success* Magazine Goal-Setting Guide," *Success!*, January 1983, p. A10.

[2] David L. Watson and Roland G. Tharp, *Self-directed Behavior: Self-modification for Personal Adjustment,* 2nd ed. (Monterey, CA: Brooks/Cole Publishing Company, 1977), p. 26.

[3] George S. Odiorne, *The Effective Executive's Guide to Successful Goal Setting* (Westfield, MA: MBO, Inc., 1980), p. 7.

[4] David Campbell, *If You Don't Know Where You're Going, You'll Probably End Up Somewhere Else* (Niles, IL: Argus Communication, 1974), p. 12.

[5] Ann Ellenson, *Human Relations* (Englewood Cliffs, NJ: Prentice-Hall, 1973), p. 124.

[6] Based on Campbell, *If You Don't Know,* pp. 36–40.

[7] Ibid., p. 41.

[8] Miriam Erez, P. Christopher Earley, and Charles L. Hulin, "The Impact of Participation on Goal Acceptance and Performance," *Academy of Management Journal,* March 1985, pp. 50–66.

[9] Peter Gibb, "Appraisal Goals and Controls," *Personnel Journal,* August 1985, pp. 89–93.

[10] Stephen Sprinkel, "Not Having Fantasies Can Be Hazardous to Your Health, Counselor Says," Gannett News Service story, April 10, 1982.

[11] The original statement of this famous explanation of human motivation is Abraham H. Maslow, "A Theory of Human Motivation," *Psychological Review,* July 1943, pp. 370–396. See also, Maslow, *Motivation and Personality* (New York: Harper & Row, 1954).

SOME ADDITIONAL READING

"A Sense of Control: PT Conversation with Judith Rodin." *Psychology Today,* December 1984, pp. 38–45.

ACKERMAN, LEONARD, and JOSEPH P. GRUENWALD. "Help Employees Motivate Themselves." *Personnel Journal,* July 1984, pp. 54–62.

EREZ, MIRIAM, and FREDERICK H. KANFER. "The Role of Goal Acceptance in Goal Setting and Task Performance." *Academy of Management Review,* July 1983, pp. 454–463.

FORD, GEORGE A., and GORDON L. LIPPITT. *Planning Your Future: A Workbook for Personal Goal Setting.* La Jolla, CA: University Associates, 1976.

KIM, JAY S. "Effect of Behavior Plus Outcome Goal Setting and Feedback on Employee Satisfaction and Performance." *Academy of Management Journal,* March 1984, pp. 139–149.

MACKENZIE, R. ALEC. "The 'To Do' List is Obsolete." *Supervisory Management,* September 1985, pp. 41–43.

REBER, ROBERT A., and JERRY A. WALLIN. "The Effects of Training, Goal Setting, and Knowledge of Results on Safe Behavior: A Component Analysis." *Academy of Management Journal,* September 1984, pp. 544–560.

ROSENBAUM, BERNARD L. *How to Motivate Today's Workers: Motivational Models for Managers and Supervisors.* New York: McGraw-Hill, 1982.

3

Solving Problems and Making Decisions

Learning Objectives

After studying the information and doing the exercises in this chapter, you should be able to:

- Solve problems and make decisions more effectively
- Understand how your personal characteristics influence your approach to solving problems and making decisions
- Recognize that some people are systematic while others are intuitive in their basic problem-solving approaches
- Take a more creative approach to problem solving and decision making

WHAT IS THE DIFFERENCE BETWEEN SOLVING PROBLEMS AND MAKING DECISIONS?

Alison and Brad were seated by a campfire, roasting frankfurters. With a gulping sensation in his throat, Brad turned to Alison and said, "Alison, I'm in love with you. How about you and I getting married? I know we'd be very happy as a lifelong team."

Immediately, Alison felt a surge of emotion. She now faced a major problem: Brad's proposal had placed an obstacle in her path to leading the type of life she wanted for now. "If I say yes to Brad, that will mean an end to dating other men as long as he's my fiancé or husband." Alison had to decide how to respond to Brad at that moment. "If I say yes to Brad, he'll be happy, but I'll be very uncomfortable. If I say no to Brad, I'll feel better but I might lose his friendship. If I say maybe, it will only prolong the suspense. I have to say something; I can't just sit here eating my frankfurter."

Problem solving and decision making are closely related to one another. You have a problem to solve when an obstacle blocks the path you want to take. Worded in another way, a **problem** is a gap between what exists and what you want to exist. Allison wants a nonexclusive relationship with Brad, and he has just requested a very exclusive relationship.

Decision making means selecting one alternative from the various alternatives or courses of action that can be pursued. Alison can say yes, no, or maybe to Brad. Or perhaps she can just ignore his comments (a rude alternative). Being faced with a problem forces you to make a decision. Decision making takes place after you recognize that a problem exists.

TWO MAJOR TYPES OF DECISIONS

Most of the information in this chapter is designed to help you solve unique and/or major decisions. Often such decisions are called nonprogrammed because no ready alternative exists. A **nonprogrammed decision** is thus a decision for which alternative solutions have not been prepared in advance. You have to arrive at a creative solution to the problem. Here are several examples of nonprogrammed decisions you are likely to face within the next decade:

Should I live alone or try to find a roommate?
Should I purchase a new or used car?

Which new car should I purchase?

Should we try to have another child?

In contrast to the above, a **programmed decision** is one in which the alternative solutions are known in advance. Programmed decisions are often made almost automatically. Many programmed decisions are so routine that you wouldn't be willing to devote much energy to improving your ability to make them. Among them are:

Should I sign this check with a felt tip or ball pen?

Should I renew my operator's license?

Should I pay my utility bill?

Should I order buttered or unbuttered popcorn?

Do I want ale or beer?

A word of caution: some people are so undecisive that they have problems with even the most routine decisions. The classic case concerns the man who was asked whether he wanted ketchup, mustard, or mayonnaise on his roast beef sandwich. To the bewilderment of the waitress, he replied, "I'm not sure. Let me think about it for a while."

People who are this indecisive are sometimes suffering from depression, a state in which emotions, thoughts, and bodily processes are slowed down. If depression is the cause of indecisiveness, the person will not become more decisive until the depression is treated or goes away spontaneously. The two main treatments for depression include antidepressant medication and psychotherapy.

EVALUATING YOUR PROBLEM-SOLVING TENDENCIES

Before reading more about problem solving, we recommend that you take stock of your present problem-solving tendencies. Psychologist Salvatore Didato developed the brief quiz on the following page to measure the quality of one's problem solving.

PERSONAL CHARACTERISTICS THAT INFLUENCE YOUR PROBLEM-SOLVING ABILITY

As the quiz implies, not everybody is equally adept at solving problems. Dozens of personal characteristics and traits influence the type of problem solver and decision maker you are now or are capable of

QUIZ ABOUT PROBLEM SOLVING

SCORING

All items in the quiz are examples of pitfalls common to poor problem solvers. Give yourself one point for each item you answered true. Then consider the following interpretations:

0 to 3 points: You have a solid approach to solving problems. You are the person to ask when a good solution to a problem is needed.

4 to 6 points: You are an average problem solver. Some conflicts you find easy to solve, but others are more difficult.

7 to 10 points: You are weak as a problem solver. You rely too heavily upon your assumptions instead of examining the facts. Try to be more open-minded and flexible about solutions.[1]

EXPLANATION

Many people fall into problem-solving traps. Many of us have strong tendencies to deny that problems even exist in our daily lives. This is wishful thinking and items 1 and 4 give such examples. Another trap in problem solving is to fall into a rigid mental set. This one-sided outlook hampers our flexibility to arrive at good solutions. More will be said about overcoming rigid mental sets at several places in this chapter. Problem-solving ability cannot be improved without improving mental flexibility.

Indicate if the following statements are true or false about you. Then read on for the scoring and an explanation:

____ 1. Most problems solve themselves in one way or another.
____ 2. I'm known to be a perfectionist when it comes to solving problems.
____ 3. It's usually true that the first answer that comes to mind is the one to follow.
____ 4. I often shelve vexing problems and hope that they will go away.
____ 5. I often become rattled by tough problems.
____ 6. I often let others make decisions for me.
____ 7. I would prefer a job where I didn't have the burden of making decisions.
____ 8. I've never been able to judge how well I did on an exam.
____ 9. It's hard for me to admit that a solution of mine isn't working out well.
____ 10. It's hard to accept a solution from someone who is younger than I am or below my professional level.

becoming. Fortunately some personal characteristics that influence your decision-making ability can be improved through conscious effort. For instance, if you make bad decisions because you have limited information, you can take steps to become a more knowledgeable person. Most of the personal characteristics described next can be strengthened through the appropriate education, training, and self-discipline.

Flexibility Versus Rigidity

Some people are successful problem solvers and decision makers because they approach every problem with a fresh outlook. They are able to avoid developing rigid mental sets. It has been said that uncreative people are those who suffer from a "hardening of the categories." If you can overcome the traditional way of thinking about things, you can solve some very difficult problems, as illustrated in the following situation:

> A motorcyclist was doing at least fifty miles an hour on a country road. He hit a wet, sandy spot on the road and went into a skid. As he worked his way out of the skid he left the road and veered into what he thought was a meadow. Unfortunately, the meadow turned out to be an optical illusion. It was really the top of a group of trees. The cyclist and his cycle tumbled down a ravine. His main injury proved to be a broken leg. Unable to walk, he could not make a temporary brace for himself with three branches. His solution was to tie one leg to the other with his belt, and drag himself to a clearing. He was sighted by a passerby two hours later. The motorcycle rider's flexibility in defining what can serve as a make-do cast perhaps saved his life.

The example just presented illustrates intellectual flexibility. An informal test of the flexibility of your attitudes is this puzzling situation: A doctor and his son are involved in a head-on automobile collision. The doctor is killed and his son is severely injured. When the boy is brought into the operating room, the surgeon says in anguish, "I can't operate on this boy. He is my son." How is this possible? (See footnote 2 for the answer.)

Intelligence, Education, and Experience

In general, if you are intelligent, well-educated, and well-experienced you will make better decisions than people without these attributes. Intelligence helps because, by definition, intelligence denotes the ability to solve problems. Education improves the problem-solving and decision-making process because it gives you a background of principles and facts to rely on. Consider the young man who wanted to sell an old, oversized car. While trying to compose an ad to place on a community bulletin board, he reflected upon an advertising course he had taken. A key principle covered in that course was the importance of appealing to the needs of the potential consumer. He thought to himself, "Why would anybody want to buy this hulk of a car, especially with today's gasoline prices?" The answer he arrived at resulted in a sale ten hours after the ad was posted:

> WANT A HIGH STATUS CAR THAT WILL ALSO GIVE YOU THE MAXIMUM SAFETY FOR YOUR MONEY? How about a 1978 Chrysler four-door sedan for $900? Call Jim at 375–2299.

Experience facilitates decision making because good decisions tend to be made by people who have already faced similar situations in the past. This is one of the many reasons why experienced people command higher salaries. All things being equal, would you prefer to take your problem to an experienced or inexperienced specialist?

Decisiveness

Some people are ill-suited to solving problems and making decisions because they are fearful of committing themselves to any given course of action. "Gee, I'm not sure, what do you think?" is their typical response to a decision forced upon them. If you are indecisive, this characteristic will have to be modified if you are to become a success in your field. A scientist has to take a stand on what research project to pursue. A manager has to decide which person to hire. And a photographer has to decide which setting is best for the subject. As the old saying goes, at some point "you have to fish or cut bait."

Risk-Taking Attitude

Closely related to decisiveness is the willingness to take risks.[3] Big risks takers are more willing to make yes decisions than are low risk takers. How many times have you heard a middle-aged person say, "I would have been rich today if I had only bought stock in Company X (or had gone into business with my friend) twenty years ago." No one has ever become rich, famous, or really happy without taking some risks in life. To become a risk taker, you have to start taking prudent risks early in life. Here are some examples of prudent risks that proved to have favorable long-range outcomes:

A young American couple adopted an ill and injured Korean child. Today that child is a healthy, happy young adult who both gives and receives love.

A woman purchased an abandoned house in the city for $750. With an additional investment of $8,000 and hundreds of hours of hard work, she restored the house. Three years later she sold the house for $30,000.

Two teenage men invested $250 in equipment to get started in the driveway sealing business. Within two seasons they were paying all their schooling expenses with profits from the business.

Various Emotions

Decision making sounds like a scientific process. It often is, but frequently emotions take over from your intellect. Many people marry a person totally unsuited to their lifestyles because romantic attachment to the person outweighs their rational analysis of the situation.

One twenty-year-old woman married a fifty-year-old executive because she admired his maturity and success. Within three months she decided to move back home with her parents. Her explanation: "My husband's glamor image soon wore thin. He was out of town about three nights a week. I got bored being home alone."

Emotions enter into many other decisions that can range from making major purchases to choosing a school. It is not necessarily wrong to be influenced by your emotions, but you should try to recognize when you are not being rational. You might say to yourself, for example, "Is this VCR gear really worth going into debt for? Or am I buying it just to impress my friends?"

ARE YOU INTUITIVE OR SYSTEMATIC?

Some people are predisposed to being scientific about problem solving and decision making. Other people rely more on intuition, or "gut feel." There is room in this world for both kinds of decision makers. It has even been suggested that, ideally, people should find the right type of job to fit their basic problem-solving style.

When systematic types of people face a problem, they size up the situation, identify the main problem, organize a method of solution, and devise step-by-step procedures to carry it out.[4] Generally, we have been taught to favor this scientific approach and without doubt many types of work and social situations require systematic thinking. Among the tasks calling for systematic thinking are preparing income tax returns, plugging energy leaks in a house, preparing a picnic for one hundred people, and programming a computer.

Intuitive problem solvers go about tackling tasks in a more emotional way. They rapidly try out one solution after another in their minds. Often they do not really know how they arrive at an answer. Tasks in which the predominantly intuitive problem solver would be effective include developing a new idea for a meal, designing a dress, or coming up with an advertising slogan for a new product.

How Do You Know Your Own Style?

To determine your particular style ask people who know you well whether they think you are systematic or intuitive in your thinking. Another approach is to perform a laboratory exercise and then analyze the way you arrived at your answer. Did you arrive at a systematic or intuitive solution? Here is one such exercise performed by thousands of people:

> You are one of twenty people held captive in a room by a man with a gun who shows clear signs of being deranged. You and the other prisoners are quite sure his gun is loaded and that it holds six bullets. The gunman yells that he plans to kill you all. What would you urge the group to do?[5]

Neal is an example of a man who tackled this problem systematically. He first developed a plan, and then decided on methods for putting the plan into action. Neal recalled that the police have formulated some guidelines for dealing with hostage situations, an important one being to get the gunman to talk about himself and what he hopes to achieve. Neal suggested that the group first talk to the gunman and then try to negotiate with him.

John is an example of a person who used the intuitive approach in dealing with the hostage taker. He made various suggestions such as turning out the light and jumping the gunman or having everyone throw shoes at him simultaneously. John at first thought of storming the gunman, but then rejected the idea as being suicidal.[6]

GETTING THE SCIENTIFIC METHOD ON YOUR SIDE

Whatever the nonprogrammed situation you may be trying to resolve, it is best to use the scientific method. In other words, use a systematic approach similar to that used in the physical or behavioral sciences. The decision making to be presented here does not rule out the role of intuitive or creative thinking. Rather, finding creative alternatives to your problem is actually at the heart of the method. Figure 3–1 summarizes the steps in decision making. It is based on the assumption that decision making should take place in an orderly flow of steps.

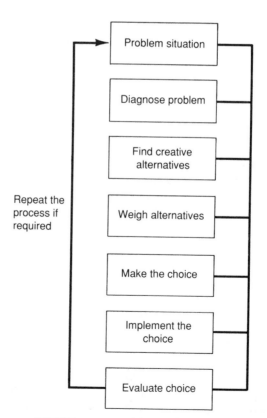

FIGURE 3–1. Decision-making steps.

Problem Situation

In most decision-making situations, problems are given to you. Alison was presented with the problem of what to do with Brad's proposal. At other times, people create their own problems to solve, or find problems. When one man decided that there were too many potholes in the streets of his town, he campaigned to force the town supervisor to take decisive action on the problem. In another case, an enterprising student set up a plant-sitting service in her neighborhood, thus creating her own problems to solve.

Diagnose the Problem

Problems should be diagnosed and clarified before any action is taken because they are not always what they seem to be on the surface. Some may be more complicated than suspected, or may even be the wrong problem you need to solve in a particular situation. The young man who found the potholes was thinking about treating the symptoms and not the real problem. Although it certainly would be advisable for the town to patch its potholes, the best solution is to attend to the cause of potholes. The town would never be able to change the weather conditions, of course, but it could strengthen all new pavement. One petroleum company, for example, has developed a webbing that dramatically reduces potholes when placed beneath the surface of a street.

If you properly diagnose a problem, your solution will probably be sound, as Exhibit 3–1 illustrates. Suppose you decided to take up a new sport in order to improve your physical condition, and your choice is racquet ball. After five months, you quit because you are bored and frustrated. Your progress was too slow. If you had diagnosed the problem you might have decided not to take up just any sport, but to take up a sport for which you had some basic aptitude. Maybe running or cycling would have been more suited to your natural talents.

Find Creative Alternatives

Here creativity and imagination enter into problem solving and decision making. Successful decision makers have the ability to think of different alternatives. The person who pushes to find one more alternative to a problem is often the person who finds a breakthrough solution. Consider the man who enrolled in a college 1,000 miles from his home. Excited about the prospects of attending this college, he had one pressing problem. "How do I go about moving my stuff down to the college? I would just hate the hassle of shipping the goods, picking them up at the railroad station, taking taxis, and looking for housing on foot."

EXHIBIT 3–1   WILLIE COPES WITH JOB BURNOUT

Willie, a youth counselor in a neighborhood center, found himself sinking into a condition of job burnout (a depressed, discouraged, and apathetic attitude that often stems from prolonged job stress). In talking about the problem, he noted, "The thing that drives me crazy is that nobody has any respect for my time. I might be in my office talking to a troubled kid, and another worker from the agency comes barging right in. Or another kid with a problem will interrupt us. I feel that I'm being jerked around without my having any control over the matter."

Once Willie talked over the problem, the solution became obvious. Although the agency was shorthanded, an arrangement was made whereby Willie's visitors were screened during the afternoons, ordinarily the peak busy period for the agency. An office assistant would sit at a desk outside Willie's office, performing the regular work while also serving as a receptionist. Visitors and agency personnel were both requested to have a seat or return later when Willie was free to see them. After two months of this new arrangement, Willie noticed that he felt less burnt out than in the past.

Willie's case example illustrates the value of clarifying a problem when trying to solve it. His real problem was that the lack of privacy and multiple interruptions were triggering a condition of burnout. When this situation was improved, Willie's mental condition also improved.

The nonstandard (creative) solution he came up with was to rent a car, using his father's credit card, with permission. In this way the man had a pleasant trip to the campus, felt like an important person, carried all the gear he wanted to, and readily found suitable housing. His rental car alternative was a good buy considering the cost of plane fare, shipment of goods, and taxi fare. Creativity plays such an important role in decision making that it will be discussed again in the next two major sections of this chapter.

Weigh Alternatives

This stage refers simply to examining the pros and cons of the various alternatives established in the previous stage. In a major decision, each alternative would have to be given serious consideration. In practice, weighing alternatives often means jotting down the key good and bad points of each possible choice. Part of Alison's list might read something like this:

Alternative 1, Agree to marry Brad

On the plus side, I would never have to go out on a blind date again, or spend time with men I do not care for. Brad is a find friend and would make a good husband. My parents would be happy to see me marry a guy with a good head on his shoulders.

On the negative side, I would give up the chance to someday find the perfect husband for me. I would be missing out on the chance to date new guys just for fun. If we had children in the first few years of marriage it would slow down my business career.

Make the Choice

Obviously the critical aspect of decision making is selecting the course of action to follow. You have to choose an alternative, even if it is not to go ahead with a new plan of action. For instance, you could decide not to buy a new stereo set, but to keep your present equipment. Experienced business executives have sometimes criticized well-educated young people for their lack of decisiveness. Trying to be very systematic, some well-educated people study a problem for a very long time before coming to a decision. How rapidly do you choose an alternative?

Implement the Choice

After you decide which course of action to take, you have to put that choice into effect. Some decisions are more difficult to implement than to make. Alison, for example, might decide that she would reject Brad's proposal and begin to date other men. When she received her first invitation from another fellow for a date, she might find it uncomfortable to accept. How many couples have you known who decide to split after an argument but soon get back together?

Some company decisions are so difficult to implement that they have to be reversed. When one executive, for example, announced the official policy that all employees would be restricted to forty-five-minute lunch breaks, few employees took the edict seriously. People continued to spend sixty minutes or so at lunch. The executive gave up and reconsidered the decision in terms of its effect on morale.

Evaluate Choice

The decision-making sequence is not complete until the decision has been evaluated. Evaluation may take a considerable period of time because the results of your decision are not always immediately apparent. Suppose you receive two job offers. It might take several months to a year to judge whether you are satisfied with the job you accepted. It would be necessary to look at the factors you think are most important in a job. Among them might be: "Is there opportunity for advancement?" "Are the people here friendly?" "Is the work interesting?" Evaluating your choice would be further complicated by the difficulty of determining how you might have fared in the job you didn't accept.

Now and then you might obtain some information to suggest what that alternative held in store for you, as did a woman who turned down a job offer with a new and promising company. She questioned that decision until she read one morning a year later that the company had gone into bankruptcy.

What happens when your evaluation of a decision is negative? You go back to the drawing board, as the line and arrow on the left-hand side of Figure 3–1 indicates. Since your first decision was not a good one, you are faced with another problem situation. Assume that a woman needs a refrigerator for her apartment. Wanting to save money, she purchases a fifteen-year-old used model for $100. Within three months the refrigerator breaks down. Her decision to purchase a used refrigerator backfired. Now she faces two new problems: how to finance a new refrigerator, and how to get the old one out of her apartment.

CREATIVE PROBLEM SOLVING AND DECISION MAKING

Creativity is the ability to developing good ideas that can be put into action, says advertising executive Edward H. Meyer. He also says that creativity is critical to success in business.[7] If you have above average creative ability you will be more adept at solving problems in both your work and personal life.

Three Myths About Creativity

Before proceeding further, it is important to dispel three myths about creativity. One myth is that people can be classified accurately as creative or noncreative. In reality, creativity is like height, intelligence, or strength. People vary considerably in these dimensions, but everyone has *some* height, *some* intelligence, and *some* strength.

A second myth about creativity is that it can only be exercised in a limited number of fields such as physical science, the arts, and advertising. Creativity, in truth, can be exercised in almost any setting. You can display creative ability in any field or subfield including manufacturing, office work, administrative work, and family life. Can you recall any creative idea that led to a whole new industry?

A third myth about creativity is that creative ideas are complex and technical. In reality, the most useful ideas are magnificently simple. Here is a classic example that answers the question you were just asked: A whole new industry was formed when two young men decided that computers could be in homes and small businesses as well as laboratories, universities, and business corporations. The two creative thinkers were Steve Jobs and Steve Wozniak, founders of Apple Computer. And here are two less dramatic examples of creativity in business that could result in millions of dollars earned or saved:

- In the mid-1980s the Internal Revenue Service started sending about 10 million taxpayers postcards instead of tax forms. The postcards are sent

to individuals as well as small businesses who used professional tax preparers in the past. People who receive the postcard can mail it back to the IRS if they want an income tax form and an instruction package. Or they can take the postcard to their tax preparer who will attach the label to the forms used in filling out the tax return. The government hopes to save about $1 million in postage and printing costs by using the postcards instead of sending out forms that are discarded. (Tax preparers usually have their own computerized forms.)

• A company was formed several years ago to lure customers from the U.S. Postal Service by selling postage stamps at a 23 percent discount. American Discount Stamps (ADS) of Houston pays full price for the stamps and affixes them to stickers about the size of a business card. Sticker space around the stamp is sold to advertisers. The sticker is resold to consumers at a discount underwritten by the advertising. The stamps are sold in packages of 20 and sometimes include coupons for the product advertised. The Postal Service approves of the ADS operation because the company pays full price for the stamps.

What Is Your Creative Potential?

One way to gain an understanding of creativity is to try out exercises used to measure creative potential. Psychologists have developed standardized tests to measure creativity, but here we confine our measurement of creative potential to the exercises presented in Exhibits 3–2 and 3–3. Do not be overly encouraged or dejected by any results you achieve on these exercises. They are designed to give only preliminary insights into whether or not your thought processes are similar to those of creative individuals.

EXHIBIT 3–2   CREATIVE PERSONALITY TEST

The following test will help you determine if certain aspects of your personality are similar to those of a creative individual. Since our test is for illustrative and research purposes, proceed with caution in mind. This is not a standardized psychological instrument. Such tests are not reprinted in general books.

Directions: Answer each of the following statements as "mostly true" or "mostly false." We are looking for general trends; therefore, do not be concerned if you answer true if they are not entirely true and false if they are not entirely false.

		Mostly True	*Mostly False*
1.	Novels are a waste of time. If you want to read, read nonfiction books.	——	——
2.	You have to admit, some crooks are very clever.	——	——
3.	People consider me to be a fastidious dresser. I despise looking shaggy.	——	——
4.	I am a person of very strong convictions. What's right is right; what's wrong is wrong.	——	——
5.	It doesn't bother me when my boss hands me vague instructions.	——	——
6.	Business before pleasure is a hard and fast rule in my life.	——	——

---

7. Taking a different route to work is fun, even if it takes longer.   ___ ___

8. Rules and regulations should not be taken too seriously. Most rules can be broken under unusual circumstances.   ___ ___

9. Playing with a new idea is fun even if it doesn't benefit me in the end.   ___ ___

10. People say that I have an excellent sense of humor.   ___ ___

11. Writers should try to avoid using unusual words and word combinations.   ___ ___

12. Detective work would have some appeal to me.   ___ ___

13. Crazy people have no good ideas.   ___ ___

14. Why write letters to friends when there are so many clever greeting cards available in the stores today?   ___ ___

15. Pleasing myself means more to me than pleasing others.   ___ ___

16. If you dig long enough, you will find the true answer to most questions.   ___ ___

Scoring the Test. The answer in the *creative direction* for each question is as follows:

1. Mostly False	7. Mostly True	13. Mostly False
2. Mostly True	8. Mostly True	14. Mostly False
3. Mostly False	9. Mostly True	15. Mostly True
4. Mostly False	10. Mostly True	16. Mostly False
5. Mostly True	11. Mostly False	
6. Mostly False	12. Mostly True	

Give yourself a plus one for each answer you gave that agreed with the keyed answers.

How Do You Interpret Your Score? As cautioned earlier, this is an exploratory test. Extremely high or low scores are probably the most meaningful. A score of 12 or more suggests that your personality and attitudes are similar to those of a creative person. A score of 5 or less suggests that your personality is dissimilar to that of a creative person. You are probably more of a conformist (and somewhat categorical) in your thinking, at least at this point in your life. Don't be discouraged. Most people can become more creative.

IMPROVING YOUR CREATIVITY ON YOUR OWN

Perhaps you did not score as highly as you would have liked in the two creativity tests. Perhaps your self-evaluation is also that you are not as creative as you would like to be. Pessimism is not necessarily in order. Techniques are available to help you develop your creative po-

EXHIBIT 3–3   RHYME AND REASON*

A noted creativity expert says that exercises in rhyming release creative energy; they stir imagination into action. While doing the following exercises remember that rhyme is frequently a matter of sound and does not have to involve similar or identical spelling. This exercise deals with light and frivolous emotions.

After each "definition," write two rhyming words to which it refers.

Examples:

1.	Large hog	Big	pig
2.	Television	Boob	tube
3.	Cooperative female	Game	dame

Now try these:

1.	Happy father	——	——
2.	False pain	——	——
3.	Formed like a simian	——	——
4.	Highest-ranking police worker	——	——
5.	Voyage by a large boat	——	——
6.	Corpulent feline	——	——
7.	Melancholy fellow	——	——
8.	Clever beginning	——	——
9.	Heavy and unbroken slumber	——	——
10.	Crazy custom	——	——
11.	Lengthy melody	——	——
12.	Weak man	——	——
13.	Instruction at the seashore	——	——
14.	Criticism lacking in effectiveness	——	——
15.	A person who murders for pleasurable excitement	——	——
16.	Musical stringed instrument with full, rich sounds	——	——
17.	Courageous person who is owned as property by another	——	——
18.	Mature complaint	——	——
19.	Strange hair growing on the lower part of a man's face	——	——
20.	Drooping marine crustacean	——	——
21.	A man, short in height, accompanying a woman.	——	——

Answers and interpretation. Obviously, the more of these rhymes you were able to come up with, the higher your creative potential. You would also need an advanced vocabulary to score very high (for instance, what is a "simian" or a "crustacean"?). Ten or more correct rhymes would tend to show outstanding creative potential, at least in the verbal area.

Here are the answers:

1.	Glad dad	12.	Frail male
2.	Fake ache	13.	Beach teach
3.	Ape shape	14.	Weak critique
4.	Top cop	15.	Thriller killer
5.	Ship trip	16.	Mellow cello
6.	Fat cat	17.	Brave slave
7.	Sad lad	18.	Ripe gripe
8.	Smart start	19.	Weird beard
9.	Deep sleep	20.	Limp shrimp
10.	Mad fad	21.	Short escort
11.	Long song		

If you can think of a sensible substitute for any of these answers, give yourself a bonus point. For example, for number 21 how about a four-foot-eight date?

---

* This rhyme and reason exercise and its interpretation are reproduced from Eugene Raudsepp with George P. Hough, Jr., *Creative Growth Games* (New York: Harcourt Brace Jovanovich, 1977).

tential, if you want to develop in that direction. We suggest several do-it-yourself techniques for improving your creativity. If you are committed to improving your creativity, formal training programs and courses such as group brainstorming should also be investigated.[8]

Loosen up Emotionally and Intellectually

All methods of creativity improvement are based on the principle of loosening up emotionally and intellectually. As long as you remain a "tight" or rigid individual, you will have difficulty giving free rein to your creative potential. On occasion an encounter group can help you to loosen up in expressing your feelings, as illustrated in Exhibit 3–4. In the process, you become a more creative problem solver and decision maker.

Overcome Rigid Mental Sets

One creativity-enhancing consequence of becoming looser intellectually is that you can overcome **rigid mental sets,** a fixed way of looking at things. Overcoming rigid mental sets is important because the major block to creativity is the inability to overcome traditional ways of looking at things. In contrast, creative ideas usually stem from looking at situations in new ways. All the creative examples presented so far in this chapter involve this process. To illustrate, the person who

---

EXHIBIT 3–4   CORA'S CREATIVE GIMMICK

Employed as an assistant to the general manager of an industrial company, Cora felt she was running out of innovative ideas. Assigned to the task of developing a new productivity campaign for the plant, Cora could only think of conventional, much-used approaches. Partly as a way of relieving her work-accumulated tensions and partly as a way of opening herself up to new experiences, Cora joined an encounter group.

The encounter group met one night a week for three hours. By the third week, Cora noticed that her thinking was becoming more expansive and free floating. Unexpectedly she arrived at a solid idea for the productivity campaign. She explains how:

> By the third session we were really emoting. Nobody seemed to be holding back anything. One fellow was talking about the way he hated being oppressed by his company and his boss. One of the women was telling how she was frightened by the prospects of having so much responsibility thrown on her on the job and at home. I was getting high on all the honest expressions of feelings running through the room. I was seeing relationships I never saw before. I could feel barriers to my thinking falling in front of me.
>
> At the high point of my high, an idea for a productivity campaign seemed to jump into view right in front of me: "Three silver dollars for three million."
>
> My idea was to give everybody in the plant three silver dollars any month that our shipments reached $3 million. It was a simple gimmick, but our plant personnel liked simple gimmicks. The general manager loved the idea. So did his boss when the campaign helped push us over the $3 million mark for the first time in the plant's history.

---

developed the postage stamp business overcame the traditional mental set of stamps being sold only at their "sticker price."

A woman improved her social life by overcoming traditional thinking about how to meet men. Her nontraditional—and therefore creative—method worked well, as described next.

> A young woman enrolled in business school decided that she wanted to enrich her social life by dating men she thought were exceptional. After pondering over many possibilities, she arrived at this unique plan. She decided to write fan letters to fellows at the school whom she knew about but did not know personally. When one man was elected president of the school association, she wrote him a congratulatory note. Among her comments were, "You can count on me for full support." She wrote the newly appointed manager of the book store a similar congratulatory note, emphasizing that "It was nice to see a young person achieve so much responsibility." Within weeks, this young woman's social calendar was filled with the kind of men she cared to be with.

Discipline Yourself to Think Creatively

Self-discipline is required for all forms of self-development, including the improvement of your creativity. To become more creative you must first believe that creativity is both important and desirable.

When you are faced with a job or personal problem calling for a creative response, one effective starting point is to sit quietly with a pencil and pad and think up possible solutions. For example, "How can I prove to my boss that I'm worthy of a 10 percent salary increase?"[9] Few people have developed the self-discipline to concentrate on a problem in this manner for more than a few moments at a time.

The type of exercises designed to measure your creativity described earlier in the chapter can also develop effective approaches for improving creativity. By disciplining yourself to perform such exercises as making up unusual rhymes you will develop more fluency in your thinking. After conducting these warm-up exercises, you should be able to tackle problems requiring creativity more readily. One example would be, "What are five different things my store could do with our used boxes?"

Conduct Private Brainstorming Sessions

Brainstorming is a technique by which group members think of multiple solutions to a problem. Thus, a group of six people might sit around a table generating new ideas for a product. During the idea-generating part of brainstorming, potential solutions are not criticized or evaluated in any way. In this way, spontaneity is encouraged. Seat belts for pets is one product that stemmed from brainstorming. How's that for making the world a safer place?

Experiments have demonstrated that good ideas are forthcoming from group brainstorming. Yet valuable ideas also stem from **private brainstorming,** a modification of brainstorming conducted by yourself. The three creativity-improvement techniques already described will help you to develop the mental flexibility necessary for brainstorming. After you have loosened up your mental processes, you will be ready to tackle your most vexing problems.

An important requirement of private brainstorming is that you set aside a regular time (and perhaps place) for generating ideas. The ideas discovered in the process of routine activities can be counted as bonus time. Even five minutes a day is much more time than most people are accustomed to thinking creatively about job problems. Give yourself a quota with a time deadline.

Hal was a part owner of a hardware store. He had agreed to take on the assignment of thinking of an effective way of raising some quick cash for his store. Hal allowed himself six days to find a solution to this problem. His proposed solutions were: (1) pawn some expensive merchandise, (2) borrow money from a bank or loan company, (3) establish a fix-it service for minor household repairs, and (4) hold a garage sale for damaged or slow-moving merchandise.

The garage sale idea proved to be a winner that was subsequently copied by other merchants in the area. Hal and his co-owner were able to raise several thousand dollars in needed cash and simultaneously clear some of the clutter from their store. As a result, Hal increased his confidence in his ability to think creatively about job problems.

Be Curious

Curiosity is often the driving force behind creative ideas. The person who routinely questions why things work or why they don't work is on the way toward developing a creative suggestion to improve what already exists. Many new ideas for products and services stem from the curiosity of their developers. An office supervisor in a plumbing supply company encouraged his firm to develop a new mechanism that would prevent water closets from leaking. His suggestion stemmed from his curiosity as to why many places he visited had trouble with running toilets. The product that resulted is built on a new principle. It uses water pressure to replace the troublesome floating bulb arrangement found in most water closets (in the tank over the toilet bowl).

Maintain (and Use) an Idea Notebook

It is difficult to capitalize on your creative ideas unless you keep a careful record of them. A creative idea entrusted to memory may be forgotten under the pressures of everyday living. An important new idea kept on your list of daily errands or duties may become lost. Because creative ideas carry considerable weight in propelling your career forward, they deserve to be recorded in a separate notebook.

Do Not Fear Failure

If you try a large number of ideas, projects, or other things, a large number of them will probably fail. Yet your number of "hits" will be much higher than if you tried only a few creative ideas and all of them were successful. It is the absolute number of successes that counts the most—not the percentage of successes.[10] Both successful companies and individuals have many failed ventures in their files. For example, the vast majority of new products fail. Instant mashed potatoes is one well-known failure. Can you think of another?

Borrow Creative Ideas

Copying the successful ideas of others is a legitimate form of creativity. Be careful, however, to give appropriate credit. Knowing when and which ideas to borrow from other people can help you behave as if you were an imaginative person. Creative ideas can be borrowed through such methods as:

Speaking to friends, relatives, classmates, and co-workers

Reading newspapers, newsmagazines, trade magazines, textbooks, non-fiction books, and novels

Watching television and listening to radio programs

Subscribing to computerized information services (very expensive but worth it to many ambitious people)

SUMMARY

Problem solving occurs when you try to remove an obstacle blocking a path you want to take, or when you try to close the gap between what exists and what you want to exist. Decision making takes place after you encounter a problem. It refers to selecting one alternative from the various courses of action that can be pursued.

A nonprogrmamed decision is one in which the alternatives are not known in advance. Nonprogrammed decisions therefore are unique and often complex. A programmed decision has the alternatives already specified and usually involves a routine matter, such as affixing the right postage to a package.

One of the major pitfalls in solving problems is having a rigid mental set. This one-sided outlook hampers our flexibility to arrive at good solutions. Most creativity-building exercises are aimed at helping people become more flexible thinkers.

Dozens of traits and characteristics influence the type of problem solver and decision maker you are now or are capable of becoming. Among them are: (1) flexibility versus rigidity; (2) intelligence, education, and experience; (3) decisiveness; (4) risk-taking attitude; and (5) various emotions.

Two main types of problem solvers and decision makers are systematic and intuitive. Systematic people carefully evaluate a problem and devise step-by-step procedures for resolving it. Intuitive problem solvers rely more on hunches and emotion. Often they are not aware of how they arrived at a solution to a problem.

The decision-making process outlined in this chapter uses both the scientific method and intuition for making decisions in response to problems. Decision making follows an orderly flow of events:

1. You are faced with a problem or create one of your own.
2. You diagnose the problem.
3. You search for creative alternatives.
4. You weigh the alternatives.
5. You make the choice.

6. You implement the choice.
7. You evaluate whether you have made a sound choice. If your choice was unsound, you are faced with a new problem and the cycle repeats itself.

Creativity is the ability to develop good ideas that can be put into action and is related to success in both work and personal life. Most people have some creative ability, and creativity can be exercised in almost any setting. Many creative ideas are magnificently simple. Tests of creativity can provide tentative ideas about your creative potential.

Eight ways of improving creativity on your own are: (1) loosen up emotionally and intellectually, (2) overcome rigid mental sets, (3) discipline yourself to think creatively, (4) conduct private brainstorming sessions, (5) be curious, (6) maintain an idea notebook, (7) do not fear failure, and (8) borrow creative ideas.

QUESTIONS AND ACTIVITIES

1. Give three examples of decisions you have faced, or will face, that should be put through the decision-making steps.
2. Potential new-car buyers face the decision of whether to buy or lease a new car. Explain whether they are facing a programmed or a nonprogrammed decision.
3. Ask any manager the steps he or she follows in making a major decision. Compare the manager's method to the decision-making steps.
4. How might impulsiveness interfere with effective problem solving and decision making?
5. How can you tell if someone's attitude is so rigid that it interferes with problem solving?
6. How can you tell if somebody is a low or high risk taker?
7. Do you think it would be better to be intuitive or systematic in selecting a life partner? Explain your reasoning.
8. After studying about creativity, one person said, "Creativity won't do me any good. I have a routine job." How would you respond to this person?
9. What do you think are one or two potential disadvantages of being creative on the job?
10. How does one know if the alternative solution chosen to a problem is a good one?

A HUMAN RELATIONS CASE PROBLEM:
THE TRADITIONAL THINKERS

Laura Madison, president of Elgin's department store, met with her team of managers at a Sunday brunch. After the meal was served, Madison began her formal presentation with these words:

> I've called this special meeting only because I have to deal with a topic that is better handled in person than by memo. Elgin's has reached a crossroads, and its fate is in your hands. Our share of the market in all five locations has shown a steady decline over the past five years. We have got to do something about this problem, or we will be closing our doors within several years.
>
> As you know, we've conducted consumer surveys to find out what our customers like about us and what they don't like. The message I get from this survey is that Elgin's lacks imagination. Some customers think we are a bland store that has become blander. If we are to survive, we have to freshen our thinking. We have become too set in our ways.

After Madison continued on for ten minutes about the importance of Elgin's becoming a more imaginative store, she asked the group for questions. Dan Battles, the advertising director, was the first to raise his hand:

"Laura, we have heard your charges about Elgin's being bland and lacking imagination. Could you please give us a few specifics?"

"I don't want to offend anybody in particular, but I guess I will have to be more specific," said Madison. "Above all, we don't do anything unusual as a store. Take this Christmas season as a good example. The motif our store chose was to decorate the store with Santa Claus, reindeers, and elves. How traditional can you be?

"Another example is that our special sales are just like everybody else's. We run ads announcing that everything in the store is marked down by a certain percent. How mundane can you be? Furthermore, our stores are not distinctive. They remind me of an average main street department store.

"I'm afraid we have become dull, dull, dull! If I don't get some fresh ideas from you people soon, I'm going to have to hire some creative talent from the outside.

"Next question please," said Laura Madison as her management group looked stunned.

After two minutes of silence, Mary Jo Fenton, a merchandising coordinator, asked: "Laura, you set the tone for new ideas in this store. We expect you to take the lead in pointing us in new directions."

"Maybe you have a point, Mary Jo. You now know that I want Elgin's to move forward with more innovation."

Questions

1. What do you think of Madison's conclusion that her managers are traditional thinkers?
2. If her diagnosis of the problem is correct, what steps could be taken to help the managers become less traditional in their thinking?
3. What do you think of Madison's approach to solving the problem of limited imagination?
4. What do you think of Madison's idea of threatening to hire some creative talent from the outside?
5. Is Mary Jo Fenton justified in assuming that the president should be setting the tone for the store?

A HUMAN RELATIONS EXPERIENTIAL ACTIVITY: GROUP BRAINSTORMING

The class organizes itself into groups to brainstorm a few relevant problems. Any problem that does not require expertise is of potential value. Here are a few possibilities: How to raise extra money for yourself; how to improve your social life; how to save money on food; how to save money on car fuel. To carry out brainstorming, follow these basic rules:

1. Use groups of about five to seven people.
2. Encourage the spontaneous expression of ideas. All suggestions are welcome, even if they are outlandish or outrageous. The least workable ideas can be edited out when the idea generation phase is completed.
3. Quantity and variety are very important. The greater the number of ideas, the greater the likelihood of a breakthrough idea.
4. Encourage combination and improvement of ideas. This process is referred to as "piggybacking" or "hitchhiking."
5. One person serves as the secretary who records the ideas, perhaps posting them on a chalkboard.
6. Do not overstructure by following any of the above five rules too rigidly. Brainstorming is a spontaneous process.

REFERENCES

[1] This section of the chapter is reprinted and adapted with permission from Salvatore Didato, "A Mind-Set Can Impede Our Problem-Solving Abilities," Gannett Newspaper feature, June 15, 1985.

[2] The surgeon is the boy's mother.

[3] Jack Halloran, *Applied Human Relations: An Organizational Approach* (Englewood Cliffs, NJ: Prentice-Hall, 1978), p. 278.

[4] The discussion of systematic and intuitive thinking is based on David D. Ewing, "Discovering Your Problem-Solving Style," *Psychology Today*, December 1977, pp. 68–73, 138.

[5] Ibid., p. 69.

[6] The thinking of Neal and John is presented in Ibid.

[7] Edward H. Meyer, "Creativity in Business," *BusinessWeek's Guide to Careers*, September 1985, p. 27.

[8] A current program is described in Jerry Conrath, "The Imagination Harvest: Training People to Solve Problems Creatively," *Supervisory Management*, September 1985, pp. 6–10.

[9] The best answer here is to prove to your boss that your accomplishments are worthy of more money than you are receiving at present.

[10] Priscilla Petty, "Break Out! Routine Thinking Can Be Hazardous to On-the-Job Creativity," *Rochester Democrat and Chronicle*, November 22, 1983, p. 1D.

SOME ADDITIONAL READING

BARTIMO, JIM. "Software to Help You Think." *Success!*, July/August 1985, pp. 94–95.

"Creativity: A Special Report." *Success!* March 1985, pp. 54–61.

KEIL, JOHN M. *The Creative Mystique: How to Manage It, Nurture It, and Make It Pay.* New York: John Wiley & Sons, 1985.

LEIGH, ANDREW. *Decisions, Decisions! A Practical Guide to Problem Solving and Decision Making.* Brookfield, VT: Gower Publishing, 1985.

RAY, DARRELL W., and BARBARA L. WILEY. "How to Generate New Ideas." *Supervisory Management*, November 1985, pp. 8–12.

TAYLOR, RONALD N. *Behavioral Decision Making.* Glenview, IL: Scott Foresman and Company, 1984.

WEISS, W. H.   "Cutting Down the Risks In Decision Making." *Supervisory Management,* May 1985, pp. 14–16.

VON OECH, ROGER.   *A Whack on the Side of the Head.* New York: Warner, 1984.

4

Dealing with Stress and Burnout

Learning Objectives

After studying the information and doing the exercises in this chapter you should be able to:

- Define and understand the technical meanings of the terms stress and burnout
- Identify several positive and negative consequences of stress
- Pinpoint the stressors in your personal and work life
- Recognize the importance of placing yourself under the right amount of stress
- Know what can be done to prevent and treat burnout
- Select several strategies for dealing with the negative effects of stress

Infuriated, the soccer-team coach asked the goalie why he just stood there and watched the winning goal whiz past his ear. The goalie replied, "Who knows? I just choked. I couldn't take the pressure of the game hanging on one shot."

A sales representative said to her friend, "I've just been promoted, and I got the big raise I needed. But my heart is thumping, my mouth is dry, and I have the shakes. I'm happy, yet all stressed out."

The above anecdotes illustrate two important facts about stress. First, most people are aware of stress. The goalie talked about his stress symptom of choking under pressure, while the sales rep mentioned she was "stressed out." Second, we can experience stress in response to both positive and negative, or winning and losing, conditions.

The term stress has several accepted meanings. A particularly useful definition is that **stress** is an internal reaction to any force that threatens to disturb a person's equilibrium. The internal reaction usually takes the form of emotional discomfort. And the force is usually something that we doubt we can successfully handle.

A **stressor** is the force that creates the stress. The force can be internal as well as external including personal conflicts and physical injuries. How you perceive things heavily influences whether or not a given event is stressful. Most people perceive getting a driver's license to be stressful; a small minority find it to be a routine event. Most people find giving a speech before a large audience to be a stressor; yet some experienced speakers regard the event as "no sweat." There are some events, however, that are perceived as stressors by almost everybody. These stressors include being mugged, almost hit by a car while walking, attacked by a large dog, or fired. Can you add to this list of universal stressors?

In this chapter we study both stress and one of its most serious job-related consequences, burnout. First we provide details about the physiology, consequences, and causes of stress. Second we examine burnout and how it can be treated and prevented. Third is the major emphasis of the chapter—how to treat and prevent stress in your work and personal life.

THE BASIC PHYSIOLOGY OF STRESS

Stress and burnout cannot be understood without examining the underlying physiology of stress. Surprisingly, the physiological changes within the body that result in stress are almost identical for most stressors. Riding a roller coaster, falling in love, or being fired, for example, make you feel about the same inside. The experience of stress helps activates hormones that prepare the body to fight or run when faced with a challenge. This battle against the stressor is referred to as the **fight or flight response.** (The "response" is really a conflict because one is forced to choose between struggling with the stressor of fleeing from the scene.) It helps you deal with emergencies.

The activation of hormones in turn produces a short-term physiological reaction. Among the most familiar are an increase in heart rate, blood pressure, breathing rate, perspiration, and blood clotting. The body functions become so accelerated under heavy stress that some people carry out feats of strength they would not be able to accomplish under ordinary circumstances. An example is a 148-pound man who rolled an 800-pound concrete sewer pipe section off the leg of a child pinned under it. After the child was saved the man tried to move the pipe again but could not budge it even a quarter inch. His supply of adrenalin had returned to a normal level.

If stress is continuous and accompanied by these short-term physiological changes, annoying and life-threatening conditions can occur. Among them are heart attacks, high blood pressure, increased cholesterol level, migraine headaches, ulcers, allergies, and cancer. Another problem is that stress increases the severity of many diseases and disorders. For example, if you are under stress it may take you much longer to recover from a common cold or a broken bone.

Despite all the problems just mentioned, stress also plays a positive role in our lives. The right amount of stress prepares us for meeting difficult challenges, and spurs us on to peak intellectual and physical performance.

THE BENEFICIAL CONSEQUENCES OF STRESS

Few people can escape stress in work and personal life. This is fortunate because escaping all stress-inducing situations would be undesirable for most people. An optimum amount of stress exists for most people and most tasks. A team entering a dance contest should experience some feelings of pressure or high challenge. If the couple is confident, they are likely to exhibit maximum performance when the competition is keen. Note, however, that we did not say when the competition is *overwhelming*.

In general, performance tends to be best under moderate amounts of stress. If the stress is too great, people become temporarily ineffective; they may freeze or choke. Under too little stress, people may become lethargic and inattentive. Figure 4–1 depicts the relationship

FIGURE 4–1. THE RELATIONSHIP BETWEEN STRESS AND JOB PERFORMANCE

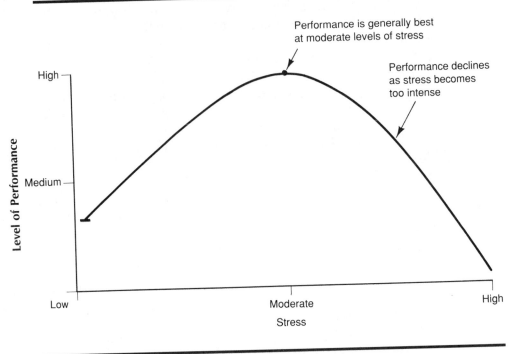

NOTE: Extremely uncomfortable stressors may show a negative relationship to job performance.

between stress and performance. An exception to this relationship is that certain negative forms of stress are likely to lower performance even if the stress is moderate.[1] For example, the stress created by an intimidating boss or worrying about radiation poisoning—even in moderate amounts—will not improve performance.

The optimum amount and type of stress is a positive force that is the equivalent of finding excitement and challenge. Your ability to solve problems and deal with challenge is enhanced when the right amount of adrenaline flows in your blood to guide you toward peak performance. In fact, highly productive people are sometimes said to be hooked on adrenaline. Let us look at several of these beneficial consequences of encountering the right type and amount of stressors:

1. *Greater strength and physical coordination.* Visualize yourself competing against another person in an individual activity such as tennis, ski racing, or chess. You will probably perform at your best if your opponent is at or above your level. It is difficult to perform well against too easy an opponent because the challenge is lacking.

2. *Increased motivation*. How many students have you heard say, "I can't study unless I have an exam coming up"? or "I never get started on a paper unless it's close to the deadline. I work best under pressure." Self-motivated people, in contrast, are able to establish their own deadlines. They keep pressure on themselves by constantly establishing new goals.

3. *Better problem-solving ability and decision making*. Laboratory experiments have shown repeatedly that people solve problems more readily when pressure is moderate. The pressure might take the form of having to race the clock. People solve problems less well when the time limits are too loose or too tight. Similarly, you might make the most satisfactory decision if you were given a week, rather than a day or a month, to find a new dwelling. As mentioned above, however, stressors that result in very unsatisfying stress always impede performance.

4. *Increased creativity*. In the same way, creativity improves when people are placed under the right amount of stress. In the words of the old adage, "Necessity is the mother of invention." People tend to be creative when life circumstances demand creativity. Many creative approaches to reducing the cost of making a product only come about under the pressure of reduced business or severe inflation. Several of the modern American-made automobiles were created in response to the competition of low-priced, high-quality Japanese cars.

5. *Better use of time*. Have you ever noticed how much you can accomplish under pressure? One of the many reasons is that you are energized to the point of being a more efficient and productive machine. When the pressure diminishes, most people lapse into a mode of once again squandering time. Again, many people need to have pressure imposed on them by others to be really productive.

THE NEGATIVE CONSEQUENCES OF STRESS

Heavy doses of stress can lead to physical and psychological ailments, can shorten life, and can make you forgetful about everyday things. Several of these negative stress symptoms have already been mentioned in this chapter. Turn to Exhibit 4–1 to determine whether you might be experiencing too many negative consequences of stress. It is helpful to divide these consequences into five types of categories or symptoms:

1. *Negative emotions and feelings*. Among these are anxiety, aggression, apathy, depression, fatigue, frustration, guilt and shame, irritability and bad temper, moodiness, low self-esteem, nervousness, loneliness, and tension. You can almost always count on being tense when placed under stress.

2. *Negative behavior*. A wide variety of negative behaviors are linked to excessive stress. Among the more frequent are emotional outbursts, nervous

EXHIBIT 4–1 HOW MUCH STRESS ARE YOU FACING?

Here's a brief questionnaire to roughly estimate if you are experiencing too many negative consequences of stress (or too much distress). Apply each question to the last six months of your life. Answer each question Mostly Yes or Mostly No.

		Mostly Yes	Mostly No
1.	Have you been feeling uncomfortably tense lately?	——	——
2.	Are you engaged in frequent arguments with people close to you?	——	——
3.	Is your romantic life very unsatisfactory?	——	——
4.	Do you have trouble sleeping?	——	——
5.	Do you feel lethargic about life?	——	——
6.	Do many people annoy or irritate you?	——	——
7.	Do you have constant cravings for candy and other sweets?	——	——
8.	Is your cigarette consumption way up?	——	——
9.	Are you becoming addicted to soft drinks or coffee?	——	——
10.	Do you find it difficult to concentrate on your work?	——	——
11.	Do you frequently grind your teeth?	——	——
12.	Are you increasingly forgetful about little things like mailing a letter?	——	——
13.	Are you increasingly forgetful about big things like appointments and major errands?	——	——
14.	Are you making far too many trips to the lavatory?	——	——
15.	Have people commented lately that you do not look well?	——	——
16.	Do you get into verbal fights with other people too frequently?	——	——
17.	Have you been involved in more than one physical fight lately?	——	——
18.	Do you have more than your share of tension headaches?	——	——
19.	Do you feel nauseated much too often?	——	——
20.	Do you feel light-headed or dizzy almost every day?	——	——
21.	Do you have churning sensations in your stomach far too often?	——	——
22.	Are you in a big hurry all the time?	——	——
23.	Are far too many things bothering you these days?	——	——

Scoring: The following guidelines are of value only if you answered the questions sincerely:

0–5 Mostly Yes answers: You seem to be experiencing a normal amount of stress.

6–15 Mostly Yes answers: Your stress level seems high. Become involved in some kind of stress management activity, such as the activities described later in this chapter.

16–21 Mostly Yes answers: Your stress level appears much too high. Seek the help of a mental health professional or visit your family doctor (or do both).

laughter, restlessness, trembling, stuttering or other speech difficulties, nervous ticks, and increased use of cigarettes, alcohol, and illegal drugs.

3. *Intellectual problems.* Thinking can be impaired under too much negative stress. Among the problems are inability to make decisions and concentrate, frequent forgetfulness, oversensitivity to criticism, mental blocks, and poor judgment.

4. *Adverse physiological symptoms.* Negative physiological conditions include increased blood glucose level, dilation (widening) of the pupils, difficulty in breathing, hot and cold spells, lump in the throat, numbness and tingling in parts of the limbs, poorer vision and hearing, and need for frequent elimination.

5. *Problems for employers.* Employers suffer also when employees experience too much stress. The problems include increased absenteeism, lowered productivity, disputes between management and labor, high accident rates, high turnover and tardiness, bickering among employees and supervisors, and increased medical costs.[2]

SOURCES OF STRESS IN PERSONAL LIFE

Almost any form of frustration, disappointment, setback, inconvenience, or crisis in your personal life can cause stress. One way of classifying the different sources of stress encountered in personal life is to extend the format we used for classifying personal goals: significant life changes in general; everyday annoyances; social and family problems; disappointments with hobbies, interests, and sports; physical and mental health problems; financial problems, school-related problems; and terrifying experiences.

Significant Life Change

A general stressor that encompasses both work and personal life is having to cope with significant change. A pioneering series of studies on stressful life events was conducted by Thomas Holmes and Richard Rahe over a period of twenty-five years. Their research, and similar studies, showed repeatedly that the necessity of significant change in the life pattern of an individual created stress.

The research on life changes resulted in the assigning of scale values to the impact of changes in forty-two life events. These values, called **life-change units,** were taken to represent the average amount of social readjustment considered necessary to cope with a given change. The more significant the change one has to cope with in a short period of time, the greater the probability of experiencing a stress disorder. According to the Holmes-Rahe scale, the maximum negative change (death of a spouse) is assigned 100 points.[3] An example of a

TABLE 4–1. STRESS IMPACT OF LIFE CHANGES AS MEASURED
BY LIFE-CHANGE UNITS

Life Event	Mean Life-Change Units
Death of spouse	100
Divorce	73
Marital separation	65
Imprisonment	63
Death of close family member	63
Marriage	50
Fired from job	47
Marital reconciliation	45
Pregnancy	45
Retirement	45
Sexual difficulties	39
Gain of new family member	39
Major business readjustment	39
Death of close friend	37
Change to a different career	36
Buying a house	31
Trouble with in-laws	29
Beginning or ending formal schooling	26
Trouble with boss	23
Change in residence	20
Change in eating habits	15
Vacation	13
Minor violation of the law	11

SOURCES: Rabi S. Bhagat, "Effects of Stressful Life Events on Individual Performance and Work Adjustment Processes within Organizational Settings: A Research Model," *Academy of Management Review*, October
1983, pp. 660–671. The values reported in Bhagat are an updating of
Thomas H. Holmes and Richard H. Rahe, "The Social Adjustment
Rating Scale," *Journal of Psychosomatic Research*, 15, 1971, pp. 210–
223.

change in life that would produce modest stress for most people is a
minor violation of the law (11 points). The life-change units assigned
to a number of events are listed in Table 4–1.

Individual differences are important in understanding the stressful impact of life changes. The mean values listed in Table 4–1 do not
hold true for everybody. For example, if a person were on parole, a
minor violation of the law might have a considerably higher value
than 11.

Everyday Annoyances

Managing everyday annoyances can have a greater impact on your
health than major life catastrophes. Sweating the small stuff can hurt

you more than dealing with the significant changes mentioned above, according to several studies.[4] Everyday annoyances that create stress for many people include concerns about weight, the health of a family member, inflation, home maintenance, overcrowded schedules, yard work and outside maintenance, taxes, crime, and physical appearance. Several of these hassles are discussed here as separate categories.

An important finding of these studies is that people who are able to cope well with daily hassles tend to have good health. They are able to tailor-make a coping strategy for each hassle they face, such as overcoming a billing error made by a credit-card company. Another method of coping with this general category of stress is to recognize that these annoyances happen to everybody. You are not being singled out for harassment; you are not a loser; it's just part of modern living.

Social and Family Problems

Friends and family are the main source of love and affection in your life. But they can also be the main source of stress. Most physical acts of violence are committed among friends and family members. One of the many reasons we encounter so much conflict with friends and family is that we are emotionally involved with them. Here are two examples of the type of stressors found in social and family life:

> A young woman sat in the office of her guidance counselor, sobbing. She put it this way, "My father threw me out of the house because I bleached my hair. I don't know where to go."
>
> A man asked his family doctor for drugs to calm him down. In his words, "My wife left me and the two kids. I don't think I can handle the situation."

Disappointments with Hobbies, Interests, and Sports

People take their pastimes seriously in our culture. The greater the emotional investment, the higher the probability that setbacks in these areas will create stress for you. Stressors of this general category include a motorcross bike blowing an engine, a favorite horse developing arthritis, a favorite painting being slashed, a camera lens being smashed, or your losing the finals of a racquet-ball tournament. Stress associated with losing in competition can often be decreased by placing less emphasis on winning.

Physical and Mental Health Problems

Prolonged stress produces physical and mental health problems, and the reverse is also true. Physical and mental illness can act as stressors—the fact of being ill is stressful, as one man discovered when he developed a severe case of gingivitis (infection of the gums). One by one his teeth fell out until treatment finally halted the process. He found the situation so stressful that he made some errors on the job. If you receive a serious injury, that too can create stress. The stress from being hospitalized can be almost as severe to some patients as the stress from the illness or injury that brought them to the hospital.

We are implying that stress operates in a cycle: stress can bring about illness and injury; the illness and injury, in turn, serve as stressors themselves, thus elevating the discomfort. You must learn to break the cycle by using the appropriate method of stress management.

Financial Problems

A major source of friction (and therefore stress) in life is financial problems. Although you may not be obsessed with money, not having enough money to take care of what you consider the necessities of life can lead to anxiety and tension. If you do not have enough money to replace or repair a broken-down pocket calculator, television set, or automobile, the result can be stressful. Even worse, imagine the stress of being hounded by bill collectors. Lack of funds can also lead to embarrassment and humiliation (both stressors). A photography student once showed up on a field trip without a tripod for his camera. The instructor said, "What's the matter, can't you afford a tripod?" The student responded, "No I can't afford one." Unthinkingly, several class members laughed at the financially troubled student.

School-Related Problems

The life of a student can be stressful. Among the stressors to cope with are exams in subjects you do not understand well, having to write papers on subjects unfamiliar to you, working your way through the complexities of registration, or having to deal with instructors who do not see things your way. Another source of severe stress for some students is having too many competing demands on their time. On most campuses you will find someone who works full-time, goes to school full-time, and has a family. This type of three-way pull often leads to marital problems. You do not have to be a middle-aged executive to develop ulcers!

Terrifying Experiences

Unfortunately, many readers of this book may have already experienced this category of stressor. Among these once-in-a-lifetime adversities are being involved in a house fire or a fatal automobile accident, being caught in a tornado, being raped or shot at, or having your house washed out from under you in a flood. The stress reaction to these events is predictable. As described in an abnormal psychology text, "People exposed to plane crashes, automobile accidents, explosions, fires, earthquakes, tornadoes, sexual assault, or other terrifying experiences frequently show psychological 'shock' reactions."

The extent to which you deteriorate under the influence of a terrifying experience depends partly on how strong a person you were before the catastrophe struck. Your reaction also depends on how much emotional first aid you received from friends or professionals right after the terrifying experience. As a result, a relatively new procedure is for mental health workers to counsel hostages immediately after they are released by their captors.

PERSONALITY FACTORS AND STRESS

Some people are more stress prone than others because of factors within their personalities. Important examples are emotional insecurity and low self-confidence. If you worry a lot about making mistakes, any demanding task will create stress. Two well-studied personality factors predisposing people to stress are Type A behavior and a belief that much of their life is controlled by external forces.

Type A Behavior

People with **Type A behavior** characteristics have basic personalities that lead them into stressful situations. Type A behavior has two main components: One is a tendency to try to accomplish too many things in too little time. This leads the Type A individual to be impatient and demanding. Two is free-floating hostility. Because of this combined sense of urgency and hostility, these people are irritated by trivial things. On the job, people with Type A behavior are aggressive and hardworking. Off the job, they keep themselves preoccupied with all kinds of errands to run and things to do.[5]

Type A personalities frequently have heart attacks and other stress-related illnesses at an early age. Recognize, however, that not every hardworking and impatient individual is prone to severe stress disorders. Hard chargers who like what they are doing—including many top executives—are remarkably healthy and outlive less competitive people. Also, new evidence indicates that people who exhibit Type A behavior recover as quickly from heart attacks as do other people.[6]

The vast majority of people reading this book probably are Type B personalities—those who are easygoing and can relax readily. People who display Type B behavior rarely suffer from impatience or a sense of time urgency, nor are they excessively hostile.

Belief in External Locus of Control

If you believe that your fate is controlled more by external than internal forces, you are probably more susceptible to stress. People with an **external locus of control** believe that external forces control their fate. Conversely, people with an **internal locus of control** believe that fate is pretty much under their control.

The link between locus of control and stress works in this manner: If people believe they can control adverse forces, they are less prone to the stressor of worrying about them. For example, if you believed that you can always find a job, you will worry less about unemployment. At the same time, the person who believes in an internal locus of control experiences a higher level of job satisfaction. Work is less stressful and more satisfying when you perceive it to be under your control.

What about your locus of control? Do you believe it to be internal? Or is it external?

SOURCES OF STRESS IN WORK LIFE

No job is without potential stressors for some people, and dozens of different sources of stress on the job have been identified. Here we discuss five different sources of job stress that you might encounter or have already encountered: frustrated ambitions, work overload or underload, confusing directions and conflicting demands, uncomfortable working conditions, and computer stress.

Frustrated Ambitions

Many people experience frustration and stress because they fail to attain their career goals. This problem is particularly true for middle managers who want to make it to the top of the organization. The problem of frustrated ambitions is becoming more widespread as the baby boom generation faces the 1990s. Too many competent young people are striving for a decreasing number of managerial jobs.

People suffer from the stress of frustrated ambitions in many fields. Many professional ballplayers do not get enough playing time, many actors and actresses never get leading roles, and many restaurant owners never build a prosperous restaurant. Setting realistic goals can help prevent the stress of frustrated ambitions.

Work Overload or Underload

Having too much or too little to do can create job stress. A burdensome work load can create stress for a person in two ways. First, the person may become fatigued and thus be less able to tolerate annoyances and irritations. Think of how much easier it is to become provoked over a minor incident when you lack proper rest. Second, a person subject to unreasonable work demands may feel perpetually behind schedule, a situation that in itself creates an uncomfortable, stressful feeling.

Heavy work demands are considered part of an executive's or a professional's work life. Many employees of lesser rank and income are also asked to give up much of their personal freedom and work under continuous pressure during working hours. Jeff, a country-western bar manager describes his experience with an overwhelming job:

> I took over as manager of the Roaring Brook Inn because I needed the money and the experience. It quickly dawned on me that the job was no picnic. The owner tried to squeeze all the profit he could out of the place. This meant that he tried to get by with the minimum amount of help possible. The bar really hopped on Friday and Saturday nights. The bartenders could hardly manage the load. The owner told the bartenders they were to push the more expensive drinks on customers. This led to a lot of hassles the bartenders didn't care for. I was responsible for an exact inventory count every night. That meant the money in the till had to equal the drinks dispensed. Somehow the thing almost never came out right. When the cash was too low, the owner would berate me and call me a cheat. As the manager, I was supposed to come in during off-hours and make minor repairs, and do any needed painting. Since we had a rough crowd, there were plenty of minor repairs to make. One week I worked about ninety hours for which I received just a little over the minimum wage. According to the owner, since I was the manager I wasn't eligible for overtime pay. When I complained, the owner told me I could quit if I didn't like it. So I quit.

A disruptive amount of stress can also occur when people experience **role underload,** or too little to do. People find role underload frustrating because it is a normal human desire to want to work toward self-fulfillment. Also, making a contribution on the job is one way of gaining self-respect. As with any facet of human behavior, there are exceptions. Some people find it relaxing not to have much to do on the job. One direct benefit is that it preserves their energy for family and leisure activities.

Confusing Directions and Conflicting Demands

"I'm really not sure I know what I'm supposed to be doing around here" is a common complaint heard from employees in all types of jobs. People in many different places of work find now and then that their job expectations are sloppily defined. As one store clerk said, "My boss left for a week's vacation. Her parting words were, 'Just take care of things while I'm away.'"

In addition, many employees receive conflicting demands from two or more bosses. Imagine being told by your boss to take Thursday off, and then being told by your boss's boss that you are needed for a special assignment on Thursday. It's often up to you to resolve such a conflict. If you don't, you will experience stress.

Uncomfortable Physical Working Conditions

Physical as well as psychological aspects of the job can serve as stressors. Temperatures can be too high or too low, noxious fumes might be present, employees might be cramped together in a small office, or physical danger might be present. In a few cases, however, it

is possible to adapt to the stress stemming from uncomfortable working conditions. John shares his experiences along these lines with us:

I've been a skier all my life, and I've also been interested in mechanics. So when the chance came up to work as a snow-making machine mechanic I grabbed it. I spent the fall months learning the equipment inside out. Once the ski season moved into full gear, I learned some of the rugged details of the job. Snow-making equipment doesn't break down on a crisp autumn day. It breaks down on the top of a mountain in the middle of winter with the wind-chill factor way below zero. It's a mess with the ice and the spray mist and the snow. The ski area owners are screaming because if the equipment doesn't get operating again soon, they could lose business. You try to work with gloves the best you can, but some of the fixing can only be done by using your bare hands. The first few times I went out on an equipment-failure assignment, I felt sick all over. As I became more skilled at what I was doing, the job became less overwhelming. By the end of the season, the misery had changed to excitement. I'm now proud to be a troubleshooter.

Observe how John's story illustrates the fine line between a situation being a stressor or a challenge. Once you conquer your fears about a situation and acquire the needed skills, it may no longer produce distress. Instead it produces **eustress,** a positive stress that elevates performance.

Computer Stress

Computer stress is a strong negative reaction to being forced to spend many more hours working at a computer than one desires. Among its symptoms are a glassy-eyed, detached look; aching neck muscles; and a growing dislike for high technology. Working for long periods of time at a VDT (video display terminal) appears to be the major contributor to computer stress. Part of the problem is that VDT users often suffer from eyestrain and physical discomfort in the back of the neck, the back, arms, and legs.

An indicator that computer stress really exists is that heavy VDT users are absent more frequently than employees who do not work with computers. One study showed that VDT users were absent from work three or four more times a year than were other employees.[7] The implication is that computer stress contributed to these poor absenteeism records.

Up to this point in the chapter we have described the nature and causes of stress. Next, we turn to a condition that can result from prolonged job stress.

BURNOUT

Burnout is a condition of emotional exhaustion and cynicism toward work in response to longstanding job stressors. Psychoanalyst and author, Herbert Freudenberger says that burnout is the final stage of an adverse reaction to stress. Physical signs of burnout include lingering colds, headaches, backaches, sleep problems, complexion problems, and stomach distress. Mental symptoms of burnout include cynicism, irritation, frustration, procrastination, and difficulties in concentration.[8]

Originally, burnout was observed primarily among people helpers including teachers, nurses, social workers, and police workers. It then became apparent that people in almost any occupation could develop burnout. Conscientiousness and perfectionism contribute to burnout. If you strive to be highly competent or perfect, you stand a good chance of being disappointed about not achieving everything you want. Organizations also play a role in contributing to burnout. If your efforts go unappreciated and you are given very little emotional support, your chances for burnout increase.

Before reading further about burnout, answer the burnout checklist shown in Exhibit 4–2. The remainder of our discussion about burnout concerns the behavior of burnout victims, and tactics for managing burnout.

EXHIBIT 4–2   THE BURNOUT CHECKLIST

Directions.   Check each one of the following statements that generally applies to you.

1. I feel tired much more frequently than I used to.   ____
2. I get very irritated at people lately.   ____
3. I suffer from a number of annoying physical problems such as neck aches and backaches.   ____
4. I often feel that I am losing control of my life.   ____
5. I'm feeling pretty depressed these days.   ____
6. I get down on myself too often.   ____
7. My life seems to be at a dead end.   ____
8. My enthusiasm for life has gone way down.   ____
9. I'm tired of dealing with the same old problems.   ____
10. Lately I've kind of withdrawn from friends and family.   ____
11. Not much seems funny to me anymore.   ____
12. There's really nothing for me to look forward to on the job or at school.   ____
13. It's difficult for me to care about what's going on in the world outside.   ____
14. My spark is gone.   ____

15. I know that I have a problem but I just don't have the energy to do anything about it.   ____
16. I can't think of the last time I didn't dread going to work or school.   ____
17. Friends say that my temper is getting pretty short.   ____
18. I don't get nearly enough appreciation from my boss.   ____
19. I don't see any good alternatives ahead of me for improving my life.   ____
20. I think I have reached a dead end in life.   ____

Total   ____

Interpretation. The more of these statements that accurately apply to you, the more likely it is that you are experiencing burnout. If you checked 15 or more of these statements, it would be helpful to discuss your feelings with a mental health professional.

Behaviors Associated with Burnout

Several symptoms of burnout have already been mentioned above. To expand upon them, there are three major signs indicating that burnout is present:

1. Emotional exhaustion. Burnout victims are emotionally exhausted. When asked how they feel, burned-out employees typically answer that they feel drained or used up, at the end of their rope, and physically fatigued. Often the burnout victim dreads going to work in the morning even though that person was once idealistic about what could be accomplished.

2. Withdrawing from people. Burnout victims try to cope with emotional exhaustion by becoming less personally involved with other people on the job. "She or he develops a detached air, becomes cynical of relationships with others, and feels callous toward others and the organization."

3. Low personal accomplishment. The third and final aspect of burnout is a feeling of low personal accomplishment. The once idealistic employee begins to realize that there are too many barriers to accomplishing what needs to be done. Often he or she lacks the energy to perform satisfactorily. Managers suffering form burnout hurt the organization because they create a ripple effect, spreading burnout to their subordinates.[9]

Treating and Preventing Burnout

Dealing with burnout follows many of the same approaches as dealing with stress, to be described in the following three sections. The major reason is that burnout is the end-product of stress. If you are burned out you will therefore have many stress symptoms. The physical symptoms of burnout, however, are generally less severe than those associated with other major stress problems. Despite the similarities between dealing with stress and burnout, three specific approaches are worth noting:

An important method for both overcoming and preventing burnout is to develop realistic expectations. One of the reasons employees develop burnout is that they try to be "miracle workers." If you establish realistic expectations in any job, you are less likely to be crushed when you achieve modest goals. For instance, a financial counselor might say, "If I can help three families a month develop sensible spending habits, I'll consider it a victory."

A second important suggestion is to reward yourself (just as in self-motivation). Burnout often comes about because we feel that our efforts are unappreciated. A useful antidote is therefore to reward yourself, such as treating yourself to a fine meal, when you accomplish something worthwhile. In short, take care of yourself rather than waiting for others to give you the reward you deserve.

Third, build a network of social support.[10] Burnout victims often feel isolated from others. If you can develop a group of friends who will give you emotional support and reassurance, you can soften these feelings of isolation. And as with any personal problem, just talking it out with a friend helps.

DEALING WITH STRESS BY ATTACKING ITS SOURCE

Stress and burnout can be dealt with in the short range by indirect techniques such as learning to relax, as described later in this chapter. However, to manage stress in the long range, you must also learn to deal directly with stressors. Three direct approaches are: eliminating the stressor putting the situation in proper perspective, and gaining control of the situation.

Eliminating the Stressor

The most potent method of managing stress is to eliminate the stressor giving you trouble. Assume that your roommate has become a stressor in your life because he or she plays the stereo at six in the morning. The early-morning noise gets you off to a bad start but you don't want to hurt your roommate's feelings by confronting the situation. Instead you engage in physical exercise and take a hot shower each morning to calm you down. This method will work to some extent, but ultimately you will again become enraged about the early-morning music.

You then decide to damage the stereo, but not mention your hostile act to your roommate. Ultimately, the stereo will be repaired or replaced and your stressor will return. You might also experience stress caused by guilt. The preferred approach is to negotiate a compromise with your roommate about early-morning music.

A helpful way to attack the cause of a stressor is to follow the steps in problem solving and decision making. You clarify the problem, identify the alternatives, weigh the alternatives, select one alternative, and so forth. One difficulty, however, is that your evaluation of the real problem could be inaccurate. There is always a limit to self-analysis. One woman thought the source of her job stress was the typewriter she was forced to work with. Reluctantly, her supervisor replaced the typewriter with one from another department. The secretary's stress symptoms continued. In talking the problem over with a personnel specialist, it was concluded that the woman's *real* stressor was her boss. A transfer to another department was arranged and the woman's stress symptoms quickly disappeared.

Place the Stressful Situation in Perspective

You will recall that stress comes about because of our perception of the situation. If you can alter your perception of a threatening situation, you are attacking the source of stress. A potentially stressful situation can be put into perspective by asking, "What is the worst that could happen to me if I fail in this activity?"[11]

The answer to the above question is found by asking a series of questions, starting with the grimmest possibility. For instance, you are late with a report that is due this afternoon. Consider the following questions and answers: (1) Will my reputation be damaged permanently? No. (2) Will I get fired? No. (3) Will I get reprimanded? Perhaps, but not for sure. (4) Will my boss think less of me? Perhaps, but not for sure. Only if the answer is yes to either of the first two questions is negative stress truly justified.

The thought process just described allows stressful situations to be properly evaluated and kept in perspective. You therefore avoid the stress that comes from overreacting to a situation.

Gaining Control of the Situation

Feeling that a bothersome situation is out of one's control is almost a universal stressor. A key method of stress management is therefore to attack the source of stress by gaining control of the situation. Robert Karasek, an industrial engineering professor, has conducted studies illustrating the importance of gaining control. He discovered that employees who have little control over their jobs, such as cooks and assembly-line workers, have higher rates of heart disease than employees who can control their work pace.[12]

How can you capitalize upon the fact that gaining control of a situation helps reduce stress? One practical approach is to improve your work habits and time management, as described in Chapter 12. By being "on top of things," you can make heavy work and school demands less stressful.

HANDLING STRESS BY GETTING CLOSE TO PEOPLE

An ideal way of managing stress is one that gives you some side benefits. Getting close to others falls into this category. You will reduce some of your tension and form a healthy relationship with another human being in the process. Closeness is a relatively vague concept. It is not as easy to define as deadline, goal, or decision. Closeness suggests getting in touch with your feelings or turning in to others. If you want to be close to someone else, and therefore relieve some of your stress, you may first have to get close to yourself.

Closeness to Yourself

Freudenberger advises us that most people seem to be running away from rather than toward themselves:

> We run from ourselves every chance we get. Think about it. When did you last spend time by yourself, with yourself, doing something you enjoy? *With* yourself is the important thing to check, because much of the time we're alone we shut off our minds and feelings. We get involved in a television program or have a couple of drinks and fall asleep. We're not really there for ourselves in a related kind of way. We're merely alone. Being alone *with* yourself, however, means your senses are alive, your thoughts are keeping you company, you're sitting in that room or going to that art gallery with a person, not just an empty body. You're sharing an experience *with* yourself, and you're enjoying it.[13]

Just being by yourself, perhaps walking the city streets or through an open field, or along a beach, can be tension reducing. As you let your mind wander it might be useful to also start formulating a plan of action to deal with the biggest stressor you are facing. But try not to worry too much.

Receiving Social Support from Others

Getting close to others helps you realize that there is someone out there to help you. You are not alone in facing your work or personal problems. The people you get close to could be other students, co-workers, neighborhood friends, family members. Many people in turmoil reach out to strangers in order to discuss personal problems. Have you ever traveled on a bus, airplane, or train and found yourself listening to the personal problems of a passenger seated next to you? Some people find solace in sharing their problems with someone who has no personal stake in those problems. Talking out your problems is a standard method of reducing tension.

Social support has been defined as the "friendly, approachable, trustworthy, cooperative, and warm attitude of the social network to which a person belongs."[14] In everyday language, it means someone is there to turn to for help. The way to develop this support network is to become a good listener yourself, so the other person will reciprocate.

A natural way to relieve tension is to do the talking yourself while the other person does the listening. This is the usual procedure when you go to a friend or a mental health professional, or your clergyperson for help. Switching roles can also be tension reducing. Listening to other people—getting close to them—will make you feel better in the same way that a therapist feels better after listening (and therefore helping) a patient. A natural way to become close to another person is to listen carefully to that person's feelings, desires, concerns, worries, or problems.

RELAXATION TECHNIQUES FOR HANDLING STRESS

"Why don't you relax?" or "You need a good vacation to unwind" is the kind of advice doctors, relatives, and friends have been offering for years to the person under stress. Today, hundreds of stress experts give us similar advice. The difference is that the experts' advice is a little more specific and is generally based on research rather than common sense. Here we will mention a half-dozen do-it-yourself techniques that can help you to relax—and thereby reduce distress and tension. If you are experiencing stress and tension, try the technique that you think best fits your personal preferences. Exhibit 4–3 distills a vast amount of knowledge about relaxation techniques into thirteen practical suggestions. They should be considered part of your strategy for learning how to reduce distress through relaxation.

On-the-Spot Relaxation

You can learn to allow your entire body to relax instantly under such stress-inducing situations as making a presentation in front of the

EXHIBIT 4–3 THIRTEEN SUGGESTIONS FOR RELAXATION AND TENSION REDUCTION*

1. Plan to have at least one idle period every day.
2. Learn to listen to others without interrupting them.
3. Read books and articles that demand concentration, rather than trying to speed-read everything.
4. Learn how to savor food by taking your time when eating pleasant food.
5. Have a quiet place for retreat at home.
6. Plan leisurely vacations so that virtually every moment is not programmed.
7. Concentrate on enriching yourself in at least one area other than work or school.
8. Live by the day or week, not by a stopwatch.
9. Concentrate on one task at a time rather than thinking of what assignment you will be tackling next.
10. Avoid irritating, overly competitive people; they tend to bring out the worst in another competitive person.
11. Stop drinking so much coffee, soft drinks, or alcoholic beverages. Try fruit juice or water instead.
12. Stop to smell the flowers, make friends with a preschool child, or play with a kitten once in awhile.
13. Smile at least five minutes every day.

* The first ten suggestions are based on Meyer Friedman and Ray H. Rosenman, *Type A Behavior and Your Heart* (Greenwich, Conn.: Fawcett Crest, 1975), pp. 207–271.

class or figuring out where you made a big error in balancing your checkbook. Stress specialist Karl Albrecht tells you how.

> If you happen to have a few moments alone before entering the challenge situation, you can relax yourself somewhat more thoroughly. Sit down, if possible, get comfortable, and close your eyes. Use your built-in muscle memory to bring back the feeling of deep relaxation and hold it for about a full minute. Then open your eyes and, as you go about the task at hand, try to retain the feeling of calmness that came with the relaxation.[15]

Physical Exercise

The right amount of physical exercise helps you deal with stress. Jogging and running, for example, have gained their places as very accessible, natural methods of reducing stress. So long as you avoid a bone injury to your feet or legs, jogging or running is almost an ideal stress antidote. Jogging and running, along with other aerobic physical exercises, relieve tension for chemical reasons. Strenuous physical

exercise releases natural biochemicals in the body that result in an emotional and physical high. It is reassuring to know that walking is now considered an excellent form of physical exercise and mental relaxation.

Here are a few comments from people who frequently use physical exercise to relieve stress and its accompanying tension. Observe how each comment ties in with stress:

> A high-ranking business executive reports, "On weekends I love to put the axe to trees on my lot. It's my best way of unwinding."
>
> A burly man enrolled in a business course: "When I'm uptight, I pound the ＿＿＿ out of the punching bag. Then I feel great."
>
> A stockbroker: "I'm out at the squash courts at least three nights every week. It's about the only way I can handle the phone jangling in my ears all day. In this business it's either take care of your tensions or wind up in the hospital."

Proper Diet

Eating nutritious foods is valuable for mental as well as physical health. Improper diet can weaken you physically, thus making you susceptible to stressors. Furthermore, some foods agitate you, making it difficult to relax. Agitating food and food substitutes include: salt, caffeine, preservatives, excessive amounts of sugar, spices, and excessive amounts of alcohol. Relaxing foods include skim milk, poultry, fish, fresh fruits, nuts, and *moderate* amounts of alcohol. A note of caution: Some of the foods we label "relaxing" may only be relaxing because they help avoid cardiac disease.

Relaxation Response

A standard technique for reducing stress is to achieve the relaxation response. The **relaxation response (RR)** is a bodily reaction in which you experience a slower respiration and heart rate, lowered blood pressure, and lowered metabolism. The response can be brought about in several ways, including meditation, exercise, or prayer. By practicing the RR, you can counteract the fight or flight response associated with stress.[16]

According to cardiologist Herbert Benson, four things are necessary to practice the RR: a quiet environment, an object to focus on, a passive attitude, and a comfortable position. You are supposed to practice the relaxation response ten to twenty minutes, twice a day. To evoke the relaxation response, Dr. Benson advises you to close your eyes. Relax. Concentrate on one word or prayer. If other thoughts come to mind, be passive, and return to the repetition.[17]

Similar to any other relaxation technique, the RR is harmless and works for most people. However, some very impatient people find it annoying to disrupt their busy day to meditate. Unfortunately, these may be the people who most urgently need to learn to relax.

Napping

The old-fashioned remedy of napping to achieve relaxation and thereby decrease tension has considerable merit. It yields some of the benefits that one might derive from formal relaxation techniques. Research has found that the brain waves of nappers are similar to those of people engaged in meditation (such as the RR).[18] One working couple reports that they meet together at midday to nap in their car. They find the experience relaxing despite the cramped conditions of napping while seated in a subcompact. Napping, however, has the same disadvantage as the relaxation response as a daytime method of stress management. Many career-minded employees feel guilty about napping during the day, even at lunchtime.

Visualizing a Pleasant Experience

Perhaps the most effortless and enjoyable relaxation technique when under stress is to visualize a calm and pleasant experience. **Visualization** means to picture yourself doing something that you would like to do. Whatever fantasy suits your fancy will work, according to the advocates of this relaxation technique. Visualizations that work for some people include: trout fishing on a sunny day, floating on a cloud, caressing a baby, petting a kitten, and walking in the woods. Notice that all of these scenes are relaxing rather than exciting. What visualization would work for you?

Rehearsal of the Stressful Situation

Akin to visualization is the technique of rehearsing a stressful situation in your mind. Imagine that you have the unpleasant task of having to resign from one job in order to take a better one. You are tense and your tension level increases as the day progresses. One approach to relaxing enough to handle this situation is to mentally rehearse this scenario. Most important, rehearse your opening line, which might be something like, "Mr. Gordon, I've asked to see you to discuss something very important," or "Mr. Gordon, the company has been very nice to me, but I've decided to make an important change in my life."

It is also helpful to anticipate other aspects of the scenario, such as what you would do if Mr. Gordon told you that he would not accept your resignation, or what you would say if Mr. Gordon turned on you and began to call you ungrateful and unappreciative. Or, what you would do if Mr. Gordon begged you to give the company one more chance.

Speech teachers recommended the rehearsal techniques for years, long before it became part of stress management. Visualizing yourself in front of the audience adds to your ability to relax. An added relaxation-inducer is to rehearse the presentation in the room or auditorium in which the talk will be given.

Muscle Monitoring

An important part of many stress reduction programs is to learn to relax your muscles. Learn to literally loosen up and be less uptight. Muscle monitoring involves becoming aware that your muscles have tightened and then consciously relaxing them. If your jaw muscles are tightening up in a tense situation, you learn to relax your jaw enough to overcome the stress effects.

Try to determine whether muscle tautness occurs in association with some recurring event. It is recommended that you pay attention to the tautness of your muscles on those occasions.[19] For example, you might experience a tightening of your neck muscles whenever it is the time of the month to pay your rent. Take a few moments to be aware of that muscle tension. After a while you will learn to relax when the last day of the month arrives and your rent (and other bills) are due.

SUMMARY

Stress is an internal reaction to any force that threatens to disturb a person's equilibrium. A stressor is the force that creates the stress. Your perception of an event influences whether it is stressful. The body's battle against a stressor is the fight or flight response. Stress always involves physiological changes such as an increase in heart rate, blood pressure, and breathing rate.

The right amount of stress can be beneficial. In general, performance tends to be best under moderate amounts of stress. An exception is that certain negative forms of stress are likely to lower performance even if the stress is moderate. Among the positive consequences of the right kind and amount of stress are: (1) greater strength and physical coordination, (2) increased motivation, (3) better problem solving and decision making, (4) increased creativity, and (5) better use of time.

Among the negative consequences of stress are: (1) negative emotions and feelings such as anxiety and depression, (2) negative behavior, (3) intellectual problems, (4) adverse physiological symptoms such as difficulty in breathing, and (5) problems for employers.

Almost any form of frustration, disappointment, setback, inconvenience, or crisis in your personal life can cause stress. The categories of situations that can produce stress include: significant life changes; everyday annoyances; social and family problems; disappointments with hobbies, interests, and sports; physical and mental health problems; financial problems; school-related problems; and terrifying experiences.

People with Type A behavior are impatient and demanding, and have free-floating hostility. They are rarely able to relax and frequently have heart attacks and other stress-related illnesses at an early age. The behavior of Type B personalities, the relaxers, is basically the opposite. Another personality factor related to stress is locus of control. If you believe that your fate is controlled more by external than internal forces, you are more susceptible to stress.

Sources of job stress are quite varied. Among them are frustrated ambitions, work overload or underload, confusing directions and conflicting demands, uncomfortable working conditions, and computer stress.

Burnout is a condition of emotional exhaustion and cynicism toward work in response to longstanding job stressors. Behaviors associated with burnout include: emotional exhaustion, withdrawing from people, and low personal accomplishment.

Dealing with burnout follows approaches similar to those used for dealing with stress, including: developing realistic expectations, rewarding yourself, and building a network of social support.

To successfully manage stress in the long range you have to deal with stressors directly. Three direct approaches are: eliminate the stressor; put the situation into proper perspective; and gain control of the stressful situation.

Getting close to people is another useful strategy for managing stress. Closeness involves both getting close to yourself and receiving social support from others. It is tension-reducing to discuss your problems with others.

Eight relaxation techniques for reducing stress are: on-the-spot relaxation, physical exercise, proper diet, the relaxation response, napping, visualizing a pleasant experience, rehearsal of the stressful situation, and muscle monitoring.

QUESTIONS AND ACTIVITIES

1. What is the biggest stressor in your life. What are you doing about it?
2. What are the three leading stressors students face in school?
3. Relatively few workaholics (people addicted to work) suffer from stress-related disorders. What do you think accounts for their low rate of stress disorders?
4. Why is boredom a source of stress to many people?
5. Many wealthy and famous people in the entertainment and sports fields are under so much stress that they require professional help. What stressors do you think these people face?
6. Dentists and psychiatrists are supposed to have among the highest suicide rates of professional people. What do you think are the key stressors faced by dentists and psychiatrists?

7. What is the difference between fatigue and burnout?

8. Burnout has been called the modern cop-out because many people blame their poor performance on burnout. To what extent do you believe that burnout is a cop-out?

9. Orientals appear to have many fewer stress disorders than Westerners. Why might this be true?

10. Interview a person who is successful in any field. Ask that person to describe the stress-management techniques he or she favors. Be prepared to discuss your findings in class.

A HUMAN RELATIONS CASE PROBLEM: THE BATTLE-WEARY SERVICE MANAGER

Maurice LaChance works as an assistant manager in the service department of a large automobile dealership, a position he has held for six months. His boss is Charlie Kennelworth, a twenty-five year veteran with the dealership. Maurice values his job because he sees it as a stepping stone to becoming the service manager in this or a larger dealership. However, Maurice has become increasingly discouraged with his relationships with Kennelworth.

Recently Maurice was giving a customer a price estimate for a new transmission on her car. While engaged in conversation with the customer, Charlie strolled by. He said to Maurice, "Don't blow this one, kid, like you did the last two transmission estimates. It's getting pretty expensive training you." Embarrassed, Maurice said to the customer, "My boss is a great joker. He really has a lot of faith in my estimates."

After finishing up with the customer, Maurice thought to himself: "This situation with Charlie is getting out of hand. He's so cynical that it's making him a terrible manager. I've asked him politely not to criticize me in front of customers, but he ignores me. The one thing left for me to do is to speak to the Mr. Thornell (the general manager of the dealership)."

Maurice followed up his idea by making an appointment with Brad Thornell, Thursday morning at 11. "What can I do for you Maurice?" said Thornell.

"I feel uncomfortable coming to you like this," said Maurice. "It's not in my nature to be a complainer. The truth is though that I'm having a terrible time with Charlie Kennelworth. I know he's done a lot for the dealership over the years, but something's bothering him. I think he's burned out."

"What makes you think Charlie is burned out?" asked Thornell.

"It's his whole approach as a manager. Half the time he sits in his office with a discouraged look on his face. He's hardly interested in what's going on in the shop. Whether or not he's interested in his job is not a big concern to me.

"What does bother me is that he's so cynical and angry. He chews out me and other employees right in front of customers. He never says anything nice about anybody. I've asked him not to criticize me in front of customers but he ignores me. Since he's my boss, I can't protest too much."

"Young man," said Thornell, "you have a lot to learn about this business. Charlie has made quite a contribution to this dealership. I know he barks and snaps a lot but he has a good heart and a good business sense. He may show a few signs of battle fatigue. He's been fighting the same battles for many years. But I doubt that he's burned out.

"My advice to you for now is to get along with Mr. Kennelworth. You can learn a lot from him."

"Thank you for your time Mr. Thornell," said Maurice as he got up from his chair. As he left the office he thought to himself, "What I can learn from Charlie is how not to manage people. In the mean time, what do I do next?"

Questions

1. Do you think Charlie Kennelworth is a burnout victim? Why or why not?
2. If Charlie is really a burnout victim, how can Maurice get either Charlie or Brad Thornell to do something about the problem?
3. What should Maurice do next?
4. How does stress fit into this case?

A HUMAN RELATIONS ROLE PLAY: THE DISTRESSED ASSISTANT MANAGER

Maurice LaChance, the assistant manager in the above case, comes home to his wife one night after a long and difficult day at the shop. Because of a heavy backlog of work, customers are being asked to postpone service on their autos and trucks. Several customers have taken out their anger on Maurice. Even more stressful to Maurice, his boss Charlie Kennelworth has been criticizing him in front of customers.

Maurice's wife, Bonnie, has had a difficult day at her office, where she works as a tax accountant. Bonnie decides that Maurice is suffering more stress than she is at the moment, so she decides to try to get Maurice to calm down and relax.

One student plays the role of Maurice. Another student plays the role of Bonnie. Maurice doesn't realize how much he is displaying stress symptoms, yet Bonnie thinks it is imperative that Maurice calm down before he develops a stress disorder.

REFERENCES

[1] R. Douglas Allen, Michael A. Hitt, and Charles R. Greer, "Occupational Stress and Perceived Organizational Effectiveness: An Examination of Stress Level and Stress Type," *Personnel Psychology,* Summer 1982, pp. 359–370.

[2] T. Cox, *Stress* (Baltimore: University Park Press, 1978), as quoted in John M. Ivancevich and Michael T. Matteson, *Stress and Work* (Glenview, IL: Scott Foresman & Co., 1980), pp. 13–14.

[3] Rabi S. Bhagat, "Effects of Stressful Life Events on Individual Performance and Work Adjustment Processes Within Organizational Settings: A Research Model," *Academy of Management Review,* October 1983, pp. 660–671.

[4] Research reported in Sally Squires, "Daily Hassles May Add Up to Poor Health," Newhouse News Service Report reprint in *Democrat and Chronicle,* Rochester, NY, August 21, 1981, p. 1C.

[5] "Stress: Can We Cope?" *Time,* June 6, 1983, p. 52; Meyer Friedman and Ray H. Rosenman, *Type A Behavior and Your Heart* (New York: Fawcett, 1975), pp. 100–103.

[6] Study from *New England Journal of Medicine,* reported in Erik Gunn, "Type A Life Isn't Harder on Heart, Study Concludes," *Democrat and Chronicle,* Rochester, NY, March 21, 1985, pp. 1A, 8A.

[7] Robert C. Miljus and Brian W. Sholly, "How Safe Are Video Display Terminals?" *Personnel Journal,* March 1985, p. 36.

[8] Carol Turkington, "Freudenberger Views Stress," *Monitor,* October 1983, p. 24.

[9] Susan E. Jackson and Randall S. Schuler, "Preventing Employee Burnout, "*Personnel,* March–April 1983, p. 59.

[10] Robert A. Baron, *Understanding Human Relations: A Practical Guide to People at Work* (Newton, MA: Allyn and Bacon, 1985), p. 294.

[11] This section follows closely Phillip Morgan and H. Kent Baker, "Building a Professional Image: Dealing With Job Stress," *Supervisory Management,* September 1985, p. 38.

[12] Cited in "Stress: Can We Cope?" p. 52.

[13] Herbert J. Freudenberger (with Geraldine Richelson), *Burn Out: The High Cost of High Achievement* (Garden City, NY: Anchor Press/Doubleday, 1980), p. 124.

[14] Arthur P. Brief, Randall S. Schuler, and Mary Van Sell, *Managing Job Stress* (Boston: Little, Brown & Co., 1981), p. 99.

[15] Karl Albrecht, *Stress and the Manager; Making It Work for You* (Englewood Cliffs, NJ: Prentice-Hall, 1979), p. 199.

[16] Herbert Benson, *The Relaxation Response* (New York: Morrow, 1975).

[17] Herbert Benson (with William Proctor), *Beyond the Relaxation Response* (New York: Berkley Books, 1985), pp. 96–97.

[18] James Hassett, "Teaching Yourself to Relax," *Psychology Today*, August 1978, p. 30.

[19] Ivancevich and Matteson, *Stress and Work,* p. 222.

SOME ADDITIONAL READING

DAVIDSON, MARILYN, and CARY COOPER. *Stress and the Woman Manager.* New York: St. Martin's Press, 1983.

GLICKEN, MORLEY D., and KATHERINE JANKA. "Beyond Burnout: The Cop-Out Syndrome." *Personnel,* November–December 1984, pp. 65–70.

LAGRECA, GENEVIEVE. "The Stress You Make." *Personnel Journal,* September 1985, pp. 42–47.

LAWRIE, JOHN. "Three Steps to Reducing Stress." *Supervisory Management,* October 1985, pp. 8–10.

LEVY, STEPHEN J. *Managing the Drugs in Your Life: A Personal and Family Guide to the Responsible Use of Drugs, Alcohol, and Medicine.* New York: McGraw-Hill, 1983.

QUICK, JAMES C., and JONATHAN D. QUICK. *Organizational Stress and Preventive Management.* New York: McGraw-Hill, 1984.

SETHI, AMARJIT SINGH, and RANDALL S. SCHULER (Eds.). *Handbook of Organizational Stress Coping Strategies* (Cambridge, MA: Balinger Publishing Company, 1984).

5

Communicating with People

Learning Objectives

After studying the information and doing the exercises in this chapter, you should be able to:

- Understand the importance of effective communication for your career and personal life
- Identify and overcome many roadblocks to communication
- Send and receive more nonverbal communications than you are doing now
- Remember names and faces better
- Become a more effective communicator
- Conduct yourself more effectively in a meeting

Communication is the sending and receiving of messages. So vital is communication that it has been described as the glue that holds families and organizations together. Most marital problems and most foul-ups on the job are considered to be communication problems. Furthermore, to be successful in work or personal life, you usually have to be a good communicator. You can't make friends or stand up against your enemies unless you can communicate with them. And you can't accomplish work with or through others unless you can send and receive messages effectively.

In this chapter we will explain several important aspects of communication between and among people. A few sections of the chapter deal specifically with improving your communication skills. As with other chapters in this book, however, we hope that explanation also leads to skill improvement. If you understand the steps involved in getting a message across to another person, for example, you may be able to prevent some communication problems.

HOW COMMUNICATION TAKES PLACE

A convenient starting point in understanding how people communicate is to look at the steps involved in communicating a message. A diagram of how the process takes place is shown in Figure 5-1. Assume that Candy wishes to inform Tony, a used-car salesman, that she is willing to make an offer of $2,000 on a used car. The price tag on the car is $2,500.

Step 1: Ideation. Candy organizes her thoughts about this important problem. She wants to make an offer she can afford and she wants to be taken seriously. This stage is the point of both the origin and the framing of the idea or message in the sender's mind. Candy says to herself, "I think I'll ask Tony if he will let me have the car for $2,000."

Step 2: Encoding. Here the ideas are organized into a series of symbols (words, hand gestures, body movements, drawings) designed to communicate to the intended receiver. Candy says, "Tony, this car obviously is not in excellent condition, but I am willing to give you $2,000 for it."

Step 3: Transmission. The message is transmitted orally, in writing, or by nonverbal communication such as gestures. In this situation the sender chooses the oral mode.

Step 4: Receiving. The message is received by the other party. Tony can receive the message only if he pays attention to Candy. As an experienced used car salesman, he listens carefully to the conviction with which the price is offered. He says to himself, "Is this her final offer, or simply a starting point in negotiation?"

Step 5: Decoding. The symbols sent by the sender to the receiver are decoded. In this case, decoding is not complete until Tony hears the whole message. The opening comment, "This car obviously is not in excellent condition, but I am willing to give you $2,000 for it" is the type of statement often used by customers when buying a used car. Tony therefore listens attentively for more information. For example, does this woman really have an interest in this car?

Step 6: Understanding. Tony has no trouble understanding that Candy indeed is interested in the car. The issue remains whether or not she will pay a sensible price from the standpoint of the dealer. Since roadblocks, or barriers, to communication exist, understanding may be limited. These roadblocks, shown in Figure 5–1, can take place at any step in the communication process. Candy might, for instance, have transmitted the message, "That is a bad car." Tony might have been needlessly discouraged. Candy was really saying that it is a *baaad* car, which means "really terrific" in urban slang.

Step 7: Action. Tony understands Candy's offer, but will not accept it. He responds by saying, "I think you're smart in wanting to buy this car. It's a honey. But we'll need a little more money from you so we can cover our costs.

FIGURE 5–1. BASIC MODEL OF HOW WE COMMUNICATE

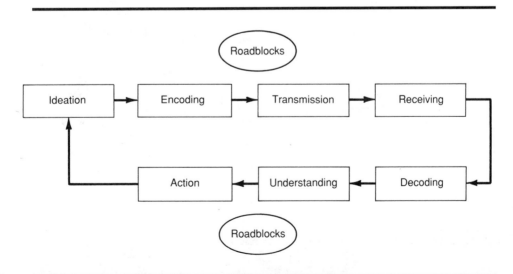

I'll take your offer back to the sales manager." Action is also a form of feed-back because it results in a message being sent back to the original sender from the receiver. If a message is not sent back, we have only one-way com-munication.

TWO-WAY VERSUS ONE-WAY COMMUNICATION

An executive telephoned his wife and said hurriedly, "Honey, no time to explain now. But my folks are visiting for the weekend. They'll be here around six this evening. Remember that 'Mumsy' doesn't want any salt in her food. Let me know if having them over is impossible."

The man who made this statement was hoping to communicate effectively with his wife. But his shutting out of messages back to him will reduce his communications effectiveness. He will not learn anything about why it might be very difficult to have his folks over this weekend. If he had stopped to listen to his wife, he would have learned that the refrigerator is broken and their son has a high fever. The executive's wife isn't even given the chance to say that his demand is impossible. He will have to deal with her resentment and anger, however, once the in-laws leave.

Effective communication is a two-way activity. An exchange of information or a transaction takes place between two people. Person A may send messages to person B to initiate communication, but B must react to A to complete the communication loop. One reason written messages frequently fail to achieve their purpose is that the person who writes the message cannot be sure how it will be interpreted. One written message that is subject to many interpretations is "Your idea is of some interest to me." (How much is "some"?) Face-to-face communication helps clarify meanings.

One-way communication sometimes takes place even when the second party responds to the first party. In such instances, the second party is not responding to what the other person is really saying. Two-way communication usually requires that the parties respond to each other's feelings. Another way of looking at the same issue is to examine the difference between a monologue and a dialogue. In a dialogue, each of the parties understands what the other is *really* saying. Exhibit 5–1 illustrates the difference between a monologue (one-way communication) and a dialogue (two-way communication).

EXHIBIT 5–1   IS IT OUR MONEY OR YOUR MONEY?

A. Monologue Between Wife and Husband

"Bill, I thought of something when I signed the joint income tax form the other day. Although all our assets are shared by state law, our three banking accounts are in your name. Why is that? Don't you trust my judgment about financial matters?"

"Why are you complaining about a technical detail like that? It's the husband's job to protect his wife from having to worry about things like bank accounts. What's for dinner?"

"The whole thing doesn't sound quite right to me. I feel left out of things."

"You find the pickiest things to complain about."

B. Dialogue Between Wife and Husband

"Bill, I thought of something when I signed the joint income tax form the other day. Although our assets are shared by. . . ."

"It sounds like you're discontented about the way I have arranged things financially. Maybe you feel you should have more power in these matters."

"Exactly. Your having total control over the bank accounts makes me feel like a second-class citizen in our marriage."

"My intent was not to make you feel like a second-class citizen. It's just been a long-held belief of mine that only one person in a marriage should be in charge of the bank accounts. How would having separate accounts appeal to you?"

"Maybe that would be a good compromise. I appreciate your not being pigheaded about the whole topic."

ROADBLOCKS TO COMMUNICATION

As the floating elipses in Figure 5–1 symbolize, communication rarely proceeds as swiftly or as effectively as we would like. Many different factors filter our message on its way to the intended receiver. Have you ever tried to make a telephone call when moisture is entrapped in the underground cables? You hear more static than voice. In this section we will look at some of the human, rather than physical or mechanical roadblocks to communication. If you are aware of their presence, you will be better able to overcome them.

Routine or neutral messages are the easiest to communicate. Communication roadblocks are the most likely to occur when a message is complex, emotionally arousing, or clashes with the receiver's mental set. An emotionally arousing message would deal with such topics as a relationship between two people or money. A message that clashes with a receiver's mental set requires that person to change his or her familiar pattern of receiving messages. Are you willing to conduct an experiment? If your answer is yes, the next time you order a meal in a restaurant order dessert first and an entree second. The waiter or waitress will probably not "hear" your dessert order because it deviates from the normal ordering sequence.

Limited Understanding of People

If you do not understand people very well, your communication effectiveness will be limited.[1] To take a basic example, if you frame your message in terms of what can be done for you, you may be in trouble. It's much more effective to frame your message in terms of what you can do for the other person. Suppose a hungry person wants five dollars for a meal from a friend. That is quite a self-centered message to send. The message could be made less self-centered:

VERY SELF-CENTERED: "You've got to let me have five dollars. I'm starving."
LESS SELF-CENTERED: "I know that you're a charitable person. Would you be willing to do the charitable act of giving me five dollars for a meal?"

Exhibit 5–2 presents some guidelines to help you overcome a limited understanding of people.

EXHIBIT 5–2   A SHORT COURSE IN HUMAN RELATIONS

The SIX most important words are "I admit I made a mistake."
The FIVE most important words are "You did a good job."
The FOUR most important words are "What is your opinion?"
The THREE most important words are "If you please."
The TWO most important words are "Thank you."
The ONE most important word is "We."
The ONE least important word is "I."

Some people who first read this "short course" react to it negatively. Among their reservations are that "It is corny," "It's so obvious. Anybody with common sense knows that," or "Good for people in kindergarten." Yet if you put these seven rules into practice, you will find they do help overcome the communications roadblock called limited understanding of people. As one example, if you use "I" too frequently in your conversation, you will create communication roadblocks.

False Assumptions about the Receiver

The assumptions you make about the receiver of your message may be false, thus serving as a communications roadblock. A parent might say to his or her child: "In order to be as successful as I am, you'll have to spend more time studying and less time partying." If the child continues with the same ratio of studying to partying, the parent will become upset. Perplexed, he or she might say silently, "I wonder why my child didn't listen to me."

The false assumption made by the message sender is, "My child wants to be as successful as I am." Furthermore, the parent assumed the child measured success in terms of job and salary. What false assumptions have you made lately when trying to communicate with another person?

Different Interpretation of Words (Semantics)

Semantics is the study of the meaning and changes in the meaning of words. These different meanings can create roadblocks to communication. Often the problem is trivial and humorous; at other times, semantic problems can create substantial communication barriers. Consider first an example of trivial consequence:

A visitor to Toronto asked a hotel employee for the name of an escort service. Obligingly, the employee wrote down the name and telephone number of Execu-

tive Escort Service. The visitor later called the firm and inquired about the price of an escort for the evening. The Executive Escort Service replied, "It depends on how fancy you want to get. Do you want six motorcycle riders and a limousine? That's the full service."

Perplexed, the executive responded, "No, thanks, I just want one young woman for drinks, dinner, and a little companionship." Finally recognizing the semantic problem involved, the voice at the other end replied, "Sir, you are talking to the wrong type of escort service. We provide escorts for funerals and other special occasions. Check the visitor's guide to Toronto for the kind of escort service you're looking for."

Of greater consequence is the experience of a plant superintendent hit in the face with a wrench by an employee. He suffered a concussion and had to have twenty-seven stitches to repair his wounds. Tensions had been building up in the factory because of a heavy work schedule and hot working conditions. An Hispanic production worker took off his T-shirt and threw it down on the floor in disgust. His supervisor shouted at him, "Hey, boy, put that shirt back on." Almost by reflex, the worker attacked the supervisor.

To the Hispanic employee, the term "boy" was an insult—it demeaned his status and he took it as a racial slur. The supervisor perceived the term to mean about the same as "son" or "young man." "Girl" and "ghetto" are other words subject to different meanings that can trigger strong emotional responses in people. What are the different meanings of the two words just mentioned?

Distortion of Information

A great problem in sending messages is that people receiving them often hear what they want to hear. Without malicious intent, people modify your message to bolster their self-respect or improve their situation. An incident that occurred between Jennifer and her mother is fairly typical of this type of communications roadblock. Jennifer asked her mother if she might have a 35 mm camera system for Christmas. Regarding the request as farfetched and beyond her means, Jennifer's mother replied, "Why should I buy you a camera system like that when you never even take pictures of your little brother with your present camera?"

Jennifer *heard* her mother say, "If you take pictures of your little brother, I would then buy you that camera system." Three weeks later Jennifer presented her mother with a surprise gift—a small album containing twenty photographs of her little brother. "Mom," said Jennifer, "Here's the album you ordered. Now let me tell you in more detail about that 35 mm outfit you said you would get me for Christmas." Her mother replied, "I never said that. Where did you get that idea?"

The reason some people are so difficult to criticize or insult is that they ward off your message just as a duck wards water off its feathers. What messages of yours has someone not heard recently? Can you think of any messages that bounced off you lately?

Different Perspectives and Experiences (Where Are You Coming From?)

People perceive words and concepts differently because their experiences and vantage points differ. On the basis of their perception of what they have heard, many Hispanic children believe that the opening line of the "Star-Spangled Banner" is "José, can you see . . ." (note that few children have *seen* the national anthem in writing).

Young people with specialized training or education often encounter communication barriers in dealing with older workers. A minority of older workers think that young people are trying to introduce impractical and theoretical ideas. It takes time to break down this type of resistance to innovation and the application of current knowledge.

Emotions and Attitudes

Have you ever tried to communicate a message to another person while that person is emotionally aroused?[2] Your message was probably distorted considerably. Another problem is that people tend to say things when emotionally aroused that they would not say when calm. Similarly, a person having strong attitudes about a particular topic may become emotional when that topic is introduced. The underlying message here is try to avoid letting strong emotions and attitudes interfere with the sending or receiving of messages. If you are angry at someone, for example, you might miss the merit in what that person has to say. Note how strong emotion creates a communication roadblock in this exchange between a headwaiter and a busboy:

BUSBOY: I've worked here for three summers, and I think I am ready to become a waiter.

HEADWAITER: I suggest you get a little more experience under your belt. You're not quite ready yet.

BUSBOY: Not ready? What kind of gratitude is that? Anytime you've asked me to come in on a moment's notice I have. I was supposed to have Father's Day off. You called me at the last minute and I came running. Now you tell me I'm not ready to be a waiter.

HEADWAITER: I say you're not ready because you're still not self-confident for the job. You blow up when things don't go your way.

BUSBOY: With a boss like you, who wouldn't blow up? I don't see why I should take this abuse any longer.

The busboy is too emotional to hear the real reasons why the headwaiter thinks he is not yet ready for promotion to waiter. His emotional state, in turn, has triggered an emotional response from the headwaiter. If this conversation continues much longer, the busboy may wind up quitting or being fired.

Timing

Many messages do not get through to people because they are poorly timed. You have to know how to deliver a message, but you must also know when to deliver it. You must be able to recognize what is an appropriate time to deliver or not deliver your message. Don't ask your boss for a raise when he or she is in a bad mood; don't ask somebody new for a date when that person has just slipped on the ice. On the other hand, do ask your boss for a raise when business has been good; do ask a new acquaintance for a date when you have just done something nice for that person, and have been thanked.

BUILDING BRIDGES TO BETTER COMMUNICATION

With awareness and determination on your part, you can become a more effective communicator. It would be impossible to remove all barriers, but they can be minimized. The following strategies represent a sampling of what can be done to build bridges to better communication.[3]

Be Aware of Roadblocks

A trainer of airplane pilots contributed to a nonfatal crash because he was not adequately aware of a possible problem in interpreting his message. As the rookie pilot navigated down the runway, the trainer shouted, "Take-off power." The pilot shut off the engine and skidded off the runway. What the trainer really meant was to *use* take-off power—a surge of energy to lift the airplane off the ground.[4]

In short, when communicating keep in mind the potential barriers you have read about in the previous section of this chapter.

Use a Multimedia Approach

If you want to send an important message to one or more people, do not rely on a single medium exclusively. Follow up your face-to-face discussion with a letter and telephone call or both. A **medium** in this sense is simply a method of transmitting the message. Your body can be another medium to help impart your message. If you agree with someone about a spoken message, say you agree and also shake hands over the agreement. Can you think of any other media by which you can transmit your messages?

Use Verbal and Nonverbal Feedback

Don't be a hit-and-run communicator. Such a person drops a message and leaves the scene before he or she is sure the message has been sent as intended. Some of the teachers you have rated as outstanding have probably been those who ask the class if there are any questions, and also ask questions themselves.

Nonverbal feedback refers to the signs other than words that indicate whether or not your message has been delivered. A blank expression on the face of the receiver might indicate no comprehension. A disturbed, agitated expression might mean that the receiver's emotions are blocking the message.

Appeal to Human Needs

People are most receptive to messages that promise to do something for them. In other words, if a message promises to satisfy a need that is less than fully satisfied, you are likely to listen. The hungry person who ordinarily does not hear low tones readily hears the whispered message, "How would you like a pizza with everything on it?" Somehow, I have always been able to communicate this message to my class: "Unfortunately the class will not meet a week from today." I wonder to which need I have been appealing.

Listen Carefully

Since communication involves sending and receiving messages, effective listening helps overcome communication roadblocks. A later section of this chapter deals with improving your receiving of messages. For now, try this advice: "Both sender and receiver should be fully aware of what the other person is trying to communicate and should concentrate on listening as if a summary of the remarks were going to be required."[5]

Use Empathy

A good communicator tries to understand the other person's viewpoint. Two modern sayings convey directly the importance of empathy. That is, if "you know where the other person is coming from" or "you can walk a mile in his or her shoes," you will be a better sender and receiver of messages. Empathy does not necessarily mean that you sympathize with the other person. Suppose you are walking down the street, and a man approaches you and says, "You've got to give me ten dollars. I lost my paycheck gambling and I'm starving." You may understand the beggar's problem (empathy), but you may not feel sorry for him (sympathy). With this attitude you might say to him, "I know where you're coming from but get lost anyway."

Repeat Your Message

In general, you can overcome roadblocks to communication by repeating your message several times. It is usually advisable to say the same thing in different ways so as to avoid annoying the listener with straight repetition. In any case, your message may not have been understood in the first form. If there is too much repetition, however, people no longer listen to the message. They think they already understand the message.

Repetition, like any other means of overcoming communication roadblocks, does not work for all people. Many people who hear the message "Drinking and driving do not mix" are not moved by it. It is helpful to use several methods of overcoming roadblocks or barriers to communication.

Use Bias-Free Language

An important implication of semantics is that certain words are interpreted by some people as signs of bias. A **bias** is a prejudgment about another person or group based on something other than fact.[6] The use of biased words is thus a form of discrimination. To avoid this type of discrimination, attempt to use bias-free language. An obvious example of a biased statement would be for a supervisor to say, "I need a real man for this job." The bias-free statement expressing the same thought would be, "I need a courageous person for this job."

Table 5–1 presents a list of biased words and terms, along with their bias-free equivalent. Recognize, however, that your choice of words can never please everybody. For example, a store manager told a new employee, "Please don't refer to me as 'Ms.' in front of customers. I prefer the title 'Miss.' 'Ms.' should be used only for correspondence."

NONVERBAL COMMUNICATION (SENDING SILENT MESSAGES TO PEOPLE)

So far we have been talking mostly about spoken communication. However, much of the communication among people includes nonspoken and nonwritten messages. These nonverbal signals are a critical part of everyday communication. As a case in point, *how* you say "Thank you" makes a big difference in the extent to which your sense of appreciation registers. In **nonverbal communication** we use our

**TABLE 5–1 BIASED TERMS AND THEIR
BIAS-FREE SUBSTITUTES**

		Usually Perceived as Biased	Usually Perceived as Bias Free
Gender-Related		Girl	Woman
		Boy	Man
		Salesman, saleswoman	Sales representative
		Woman crane operator	Crane operator
		Hotel maid	Housekeeper
		Cleaning man	Custodian, cleaner
		Flag man, flag woman	Flagger
		Chairman, chairwoman	Chairperson, chair
Disabilities		Handicapped	Physically challenged
		Deaf	Hearing impaired
		Blind	Visually impaired
		Confined to a wheelchair	Uses a wheelchair
Race		Nonwhite	Black, Afro-American, Oriental, Indian
		Whitey	White, white person, Caucasian
Nationality, ethnic background		Jewish person	Jew
		"Scottish in me"	"My frugality"
		Ethnic jokes	Jokes with nationality unspecified

SOURCE: Several of the pairs of terms above are from information in Judy E. Pickens, "Terms of Equality: A Guide to Bias-Free Language," *Personnel Journal*, August 1985, pp. 24–28.

body, voice, or environment in numerous ways to help put a message across. Sometimes we are not aware how much our true feelings color our spoken message.

One problem of paying attention to nonverbal signals is that they can be taken too seriously. Just because some nonverbal signals (such as yawning or looking away from a person) might reflect a person's real feelings, not every signal can be reliably connected with a particular attitude. Jason may put his hand over his mouth because he is shocked; Lucille may put her hand over her mouth because she is trying to control her laughter about the message, and Ken may put his hand over his mouth as a signal that he is pondering the consequences of the message. Here we look at six categories of nonverbal communication that are generally reliable indicators of a person's attitude and feelings.[7]

Environment or Setting

Where you choose to deliver your message indicates what you think of its importance. Assume that a neighbor invites you over for dinner to discuss something with you. You will think it is a more important topic under these circumstances than if it were brought up when the two of you met in the supermarket. Other important environmental cues include room color, temperature, lighting, and furniture arrangement. A person who sits behind an uncluttered large desk, for example, appears more powerful than a person who sits behind a small, cluttered desk. This illusion of power may persist even if the two people express the same message, such as "We think you have a future with us."

Another aspect of the environment that can communicate information about you is your choice of restaurants and your selection of food. According to speculations contained in the book *Power Lunching,* business luncheons can be used to communicate power. To acquire the power balance over your luncheon partner you must choose the restaurant. Next, you must be careful to choose "power food" rather than "wimp food." A culinary guide to power follows:

POWER FOOD	WIMP FOOD
Anchovies	Apple sauce
Artichokes	Avocado
Baked potato	French fries
Boeuf bourguignon	Beef Wellington
Bleu Cheese	Gouda
Bloody Mary	Perrier water
Caesar salad	Chef salad
Caviar	Cantaloupe
Chicken livers	Chicken Kiev
Chili	Corned beef
Eggs (scrambled or fried)	Quiche
Hamburger	Ham
Horseradish dressing	Bacon
Lamb chops	Rack of lamb
Lobster	Lobster Newberg
Steamed clams	Frog legs
Soft shell crabs	Crab legs
Sushi	Shrimp cocktails
Tea	Iced tea
Tongue	Tuna

The above list contains a large element of tongue-in-cheek.[8] Yet the idea of power lunching does communicate an important fact: Almost anything about your behavior can send messages to others.

Distance from the Other Person

How close you place your body relative to another person's also conveys meaning when you send a message. If, for instance, you want to convey a positive attitude toward another person, get physically close to him or her. Putting your arm around someone to express interest and warmth is another obvious nonverbal signal. Cultural differences must be kept in mind in interpreting nonverbal cues. To illustrate, a French male is likely to stand closer to you than a British male, even if they had equally positive attitudes toward you. A set of useful guidelines has been developed for estimating how close to stand to another person (at least in North America!):

Intimate distance covers actual physical contact to about 18 inches. Usually it is reserved for close friends and loved ones or other people you feel affectionate toward. Physical intimacy is usually not called for on the job, but there are exceptions. For one, confidential information might be whispered within the intimate distance zone.

Personal distance covers from about 1.5 to 4 feet. In this zone it is natural to carry on friendly conversation and discussions. Also, you can touch the other person if you wish to maintain a feeling of privacy. When people engage in a heated argument, they sometimes enter the personal distance zone. One example is a baseball coach getting up close to an umpire and shouting in his face.

Social distance covers from 4 to 8 feet and in general is reserved for interaction that is businesslike and impersonal. We usually maintain this amount of distance between ourselves and strangers such as retail store clerks and cab drivers.

Public distance covers from 12 feet to the outer limit of being heard. This zone is typically used in speaking to an audience at a large meeting or in a classroom, but a few insensitive individuals might send ordinary messages by shouting across a room. The unstated message suggested by such an action is that the receiver of the message does not merit the effort of walking across the room.[9]

People sometimes manipulate personal space in order to dominate a situation. A sales representative might move into the personal or intimate circle of a customer just to intimidate him or her.[10] Many people become upset when you move into a closer circle than the situation calls for. They consider it an invasion of their personal space, or their "territorial rights." How would you feel if, while waiting in line at the post office, a complete stranger stood within 4 inches of your face?

Posture

Certain aspects of your posture communicate a message. Leaning toward another individual suggests that you are favorably disposed toward his or her message. Leaning backwards communicates the opposite. Openness of the arms or legs serves as an indicator of liking or caring. In general, people establish closed postures (arms folded and legs crossed) when speaking to people they dislike. Standing up straight generally indicates high self-confidence. Stooping and slouching could mean a poor self-image. In any event, there is almost no disadvantage to standing up straight.

Gestures

A rather obvious form of body language is gestures. Hand gestures are universally recognized as conveying specific information to others. If you make frequent hand movements, you will generally communicate a positive attitude. If you use few gestures, you will convey dislike or disinterest. An important exception here is that some people wave their hands vigorously while arguing. Some of their hand movements reflect anger. Another example is that open-palm gestures toward the other person typically convey positive attitudes.

Head, Face, and Eye Signals

"Here comes a live one," said one fellow to another at a singles bar. "I can tell she's interested in getting to know me. Just look into her eyes and at the expression on her face." The young man who spoke these words may have a valid point. When used in combination, the head, face, and eyes provide the clearest indications of attitudes toward other people. Lowering your head and peering over your glasses, for instance, is the nonverbal equivalent of the expression, "You're putting me on." As is well known, maintaining eye contact with another person improves communication with that person. In order to maintain eye contact, it is usually necessary to correspondingly move your head and face. Moving your head, face, and eyes away from another person is often interpreted as a defensive gesture or one suggesting a lack of self-confidence. Would you lend money to someone who didn't look at you directly?

The face is often used as a primary source of information about how we feel. We look for facial cues when we want to determine another person's attitude. You can often judge someone's current state of happiness by looking at his or her face. The expression "sourpuss" attests to this observation. Happiness, apprehension, anger, resentment, sadness, contempt, enthusiasm, and embarrassment are but a few of the emotions that can be expressed through the face. Exhibit 5–3 shows how the ability to interpret head, face, and eye signals can be an asset on the job.

EXHIBIT 5–3   REAL ESTATE AGENT SYLVIA INTERPRETS BODY LANGUAGE

Real estate agent Sylvia works out of an office in a large apartment complex. A bothersome part of her job of renting luxury apartments is taking people who have no real interest in the apartments on tours of them. She explains how she uses nonverbal cues to assist her with this problem:

We get hundreds of people who are just out for a Sunday afternoon or an early evening of fun. Among this group of fun seekers are a small percentage of legitimate prospects. I try to spend as little time as possible with the time wasters, short of being rude to them. Any casual looker could conceivably send around a friend who is a legitimate prospect.

After about twenty minutes of taking a person on a tour, I tell that person directly that he or she could move in within thirty days or sooner if necessary. I then watch carefully their body or eyes. If the prospect moves toward me or develops an intrigued, excited expression, I know I've got a live one on the hook. But if the person tightens up or turns his or her body away, I know I've got a time waster on my hands.

Sylvia's situation illustrates how understanding nonverbal communication can be an asset on the job. By interpreting the head, face, and eye signals of prospective renters, Sylvia is able to sort out the good prospects from the poor ones without appearing rude. For example, asking a person "Are you really interested in renting an apartment?" might create a strained relationship between Sylvia and that person. As Sylvia observes, any person is capable of making a referral at some time in the future. No enemies needed!

Tone of Voice

We often attach more significance to the *way* something is said than to *what* is said. Closely related to voice tone are volume, pitch, and rate of speaking. As with all nonverbal cues, there is a danger in making too much out of one aspect of voice. A friend of yours might speak to you about your broken portable TV in a high-pitched voice. You think you are being tipped off to guilt, but in reality your friend has laryngitis.

Anger, boredom, and joy can often be interpreted from voice quality. Anger is noted when the person speaks loudly, at a fast rate, and in a high pitch. Boredom is indicated by a monotone inflection. A tip-off to joy is when the person speaks loudly, with a high pitch, and fast rate. How do you sound when you are experiencing anger? Boredom? Joy?

DESCRIBING VERSUS JUDGING BEHAVIOR

Nonverbal behavior can be a subtle aspect of communication between people. Another fine point of communication is the difference between describing and judging the behavior of another person.[11] Generally communication improves when you present the most objective facts you can about a person (description) and then allow the receiver to reach a conclusion. In this way, you won't sound prejudiced or biased and communications will be improved, both in personal life and on the job. Learning the difference between description and judgment also helps you to write about people.

The difference between description and judgment can be illustrated through two comments about a man named Oscar. In trying to present a picture of Oscar, one woman says, "You'll notice a couple of unique things about Oscar's behavior. First of all, he enjoys eating food with his fingers and then licking them clean. Second, when he is introduced to a woman, he gives her quite a bear hug. Oscar is said to be facing many problems at home." Another woman says, "Watch out for Oscar, he's really a slob. I find him repulsive."

The first mode of presenting a picture of Oscar at least gives him a chance to be understood and tolerated by the recipient of the message. Not all descriptions versus judgments about people are so transparent. The exercise in Exhibit 5–4 will help sensitize you further to the distinction between description and judgment, or observation and interpretation.

EXHIBIT 5–4

Directions: Groups of three people each will discuss whether each statement describes or judges behavior. The verdict D (describes) or J (judges) will be noted in the space to the left of each statement.

_____ 1. Oh, what a beautiful day.
_____ 2. Sally has five large warts on her face.
_____ 3. Melanie is a knockout.
_____ 4. Bill is too hot tempered to work in this department.
_____ 5. Gerry tells you exactly what he thinks of your clothing and appearance.
_____ 6. Mandi is one terrific cook.
_____ 7. Jim enjoys preparing gourmet meals.
_____ 8. Miguel is a peacemaker.
_____ 9. Roosevelt finishes sentences for people.
_____ 10. Margie expresses appreciation whenever you do her a favor.

REMEMBERING NAMES AND FACES

In both social and work life, you are often faced with the challenge of trying to remember the name of a person you have been introduced to in the past. If you recall that person's face, communication is facilitated. If you cannot recall the name, a small barrier to communication is immediately erected. Two time-tested principles are particularly helpful in improving your ability to remember people's names and faces. Nobody intent on creating a positive impression on others or communicating effectively with them can afford to forget people's names and faces.

Learn the Name Through Rehearsal

At a business meeting, Joe was introduced to a new designer on the staff, Giuseppe Zavaglia. Joe said, "Hi, pleased to meet you." The next day the two men passed each other in the hall. Giuseppe said, "Hi, Joe, how are things going?" Joe replied, "Oh, just fine. Say, I've forgotten your name."

Joe must be credited for his candor in admitting that he did not know the other man's name. However, Joe was giving misinformation. He did not forget Zavaglia's name. He never learned it. Upon meeting Giuseppe, he should have said, "Nice to meet you, Giuseppe Zavaglia. I'll try to remember your name." At the end of the meeting he should have said, "So long, Giuseppe, I enjoyed meeting you." Two quick rehearsals are an effective way of learning someone's name.

Form a Humorous Association

A widely practiced simple memory device for remembering names is to make a humorous, or even absurd, association between that person's name and a familiar object. Assume that Peg meets Teena Stein, one of the young women in her physical fitness program at the community center. (Peg is new to town and wants to make some friends. It is therefore in her best interest to remember the names of people she meets.)

As Peg looks at Teena, she silently says her name and thinks up an easily remembered image: a woman with a small (tiny like Teena) beer stein (same as Stein) perched on her head. As long as Peg doesn't call her new acquaintance "Teena Beer" on their next meeting, her system will work.

IMPROVING YOUR SENDING OF MESSAGES

Most of the information already presented in this chapter will aid you in your attempt to send messages more effectively. If you know how to build better bridges to communication, for example, you will get more messages across to people. Here we are concerned with a few specific tips for communicating orally and nonverbally.

Oral Communication

Most people could stand improvement in public speaking, but few people have jobs that actually call for much speech making. Even as a club or association member you will be called upon to make a speech or address a group on relatively few occasions. We are not saying that public speaking skills are unimportant, just that they are rarely used. What most people do need is to improve their ability to express ideas and feelings in face-to-face encounters. Among these encounters are meetings at work, problem-solving discussions, and two-way conversations in general. Any course in conference leadership would help you achieve this end. Five practical suggestions, if carried out, should help you improve your face-to-face speaking skills.

1. Take the opportunity to speak in a meeting or class whenever it arises. Volunteer comments in class and committee meetings, and capitalize on any chance to be a spokesperson for the group. But avoid the extreme of monopolizing the time available for comments.

2. Obtain feedback by listening to tape recordings or dictating equipment renditions of your voice. Attempt to eliminate vocalized pauses and repetitious phrases (such as "OK" or "you know," or "really") that detract from your communication effectiveness. Ask a knowledgeable friend for his or her opinion on your voice and speech.

3. Use appropriate models to help you develop your speech. A television talk show host or commercial announcer may have the type of voice and speech behavior that fits your personality. The goal is not to imitate that person but to use him or her as an approximate guide to generally acceptable speech.

4. Practice interviewing and being interviewed. With a friend take turns conducting a simulated job interview, or a discussion with a store manager about returning defective merchandise. Interview each other about a controversial current topic or each other's hobby.

5. Practice expressing the feelings behind your factual statements. For example you might rehearse an imaginary situation in which a neighbor's dog has dug up your garden. A factual statement might be, "I think Rex tore up my lawn." A statement that combines facts with feelings is "I

think Rex tore up my lawn. And I'm very upset about it. How are you going to help me get my garden back in shape?" Expressing your feelings in a mature manner is so important for personal success that it is the subject of the next chapter.

Nonverbal Communication

To improve your effectiveness in sending messages, it is important to support words with appropriate forms of nonverbal communication. Since less reliable information is known about silent than about verbal messages, the following five suggestions are somewhat tentative.

1. Obtain feedback on your body language by asking others to comment on the gestures and facial expressions that you use in conversations. Have a video tape prepared of you conferring with another individual. After studying your body language, attempt to eliminate those mannerisms and gestures that you think detract from your effectiveness (such as moving your knee from side to side when being interviewed).

2. Learn to relax when communicating with others. Take a deep breath and consciously allow your body muscles to loosen. The relaxation techniques discussed in Chapter 4 should be helpful here. A relaxed person makes it easier for other people to relax. Thus you are likely to elicit more useful information from other people when you are relaxed.

3. Use facial, hand, and body gestures to supplement your speech. (But do not overdo it.) A good starting point is to use hand gestures to express enthusiasm. You can increase the potency of enthusiastic comments by shaking the other person's hand, nodding approval, smiling, or patting him or her on the shoulder.

4. Avoid using the same nonverbal gesture indiscriminately. To illustrate, if you want to use nodding to convey approval, do not nod with approval even when you dislike what somebody else is saying. Also, do not pat everybody on the back. Nonverbal gestures used indiscriminately lose their communications effectiveness.

5. Use role-playing to practice various forms of nonverbal communication. A good starting point would be to practice selling your ideas about an important project or concept to another person. During your interchange, supplement your spoken messages with appropriate nonverbal cues such as posture, voice intonation, gestures, and so forth. Later, obtain the other person's perception of the effectiveness of your nonverbal behavior.

Written Communication

Most readers of this book have already taken one or two courses designed to improve writing skills, and many other courses have a writing component. Nevertheless, since written communication is so important in business, five brief suggestions are in order. In addition, avoid the common writing mistakes noted in Exhibit 5–5.

EXHIBIT 5–5   COMMON WRITING MISTAKES TO AVOID

Frank Edmund Smith, a professor of business writing, observes that any piece of writing sends at least two messages. The literal message is found in the words themselves, and the other message is conveyed through unconscious signals. Writing sends information not only about the message but also about the writer. Some of these signals are obvious, such as the quality of paper used for letters or job résumés.

When it comes to matters of grammar, usage, and style, the kind of people who make it to the executive suite are often stricter than the most rigid grade school teacher. Executives expect high-quality written documents from their employees. Professor Smith has noticed several signals of the wrong sort that are sent regularly in business writing. He bases his conclusions on the thousands of pieces of business correspondence he has reviewed in recent years.

1. *Possessives and plurals.* Many people completely confuse possessives and plurals. The most common mix-up occurs between "its" (the possessive) and "it's" (the contraction of it is). Every business writer who is concerned with accuracy will be quick to identify the confusion that can result if the expression "the manager's position" is written as "the managers' position." The manager's position refers to the position taken by one manager, while the second is the position taken by more than one manager.

2. *Collective nouns.* The possessive-plural confusion suggests another frequent error in business correspondence—treating collective nouns as plurals. An expression such as "The corporation has decided to move their headquarters," ignores the fact that a business is a single entity. The correct expression is, "The corporation has decided to move *its* headquarters."

3. *Double negatives.* Double negatives such as "I haven't seen nobody" are really positives. They cause no real confusion since nobody actually interprets a double negative as a positive. However, the use of a double negative says something negative about the writer.

4. *Homonyms.* An increasingly common misusage is the substitution of words that sound almost alike. But do we feel comfortable doing business with someone who does not know the difference between "insure" (to obtain financial protection against risk) and "ensure" (to make certain)?

5. *Right justification on the word processor.* Professor Smith believes that right margin justification (or "block writing") makes a letter or memo look cold, impersonal, and uninviting. Right margin justification is therefore best used for overdue payment letters and information about machine parts.

Don't rely on even the best secretary to catch all of these mistakes. In fact, some of the above problems would not necessarily be spotted as "mistakes" except by the person for whom the message is intended.

SOURCE: Excerpted and paraphrased from Frank Edmund Smith, "Does Your Writing Send the Wrong Signals?" *Personnel Journal*, December 1985, pp. 28–30. Reprinted with permission of *Personnel Journal*, Costa Mesa, California; all rights reserved.

1. Read a book about effective business report writing and attempt to implement the suggestions it offers.[12]

2. Read material regularly that is written in the style and format that would be useful to you in your career. The *Wall Street Journal* and *BusinessWeek* are useful models for most forms of job-related writing. Managerial and staff jobs require you to write brief, readily understandable memos and reports. If your goal is to become a competent technical report writer, continuously read technical reports in your specialty.

3. Practice writing at every opportunity. As a starting point, you might write letters to friends and relatives or memos to the file (those placed directly in the file). Successful writers constantly practice writing. If you do not write frequently you run the risk of getting out of "writing shape."

4. Get feedback on your writing. Ask a co-worker or classmate to critique a rough draft of your reports and memos. Offer to reciprocate. Editing other people's writing is a valuable way of improving your own. Feedback from a person with more writing experience and knowledge than you is particularly valuable. For instance, comments made by an instructor about a submitted paper are usually extremely useful.

5. Learn to use a word processor or an electronic typewriter with a memory. Writing will always be a tedious process unless you mechanize the process. Typing in place of writing by hand is one moderate step forward. Learning to use a word processor or an advanced electronic typewriter is a giant step forward. The vast majority of professional writers today use a word processor. Also, many employees are expected to prepare their own memos and brief reports on a word processor.

People often think of word processing as a method of increasing the speed of one's writing. My observation is that the biggest payoff may be in writing quality, rather than speed—although the gains in speed may also be impressive. Writing quality improves because it is so easy to correct mistakes and edit your writing as you go along.

The majority of spelling mistakes can be corrected by using the spelling function included in most word processing programs. (Most electronic spellers cannot spell technical terms or last names unless you add these terms and names to their memory.) Some electronic spell-checkers also spot grammatical errors. You can also rearrange your paragraphs. When it comes time to do a second draft of your paper, you simply recall the original document from the computer memory and re-edit.

My one caution to the reader, however is that word processors are much more temperamental than typewriters or writing pads. Use the save command after every few paragraphs of writing. After every two pages of written input, command the computer to print. At this stage of their development, many word processors sometimes refuse to store or retrieve input. Or the disks used in microcomputers and personal computers sometimes fail.

IMPROVING YOUR RECEIVING OF MESSAGES

Many people are surprised to discover that they have developed the reputation of being "good communicators" simply because they are good at receiving messages. Yet receiving messages is a basic part of the communication process. Unless you receive messages as they were intended, you cannot properly perform your job or be a good social companion. A major step forward in your listening skill would be to improve your concentration. Much is forgotten because a message was never received correctly in the first place. (Do you remember the incident with Giuseppe Zavaglia?) Receiving messages, however, involves much more than listening. To simplify matters, we have organized improving your receiving of messages into five different skills: basic listening, paraphrasing, verbal following, open-ended questioning, and summarization.

Basic Listening

Your listening skill in face-to-face situations (rather than listening to a formal speaker) will improve if you follow these several tips:

1. *Hold your fire.* A common barrier to effective listening is the habit of mentally preparing an answer while another person is speaking.[13] Therefore learn not to get too excited about the sender's point, pro or con, until you are sure you understand it. Do not make up your mind immediately whether the message sender is good or bad.

2. *Listen for key ideas.* Facts serve as documentation for ideas of broader significance. When your roommate tells you that your desk is messy, he or she may also be telling you that you are messy in a number of ways. Simply cleaning up your desk will not cure the problem.

3. *Resist external distractions.* Aside from distractions taking place inside your head, external distractions also have to be resisted. While listening to the speaker, try to ignore the low-flying plane or that physically attractive person adjacent to you. A good listener intuitively combats distractions.

4. *Capitalize on thought speed.* The average rate of speech for English is 125 words a minute. We think, and therefore listen, at almost four times that speed. Be careful not to let your mind wander while you are waiting for the person's next thought. Instead, try to listen between the lines. Try to interpret the speaker's nonverbal communication. For instance, did the sender of the message look sincere when he or she said, "You're

doing great"? (Review the section "Use Verbal and Nonverbal Feedback" presented earlier in the chapter.)

5. *Listen for total meaning.* As discussed in relation to monologues versus dialogues, listen for feeling as well as fact. In other words, try to "get inside your speaker's head." Suppose that your boss says, "I wonder if we're putting you under too much pressure." Find out if the boss means that you look as though you're faltering under the pressure. Your boss might simply think that you have been carrying an unfair burden.[14]

Paraphrasing

One human relations specialist contends that paraphrasing is the keystone to receiving messages. Restating in your own words what the sender says, feels, and means, improves communication in a couple of ways: "First it helps you avoid judging and evaluating. When you are restating you are not passing judgment. Second, restating gives the sender direct feedback as to how well you understand the messages. If you do not fully understand, the sender can add messages until you do."[15]

It is conceivable that you will feel awkward the first several times you try paraphrasing. Therefore, first try it with a good friend, spouse, or parent. With some practice, it will become a natural part of your communication skill kit. Here is an example of how you might go about paraphrasing:

OTHER PERSON: I'm getting ticked off at working so hard around here. I wish somebody else would pitch in and do a fair day's work.

YOU: You're saying that you do more than your fair share of the tough work in our department.

OTHER PERSON: You bet. Here's what I think we should be doing about it.
. . .

Or, try this example:

YOU (READER): How many more suggestions for improving your communication are there in this chapter?

ME (AUTHOR): You're beginning to think that this chapter is getting a little long.

YOU: You got it.

ME: It will be over in a few pages.

Verbal Following

In verbal following you try to follow carefully the verbal messages people are saying. It involves the exact repetition of a person's last few words, the use of "um-hmmms," "I follow you," "I understand," "Yes," and other such verbal encouragers. To the person with whom you are trying to communicate, too much verbal following will seem like a mental health counselor's approach. The effect could be annoying.

Open-Ended Questions

Developing this skill can aid in verbal following and can also bring forth new information.[16] Closed-ended questions frequently begin with words such as "did," "is," or "aren't you?" They can be too easily answered by a "yes" or "no" that shuts off further communication. "How have you enjoyed your new job so far?" is an open-ended question. It leads to more communication than "Do you like your new job?"

Summarization

The final basic message-receiving skill deals with summarizing what you heard from the other person during your communication session. When you summarize, you pull together, condense, and thereby clarify the main points communicated about the other person. It allows for further clarification on the part of the sender. Here are two basic summarization statements:

> "Lynn, what I've heard you say during our meeting is that. . . ."
> "Les, as I understand you, your position is that. . . ."[17]

HOW TO CONDUCT YOURSELF AT A MEETING

A substantial amount of communication in organizations takes place at formal meetings among small groups of people. In your community or on the job you need to be able to communicate effectively in meetings. Virtually all of the information about nonwritten communication presented so far in this chapter applies to meetings. Here we provide some additional suggestions geared specifically toward increasing one's effectiveness at meetings.[18] We emphasize participation at meetings, yet most of the suggestions also apply to conducting or leading a meeting.

- ☐ Volunteer to attend meetings about topics in which you are interested and knowledgeable. You are likely to perform the best in a meeting under the conditions just stated. However, do your best when you are assigned to attend meetings of little interest to you.
- ☐ Display your best spoken and nonverbal communication skills during the meeting. You will be perceived negatively if you commit such errors as

having slurred speech, using repetitive and meaningless phrases such as "You know," or displaying poor posture.

☐ Make the right number of contributions. The person who hogs a meeting is perceived just as negatively as the noncontributor. Give other people a chance to contribute, but do not be so polite that you become passive.

☐ Be punctual and stay until the leader says that the meeting is over. If you will be late or have to leave early, let the leader know in advance.

☐ Keep your comments brief and to the point. One of the major problems facing the meeting leader is to keep conversations on track. Help the leader by setting a good example for the other participants.

☐ Avoid leaving the meeting except for emergencies. Instruct your co-workers and friends not to call you out of a meeting except for legitimate emergencies.

☐ Be supportive toward other members. If another participant says something of value, give that person your approval by such means as nodding your head or smiling. Support of this type encourages the free flow of ideas. Being supportive includes being tolerant of viewpoints considerably different than yours.

☐ Listen carefully to the leader and other participants. Show by your nonverbal behavior that you are concerned about what they are saying. For example, look attentive.

☐ Take your turn at being the leader during the meeting. To accomplish this you might volunteer to make a report during the meeting or head a subcommittee that will report back to the group later.

☐ Respond to the comments of other participants. Interacting with others is important because it has a brainstorming effect—new ideas build on the ideas of others.

☐ Avoid disruptive behavior such as belittling another participant, frequent outbursts of laughter, nail clipping, wallet cleaning, newspaper reading, napping, or yawning.

☐ Bring refreshments to the meeting only if such behavior is agreed upon in advance. For instance, many meetings held at midday are "brown-bag" events. If you cannot get through a meeting without refreshments, bring enough food and beverage with you to supply the other participants.

SUMMARY

Communication is the sending and receiving of messages. Almost anything that takes place in personal or work life therefore involves communication. The steps involved in communication are: ideation, encoding, transmission, receiving, decoding, understanding, and action.

Two-way communication is generally superior to one-way communication. For two-way communication to take place, both parties must respond to one another's feelings as well as the content of the message.

Many potential roadblocks or barriers to communication exist. These roadblocks are most likely to occur when messages are complex, emotional, or clash with the receiver's mental set. Communication roadblocks include: limited understanding of people, false assumptions about the receiver, semantics, distorting information, different perspectives and experiences, emotions and attitudes, and improper timing of the message.

Strategies to overcome communication roadblocks include: be aware they exist, use more than one medium, use verbal and nonverbal feedback, appeal to human needs, listen carefully, use empathy, repeat your message, and use bias-free language.

Nonverbal communication, or silent messages, are important parts of everyday communication. Nonverbal communication includes the environment or setting in which the message is sent; distance from the other person; posture; gestures; head, face, and eye signals; and voice tone.

Communication of information about people is generally improved when you describe rather than judge behavior. In this way the receiver of the messages is allowed to reach his or her own conclusion about the individual described. Remembering names and faces also improves communication between people. Two helpful principles are: (1) learn the name through rehearsal and (2) form a humorous association between the name and the person.

To improve your face-to-face speaking ability, you should: practice, obtain feedback, use appropriate people as models, conduct practice interviews, practice expressing your feelings. Nonverbal communication skills can be improved by obtaining feedback, relaxing when communicating, using gestures, avoiding indiscriminate use of gestures, and role playing.

Methods of improving written communication include: reading about effective writing, modeling good writing in your field, practice your writing, get feedback on your writing, and use a word processor (or electronic typewriter with a memory). Also avoid common mistakes such as confusing possessives and plurals.

Your receiving of messages can be improved by working on your basic listening skills, paraphrasing what people tell you, verbal following, open-ended questioning, and summarization.

Handling yourself well at meetings is an important part of being a good communicator. Suggestions along these lines include: speak at your best during meetings; contribute the right amount; make brief, pointed comments; be supportive toward other members; take your

turn at being a leader during the meeting; and respond to other participants.

QUESTIONS AND ACTIVITIES

1.   How can a person tell if he or she is a good communicator?
2.   What information in this chapter would be particularly important
     for a hearing impaired individual?
3.   How does the "generation gap" contribute to communication prob-
     lems?
4.   What would you suggest for getting through to a person who is
     already overloaded with information?
5.   How important is nonverbal communication for actors and ac-
     tresses? Explain your answer.
6.   Why is it that "better communication between the parties in-
     volved" is offered as a solution to so many family and work prob-
     lems?
7.   Elementary and high school students allegedly spend about 1,000
     hours per year watching television. What is the probable effect of
     this much television watching on their communication skills?
8.   Think of the last time you shopped for a major purchase. What
     kind of body language did the salesperson use to try to influence
     you to make a purchase.
9.   What barriers to communication typically exist in a classroom?
     What can be done to reduce these barriers?
10. Attend, or watch on television, a presentation by an executive or
     political figure. Analyze what that person does right or wrong
     based on any points about effective communication made in this
     chapter. Be prepared to discuss your findings in class.

A HUMAN RELATIONS CASE PROBLEM:
MEMO WARFARE

Jerry Prince, owner and president of Prince Travel, observed that too
much money was being spent on photocopying at his travel agency.
The memos written in response to this problem are as follows:

OFFICE MEMO

To: Office staff of Prince Travel

From: Jerry Prince

Subject: Budget overrun on photocopying

It has been brought to my attention that we are now 24 percent over budget on photocopying expenses, with one-third of the year remaining. This abuse of photocopying privileges must stop. I see three alternatives facing us. Number one, we can close down the agency for the year, thus avoiding any more copying expenses (an alternative *most* of you would not desire). Number two, we can stop making photocopies for the rest of the year. Number three, we can all develop a responsible and mature approach to budget management by making more prudent use of the photocopier.

OFFICE MEMO

To: Jerry Prince

From: Sheila LaVal

Subject: Your memo about photocopying

I read your recent memo with dismay, since it is my department that makes extensive use of the photocopying machine. We use copies mostly for important purposes like getting trip information to clients in a hurry. Are we in the business of taking care of the travel needs of clients or in the business of pinching pennies on photocopy costs?

OFFICE MEMO

To: Sheila LaVal

From: Jerry Prince

Subject: Your response to my memo about photocopying

It is obvious to me, Sheila, that you are resisting the philosophy of budgeting. In today's business world, both the IBMs and the Prince Travel agencies must learn to respect the limits imposed by budgets. Perhaps it is time you and I had a serious discussion about this matter. Please make an appointment to see me at your earliest convenience.

Questions

1. What disadvantages to written communication are suggested by the above case?
2. What feelings did Prince's first memo communicate to Sheila?
3. What feelings did LaVal's memo communicate to Prince?
4. So far what actions have been prompted by Prince's memos?
5. What can be done to convert this situation into a successful communication event?

A HUMAN RELATIONS ROLE PLAY:
DISCUSSING A CONTROVERSIAL MEMO

This role play is a follow-up to Prince's last memo. Prince and LaVal get together to discuss the problems mentioned in the memo. One person plays the role of Prince. He is irritated that LaVal seems so unsympathetic to the need for a balanced photocopy budget. He wants to communicate this irritation to Sheila, yet he does not want to create needless conflict. As the president of the agency, he wants to retain harmony in the work group.

Another person plays the role of LaVal, who is very upset about Prince's memos. She believes strongly that Prince is pinching pennies at the expense of customer goodwill. LaVal wants to get this important message about customer goodwill across to Prince.

In conducting this role play, use both verbal and nonverbal communication. Both players should also make an effort to overcome communication barriers.

REFERENCES

[1] Jitendra M. Sharma, "Organizational Communications: A Linking Process," *Personnel Administrator,* July 1979, p. 37.

[2] Barry L. Reece and Rhonda Brandt, *Effective Human Relations in Business* (Boston: Houghton Mifflin, 1981), p. 30.

[3] The term "building bridges" in relation to communication is from Ann Ellenson, *Human Relations* (Englewood Cliffs, NJ: Prentice-Hall, 1973), p. 83.

[4] Anecdote contributed by Robert Paul.

[5] G. James Francis and Gene Milbourn, Jr., *Human Behavior in the Work Environment: A Managerial Perspective* (Santa Monica, CA: Goodyear Publishing Company, 1980), p. 230.

[6] Judy E. Pickens, "Terms of Equality: A Guide to Bias-Free Language," *Personnel Journal,* August 1985, p. 24.

[7] This section is based on two sources: John Baird, Jr., and Gretchen Wieting, "Nonverbal Communication Can Be a Motivational Tool," *Personnel Journal,* September 1979, pp. 607–610, 625; Walter D. St. John, "You Are What You Communicate," *Personnel Journal,* October 1985, pp. 40–43.

[8] E. Melvin Pinsel and Ligita Dienhart, *Power Lunching* (New York: Rawson Wade, 1984).

[9] Edward T. Hall, "Proxemics—A Study of Man's Spatial Relationships," in *Man's Image in Medicine and Anthropology* (New York: International Universities Press, 1963).

[10] Reece and Brandt, *Effective Human Relations in Business,* p. 32.

[11] David W. Johnson, *Human Relations and Your Career: A Guide to*

Interpersonal Skills (Englewood Cliffs, NJ: Prentice-Hall, 1978), pp. 125–128. The exercise is also adapted from Johnson.

[12] One of many good books on this topic is William Repp, *Complete Handbook of Business English* (Englewood Cliffs, NJ: Prentice-Hall, 1983).

[13] Robert Maidment, "Listening—the Overlooked and Underdeveloped Other Half of Talking," *Supervisory Management,* August 1985, p. 10.

[14] Most of the above list is based on and adapted from Ralph G. Nichols, "Listening is a 10-Part Skill," in *Managing Yourself,* presented by the editors of *Nation's Business,* not dated.

[15] Johnson, *Human Relations and Your Career,* p. 136.

[16] D. Keith Denton, "A Manager's Toughest Job: One-on-one Communication," *Supervisory Management,* May 1985, p. 37.

[17] This and some of the previous suggestions are presented in John F. Kikoski, "Communication: Understanding It, Improving It," *Personnel Journal,* February 1980, pp. 129–131.

[18] Based on Andrew J. DuBrin, *Contemporary Applied Management: Behavioral Science Techniques for Managers and Professionals,* 2nd ed. (Plano, TX: Business Publications, 1985), pp. 139–153.

SOME ADDITIONAL READING

BERRY, WALDRON.   "Group Problem Solving: How to Be an Effective Participant." *Supervisory Management,* June 1983, pp. 13–19.

BOOTH-BUTTERFIELD, MELANIE.   "She Hears . . . He Hears: What They Hear and Why." *Personnel Journal,* May 1984, pp. 36–43.

DAVIS, KEN.   *Better Business Writing: A Process Approach.* Columbus, OH: Charles E. Merrill, 1983.

ELSEA, JANET G.   "Strategies for Effective Presentations." *Personnel Journal,* September 1985, pp. 31–34.

FRANK, ALLAN D.   "Trends in Communication: Who Talks to Whom?" *Personnel,* December 1985, pp. 41–47.

JOSEPH, BUCK.   "Business Writer's Block." *Supervisory Management,* October 1985, pp. 25–31.

SIGBAND, NORMAN B.   "Meetings With Success." *Personnel Journal,* May 1985, pp. 48–55.

STECKLER, NICOLE A., and ROBERT ROSENTHAL.   "Sex Differences in Nonverbal and Verbal Communication with Bosses, Peers, and Subordinates." *Journal of Applied Psychology,* February 1985, pp. 157–163.

ST. JOHN, WALTER D.   "Plain Speaking." *Personnel Journal,* June 1985, pp. 83–90.

6

Being Assertive with Others

Learning Objectives

After studying the information and doing the exercises in this chapter you should be able to:

- Understand the benefits of being assertive
- Become more aware of your feelings and be able to express them more directly
- Develop some techniques for becoming less shy if you think shyness is a problem for you
- Develop a strategy for becoming more assertive with people
- Develop an awareness of when to be assertive and when to be nonassertive

"I'm tired of being victimized all the time," said the interior designer. "My husband and I both have full-time careers, but I'm always stuck doing most of the homemaking."

"I've had it up to my neck," said the football tackle. "I'm treated like a practice dummy. Something's got to change or I'm finding a new job."

The interior designer and the football player just quoted are both suffering from the same problem. Something important is bothering them, but they haven't developed skills they need to make their demands known. Both have negative feelings about what is happening to them, yet they grumble instead of taking action. If they were truly assertive, they would be able to make their feelings and demands known in an effective way. The interior designer might not scream for a divorce, but she would have her share of time off from household chores and child care. The tackle would demand less shabby treatment during practice sessions.

Learning to express your feelings and make your demands known is an important aspect of becoming an effective individual. Many of the stress-related problems described in Chapter 4 can be avoided if you express your feelings. If you rarely let others know what is bothering you, the tension will lead to serious internal problems. Expressing your feelings also helps you establish good relationships with people. If you aren't sharing your feelings and attitudes with other people, you will never get close to them. After all, what is a good friend for?

Another benefit from being emotionally expressive, and therefore assertive, is that you get more of what you want in life. If you are too passive, people will neglect giving you what you want. Often it is necessary to ask someone when you want a raise, promotion, date, or a better deal on a bank loan. Successful people usually make their demands known, yet do not throw tantrums and are rarely considered hotheads. Exceptions include theatrically inclined trial lawyers and a few athletic coaches. Very few occupations call for displays of this nature.

BECOMING MORE AWARE OF YOUR FEELINGS

You must first become aware of your feelings in order to develop the ability to express them in a beneficial way. In general, people do not have much trouble making facts known to other people. Your interpre-

tation of those facts (your feelings and attitudes) creates the problem. It is easier to say to a store clerk, "This blouse is made in a foreign country," than to say, "My attitude toward foreign merchandise is negative." You may be wrong, but those are your true feelings (which underlie your attitude).

So far we have been using the term "feeling" in several ways. The term feeling generally refers to any emotional state or disposition, such as happiness or sadness. A feeling is also said to be an internal reaction—such as butterflies in your stomach—based on your experience.[1] Suppose you see a tiger cat walking toward you. All your life, you have liked cats. Immediately you experience positive internal sensations. Your friend may start to cringe and have feelings of fright upon seeing the same tiger cat. Your friend knows from experience that he or she is allergic to cats. To gain some practice in becoming aware of your feelings, try the exercise presented in Exhibit 6–1.

EXHIBIT 6–1   THE PERSONAL REACTION LIST

Directions: Write down how you feel (your reactions) toward each of the following twelve statements. Any answer but "This could never happen to me" is acceptable. It is essential to state clearly the kind of emotion you are experiencing for each statement.

1. While I'm standing in line at the bank, an attractive stranger winks at me and says hello.

   _____

   _____

2. My dentist informs me that I need $600 worth of root canal work (a complicated type of oral surgery).

   _____

   _____

3. I apply for a job I want very much. The company official says, "Sorry, we need somebody brighter for this job."

   _____

   _____

4. My doctor confirms the fact that I will be completely bald within two years.

   _____

   _____

5. A clean, well-groomed puppy licks my face.

   _____

   _____

6. An eighty-year-old woman holds my arms and says, "Please don't go; I need your company." If you do not leave now you will be late for work (or class).

   _____

   _____

---

7. I run over a rabbit with the car I am driving. The rabbit lies in the road quivering and struggling to move.

8. A drunk old man, dressed in rags, unshaven, and toothless puts his arm around my shoulder and asks me for a dollar.

9. A six-year-old-girl makes me a birthday card and writes on it, "I love you."

10. I read in the newspaper that a close friend of mine died last night in a house fire.

11. I am about to pay my bill at an expensive restaurant and I discover that my wallet is missing. Since it was my treat, my companion did not bring along money.

12. Although I am totally innocent, two police workers come to my door and inform me that I am under arrest for suspicion of grand larceny.

After you have completed the above exercise you will have gained some experience in describing your feelings to yourself. At some point in the near future, perhaps the next class session, it is recommended that you participate in the group exercise presented in Exhibit 6–2, which is about expressing your feelings. The exercise is designed to help you feel comfortable expressing your feelings to others.

EXHIBIT 6–2   THE FEELING CIRCLE

The class will organize itself into groups of about seven to ten people. Before the group experience begins, each participant thinks up a "feeling subject" for the group. One by one, in a clockwise direction, people will respond to your question "How would you feel if _____?" You can complete the sentence with any situation or experience you think will be useful in disclosing feelings.

Among the numerous possibilities are:

> "How would you feel if your parents told you they were getting a divorce?"
> "How would you feel if you flunked out of school?"
> "How would you feel if a special friend of yours wrote you a poem expressing his or her love to you?"

After the "How would you feel" question is introduced, each group member in turn (clockwise direction) reports his or her feelings. In this way each person in the group will be able to respond to the questions asked by every other participant in the group. Finally, the person who asked the "How would you feel" question should respond to his or her own question.

After everyone has had a turn, the group members discuss what they learned from the experience. The class instructor might then report to the group what he or she saw happening.

EXPRESSING YOUR FEELINGS DIRECTLY

Being assertive with others and expressing your feelings is a skill that people possess in different amounts. Some people are direct and forthright in expressing their feelings, almost to the point of brutality. One example would be a stranger who meets you at a party and says, "I feel uncomfortable meeting you. In fact, I find you loathsome." At the other extreme are people who keep most of their feelings bottled up. No matter how upset they are with people, they never share these feelings. Unfortunately, these are the same people who sometimes explode with rage and commit violent acts. They allow negative feelings to build up to a danger point. Or, they begin to suffer from some kind of stress disorder.

Most people fall between these extremes. Some might express their feelings in an indirect manner rather than explaining how they really feel about something. Others might attack something that is not the real issue. One example is the husband who berates his wife for being late in getting ready to attend a party. What he is really upset about is that he dislikes the way his wife looks this evening. A more direct, and mutually beneficial approach might have been to say to his wife, "I must tell you that I do not care for the dress you have chosen for tonight. My thoughts (really feelings) are that this dress does not do justice to your appearance. Chartreuse does not go well with your red hair."

Another human tendency is to attack a general situation instead of being honest with ourselves about our feelings. A young woman might say, "I hate this town. It's so dull. There is nothing to do around here." If she expressed her true feelings, she would be saying, "I'm feeling discouraged and depressed. I've lived here for six months and I've hardly made any friends." The reward in expressing true feelings is that your mental health improves, and you are better able to deal with the problem. In the example just given, if the woman admitted to herself that her negative feelings stem from loneliness—not the town—she could take remedial action. It is much easier to plan a campaign of meeting new friends than to move to another town.

Following are several examples of the differences between direct and indirect expression of feelings. In the last two examples, you decide which are the direct and indirect alternatives.

> *Indirect:* Business statistics is really a waste of time. You never need it in the real world.
> *Direct:* I'm not very confident of my abilities in statistics. I'm also afraid of failing.
> *Indirect:* Are you sure you want to wash and wax your car right now?
> *Direct:* I wish you wouldn't wash and wax your car right now. I'm lonely and I want your companionship.
> *Indirect:* You're a talented person. I bet you have loads of friends.
> *Direct:* I like you.
> ——: Let's not go to this restaurant. I've heard it's overpriced.
> ——: I'm embarrassed to say that I can't afford this restaurant.
> ——: I'm angry that I don't play better tennis in the wind.
> ——: This darn wind is driving me crazy. How can anybody play tennis in a wind like this?[2]

SHYNESS: A PROBLEM IN BEING ASSERTIVE

Shyness is the most common major adjustment problem people face in everyday life. Psychologist Philip Zimbardo found that 40 percent of the 10,000 adults he surveyed consider themselves shy. About 15 percent of the population feel that they are "painfully shy." Shy people have a difficult time expressing their feelings, attitudes, and opinions to people—particularly to strangers.[3]

Shyness, of course, involves more than not being emotionally expressive. It sometimes involves trying to minimize contact with people for such matters as asking directions, exchanging purchases, or asking for dates. Many shy people also have relationship problems because they find intimacy embarrassing.

Before discussing methods of overcoming shyness and becoming more assertive, it is helpful to examine the consequences of the problem. The consequences can be divided according to their affects on career and personal life, although the two are related.

Career Consequences of Shyness

Zimbardo found that shyness is a great liability on the job: "Although they do succeed if they are outstanding performers, shy people usually earn less, receive fewer promotions and report less job satisfaction than those who are outgoing. They have a higher rate of absenteeism and are less likely to hold positions of leadership in their field."[4]

Shy people have job problems, according to Zimbardo, because they are overly concerned about being evaluated and are low risk takers. Usually, as children they were severely criticized by their parents and teachers whenever they made mistakes, so shy people often settle for jobs below their capabilities.

The underdeveloped social skills of shy people also retard their career advancement. Zimbardo says shy people do not know how to make small talk, so they avoid going to lunch with people in their fields who could advance their careers. Because few people know them, their names never come up when job openings occur.

Nevertheless, being shy is not a negative behavior pattern in all work situations. Many technical, scientific, and scholarly people are socially shy. During working hours their attention is focused more on their work and inner thoughts than on other people.

Personal Consequences of Shyness

In a study of college students, Zimbardo found that three-fourths of shy people reported they did not like being shy. Most of these people thought that shyness is a definite personal problem. People break down the consequences of shyness into seven categories.

1. Difficulties in meeting new people and making friends, or getting the most out of personal relationships.
2. Negative emotional feelings, such as feeling depressed and lonely.
3. Difficulty in being assertive enough or expressing personal opinions and values.
4. Creating a false negative impression on others. Shyness often clouds a person's true assets.
5. Creating a poor initial impression. A shy person is often interpreted as being weak, unfriendly, or tense.
6. Difficulty in thinking clearly and communicating effectively in the presence of others.
7. Self-consciousness and an overpreoccupation with one's personal feelings and thoughts.[5]

There are two general strategies for becoming a more assertive and less shy individual. One is to engage in exercises by yourself that often improve your ability to express your feelings and make your demands known. Another strategy is to attend assertiveness training (AT). The balance of this chapter deals with these two approaches to becoming more assertive.

BECOMING MORE ASSERTIVE AND LESS SHY ON YOUR OWN

There are a number of everyday things a person can do to overcome **shyness** and lack of assertiveness. Those described here are such that even if they do not elevate your social skills, they will not backfire and cause you pain. After reading about the following techniques, you might be able to think of others that will work for you.

Legitimate Telephone Calls to Strangers

Telephone conversations with strangers that have a legitimate purpose can help you start expressing yourself to people you do not know well. You might call numbers listed in classified ads to inquire about articles listed for sale. Try a positive approach like, "Hello, my name is ___. I'd like to know about the condition of that piano you have for sale." Call the gas and electric company to inquire about a problem with your bill. Make telephone inquiries about employment opportunities in a firm of your choice. Call the library with reference questions. Call the federal government bureau in your town with questions about laws and regulations.

With practice, you will probably become more adept at speaking to strangers. You will then be ready for a more challenging self-improvement task.

Anonymous Conversations

Try starting a conversation with strangers in a safe setting such as a waiting line for tickets at a concert, a political rally, the waiting room of a medical office, a waiting line at the post office, or in a laundromat. Begin the conversation with the common experience you are sharing at the time. Among them might be:

"I wonder if there will be any tickets left by the time we get to the box office?"

"How long does it usually take before you get to see the doctor?"

"Where did you get that laundry basket? I've never seen one so sturdy before."

Greeting Strangers

For the next week or so, greet every person you pass. Smile and make a neutral comment such as "How ya doing?" "Great day, isn't it." Since most people are unaccustomed to being greeted by a stranger, you may get a few quizzical looks. Many other people may smile and return your greeting. A few of these greetings may turn into conversations. A few conversations may even turn into friendships. Even if the return on your investment in greetings is only a few pleasant responses, it will boost your confidence.

Dress and Groom for Assertiveness

Clothing and appearance can help you become more assertive for several reasons. As a form of nonverbal communication, the right attire can project the image that you feel good about yourself and are interested in relating to others. If you are satisfied with your appearance, your confidence might be boosted just enough to help you make that all-important initial contact with another person. The shyness manual we have been referring to here recommends:

> Figure out what clothes look the best on you; if you don't know, ask your friends. What are your best colors? Use them. Make sure your clothes are clean and pressed. When you dress assertively (and comfortably), you will naturally start feeling more assertive. At the very least, you should minimize or eliminate this source of apprehension.[6]

The three techniques described next help you to assert yourself when you think you are being manipulated by another person. By asserting yourself you will behave less shyly. The manipulation could take the form of being pressured to do something against your will or being criticized.[7]

Broken Record

The assertion skill called broken record teaches you to persist until you get your way. **Broken record** consists of calmly repeating your position over and over again without showing signs of anger or irritation. The person trying to persuade you will usually give up after a few minutes of hearing your "broken record." Acquiring this skill can help a shy person learn to say no, and not to give up after hearing the first no from another person.

Imagine this scenario. It is Sunday afternoon and you are busily preparing a report that is due Monday morning. A neighbor of yours, Tammy, rings your doorbell. After you open the door she says, "The whole gang is going to play volleyball this afternoon. We need you to join us. Could you be ready in fifteen minutes?" You decide that working on your report is more important than playing volleyball this afternoon. The broken record technique might proceed in this manner:

YOU: Thanks anyway, but I'll have to decline your offer. I'm working on an important report this afternoon.

TAMMY: You must be kidding. It's too nice a day to stay inside and work on a report.

YOU: No, I'm not kidding. I'll have to decline your offer.

TAMMY: How about taking a two-hour break? I promise you that the game will be over in two hours.

YOU: No, I'll have to decline your offer.

TAMMY: What kind of a neighbor are you? The whole gang will be disappointed. Can't you please join us?

YOU: No, I'll have to decline your offer.

TAMMY: Thanks, anyway. Maybe we can catch you next time.

YOU: Sounds good. Have a nice day.

In the example just cited, your nonverbal behavior must correspond to your verbal statements. For example, your facial expressions and the tone of your voice must communicate the thought that you really do not want to be disturbed from your work. Sounding like a broken record may not be part of your self-image. However, it is preferable to being manipulated into doing something you prefer not to do.

Negative Inquiry

Shy people have difficulty managing criticism. The technique of negative inquiry helps you deal with criticism. **Negative inquiry** is the active encouragement of criticism in order to elicit helpful information or exhaust manipulative criticism. At the same time you prompt your critic to be more assertive and less manipulative. Negative inquiry involves asking a series of questions to get at the true nature of the criticism.

Assume that Pedro, a co-worker of yours, expresses displeasure with your performance in a recent department meeting. You find his criticism uncomfortable and undeserved. Here is how negative inquiry might be used:

PEDRO: That was a pretty bad show you put on in yesterday's meeting.

YOU: What was bad about it?

PEDRO: You took up too much of the meeting pushing your own ideas.

YOU: Whose ideas was I supposed to push?

PEDRO: I'm not sure. I just know that you pushed too many of your own ideas.

YOU: What is it that you disliked about my pushing my own ideas?

PEDRO: I guess I wanted you to tell the boss about some of the great ideas I had. I wanted some credit too.

YOU: Now I see why you're upset with me.

Negative inquiry, as illustrated above, helped you discover the true nature of Pedro's problem. Since the truth is out, Pedro can no longer manipulate you by making you feel bad about actively contributing to the meeting.

Fogging

When criticized, most people become defensive and anxious. Shy people experience this problem to an even greater extent. The technique of fogging helps us receive criticism comfortably without becoming anxious or defensive. At the same time it avoids giving a reward to those using manipulative critism.[8] **Fogging** involves accepting manipulative criticism by calmly acknowledging that the criticism contains an element of truth. Since you agree in part with the criticizer, he or she does not get the reward of watching you become anxious and defensive. The reference to a fog means that the criticism passes right through you.

Fogging can be used in defending yourself against criticism from superiors, co-workers, friends, and family members. Here is an illustration of fogging in response to personal criticism:

CRITIC: I see that you are wearing the same drab old color again today.

PERSON BEING CRITICIZED: Yes, I am wearing gray again today.

CRITIC: Gray makes you look like a very conservative person.

PERSON BEING CRITICIZED: You're right. I do look like a conservative person.

CRITIC: When you dress so conservatively, it makes you look too old.

PERSON BEING CRITICIZED: I get your point. I do look mature when I'm wearing gray.

CRITIC: Let's talk about something else.

ASSERTIVENESS TRAINING: A PROGRAM FOR MAKING YOUR DEMANDS KNOWN

Many people need to develop skills in expressing their feelings and thoughts in a way that will achieve what they want. A form of human relations training has been developed to help people develop these skills. **Assertiveness training (AT)** is a self-improvement training program that teaches people to express their feelings and thoughts and to act with an appropriate degree of openness. The goals of AT typically include:

Recognize your feelings
Say what you want
Get what you want

Learn how to handle conflict positively
Communicate more clearly, directly, and persuasively
Deal with difficult people more confidently
Project a strong professional image[9]

Passive, Aggressive, and Assertive Behavior

AT programs are based on a distinction that has been made among three types of behavior. **Assertive** people state clearly what they want or how they feel in a given situation without being abusive, abrasive, or obnoxious. People who are assertive are open, honest, and "up front" because they believe that all people have an equal right to express themselves honestly.[10]

Passive, or nonassertive, people let things happen to them without letting their feelings be known. **Aggressive** people are obnoxious and overbearing. They push for what they want with almost no regard for the feelings of others.

Another way of explaining these differences is to say that the nonassertive person is stepped on and the aggressive person steps on others, while the assertive person deals with a problem in a mature and direct manner. Suppose a stranger invites you to a party and you do not wish to go with that person. Here are the three ways of responding, according to AT:

PASSIVE: I'm not sure. I might be busy. Could you call me again? Maybe I can make it, but I'm not sure.

AGGRESSIVE: I'd like to go to a party, but not with you. Bug off.

ASSERTIVE: Thank you for the invitation, but I prefer not to go.

Thirteen Steps to Assertiveness

One way of explaining how people can become more assertive is to describe the basics of an AT program developed by leading authorities.[11] Although attending such a program would be more beneficial than merely reading about it, you can profit from a careful study of these steps. Many of them can be put into practice with the proper amount of self-discipline.

Step 1: Observe your own behavior. Are you asserting yourself adequately? Or are you being too pushy, obnoxious, abusive, or uncompromising? Do you believe you get what you want when you want it, without stepping on the rights of others? Exhibit 6–3 will provide some clues to your tendencies toward assertiveness.

Step 2: Keep a record of your assertiveness. Devote an entire week to this project, keeping a careful log or diary of situations in which assertive behavior might have been called for. Record each day when you behaved assertively, when you were too passive or too aggressive. Also, look carefully at situations that you avoided altogether in order to avoid confrontation. Such a diary entry might be, "A friend of mine borrowed my color TV for the weekend. He told me he needed it a little longer. I wanted it back, but I said nothing. All I did was grumble to myself. I guess I should have demanded that my set be returned as promised." It is important to be candid and systematic in keeping this diary.

EXHIBIT 6–3   ARE YOU PASSIVE, ASSERTIVE, OR AGGRESSIVE?

The following questionnaire is designed to give you tentative insight into your current tendencies toward passivity, assertiveness, or aggressiveness. As with other questionnaires presented in this book, the Assertiveness Scale is primarily a self-examination and discussion device. Answer each question Mostly True or Mostly False, as it applies to you.

		Mostly True	*Mostly False*
1.	It is extremely difficult for me to turn down a sales representative when that individual is a nice person.	___	___
2.	I express criticism freely.	___	___
3.	If another person were being very unfair, I would bring it to that person's attention.	___	___
4.	Work is no place to let your feelings show.	___	___
5.	No use asking for favors, people get what they deserve on the job.	___	___
6.	Business is not the place for tact; say what you think.	___	___
7.	If a person looked like he or she were in a hurry, I would let that person in front of me in a supermarket line.	___	___
8.	A weakness of mine is that I'm too nice a person.	___	___
9.	If my restaurant bill is even 25¢ more than it should be, I demand that the mistake be corrected.	___	___
10.	I have laughed out loud in public more than once.	___	___
11.	I've been described as too outspoken by several people.	___	___
12.	I am quite willing to have the store take back a piece of furniture that contains a scratch.	___	___
13.	I dread having to express anger toward a co-worker.	___	___
14.	People often say that I'm too reserved and emotionally controlled.	___	___
15.	Nice guys and gals finish last in business.	___	___
16.	I fight for my rights down to the last detail.	___	___
17.	I have no misgivings about returning an overcoat to the store if it doesn't fit me properly.	___	___
18.	If I have had an argument with a person, I try to avoid him or her.	___	___
19.	I insist on my spouse (roommate, or partner) doing his or her fair share of undesirable chores.	___	___
20.	It is difficult for me to look directly at another person when the two of us are in disagreement.	___	___
21.	I have cried among friends more than once.	___	___

	Mostly True	Mostly False
22. If someone near me at a movie kept up a conversation with another person, I would ask him or her to stop.	——	——
23. I am able to turn down social engagements with people I do not particularly care for.	——	——
24. It is in poor taste to express what you really feel about another individual.	——	——
25. I sometimes show my anger by swearing or belittling another person.	——	——
26. I am reluctant to speak up in a meeting.	——	——
27. I find it relatively easy to ask friends for small favors such as giving me a lift to work when my car is being serviced or repaired.	——	——
28. If another person was smoking in a restaurant and it bothered me, I would inform that person.	——	——
29. I often finish other people's sentences for them.	——	——
30. It is relatively easy for me to express love and affection toward another person.	——	——

Scoring and Interpretation. Score yourself plus 1 for each of your answers that agrees with the scoring key. If your score is 15 or less, it is probable that you are currently a nonassertive individual. A score of 16 through 24 suggests that you are an assertive individual. A score of 25 or higher suggests that you are an aggressive individual. Retake this score about 30 days from now to give yourself some indication of the stability of your answers. You might also discuss your answers with a close friend to determine if that person has a similar perception of your assertiveness. Here is the scoring key.

1.	Mostly False	16.	Mostly True
2.	Mostly True	17.	Mostly True
3.	Mostly True	18.	Mostly False
4.	Mostly False	19.	Mostly True
5.	Mostly False	20.	Mostly False
6.	Mostly True	21.	Mostly True
7.	Mostly False	22.	Mostly True
8.	Mostly False	23.	Mostly True
9.	Mostly True	24.	Mostly False
10.	Mostly True	25.	Mostly True
11.	Mostly True	26.	Mostly False
12.	Mostly True	27.	Mostly True
13.	Mostly False	28.	Mostly True
14.	Mostly False	29.	Mostly True
15.	Mostly True	30.	Mostly True

Step 3: Concentrate on a specific situation. The instructions here are to spend a few moments with your eyes closed, recalling how you handled a specific incident (being short-changed at the supermarket, having a friend keep you on the telephone when you had too much to do, letting the boss make you feel petty over a small mistake). Imagine vividly the actual details, including your specific feelings at the time and afterward.

Step 4: Review your responses. Write down your behavior in Step 3 in terms of nonverbal communication such as posture, gestures, facial expression, and voice tone. Did my body language communicate how I really felt about the situation? Did I look disappointed about being asked to work late on Friday afternoon? Did I express my disagreement in a forceful, well-modulated conversational statement? Or did I murmur or fly off the handle? Was I able to look my boss straight in the eye? Did I state clearly that I had already made plans for a dinner date before I was asked to work late?

As you review your responses, it is helpful to note the things you did right. For instance, you might have said to your boss "I find this request disappointing."

Step 5: Observe an effective model. People who attend AT training programs are encouraged to observe another person in action who appears to be assertive. It is as important to observe that person's style as to note what that person says. Observing an assertive person on the job is one method of finding an appropriate model. Interviews shown on television are useful in providing a variety of effective models. Some public figures are adept at behaving assertively when interviewed by a television reporter.

Style refers to body language rather than content. The timing of messages is also part of a person's style. A good person to model is one who times his or her assertions well. It is poor practice to behave assertively with your boss, for example, when the both of you are around others in the office. The boss may be forced to behave defensively in such a situation.

Step 6: Consider alternative responses. Think of a situation you recently handled. How else could it have been handled? Audrey was using a coin-operated photocopying machine at a library. Those people waiting in line in back of her could readily see that she had a large stack of papers to be copied. Four different people said something to the effect, "Do you mind if I jump in for a second and use the machine? I only have two pages to copy." Audrey did mind, but each time her response was "Well, okay, if you only have one or two pages."

An assertive response Audrey might have tried would be, "It may not be what you prefer. But you will have to wait ten minutes until I've completed my copying. My time is very valuable today."

Step 7: Imagine yourself handling the situation. Close your eyes and visualize yourself behaving assertively in the situation reported in Step 6. You might act similarly to the model you have used for Step 5. It is important to be assertive but not to behave in a manner out of character with yourself. This step is much like a rehearsal or role play, except that it takes place while you are alone. You might also practice saying assertively "I appreciate your asking me first, but I cannot let other people in to use this machine until I have finished. My time is very valuable today."

At this point, some readers will think, "AT is much like the old standby, 'I should have said' when you have recently argued with somebody." The difference is that in AT, you relive the past *and* rehearse the future.

Step 8:   Try it out. Now that you have examined your own behavior, explored alternatives, and observed a model of an assertive individual, you are prepared to begin trying out assertive behavior in a specific problem situation or two. It may be helpful to repeat Steps 5 through 7 until you are ready to proceed. Prior to trying out your new assertive behavior, it may be beneficial to role play the situation with a friend.

One engineer used role playing to prepare herself to assertively handle an annoying situation at work. Although she was equal in organizational rank to other engineers in her department, her boss typically introduced her to strangers by her first name only: "This is Pam, one of our mechanical engineers." Males were introduced to visitors in a manner such as "This is Pete Nowacki, one of our mechanical engineers." Pam's assertive response to her boss was: "Gerry, something has been troubling me. I notice that when I'm introduced to visitors, you only use my first name. When you introduce male engineers to visitors, you use their first and last names. I would like to be given the same courtesy as males." Pam's boss apologized and never repeated this personal slight.

Step 9:   Obtain feedback. Here you try to obtain feedback on how well you did in trying out the assertive behavior. Step 4 called for the same type of self-examination. In this step you emphasize what you did right. Pam might provide herself with this type of feedback, "You handled things well. You leveled with Gerry in a way that did not make him defensive or retaliatory. I now feel much more comfortable when Gerry introduces me to new people. Although I thought I would appear nervous in making my assertion, I came across pretty cool."

Step 10:   Mold your behavior gradually. Steps 7 through 9 should be repeated as often as necessary to point your behavior in the desirable direction. Step by step you build up toward the final desired result—the point at which you can feel comfortable dealing in a self-enhancing manner with a situation that was bothersome in the past. Suppose you work for a superior who characteristically tells you, "Don't you see that my way is better." Your final goal might be to say, "I must disagree. Your way has some merit, but my careful analysis of the situation reveals. . . ." Since you are somewhat fearful of disagreeing with someone in a position of authority, you may have to begin with a mild assertion such as, "You could be right. But could you explain your position to me more fully?"

Step 11:   Delay no further in trying out the assertive behavior. The illustrations presented above indicate that many people will have put their AT to actual use from Step 8 onward. Some particularly nonassertive people, however, may still be restricting their assertive behavior to practice sessions.

Rehearsals and role plays are a relatively secure environment. It is now time to do what Pam did—behave assertively in a natural setting. As a final preliminary, some people will try out AT in low-stake situations such as demanding a larger portion of French fries at a restaurant, or asking a clerk in a dry cleaning store to replace a button broken during the dry cleaning process. People who still cannot behave assertively through Step 11 may need professional assistance in defending their rights and expressing what they think and feel. An example of how AT helped one individual to deal with discontent in a personal relationship is presented in Exhibit 6–4.

EXHIBIT 6–4   CISSIE EXPRESSES HER ANGER

Cissie is talking on the phone, telling Lem about some pleasant experiences of the week. As far as she is concerned, it's just chit-chat. As she talks, she laughs, often punctuating her comments with: "It was really so funny," "We all broke up," and "You wouldn't believe it." She feels lighthearted and enjoys telling Lem about these minor events.

Lem is quiet as she chats, and suddenly remarks, "You certainly don't miss many opportunities to have fun." Something about Lem's tone of voice makes Cissie suddenly feel as though he has struck her. She is puzzled because his statement is actually true. She *doesn't* miss many opportunities to have fun. Why should she? But why does she suddenly feel so deflated? It makes no sense to her. All she knows is that she feels uncomfortable, and she doesn't want to continue the conversation. They talk a little further, and then, "I have to go now," she says. "I'll see you tomorrow night," and hangs up.

Cissie sits at the phone, frowning. She doesn't have "to go" anyplace. She just didn't want to talk with Lem anymore. She feels bad, but does not know why. She remembers that she often feels this way when they talk or when they are doing something together. The feeling seems to come on suddenly, and then she forgets about it. But it seems to be happening more and more.

Thinking about it, Cissie recognizes the uncomfortable feeling as irritation. "I'm angry," she exclaims. "I'm angry at him, but I don't see what I'm angry about."

In thinking about the conversation, she locates the moment when he said, "You certainly don't miss many opportunities to have fun." Thinking further, she finds herself becoming more annoyed. "He has a nerve," she finally bursts out. But she remains just as puzzled. Why does he have a nerve? And then: "It's the way he said it. It was a put-down. By the tone of his voice, I felt he was saying, " 'What are you doing finding all that enjoyment in such trifles? Only dummies have fun like that. Don't you have a better way to spend your time?'"

Lem's voice was cold and critical, she feels. And in being critical, he hurt her feelings. This spoiled the pleasure in sharing her experiences with him. Cissie thinks his criticism is entirely unwarranted. Having been through assertiveness training recently, she decides to do something about her feelings. Cissie now plans to meet with Lem and confront him with her feelings of hurt and anger.

Cissie has several alternatives. She can write a letter, speak on the telephone, go to Lem's home, or meet in a restaurant. Cissie phones Lem and says, "Will you meet me at Tom's Restaurant on Tuesday at 7?" When Lem asks the purpose of the meeting, Cissie assertively replies, "I have something I want to talk to you about, but I don't want to discuss it now." When they meet at the restaurant, Cissie explains exactly how she feels. She begins "Lem, there is some aspect of our relationship that angers me and I want to talk to you about it." She then reviews the phone conversation and related instances. Among her comments are, "Lem, I felt you were putting me down in a recent phone conversation."

Cissie now feels better because she confronted Lem with her feelings in a forthright manner. If Cissie did not take the initiative to discuss these feelings (as was her pattern prior to AT) her discontent would have simmered. And simmering discontent often leads to broken relationships both in personal life and work.

_____

* Adapted from Helen A. De Rosis, _How To Be Assertive without Putting Someone Down_ (New York: Bonomo Contemporary Living Series, 1977), pp. 8–33.

Step 12: _Continue further training if necessary._ The developers of this program of AT state, "You are encouraged to repeat such procedures as may be appropriate in the development of the behavior pattern you desire." Some people will repeat steps 1 through 11 for one or two other situations in life that call for assertiveness. A person with a work-related problem of assertiveness might want to repeat the same process for a bothersome personal problem.

Step 13: _Receive reward._ No program of self-development will work unless you are rewarded for your new behaviors. As you practice assertive behavior, observe the beneficial consequences. (For example, "Yes, it felt great to patiently explain to my boss that I want to be considered for promotion to another division even if I have a husband and three children.") Positive comments from other people about your assertions will prove of more value than self-rewards. A shy manufacturing clerk went through a program of assertiveness training. He practiced the new skills back on the job with apparent success. His self-confidence elevated a notch when he overheard the comment, "Whatever happened to Tim? He's a new man these days. He lets people know exactly what he thinks of their work requests."

How Often Should You Be Assertive?

If everyone were assertive all the time, everybody would always be trying to get what he or she wanted. Many locked horns would be the result. It is therefore unrealistic to be assertive all the time. In many situations, a listening posture is appropriate. For example, why be assertive when listening to a friend or co-worker lean on you for emotional support? It would be more appropriate to be passive. In rare instances, it may be appropriate to be obnoxious and overbearing—such as when trying to frighten away a mugger.

W. Alan Randolph and Ruth Anne Randolph developed approximate guidelines for how frequently to be assertive on the job. As shown in Figure 6–1, the area under the bell-shaped curve represents the proportion of time appropriate for each behavior in the workplace. The two researchers offer this explanation of the different forms of assertiveness:

Understanding/assertive behavior focuses more attention on hearing the other person's ideas, and less on asserting your own ideas.

Assertive/understanding behavior is just the opposite. This type of behavior focuses more on asserting your own ideas.

FIGURE 6–1   PROPORTION OF TIME APPROPRIATE FOR ASSERTIVE BEHAVIORS

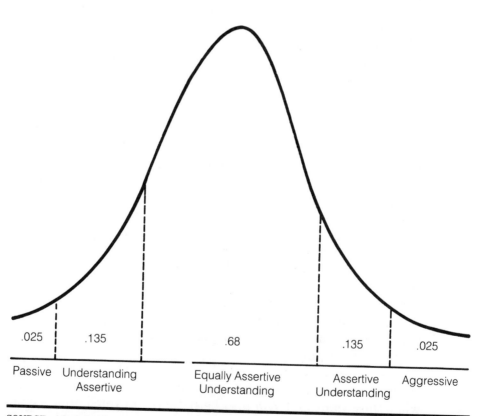

SOURCE: Adapted with permission from W. Alan Randolph and Ruth Anne Randolph, "Asserting Your Way to Better Planning," *Supervision Training Update,* Spring 1985, p. 4. (A McGraw-Hill Training Systems Publication.)

Equally/assertive understanding behavior is a balance between asserting your ideas and hearing the other person's ideas. If understanding disappears, you move into aggressive behavior. However, when assertive behavior disappears, the behavior shifts to passive.

About 95 percent of the time, one of the three assertive and understanding behaviors will lead to a more productive interaction with another person. Randolph and Randolph report that "When people learn to use appropriate behaviors, they become better planners, better team members, better implementers, and better communicators with their boss. And, that enhances all work relationships and the ability to get the job done."[12]

SUMMARY

Assertive people make their demands known in an effective way. Being able to express your feelings helps prevent some stress-related problems. It also helps you develop good relationships with people and get more of what you want out of life.

To become more assertive you must first become more aware of your own feelings. A feeling is an emotional state or disposition, and can also be considered an internal reaction based on your experience. Feelings can be expressed directly or indirectly. When you express feelings indirectly, you often attack something that is not the real issue. Or you might say positive things about a situation or person without expressing your actual emotion.

Shyness is the most common major adjustment problem people face in everyday life. Being shy can also be a job and career liability. However, shyness is not a negative behavior pattern unless it causes you discomfort or interferes with reaching your goals. Among the exercises to modify shyness on your own are: telephone calls to strangers for a legitimate purpose, talk to strangers in safe settings, greet strangers, and dress and groom for assertiveness.

Shy people often have difficulties facing up to manipulation by others. Three techniques to assert yourself when you think you are being manipulated by another person are: broken record, negative inquiry, and fogging.

Assertiveness training (AT) is designed to help people develop skills in expressing their feelings and thoughts in a way that achieves what they want. AT can also be helpful in overcoming shyness. Programs of this type are based on the differences in passive, aggressive, and assertive behavior. An assertive person makes a clear statement of what he or she wants, or how he or she feels. Passive or nonassertive people let things happen to them without expressing their feelings. Aggressive people are obnoxious and overbearing, or "pushy."

The AT program described here consists of thirteen steps, most of which you can begin practicing on your own. Briefly, they are:

1. Observe your own behavior.
2. Keep a record of your assertiveness.
3. Concentrate on a specific situation.
4. Review your responses.
5. Observe an effective model.
6. Consider alternative responses.
7. Imagine yourself handling the situation.
8. Try it out.
9. Obtain feedback.
10. Mold your behavior gradually.
11. Delay no further in trying out the assertive behavior.
12. Continue further training if necessary.
13. Receive reward.

Although assertiveness is valuable, many times it is important to modify your assertive behavior to include understanding and listening to the other person. About 95 percent of the time some combination of assertiveness and understanding will lead to productive interaction with people.

QUESTIONS AND ACTIVITIES

1. Are people from certain geographic areas more emotionally expressive and outgoing than others? Give a couple of examples.
2. Why is it generally easier to build a friendship with an emotionally expressive than a reserved individual?
3. Identify three occupations in which many of the successful people are emotionally expressive and outgoing.
4. Identify three occupations in which many of the successful people are emotionally reserved and not outgoing.
5. Identify two prominent people who seem more shy than outgoing.
6. Of what value might assertiveness training be in improving your social life?
7. Describe how AT might help you obtain a bigger raise.
8. Some successful people are apparently "aggressive." Why, then, the big emphasis on being assertive?

9. Interview an experienced higher-level worker. Ask that person how important he or she thinks assertiveness is for career success. Be prepared to discuss your findings in class.

10. Ask ten consecutive people whether or not they are shy. Bring the results of your minipoll back to class. Combine data for the entire class and calculate the percentage of shy people in your sample.

A HUMAN RELATIONS CASE PROBLEM:
THE COMPLAINT LIST

Beth has been dating Jeff for about a year. As Beth sees the relationship, the two of them are headed toward marriage. A feeling of hesitancy about the relationship has been building up within Beth. She thinks she loves Jeff, but she does have some concerns about some of his habits. One day, over coffee, she discusses her concerns with a good friend, Corinne. After listening carefully, Corinne offers this advice:

"Beth, you've come to the right person. I've been taking this fascinating human relations course. The instructor is a with-it gal who encourages us to tell things like they are. Lay your problems right out on the table. Why don't you make up a complaint list about Jeff? Bring it to him and tell him that you want to discuss all your reservations about him."

Partly convinced, Beth thanks Corinne for her advice and that evening composes her complaint list about Jeff. The following evening, she says to Jeff, "There is something we have to talk about. You're a wonderful guy, but I have some complaints about you. In fact, I've brought a whole list of these complaints for you to read this evening."

Perplexed, Jeff grabs the list. It reads:

1. I wish you would not use toothpicks in public.
2. Give me more than a day's notice about where we are going on Saturday night.
3. When you tell me that you love me, please turn off the television set.
4. Please do not wear cut-off jeans in front of my parents or friends.
5. Find a job with a future.
6. Do a better job of cleaning your fingernails.

Moments after reading the list, Jeff crumpled it in his hand and threw it on the floor. With an angry look on his face, he shouted, "If you think all these things are wrong with me, why see me any longer. We're through." Before Beth could offer an explanation, Jeff left.

Questions

1. What should Beth do next?
2. What did Beth do wrong? Or didn't she do anything wrong?

A HUMAN RELATIONS ROLE PLAY:
OVERCOMING MANIPULATION

Refer back to the chapter section on broken record, negative inquiry, and fogging to obtain the information needed for this role play. In each situation one person plays the role of the potential manipulator and the other person plays the role of the person using the antimanipulation technique.

1. Broken record. One person tries to sell the other a used personal computer and printer for $3,000. He or she needs to make this sale in order to pay rent and tuition and therefore cannot afford to let this prospect get away. The other person is mildly interested in purchasing a personal computer and printer, but thinks the price is too high and has never even heard of this brand. He or she feels manipulated, so will use the broken record technique.

2. Negative inquiry. One person plays the role of an instructor who has assigned an F grade to a remarkably sloppy and incoherent term paper. The student whose paper received the F is coming to see the instructor. Another person plays the role of the student, who is basically shy but wants to profit from this experience. The student decides to use negative inquiry to find out what the instructor *really* disliked about the paper.

3. Fogging. One person plays the role of a police officer who has caught a driver (a) speeding, (b) driving with an expired registration, and (c) passing in a no-passing lane. The officer has decided to come down hard on this law breaker. The other person plays the role of the driver, who is indeed guilty on all three counts. However, if the driver receives another moving violation his or her insurance rate will most likely skyrocket. The only thing that might save the driver is the fogging technique he or she learned in a human relations course. Go to it.

REFERENCES

[1] David W. Johnson, *Human Relations and Your Career: A Guide to Interpersonal Skills* (Englewood Cliffs, NJ: Prentice-Hall, 1978), p. 151. Most of the discussion about feelings in this chapter is based on Chapter 6 of *Human Relations and Your Career*.

[2] This exercise is based on David W. Johnson, *Reaching Out: Interpersonal Effectiveness and Self-actualization* (Englewood Cliffs, NJ: Prentice-Hall, 1972), pp. 93–98.

[3] Sharon Johnson, "Shyness Can Hamper Your Success at Work," *New York Times* reprint, October 5, 1985; Philip G. Zimbardo, Paul A. Pilkonis, and Robert N. Norwood, "The Social Disease Called Shyness," *Psychology Today,* May 1975, p. 69.

[4] Cited in Sharon Johnson, "Shyness Can Hamper Your Success at Work."

[5] Philip Zimbardo, Shyness: What It Is, What to Do About It (Reading, MA: Addison-Wesley, 1977), p. 22.

[6] This section is based on Ibid., Chapter 10.

[7] Philip I. Morgan, and H. Kent Baker, "Developing a Professional Image: Learning Assertiveness," *Supervisory Management,* August 1985, pp. 16–19; Manuel J. Smith, *When I Say No, I Feel Guilty* (New York: Bantam, 1975), Chapters 4, 6, and 7.

[8] Smith, *When I Say No, I Feel Guilty,* p. 323.

[9] Based on *Assertiveness Training for Professionals,* a program offered by CareerTrack, Inc., 1985; Lynn Z. Bloom, Karen Coburn, and Joan Pearlman, *The New Assertive Woman* (New York: Dell, 1976), p. i.

[10] Morgan and Baker, "Developing a Professional Image," p. 16.

[11] This presentation follows closely Robert E. Alberti and Michael L. Emmons, *Your Perfect Right: A Guide to Assertive Behavior,* 2nd ed. (San Luis Obispo, CA: Impact Publishers, 1974), pp. 35–38. The examples and illustrations, however, are original unless otherwise indicated by a footnote.

[12] The quotation and definitions are from W. Alan Randolph and Ruth Anne Randolph, "Asserting Your Way to Better Planning," *Supervision Planning Update,* Spring 1985, pp. 4–5.

SOME ADDITIONAL READING

ADAMS, JEROME, and JANICE D. YODER. *Effective Leadership for Men and Women.* Norwood, NJ: Ablex, 1985.

DARLING, LYNN. "The Power of Positive Influence." *Success!,* January 1985, pp. 20–21.

DYER, WAYNE W. *Pulling Your Own Strings.* New York: Avon, 1978.

MOLLOY, JOHN T. *Molloy's Live for Success.* New York: Bantam Books, 1982.

PANTE, ROBERT. *Dressing to Win: How to Have More Money, Romance, and Power in Your Life.* New York: Doubleday, 1984.

PHILLIPS, GERALD M. *Help for Shy People.* Englewood Cliffs, NJ: Prentice-Hall, 1981.

POWELL, BARBARA. *Overcoming Shyness: Practical Scripts for Everyday Encounters.* New York: McGraw-Hill, 1981.

Getting Along with Your Boss

Learning Objectives

After reading the information and doing the exercises in this chapter you should be able to:

- Recognize the impact your boss has on your future
- Select several tactics for creating a favorable impression on your present or future boss
- Select several tactics for dealing with your boss in a constructive manner
- Prepare to deal effectively with a boss whom you perceive as being intolerable

*I*mpressing your boss is the most basic strategy of getting ahead in your career. If you cannot gain favor with him or her, it will be difficult to advance to higher positions or earn much more money. Should you clash with one particular boss, you can sometimes be gracefully transferred to another department. Or you can first find a job with another firm and then quit. You will then have another chance to impress the person who recommends you for a salary increase and evaluates your work performance. The principle remains the same—you have to be seen by your immediate superior as a competent person. Your boss is always the person who is contacted first when someone wants to determine what kind of employee you are. Usually this information is sought when you are being considered for transfer, promotion, or for a position with another firm.

In this chapter we present a variety of strategies and tactics that lead to constructive relationships with an immediate superior. The strategies and tactics are grouped for convenience into three categories: creating a favorable impression on your boss, dealing with your boss directly, and coping with an intolerable boss. Some of these tactics might seem like "office politics." Many are political tactics but of a positive, sensible nature. We are decidedly *not* recommending any underhanded tricks that might prevent your boss or the company from accomplishing work.

Before reading further, study the checklist of tactics in Exhibit 7–1. They can be used along with the strategies and tactics presented throughout this chapter.

EXHIBIT 7–1   A CHECKLIST FOR GETTING ALONG WITH YOUR BOSS

Human Relations specialist David W. Johnson offers some practical tips for getting along with your boss that dovetail the strategies described in this chapter. They can be used as a brief checklist to see if you are doing the right things to cultivate your boss.

1. Begin by building good relationships with your co-workers. If they find you easy to work with, word will get to your boss quickly.
2. Let your boss know how well you are performing your job. Keep your boss informed of both your victories and your bloopers. Occasionally, ask for a few minutes to discuss how well you are performing on the job.
3. Form your own opinion of your boss. Do not be unduly influenced by the opinion of your boss expressed by other employees within the department.
4. Be sensitive about the content and timing of messages to your boss. Trust your intuition about communicating with your boss.
5. Do not be upset if your boss has a bad day once in awhile. Your boss may be under more pressure than you realize.

6. Do not go over your boss's head without first getting permission from your boss. Such "end runs" are considered a violation of both formal and informal policy.[1]

What do you think would be the advantages and disadvantages of discussing this list (and perhaps this chapter) with a present or future boss? Do you think it would build better communication bridges between the two of you? Or would it create roadblocks to communication?

CREATING A FAVORABLE IMPRESSION ON YOUR BOSS

The five strategies and tactics in this section all help you create a favorable impression on the boss. The term *impression* refers to a true impression, not a false one. Following these straightforward suggestions helps you deserve a positive reputation.

Display Good Job Performance

Job competence remains the most vital strategy for impressing your boss. Some bosses seem to be more interested in praise than performance from employees. Nevertheless, the praise—and other forms of office politics—won't do you much good if you do not back it up with job accomplishment. When any rational (or even sane) boss evaluates a subordinate's performance, the first question the boss asks is: "Is this employee getting the job done?" And you cannot get the job done if you are not competent.

Many factors contribute to whether or not you can become a competent performer. Among them are your education, training, personality characteristics, job experience, and special skills, such as being able to solve problems, resolve conflict, and organize your work. Much of this book discusses skills, techniques, and strategies that are designed to contribute to job competence.

Keep Your Boss Aware of Your Accomplishments

Good job performance usually, but not always, speaks for itself. It is therefore necessary to let your boss know of your achievements without appearing to brag about yourself. One way of tooting your own horn softly is to send your boss copies of memos summarizing your accomplishments. Another is to informally keep your boss informed of projects he or she particularly favors.[2]

Another suggestion is to send your boss a letter listing your accomplishments shortly before you are due for a performance appraisal. This will provide the boss with current information about your successes. A final—and mildly devious—tactic is to ask a friend to casually mention to your boss what you have accomplished lately. You can return the favor later.

Be Dependable and Honest

Dependability is a critical employee virtue. If an employee can be counted on to deliver as promised, and to be at work regularly, that employee has gone a long way toward impressing the boss. A boss is uncomfortable not knowing whether an important assignment will be accomplished on time. If you are not dependable, you will probably not get your share of important assignments. Honesty is tied to dependability because a dependable employee is honest about when he or she will have an assignment completed.

Dependability and honesty are as important in the secretarial pool as in the executive suite. One of the highest compliments a manager can pay a secretary is to say that she (or he) is dependable. Conversely, it is considered derogatory to call any employee undependable. As one company president put it when describing a subordinate: "When he's great, he's terrific, but I can't depend on him. I'd rather he be more consistent even if he delivered fewer peak successes—at least I could rely on him."[3]

Display Loyalty

A basic way to impress your boss is to be loyal. Loyalty can be expressed to the supervisor, the department, the division, or the entire firm. In whatever form it is expressed, loyalty tends to foster a good relationship with your immediate superior. A subordinate can express loyalty in many ways other than heaping flattery upon the boss and the department. Loyalty can be expressed through staying with the company, attending company picnics and other functions, using the company's products, or even wearing company insignia.

An important characteristic of a loyal subordinate is defending the boss when the latter is under attack by people from other departments. Defending your boss under such circumstances does not necessarily mean that you think your boss is entirely correct. You can defend what deserves credit without agreeing with the boss's entire position. Assume your boss was under attack from another department for being late with the processing of materials needed by them. Your boss contends that delays in shipments by suppliers have created the problem. You realize that inefficiencies in the department are also a contributing factor. You might publicly agree with your boss that supplier delays have created problems. In private, you might make suggestions to your boss for improving department efficiency.

Appreciate Your Boss's Strengths

You may not admire every boss you work for, particularly early in your career. Your young boss might be inexperienced and therefore less than ideal. Older bosses you work for early in your career tend to be people who have been passed over for promotion many times. In other words, the company recognizes they are not the strongest supervisors. But they are usually competent enough to perform their jobs satisfactorily.

If you focus only on the weaknesses of your boss, you will probably communicate many negative nonverbal messages to that individual. For instance, when your boss is making general suggestions you might display a bored expression on your face. Instead of thinking primarily about your boss's weakness, look for strengths. Look for answers to such questions as, "What knowledge does he or she have that can help me advance my career?" "What good points about my boss led to his or her promotion?" or "What do some of my co-workers see as my boss's strengths?"

A case in point is Bruce, a young sales representative. Recently graduated from business school, Bruce was fired up with modern techniques of selling, such as identifying the customer's most pressing problems. He was somewhat perplexed about why his boss, Arlie, was considered such an outstanding sales manager. He displayed few of the management techniques that Bruce had studied in school. Bruce then spoke to an aunt who worked in another department of the same company. "How come old Arlie is so highly regarded? He doesn't seem to know much about sales techniques or management." Bruce's aunt replied, "You could be right, Bruce. But Arlie knows how to read people and how to form good relationships. He's what is known as a good personal salesman."

From that point on Bruce began to look for techniques of forming good relationships with people that Arlie used. As he showed a sincere interest in learning more from Arlie, their relationship improved.

DEALING WITH YOUR BOSS DIRECTLY

Find Out What Your Boss Expects of You

You have little chance of doing a good job and impressing your boss unless you know what you are trying to accomplish. Understanding your immediate superior's goals and the priorities attached to those goals is a good starting point. Working toward a goal such as "Set up a filing system for our warehouse by the end of the month," will help keep you on track.

Unfortunately not every boss uses goal setting. Nor does every boss give you a clear statement of performance standards for your job. A **performance standard** is a statement of what constitutes accept-able performance. To get around this dilemma, career specialist Shir-ley Sloan Fader offers this advice: "Your boss, like most human beings, won't always spell out precisely what is expected of you. It's up to you to determine this."[4]

The answer to what is expected of you can be surprising. Jake took on a part-time job as a bouncer in a night club. Wanting to do a good job, Jake said to his boss, "I take it, the most important part of my job is to ease any troublemaker out the door?" The boss replied, "No, Jake, that's the second most important part of your job. The most im-portant part is to prevent troublemakers from getting in the place. Keep the hoodlums and roughnecks out. If somebody is giving you a hard time at the door, tell him to try another club."

Take the Initiative in Asking for Help

Many employees irritate their bosses because they are hesitant to ask for help. They flounder along until finally the boss recognizes that a major problem has developed. One major responsibility of a supervi-sor is to provide assistance to employees who are having difficulty com-pleting the job. Asking for help thus makes the boss feel needed. A competent boss regards giving help as a vital aspect of performing his or her job, not as a "bother" or "nuisance."

It is important to take the initiative in asking for help because the boss may not sense that you need help until the problem gets out of hand. Ralph, a bartender, did not know how to prepare the fancy drinks that customers occasionally requested. His solution was to quickly throw together something that looked about right. (He didn't have the time to look up the mixture in a bartender's guide when the drink was ordered.) Customer complaints gradually filtered back to the manager. When the owner confronted Ralph as to why he didn't ask for training in drink-mixing, he replied, "I thought you would think I was some kind of a jerk, if I couldn't hack making those fancy drinks." The owner was unimpressed with Ralph's explanation.

Respect Your Boss's Authority

A common complaint about modern society is that respect for au-thority is decreasing. According to this sentiment, people in positions of authority such as police workers, physicians, lawyers, politicians, teachers, and managers are not treated with as much respect today as they were in the past. Many of these people would appreciate receiving more respect for their authority. You can use this factor to help develop a good relationship with your boss. By showing appropriate respect for your boss's authority, you can win points with your boss.

Here are a few statements that might appeal to a boss's sense of authority without making you appear unduly status conscious:

"Yes, sir, that sounds like a good idea."

"Yes, ma'am, that sounds like a good idea."

"Okay, coach, what do I do now?"

"As the head of this department, what do you think we should do about this?"

"In your experience, what is the best way to go about handling this problem."

Another authority-related issue is whether or not to address your boss by his or her first name. In almost every place of work outside of medical settings, some colleges and schools, a few conservative banks, and some retail stores, subordinates are encouraged to call superiors by their first names. Local custom, of course, will prevail. You might also ask your boss how he or she prefers to be addressed. Nevertheless, you are probably safe in using a title and last name to address your boss when visitors are around. Titles include Mr., Miss, Ms., Sir, Madam, Doctor, Professor, Chief, Coach, and Captain. All of them send out the message that you respect your boss's authority. Most bosses will be pleased by that attitude.

Recognize That Your Boss Has Problems, Too

Part of a boss's job is to absorb work-related and some personal problems of subordinates. No matter how much stress the boss is facing, he or she is supposed to be immediately attentive to any problem from below. You can help cultivate a good relationship with your boss by recognizing that he or she might also be facing problems. One way to do this is not to bring routine problems to your boss when it appears that he or she is already overloaded that day. Before bringing a serious problem to your boss, check with his or her secretary or assistant. Find out if the boss would be hard pressed to tackle another problem that day. If so, schedule a conference with the boss for later that week.

A potentially valuable strategy for dealing with your boss's problem is simply to be ready to listen to those problems. A sympathetic subordinate is sometimes just the person the boss needs for thinking through a problem. To tip your boss off that you might be a good listener, stop talking about your own problems, and ask one or two open-ended questions, such as:

"How is your work going?"
"How have all these cutbacks in the firm affected your work?"
"How are you doing in selling your own house?"

Another way of displaying a willingness to listen is to show an interest whenever the boss begins to discuss work or even personal problems. If your boss says, "Those people in the home office are driving a hard bargain," you might say, "A hard bargain?" Most of the listening tips discussed in Chapter 5 would apply to relationships with the immediate superior.

Bring Forth Solutions as Well as Problems

An advanced tactic for developing a good working relationship with your boss is to bring solutions to your boss's attention, not just problems. Too often subordinates only ask to see their bosses when they have problems requiring help. A boss under pressure may thus anticipate additional pressure when a subordinate asks for an appointment. The subordinate who comes forth with a solved problem is thus regarded as a welcome relief. In short, you can ease your boss's suffering by walking into his or her office and saying, "Here's what I did about that mess that was plaguing us yesterday. Everything is under control now."

Minimize Complaints

In the previous chapter we extolled the virtues of being open and honest in expressing your feelings and opinions. Nevertheless, this type of behavior when carried to excess could earn you a reputation as a complainer. Few bosses want to have a subordinate around who constantly complains about working conditions, co-workers, working hours, pay, and so forth. An employee who complains too loudly and frequently quickly becomes labeled a pill or a pest.

Another important reason a boss usually dislikes having a subordinate who complains too much is that listening to these complaints takes up considerable time. An accurate generalization about superior-subordinate relationships is that most bosses spend a disproportionate amount of time listening to the problems of a small number of ineffective or complaining employees. Consciously or unconsciously, a boss who has to listen to many of your complaints may find a way to seek revenge.

> Diane was the supervisor of a small group of computer programmers working for an insurance company. Her biggest employee problem was Henry, a programmer with four years of job experience. Henry loudly complained about matters such as the computer owned by the company, the wages, the food in the company cafeteria, the music piped into the office, and his rate of advancement. As part of an efficiency compaign, the company decided to run the computer operations twenty-four hours a day, instead of twelve. In this way, they could get by with fewer computer employees. Diane placed Henry's name at the top of the list for assignment to the midnight to eight o'clock shift. Henry complained bitterly to Diane about his new assignment. She retorted calmly, "Go complain to your new boss, the night supervisor. But I doubt it will do you much good. He doesn't care for that shift either."

How then does an employee make valid complaints to the boss? The answer is to complain only when justified. And when you do offer a complaint, back it up with a recommended solution. Anyone can take potshots at something. The valuable employee is the person who backs up these complaints with a constructive action plan. Following are two examples of complaints, backed up by action plans for remedying the complaint:

> "I've noticed that several of us get very tired feet by the end of the working day. Maybe we could perform this work just as well if we sat on high stools."
>
> "We have a difficult time handling emergency requests when you are away from the department. I would suggest that when you will be away for more than one or two hours, one of us can serve as the acting supervisor. It could be done on a rotating basis to give each of us some supervisory experience."

Avoid Running Around Your Boss

A good way to embarrass, and sometimes infuriate, your boss is to repeatedly go to your boss's superior with your problems, conflicts, and complaints. Such bypasses have at least two strongly negative connotations for your boss. One is that you don't believe your boss has the power to take care of your problem. Another is that you distrust your boss's judgment in the matter at hand. A third is that you are secretly launching a complaint against your boss.

The boss bypass is looked upon so negatively that most experienced managers will not listen to your problem unless you have already discussed it with your immediate superior. There *are* times, however, when running around your boss is necessary, for example, when you have been unable to resolve a conflict directly with your boss (see the following section). But even under these circumstances, you should politely inform your boss that you are going to take up your problem with the next level of management.

In short, if you want to keep on the good side of your boss, bring all problems directly to him or her. If your boss is unable or unwilling to take care of the problem, you might consider contacting your boss's boss. Nonetheless, considerable tact and diplomacy are needed. Do not imply that your boss is incompetent, but merely that you would like another opinion about the issues at stake.

Stay in Touch

A surprising aspect of many jobs today is the amount of freedom from supervision they offer. If your boss is a busy manager who is frequently off to meetings in other parts of the firm or out of town you might see that person infrequently. Also, many bosses become so preoccupied with their own paperwork they neglect to spend enough time with subordinates. The employee who prefers to avoid being supervised closely would enjoy circumstances such as those just described.

Despite this absence of close supervision, it is still important to have some contact with your boss if you want to maintain a good superior-subordinate relationship. Many employees who are aware of the importance of cultivating the boss, develop a reason for seeing their boss, even if an urgent reason does not exist. Their tactics include bringing telephone messages to the boss, getting a reaction to a routine memo, or asking for clarification of a problem. A risk exists of being seen as a pest or an indecisive person if you overdo the principle of staying in touch with the boss.

What valid reasons can you think of for asking to see your boss?

Use Discretion in Socializing with Your Boss

A constant dilemma facing employees is how much and what type of socializing with the boss is appropriate. Advocates of socializing contend that off-the-job friendships with the boss lead to more natural work relationships. Opponents of socializing with the boss say that it leads to **role confusion** (being uncertain about what role you are carrying out). For example, how can your boss make an objective decision about your salary increase on Monday morning when he or she had dinner with you on Sunday? To avoid cries of favoritism, your boss might recommend you for a below-average increase.

One guideline to consider is to have cordial social relationships with the boss of the same kind shared by most employees. "Cordial" socializing includes activities such as company-sponsored parties, group invitations to the boss's home, and business lunches. Individual social activities such as camping with the boss, double-dating, and so forth, are more likely to lead to role confusion.

Socializing with the boss should not include a casual romantic involvement. Recent research has demonstrated what has been known for a long time: Romantic involvements between a superior and a subordinate are disruptive to work and morale. Co-workers usually suspect that the special friend of the boss is getting special treatment and resent the favoritism.[5]

What should you do if you and your boss seem suited for a long-term commitment? Why walk away from Mr. or Ms. Right? My suggestion is that if you do become romantically involved with the boss, one of you should request a transfer to another department. Many office romances do lead to happy marriages and other long-term relationships. At the start of the relationship, however, use considerable discretion. Engaging in personal conversation during work time, or holding hands in the company cafeteria, is unprofessional and taboo.

COPING WITH AN INTOLERABLE BOSS

Up to this point in the chapter we have prescribed tactics for dealing with a reasonably rational boss. At some point in their careers many people face the situation of dealing with an intolerable boss. What makes a boss intolerable depends—like any stressor—on your perception. Different types of intolerable bosses include those who are incompetent, mean, lacking in integrity, or rude and insensitive.[6]

Our concern here is with constructive approaches to dealing with the delicate situation of working for an intolerable immediate superior. The tactics described include profiting from the experience and easing away from the boss you cannot tolerate.

Learn from Your Boss's Mistakes

Just as you can learn from watching your boss do things right, you can also learn from watching your boss do things wrong. In the first instance, we are talking about using your boss as a positive model. "Modeling" of this type is an important source of learning on the job. Using your boss as a negative model can also be of some benefit. As an elementary example, if your boss criticized you in public, and you felt humiliated, you would have learned a good lesson in effective supervision: never criticize a subordinate in public. By serving as a negative example, your boss has taught you a valuable lesson.

Tina, an administrative assistant in a department that wrote proposals for obtaining government contracts, shows us how to learn from the boss's mistakes. She worked for a boss who responded to pressure by procrastinating. One time Tina approached her boss with an urgent problem: "We stand in danger of not getting this contract proposal out on time unless you authorize some clerical overtime."

Tina's boss responded: "Let's table that idea until tomorrow. I need time to think it over. We have to look at every decision from the total company point of view. If we rush into authorizing overtime for you, we could be weakening ourselves in another area at the same time."

Rather than become infuriated and resign or insult her boss, Tina patiently waited for a transfer. The transfer was forthcoming and Tina became an office supervisor. She is noted for her willingness and ability to give a rapid reply to any request made of her by a superior or a subordinate. Tina expresses her decision-making philosophy in this way:

> If anybody asks me a routine question—such as "Am I eligible to take out a home improvement loan through the company credit union?"—I try to get an answer within one day. When I'm asked a major question from above—such as "Can your department handle this project this quarter?"—I respond within one week.
>
> Some questions cannot be answered without doing some research, because a lot of factors have to be weighed. But even then I try to give the person requesting the information a status report on how I'm progressing in terms of answering his or her question.

Tina's case history was presented in detail because she avoided the mistake of many employees who yell at their bosses in the heat of a dispute. Exhibit 7–2 suggests an approach for dealing with this unfortunate mistake.

EXHIBIT 7–2   WHAT TO DO AFTER YOU'VE YELLED AT THE BOSS

It finally happened. You handed in your masterpiece, but instead of cheering your report the boss dumped all over it. Ripping your own twenty-five-page report to shreds and chucking it in the chief's face was not enough. You had to add a few high-decibel insults and top your tantrum with a fist through the wall.

Now what? How will you face your boss and co-workers again? Try to understand what drove you to the boiling point. Apologize, and then act like it never happened. Don't try to excuse your behavior even if you think you were right.

But nothing draws co-workers to the watercooler like a public prizefight, and they might not be willing to let the incident die. If you can't escape questions, simply tell nosy co-workers you were wrong to behave that way.

So much for damage control. There are ways to stop yourself from becoming a hothead again before it's too late:

Take as many deep breaths as you need until you calm down.

Get to the typewriter, hammer out every nasty thing that you want to say, then put the letter away. The next day chances are you'll be glad you never mailed it.

Most of all, be realistic. Don't get upset about things over which you have no control.

SOURCE: Betsy Bauer, "You Yelled at the Boss? Apologize, Then Forget It," *USA Weekend*, November 22–24, 1985, p. 28.

What to Do When Your Boss Ignores Your Suggestions

One subtype of an intolerable boss is the manager who ignores suggestions because he or she prefers to maintain the status quo. These managers see their jobs as simply running a smooth operation, and they perceive employees who continue to bring forth suggestions as troublemakers. The problem with not bringing forth innovative ideas is that you will never earn the reputation of being imaginative and ambitious.

A management research report offers several suggestions for coping with this form of intolerable boss. One approach is to implement your idea without your boss's approval. If your idea works out well, your boss may embrace your suggestion. Another tactic is to cultivate your boss's superior. Tactfully tell your boss's boss about your innovative idea. He or she might support your idea and give you the green light to implement it.[7]

A real problem with cultivating your boss's boss, is that a boss bypass is generally frowned upon. However, so long as you do not say or imply anything negative about your boss it could be worth a try. You might say to your boss's superior, "I have brought this to McHendry's (your boss) attention, but she's too busy with other projects now to dig into my proposal."

What to Do When the Boss Takes Credit for Your Accomplishments

Imagine that you have been assigned the job of making the arrangements for a company meeting. Everything runs so smoothly that at the banquet your boss is praised for his or her fine job of arranging the meeting. You smolder while the boss accepts all the praise without mentioning that you did all the work. How should you handle an intolerable boss of this type—one who takes credit for your accomplishments?

Remember, first, that in one sense your boss does deserve much of the credit. Managers are responsible for the accomplishments and failures of their subordinates. Your boss had the good sense to delegate the task to the right person. Nevertheless, a self-confident boss would share the credit with you. To get the credit you deserve for your ideas and accomplishments, try these tips:

1. *Supply the pieces, but let others fit them together.* Suppose, for example, you were talking to your boss's boss at the company meeting mentioned above. You might state, "I'm happy that people enjoyed this meeting. I enjoyed being given so much responsibility for helping our department arrange this meeting." Your boss's boss may get the point without your disputing what your boss said.

2. *Try a discreet confrontation.* The boss who is taking credit for your accomplishments may not realize that you are being slighted. A quiet conversation about the issue could prevent recurrences. You might gently ask, for example, "At what point do I get recognition for doing an assigned task well? I noticed that my name was not mentioned when our department received credit for setting up a new billing system." (It was you who did 95 percent of the work on the system.)

3. *Take preventive measures.* A sensible way to receive credit for your accomplishments is to let others know of your efforts *while* you are doing the work. This is more effective than looking for recognition after your boss has already taken credit for your accomplishments. Casually let others know what you are doing, including your boss's boss and other key people. In this way you will not sound immodest or aggressive—you are only talking about your work.

4. *Present a valid reason for seeking recognition.* By explaining why you want recognition, you will not seem unduly ambitious or pushy to your boss. You might say "I am trying to succeed in this company. It would help me to document my performance. Would it therefore be possible for my name to also appear on the report of the new billing system?"[8]

How to Gently Get Away from Your Boss

Perhaps you have tried long and hard to develop a better working relationship with your boss but the situation is still intolerable. Three alternatives remain: You can wait for your boss to leave; you can leave the company; or you can look for a job in the same firm. It generally makes the most sense to pursue the last course of action, particularly if you are satisfied with the firm.

The major strategy for getting away from your boss is to market yourself to other key managers in the company.[9] Make others aware of your accomplishments through such means as volunteering for committee work or getting your name in the company newsletter. Another method is to make personal contacts through such means as joining company teams or clubs. Chapter 13 discusses the art of making contacts (**networking**) in more detail.

While you are developing your contacts, speak to your boss about a transfer. Point out that although you are satisfied with your job, you value broad experience at this point in your career. Unfortunately, weak bosses generally are reluctant to recommend subordinates for transfer.

Another recommended approach is to speak directly to the personnel department about your dilemma. Point out gently that you want to be considered a candidate for transfer to another department. Suggest that you could make a bigger contribution if you worked for a superior who gave you more responsibility. However, never say anything derogatory about your present boss. Such a practice is strictly taboo.

SUMMARY

Developing a favorable relationship with your boss is the most basic strategy of getting ahead in your career. Your boss influences your future because he or she is often asked by other prospective bosses to present an opinion about your capabilities.

One strategy for developing a favorable relationship with your boss is to create a favorable impression. Specific tactics of this type include: display good job performance, keep your boss aware of your accomplishments, be dependable and honest, display loyalty, and appreciate your boss's strengths.

Many tactics for cultivating your boss require that you deal directly with him or her, including:

1. Find out what your boss expects of you.
2. Take the initiative in asking for help.
3. Respect your boss's authority.
4. Recognize that your boss has problems, too.
5. Bring forth solutions as well as problems.
6. Minimize complaints to your boss.

7. Avoid running around your boss.
8. Stay in touch with your boss.
9. Use discretion in socializing with your boss.

Coping with a boss you perceive to be intolerable is part of getting along with your boss. One approach is to learn from the mistakes made by the intolerable boss. When your boss ignores your suggestions you may have to take such steps as implementing your idea without approval. If your idea works, he or she might embrace your suggestion. You might also tactfully tell your boss's boss about your suggestions.

When your boss takes credit for your accomplishments, consider these tactics: give enough information to others so they can figure out what you have done, discreetly confront your boss, take preventive measures by keeping others informed of work in progress, and present a valid reason for seeking recognition.

When your relationship with your boss does not improve it may be necessary to seek a transfer. The best method is to market yourself to other key managers in the company. This may involve establishing a network of contacts. Also, speak to your boss about a transfer without speaking of dissatisfaction, and present your case to the personnel department.

QUESTIONS AND ACTIVITIES

1. Suppose your boss reads this chapter. How might this influence the effectiveness of your using the strategies and tactics described here?

2. Which several of the tactics described in this chapter are you most likely to use? Why?

3. Which tactics described in this chapter are you least likely to use? Why?

4. Should you occasionally ask your boss for help even if you don't need it? Explain.

5. Suggest a few additional ways of displaying loyalty in addition to those presented in this chapter.

6. Suppose one of your co-workers is idle much of the time. How would it affect your relationship with your boss if you brought this problem to his or her attention? Explain.

7. What are one or two situations in which you think it would be justifiable to run around your boss.

8. Suppose you and a co-worker are best friends. He or she gets promoted and becomes your boss. What should be your policy about socializing with this person?

9. How should you respond if your boss asks you for a date under these circumstances? You are not at all interested in that person socially, yet you want to maintain a good working relationship.

10. Interview an experienced manager. Ask that manager's opinion about what an employee can do to create a favorable impression. Be prepared to discuss your findings in class.

A HUMAN RELATIONS CASE PROBLEM:
NEGATIVE CHEMISTRY

Gunther Wortman looked forward to a career as a quality specialist. He began working for Micro Tech as a quality control inspector. As a result of hard work and additional study, he was promoted to quality control technician, and then to quality control supervisor. As a supervisor he now reported to Alan Tombak, manager of quality assurance. Four other supervisors also reported to Tombak.

Gunther approached his new job with his usual enthusiasm. He was proud to be a supervisor, and believed that his big career break had finally arrived. Gradually Gunther began to sense that things were not going so well for him in his new position. One day he felt particularly despondent. Ten days previously he had sent Tombak a detailed proposal for the use of a new inspection machine. So far Tombak had not even acknowledged his proposal.

Concerned about his feeling that things were not going so well between himself and his boss, Gunther decided to call Diane Garcia, a personnel specialist. He asked Diane if she would join him for lunch to discuss a career problem he was facing. Gunther and Diane agreed to meet for lunch the following Friday at a nearby sushi restaurant.

As the two dug into their fish, Gunther began to talk about his concern. "Diane, maybe you can help me," he said. "I just don't seem to be hitting it off with my boss, Alan Tombak. He hardly acknowledges my presence. He usually ignores my suggestions. He doesn't even laugh at my jokes. When I'm at a staff meeting with the other supervisors, he acts as if I don't even exist. Do you have any suggestions for handling this situation?"

Diane said, "Gunther, it sounds like you do have a problem. Either you're paranoid, or you have failed to impress Tombak. I know you well enough to be sure that you're not paranoid. So there must be a real problem between you and Tombak. What have you done about the problem so far?"

"I've put my nose to the grindstone like I have in every other assignment with Micro Tech. Nothing about me seems to impress Tombak. That's why I've asked for your help."

After thinking for a moment, Diane responded, "I have a plan. This month I'm supposed to help the managers in your area with their human resource planning. This usually involves a discussion of key employees. I'll see what Tombak has to say about you. I'll then get back to you with my findings."

Ten days later, Diane did help Alan with human resource planning. The conversation led naturally to a discussion of the strengths and weaknesses of the supervisors reporting to Tombak. "What is your evaluation of Gunther Wortman, your newest supervisor?" asked Diane coyly. "Good question," said Alan. "I don't really know what to make out of him. He does seem to try hard. But there's negative chemistry between us. The guy just doesn't turn me on as an employee. I think he's overrated. Maybe I'm missing something, but he's just a neutral entity to me. Yet, I'm certainly not trying to get rid of him. That's all I can say."

Diane thought to herself, "Tombak has been brutally honest. Gunther and he just don't hit it off. I guess it's my duty as a friend to tell Gunther. But I wouldn't want him to leave Micro Tech over this problem."

Questions

1. Should Diane give Gunther a full report of her findings?
2. What should Gunther do about this problem of negative chemistry between himself and his boss?
3. Is Diane acting ethically in her method of helping Gunther?
4. Should Gunther confront Alan directly about his problem?

A HUMAN RELATIONS ROLE PLAY: THE NEGATIVE CHEMISTRY CONFRONTATION

Assume that after hearing back from Diane, Gunther decides to confront his boss about the problem of negative chemistry. Gunther makes an appointment to discuss his problem with Tombak. He wants to improve—not worsen—his relationship with his boss. Tombak is upset by this confrontation, yet he wants to keep his cool and not prompt Gunther to quit. Tombak sees no grounds for dismissing Gunther, yet he does not see him as a star on his team. The roles to be played, of course, are Gunther Wortman and Alan Tombak.

REFERENCES

[1] Adapted from David W. Johnson, *Human Relations and Your Career* (Englewood Cliffs, NJ: Prentice Hall, 1978), p. 233.

[2] William A. Cohen and Nurit Cohen, "Get Promoted Fast," *Success!*, July/August 1985, p. 46.

[3] John J. Gabarro and John P. Kotter, "Managing Your Boss," *Harvard Business Review*, January–February 1980, pp. 92–100.

[4] Shirley Sloan Fader, "What Your Boss Wants You to Know," *BusinessWeek's Guide to Careers*, October 1985, p. 43.

[5] Carol I. Anderson and Phillip L. Hunsaker, "Why There's Romancing at the Office and Why It's Everybody's Problem," *Personnel*, February 1985, p. 62.

[6] Michael M. Lombardo and Morgan W. McCall, Jr., *Coping With an Intolerable Boss* (Greensboro, NC: Center for Creative Leadership, January 1984), pp. 1–3.

[7] *How to Win at Organizational Politics—Without Being Unethical or Sacrificing Your Self-Respect* (New York: The Research Institute of America, January 1985), pp. 7–8.

[8] Ibid., p. 15.

[9] D. Keith Denton, "Survival Tactics: Coping With Incompetent Bosses," *Personnel Journal*, April 1985, p. 68.

SOME ADDITIONAL READING

ANDRE, RAE, and PETER D. WARD. *The 59-Second Employee: How to Stay One Second Ahead of Your One-Minute Manager*. Boston: Houghton Mifflin, 1984.

COLLINS, ELIZA G. C. "Managers and Lovers." *Harvard Business Review*, September–October 1983, pp. 142–153.

DAVIS, SANDRA. "Danger! Love at Work." *BusinessWeek's Guide to Careers*, Spring/Summer Edition, 1984, pp. 45–47.

DUBRIN, ANDREW J. *Winning at Office Politics*. New York: Van Nostrand Reinhold, 1978.

FAIRHOLM, GILBERT W.   "Power Tactics on the Job." *Personnel,* May 1985, pp. 45–50.

HEGARTY, CHRISTOPHER.   *How to Manage Your Boss.* New York: Rawson Wade, 1981.

MONDY, R. WAYNE, and SHANE R. PREMEAUX.   "Power, Politics, and the First-Line Supervisor." *Supervisory Management,* January 1986, pp. 36–39.

8

Getting Along with Co-workers

Learning Objectives

After studying the information and doing the exercises in this chapter, you should be able to:

- Recognize the importance of gaining favor with your co-workers
- Describe several methods of taking the initiative to get along with co-workers
- Describe several methods of getting along with co-workers by responding constructively to their actions

Anyone with work experience is aware of the importance of getting along with co-workers. If you are unable to work cooperatively with those around you, it will be difficult for you to do your job. You need their cooperation, and they need yours. Furthermore, the leading reason employees are fired is not poor technical skill but inability or unwillingness to form satisfactory relationships with others on the job.

In this chapter we describe a number of tactics and methods designed to help you gain favor or avoid disfavor with co-workers. For convenience, these tactics and methods are divided into two categories: those requiring you to take the initiative to establish good relationships and those requiring you to react to the behavior of others.

Many of these ideas about getting along with co-workers are also applicable to your personal life. As obvious as most of these simple principles are, many people violate them. One blind spot many people have is that they believe they are experts in human relations. Have you met anyone with this misperception lately?

TAKING THE INITIATIVE TO ESTABLISH GOOD RELATIONSHIPS

The methods and tactics in this section have one common thread—they all require you to take the initiative in establishing good relationships with co-workers. Instead of reacting to the behavior of a co-worker, you launch an offensive of goodwill. Expressed another way, you are **proactive** instead of **reactive**. Later we deal with reactive methods of getting along with co-workers. Remember, however, that several of the tactics and methods could fit into either category.

Store Up a Reservoir of Good Feelings

Writer Jane Michaels correctly observes that people who are courteous, kind, cooperative and cheerful develop allies and friends in the workplace. Storing up this reservoir of good feeling involves practicing basic good manners such as being pleasant and friendly. It also involves not snooping, spreading malicious gossip, or weaseling out of group presents such as shower or retirement gifts. In addition, it is important to be available to co-workers who want your advice as well as your help in times of crisis.[1]

Maintain Honest and Open Relationships

In human relations we attach considerable importance to maintaining honest and open relationships with other people. Giving co-workers frank, but tactful, answers to their requests for your opinion is one useful way of developing open relationships. Assume that a co-worker asks your opinion about a memo that he intends to send to his boss. As you read it, you find it somewhat incoherent and filled with spelling and grammatical errors. An honest response to this letter might be: "I think your idea is a good one. But I think your memo needs more work before that idea comes across clearly."

As described in Chapter 6, accurately expressing your feelings also leads to constructive relationships. If you arrive at work upset over a personal problem and appearing obviously fatigued, you can expect some reaction. A peer might say, "What seems to be the problem? Is

everything all right?" A dishonest reply would be, "Everything is fine. What makes you think something is wrong?" In addition to making an obviously untrue statement, you would also be perceived as rejecting the person who asked the question.

If you prefer not to discuss your problem, an honest response on your part would be, "Thanks for your interest. I am facing some problems today. But I think things will work out." Such an answer would not involve you in a discussion of your personal problems. Also, you would not be perceived as rejecting your co-worker. The same principle applies equally well to personal relationships.

Be An Optimistic and Positive Person

Everyone knows that you gain more allies by being optimistic and positive than by being pessimistic and negative. Nevertheless, many people ignore this simple strategy for getting along well with others. Co-workers are more likely to solicit your opinion or offer you help when you are perceived to be a cheerful person.

From the supervisor's standpoint, an optimistic and positive employee is a greater asset than an employee with the opposite disposition. People who chronically complain are a drag on the morale of other employees in the office. People with a positive attitude tend to be asked first to try out new techniques and procedures. The reason is that they are more willing to accept change than are people with a negative outlook.

Display a Helpful Cooperative Attitude

Many jobs require teamwork. If you display a willingness to help others and work cooperatively with them, you will be regarded as a good team player. Organizations are designed with cooperation in mind. If people do not cooperate with each other, the total system breaks down. Not all your co-workers are concerned about the smooth functioning of the total organization, but they do want cooperation from you.

When evaluating your work performance, many companies include a rating of your cooperativeness. Both management and your peers value cooperative behavior. Exhibit 8–1 is reproduced from a rating form used by many companies.

EXHIBIT 8-1   COOPERATION AND CONTACTS

Goal: Rating ability to work for and with others.

Criteria: Willing to follow directions? Accept suggestions? Does he or she consider others' viewpoints? Adapt to changing situations? What is his or her attitude toward others? Does he or she respect them and earn their respect? Successful in dealing with others? Is he or she cooperative?

- ☐ Best; upper 10%
- ☐ Next 20%
- ☐ Normal; 40% of group
- ☐ Next 20%
- ☐ Bottom 10%

Now turn to Exhibit 8–2 for an exercise that can be used to suggest what impression others might have of you as a co-worker.

EXHIBIT 8–2   THE CO-WORKER IMPRESSION GROUP

The activity to be described here is another version of a growth group. Here, the task is to share impressions about what kind of co-worker you think each other might be. Each group member will receive feedback from every other group member on this topic. By this point in the course you probably have worked with other class members on group projects, or you have at least formed some impressions about the other class members. The group leader, usually the course instructor, will organize activities in the following manner:

A. The class is divided into groups of about eight to ten people. Each group carries out the co-worker impression group separately, assisted by the group leader.

B. The group arranges itself into a circle. The person seated to the left of the group leader is the first feedback recipient. Each group member, beginning with the person seated to the left of the first feedback recipient, tells that person what kind of co-worker he or she would probably make. The reasons behind this perception are shared with the person (within reason).

C. After everyone has had a turn, the person who is "it" discusses how he or she feels about these perceptions.

D. Each group member has a turn receiving feedback about the kind of co-worker he or she would probably be.

E. Guided by the instructor, the group discusses the meaning and implications of the co-worker impression group.

Be a Team Player

An essential strategy for cultivating your peers is to function in your department or task force as a **team player**. You will have to work cooperatively with others even when you reach the pinnacle of power in your company. Top executives who cannot get along with their immediate subordinates face the threat of being overruled or overthrown by them.

You can improve your status as a team player if you share credit with co-workers, give information and opinions to them, and touch base with them on important issues.

Sharing credit with co-workers is a direct method of promoting the team concept. Instead of focusing on yourself as the person responsible for a work accomplishment, you point out that the accomplishment was a team effort. A sales representative, Frank, is a good example of the team concept in action:

"We won, team, we won," said Frank excitedly to his four lunchmates. "The world's largest manufacturer of air conditioners is going to use our new electronic switch in every one of their units. I just received the good news today. Thanks to all of you for giving me so darn many good suggestions for explaining the merits of our switch. I know that the big boss will be thrilled with our sales department."

Giving information and opinions to co-workers shows that you are team-minded. This is true because one of the benefits of group effort is the fact that members can engage in a sharing of ideas. The result is often a better solution to the problem than would have been possible if people worked alone. **Synergy** is the name given to this phenomenon of group effort whereby the whole is greater than the sum of the parts.

Touching base on important issues refers to such things as keeping your co-workers informed about plans you have that could affect them. One example of this concept in action is to inform your co-workers about a suggestion that you are planning to make to management. In this way, if your proposal is accepted, you are more likely to gain the support of your co-workers in implementing your idea than if your suggestion were a big surprise.

Exchange Favors

The saying "one hand washes the other" is applicable to both work and personal life. In many places of work people unofficially exchange favors as a way of getting work accomplished. Your job, for example, might now and then require a large number of photocopies to be made in a hurry. If the person in charge of making large batches of photocopies goes out of the way to take care of your request, you owe him or her a favor. If you work in the accounting department, you might be able to help the photocopy clerk have an expense account payment processed in a hurry. Exchanging favors as a method of getting along with co-workers will remain effective only if these favors balance out in the long run.

Exchanging favors helps build relationships with co-workers because it leads to cooperation and shared concern about completing the job. The method can work to the good of the organization, as illustrated by a situation in one factory. In this particular setting, supervisors frequently exchange needed supplies with each other. If one supervisor should run out of bolts in a department, that person looks around for another department with an ample supply of bolts. The supervisor with ample bolts lends some to the supervisor short on bolts. Eventually each supervisor gives out about as many bolts as he or she receives.

The reason the supervisors go to the trouble of exchanging bolts relates to their budgets. Rather than asking for additional money to spend on bolts in a given budget period, they exchange supplies. Can you think of any way in which exchange of favors might be applied to a past or present job of yours?

Ask Advice

Asking advice is an effective way of building good relationships with co-workers and friends. If you ask a person whose job does not require giving advice for advice, you are indirectly paying that person a compliment. You are saying, "I trust your judgment enough to ask your opinion on something important to me." You are also saying, "I trust you enough to think that the advice you give me will be in my best interest."

It is important to inform the person whose advice you are seeking that although his or her opinion is sought, it will not necessarily be binding. In other words, it may not be feasible to accept and implement the advice of your friend or co-worker. You should preface your inquiry with a comment of this nature, "I would like your opinion on a problem facing me, but I can't guarantee that I'll be in a position to act on it." In this way you might be able to ward off any hurt feelings because the person wasn't listened to.

Asking for advice must be done with sensitivity for another important reason. If you are in a competitive work or school environment, the person you consult might think you are picking his or her brains for competitive gain. One example would be asking a co-worker for a good idea for cutting costs in the department. If you take the advice offered, you will get the credit from the boss. Your advice-giver might just as soon bring forward that idea to management. One student encountered considerable resentment when asking a classmate for this advice: "Our term paper is due in two weeks. I would like your advice on a good topic."

Avoid Being Abrasive

An abrasive person is someone who "rubs people the wrong way." Management psychologist Harry Levinson says this kind of person "like the proverbial porcupine seems to have a knack for jabbing others in an irritating, sometimes painful way."[2] Abrasive personalities are frequently fired from high-level positions. On the way up, they make irritating, annoying, and uncomfortable co-workers. The primary characteristics of the abrasive personality are self-centeredness, isolation from others, perfectionism, contempt for others, and a tendency to attack people.

As a co-worker, the abrasive person is commonly a source of irritation. Most abrasive people do not really understand how upsetting they are to peers. An advantage of participating in growth groups is that at a minimum you'll find out rather quickly if others consider you to be abrasive.

Here are a few examples of an abrasive person in action that could serve as a useful partial checklist of the type of behaviors to avoid if you want to maintain good peer relationships:

- A waitress drops a loaded tray on the floor while serving dinner. Her abrasive busboy shouts, "Flora, you clumsy slob, you've done it again. We'll all lose our ____ jobs if you don't shape up."
- You ask a new worker in your department to join you and two of your friends for lunch. Having an abrasive personality, she responds, "No thanks, I have better things to do on my lunch hour."
- You ask a co-worker if you can borrow his felt-tip pen to finish up a drawing you are doing for your boss. Angrily, he answers, "Bug off. I hate a mooch."

Avoid Being Despised and Hated

About 500 years ago Niccolo Machiavelli wrote *The Prince*, which is still referred to, especially by management writers. The author advised princes to take steps to ensure that they would not be despised and hated. Machiavelli believed that so long as you did not deprive other men of their property and women, you would not be hated and despised. In today's world of work, you can be despised and hated—or at least disliked—for much less. In practice, this strategy translates into getting along with your co-workers by avoiding actions that irritate most people in the office. Among such actions to avoid are the following:

Sitting on a co-worker's desk.
Bragging to others that you received a magnificent salary increase.
Placing dirty coffee containers, wads of chewing gum, or cigar butts in their ash tray.
Smugly mentioning that you forgot it was payday, so you will pick up your paycheck next week.

REACTING CONSTRUCTIVELY TO THE BEHAVIOR OF CO-WORKERS

You are often forced to react to the actions and words of co-workers. How you react influences the quality of your relationship with them. In this section of the chapter we describe a number of time-tested ways of reacting constructively to the behavior of co-workers. (**Behavior** refers to the tangible acts or decisions of people, including both their actions and words.)

Express an Interest in Their Work

Almost everyone is self-centered to some extent. Thus, topics that are favored are ones closely related to themselves, such as their children, friends, hobbies, work, or possessions. Sales representatives rely heavily on this fact in cultivating relationships with established customers. They routinely ask the customer about his or her hobbies, family members, and work activities. (Say, how's your beer can collection going?) You can capitalize on this simple strategy by asking co-workers and friends questions such as these:

How is your work going? (highly recommended)
How are things going for you?
How did you gain the knowledge necessary for your job?
How does the company use the output from your department?
How does your present job fit in with your career plans?
How well did Mitzie do in the county cat show?

A danger in asking questions about other people's work is that some questions may not be perceived as well-intentioned. There is a fine line between honest curiosity and snooping. You must stay alert to this subtle distinction. A payroll clerk once asked an administrative assistant in her department, "What did you do today?" The administrative assistant interpreted the question as intimating that administrative assistants may not have a full day's work to perform.

Be a Good Listener

After you ask questions, you must be prepared to listen to the answers. The simplest technique of getting along with co-workers, friends, and acquaintances is to be a good listener. The topics you should be willing to listen to during working hours include job problems and miscellaneous complaints. Lunch breaks, coffee breaks, and after hours are better suited to listening to people talk about their personal lives, current events, sports, and the like.

Becoming an effective listener takes practice. As you practice your listening skills try the suggestions offered in Chapter 5. The payoff is that listening builds constructive relationships both on and off the job. Too often people take turns talking rather than listening to each other. The result is that neither party feels better as a result of the conversation.

Be Courteous

Many people are rude to co-workers both in business and nonprofit firms. Consequently, if you show common courtesy to other employees (or friends and acquaintances), you may have a substantial advantage in gaining their respect and support. Two elementary suggestions can help you avoid the discourtesy trap:

Answer memos and letters. Many an employee answers memos and letters according to the rank of the sender. Correspondence from the highest rank is answered promptly; correspondence from medium-ranking personnel is answered within one week; correspondence from lower-ranking people is often ignored and discarded. Answering the memos of lower-ranking people promptly will be advantageous in cultivating their support. Answering a memo quickly generally requires only a little more time than does earmarking it for later action. A modern technique is to handwrite a quick response on the bottom of a type-written memo. A photocopy is then made for your files and the original is returned to the sender.

Return telephone calls. Neglecting to return telephone calls of sales representatives and job applicants is a common practice in many organizations. Even if you are not interested in the message that the caller has for you, saying, "No thank you, I'm not interested," will at least end the matter. Also, you will not be branded as another discourteous person. The message sender may prove to be someone who can someday help you.

Phone calls should also be returned in your personal life. Assume you receive a message that a person has called you, but you do not wish to speak to that person. It is preferable to return the call and decline that person's invitation rather than ignore him or her.

Use Appropriate Compliments

An effective way of developing good relationships with co-workers and friends is to compliment their work on something they are closely identified with, such as their children, spouse, hobbies, or pets. Paying a compliment is a form of **positive reinforcement,** rewarding somebody for doing something right. The right response is therefore strengthened, or reinforced. A compliment is a useful multipurpose reward.

Compliments to co-workers are more likely to be accepted at face value than are compliments to your boss or higher-ranking managers.

Nevertheless, a sincere compliment can help you develop a good relationship with almost anyone. Exhibit 8–3 presents an exercise to help you develop a sense of the difference between appropriate and exaggerated compliments. Appropriate compliments will be perceived as sincere; exaggerated compliments will be perceived as insincere.

EXHIBIT 8–3   APPROPRIATE VERSUS EXAGGERATED COMPLIMENTS

Complimenting others effectively is a skill that takes time to develop. To help sensitize you to the difference between appropriate and exaggerated (and therefore inappropriate) compliments, do the exercise described below.

For each of the following situations write down both an appropriate and an exaggerated compliment. Study carefully the text material to guide you in creating an effective compliment.

SITUATION A: A friend of your has just placed fifth out of 113 entrants in the company bowling tournament. You know that he is almost fanatical about bowling.

   Appropriate compliment:_____

_____

_____

   Exaggerated compliment:_____

_____

SITUATION B: A secretary in your department has just received a twenty-five year recognition pin from the company. Any employee who works for the company for twenty-five consecutive years automatically receives one of these pins.

   Appropriate compliment:_____

_____

_____

   Exaggerated compliment:_____

_____

SITUATION C: A high school senior you know well has just received a National Merit Scholarship, one of two students in her high school to accomplish this feat.

   Appropriate compliment:_____

_____

   Exaggerated compliment:_____

_____

Give Out Recognition

An inexpensive method of cultivating people, in terms of money and time, is to give them attention or any appropriate form of **recognition**. "Show people how important you think they are," contend most books about getting along with people. Similar to warnings about the importance of driving carefully, the number of people who understand the concept far exceeds the number who drive carefully. Yet investing a small amount of time in recognizing a co-worker can pay large dividends in terms of cultivating an ally. Recognition can take many forms, including sincere compliments. Here are several everyday examples of giving recognition to co-workers and friends:

You read in the local section of the newspaper that a worker in your department won an award for his 1939 Cadillac in an antique car show. You pin that article up on the department bulletin board, accompanied by the comment, "Congratulations, Charlie." And don't forget to sign your name in order to receive appropriate credit.

You find out that a woman in your department has been chosen area coordinator for the hospital building-fund drive. You write her a note saying, "I'm proud of you, Mary. Enclosed is a check for $15.00. Let me be one of the first to help you raise all the money you need for this worthwhile cause."

A friend of yours saves a drowning child. The next time you see her you give her a big hug and say, "What you did for that child is its own reward. I'm proud to be your friend."

Follow Group Standards of Conduct

The basic principle to follow in getting along with co-workers is to pay heed to **group norms.** These refer to the unwritten set of expectations for group members—what the people ought to do. Norms become a standard of what each person should do nor not do within the group. Employees learn about norms both through simple observation and direct instruction from other group members. If you do not deviate too far from these norms, much of your behavior will be accepted by the group. If you deviate too far, you will be subject to much rejection. Here is one explanation of how group norms influence work output:

When a new member works at too fast a pace the first day on the job, he or she may be subjected to derogatory comments such as "Look at old speed king (or queen) there," "Look who's trying to make us look bad," "Look who's trying to impress the supervisor," "Look who's trying to make us lose our jobs," and so on. A little of this goes a long way in obtaining compliance with group norms.[4]

Group norms also influence the social aspects of behavior on the job. Among established norms many relate to such things as the people to have lunch with, getting together with other employees for an after-hours drink on Friday, joining a department team, and the type of clothing to wear to work.

If you deviate too far from work or social norms, you run the risk of being isolated from the group. In some instances you might even be subjected to physical abuse if you make the other employees look bad. The risk of conforming too closely to group norms is that you lose your individuality. You become viewed by your superiors as "one of the guys or gals" rather than a person who aspires to move up in the organization. Getting along too well with peers has its price as well. An example of how one individual gained group acceptance appears in Exhibit 8–4.

EXHIBIT 8–4   FRANK WINS GROUP ACCEPTANCE

Frank looked forward enthusiastically to his new job as quality control technician. The company hiring him was well respected, the pay was good, the work sounded challenging, and there appeared to be good opportunities for advancement. Frank's supervisor made sure he went through the required employee orientation program and he was introduced to each of his new co-workers. In Frank's opinion they seemed friendly but not particularly eager to welcome him to the group. Frank shrugged off their reserve as typical behavior in business.

As the weeks passed Frank became increasingly concerned about the limited acceptance he was receiving from the group. His co-workers did not openly avoid him but Frank was not included in department jokes. And only on his first two days on the job was he invited to lunch by his co-workers. Frank considered the problem to be serious because he regarded the job itself as well-suited to his talents and interests. Frank did not consider himself to be a loner and did not wish to be treated as one.

Frank looked at the alternatives facing him. As he perceived the problem he could take one or more of the following actions: first, he could take no particular action and wait to see if he would eventually be accepted by the group; second, he could ask each person individually why he or she did not reach out to him; third, he could go out of his way to do favors for the group such as leaving candy on his desk for others to eat or volunteering to run errands for co-workers; fourth, he could take the initiative to show that he was interested in them; and fifth, he could ask his boss to investigate the problem.

Frank's study of human relations combined with his intuition led him to choose the fourth alternative. To implement this plan he made up a list of several questions he would ask his co-workers over the next one or two weeks. The questions were:

1. What is your specialty within the department?
2. How does your job fit into the overall picture?
3. By the way, what are your favorite activities when you are not working?

Within two weeks Frank completed his questioning of co-workers. He recognized there was a small risk associated with this course of action. Some people in the department might think he was snooping into confidential matters. Frank found the opposite to be true. Within two weeks he was accepted into the group. His co-workers now invited him to lunch, joked with him, and kept him informed of office gossip.

> **Frank made an intelligent decision by taking the initiative to use the strategy "express an interest in their work." His line of questioning was innocent enough to avoid making people defensive. We do not know that the other alternatives would not have been effective. But we do know that expressing an interest in the work of others is a psychologically sound and mature tactic for winning the acceptance of co-workers (and people in general).**

Use Tact in Dealing with Annoying Behavior

Co-workers who irritate you rarely do annoying things on purpose. Tactful actions on your part can sometimes take care of these annoyances without your having to confront the problem. Close your door, for example, if noisy co-workers are gathered outside. Or try one woman's method of getting rid of office pests: She keeps paper in her electronic typewriter and gestures to it apologetically when someone overstays a visit.[3]

Sometimes subtlety doesn't work, and it may be necessary to diplomatically confront the co-worker who is annoying you. Jane Michaels suggests that you precede a criticism with a compliment. Here is an example of this approach: "You're one of the best people I've ever worked with, but one habit of yours drives me bananas. Do you think you could let me know when you're going to be late getting back to the office after lunch?"[4]

Be Sympathetic Toward the Personality Quirks of Co-workers

Both on and off the job, many people have personality quirks that make them difficult to deal with. The manager is usually in the best position to help these people control their quirks so that job performance does not suffer. Often a personnel counselor will assist the manager in dealing with employee quirks.

Your best defense as a co-worker is to show sympathy for employees with these quirks without submitting to all of their demands. Be understanding even if you do not find all their behavior acceptable. By showing sympathy, the co-worker with the quirk may shift to more tolerable behavior. Here are several of the more frequently observed personality quirks:[5]

☐ The person who has a strong need to be always correct. Employees with this quirk set up situations so that people who disagree with them are made to look naive or foolish. For example, "All well-educated and intelligent people believe as I do that this is the way we should go on this project. If anybody disagrees, please speak up now."

(You can sympathize in this manner: "I recognize Margot, that you research everything before reaching an opinion, and that you are usually right. Nevertheless, I want to point out another perspective of this problem.")

☐ The person who has a strong need for attention, whether the attention be positive or negative. Attention-seekers may shout louder than others, play the role of the office clown, or tell co-workers all their woes.

(You can sympathize in this manner: "We all know, Gus, that you like to be in the limelight. You do deserve our attention, but now it is Amanda's turn to speak.")

☐ The person who resents control, direction, or advice from others. Employees with this quirk are so oversensitive to being controlled that they misinterpret hints as suggestions, and orders as direct challenges to their intelligence and self-worth.

(You might express sympathy—yet still get through—to a co-worker with this quirk by a statement such as, "Carlos, I know you like to be your own person. I admire you for it, but I have a teeny suggestion that could strengthen the graphics you just put together.")

By showing sympathy in all of the above situations, you will be able to work more effectively with the co-worker who has a personality quirk.

SUMMARY

Getting along with co-workers is important for performing your job satisfactorily or better. Methods and tactics for getting along with people on the job are also useful in personal life. Methods and tactics that center around taking the initiative to establish good relationships include:

1. Store up a reservoir of good feelings (develop allies on the job).
2. Maintain honest and open relationships (be frank but tactful).
3. Be an optimistic and positive person (smiling helps).
4. Display a helpful and cooperative attitude (many jobs require teamwork).
5. Be a team player (emphasize "we" instead of "I").
6. Exchange favors (use unofficial bargains to get the job done).
7. Ask advice (show people you respect their opinion).

8. Avoid being abrasive (one who attacks others and rubs them the wrong way).

9. Avoid being despised and hated (doing a variety of things that "bug" other people).

Methods and tactics of getting along with co-workers that center around reacting constructively to their behavior, include:

1. Express an interest in their work (asking questions helps).

2. Be a good listener (an indispensable tactic).

3. Be courteous (for example, answer memos and letters, and return telephone calls).

4. Use appropriate compliments (be specific, and do not exaggerate the person's accomplishment).

5. Give out recognition (recognize people for their accomplishments).

6. Follow group standards of conduct (go along with what the group considers acceptable behavior).

7. Use tact in dealing with annoying behavior (do not insult or be rude to annoying co-workers).

8. Be sympathetic toward the personality quirks of co-workers (accept their needs but do not necessarily give in to their demands).

QUESTIONS AND ACTIVITIES

1. A critic of this chapter said, "A lot of ruthless people get ahead in business. So getting along with your co-workers may not really be all that important." What do you think?

2. What are three questions you might ask the instructor of this course to show that you are interested in his or her work?

3. Which three of the tactics described in this chapter do you think would be the most effective for you? Explain your reasoning.

4. Which three of the tactics described in this chapter do you think would be the least effective for you? Explain your reasoning.

5. Do you agree that one should be sympathetic toward the personality quirks of co-workers?

6. Identify another personality quirk that you have found among a number of workers or students.

7. What additions can you make to the "despised and hated" list?

8. Interview a successful employed person. Obtain his or her advice on getting along with co-workers, and be prepared to discuss your findings in class.

A HUMAN RELATIONS CASE PROBLEM:
THE UNPOPULAR INVENTORY AUDITOR

Lynn Diamond looked forward to a career in retailing for many years. While in high school and vocational technical school she worked as a sales clerk for Silver Triangle, a chain of discount department stores. Although her performance reviews were not outstanding, Lynn performed well enough to be invited back as a full-time employee after graduation.

Silver Triangle management offered Lynn a position as an inventory auditor. A company official told her that the auditor position would be a good broadening experience. It would expose Lynn to all the stores in her area, thus helping prepare her for a store manager position in the future. Lynn's primary job is to count inventory in each store to see if any inventory is missing that cannot be accounted for by sales figures. (An important part of loss control in a retail store is to keep careful track of inventory. If any inventory cannot be accounted for by sales, it could mean that employees or customers are misappropriating inventory.)

After two months on the job, Lynn was asked how she was doing in her new assignment by a friend who worked at Silver Triangle regional headquarters. "Not nearly as well as I would like to be doing," replied Lynn. "I'm learning how to do a first-rate inventory audit, but I'm certainly not making many friends."

"How do you know that you're not making friends?" asked her friend.

"It's the comments about me that I've heard, and the cold shoulders that I've been getting. Just last week I was auditing a big stack of tennis balls. I overhead the assistant store manager ask one of the clerks if he had seen me today. The clerk said 'Yes, Miss Pits was sneaking around the department.' Then they both laughed.

"Another problem is that hardly anybody in the stores treats me with any kindness. I know that people don't naturally love an auditor, but I'm just doing my job. Hardly anybody at the stores ever invites me to lunch."

Lynn's friend said, "What can I do to help you?"

Lynn replied, "Help me find out how I can become better liked as an auditor."

Questions

1. What advice should Lynn's friend give her?
2. Is Lynn asking a realistic question? Could it be that the problem is her

job, and not her behavior or personal characteristics, that leads her to be disliked?

3. What might Lynn do to diagnose the reasons for her problem?

4. What general suggestions can you offer Lynn until she finds out the underlying reasons for her problem?

A HUMAN RELATIONS ROLE PLAY: GETTING ALONG WITH CO-WORKERS

Lynn Diamond decides that she wants to take immediate action toward getting along better with co-workers. During her next several visits to Silver Triangle stores, she will try a few of the methods and tactics recommended for improving relationships with co-workers. In each of the following three scenarios, one person plays the role of Lynn the inventory auditor. Another person plays the role of the store employee whom Lynn is trying to cultivate.

Scenario A: Exchanging Favors

Lynn decides to strike up a bargain with a store clerk. (The role player decides what this exchange of favors should be.) Unknown to Lynn, the clerk is concerned about an inventory audit because he is worried about being accused of stealing merchandise.

Scenario B: Avoid Being Despised and Hated

Lynn takes the initiative to see if she is doing anything on the job that might be irritating store employees. She brings up this topic during a coffee break with Rita, a store manager.

Scenario C: Express an Interest in Their Work

Lynn uses the most reliable tactic of all in order to form better relationships with store personnel. She tries "express an interest" first on Clyde, a slow-moving, slow-thinking warehouse clerk. Clyde is being paid the minimum wage and suffers from low job satisfaction.

REFERENCES

[1] Jane Michaels, "You Gotta Get Along to Get Ahead," *Woman's Day*, April 3, 1984, p. 58.

[2] Harry Levinson, "The Abrasive Personality at the Office," *Psychology Today*, May 1978, pp. 78–84.

[3] Michaels, "You Gotta Get Along," p. 60.

[4] Ibid.

[5] Michael E. Cavanagh, *Personnel Journal,* March 1985, pp. 55–64.

SOME ADDITIONAL READING

CARNEGIE, DALE.   *How to Win Friends and Influence People.* New York: Pocket Books (a classic reprinted every several years).

DuBRIN, ANDREW J.   *Winning at Office Politics.* New York: Ballantine Books, 1978, Chapters 6 and 7.

MACHER, KEN.   "The Politics of People." *Personnel Journal,* January 1986, pp. 50–53.

SANDLER, LEONARD.   "The Successful and Supportive Subordinate." *Personnel Journal,* December 1984, pp. 40–45.

SCHWARTZ, JUDITH D.   "The Psychology of a Winning Team," *Success!* December 1985, pp. 42–45.

STEIL, LYMAN K., JOANNE SUMMERFIELD, and GEORGE DEMARE.   *Listening: It Can Change Your Life.* New York: John Wiley, 1983.

WIEDER, ROBERT S.   "Dr. Truth." *Success!,* February 1985, pp. 56–59.

WINTER, CARYL.   *Present Yourself with Impact: Techniques for Success.* New York: Ballantine Books, 1983.

Handling Conflict with Others

Learning Objectives

After studying the information and doing the exercises in this chapter, you should be able to:

- Understand why conflict takes place so often in work and personal life
- Pinpoint several helpful and harmful consequences of conflict
- Understand how to deal constructively with anger
- Do a better job of negotiating with yourself
- Know how to deal with sexual harassment

As long as you are willing or interested in standing up for what you think are your rights, you will run into conflict both on the job and in personal life. Conflicts can take various forms, including such incidents as these:

- Your boss wants you to work on Saturday, but you want to go fishing.
- Your boyfriend or girlfriend wants to become engaged but you want to keep the relationship alive without becoming engaged.
- The Internal Revenue Service says you owe $150 for last year's taxes, and you claim you already paid that amount with a money order.

All three situations illustrate the underlying nature of **conflict**: two sets of demands, goals, or motives are incompatible.[1] You cannot work on Saturday and go fishing at the same time; you cannot be engaged and not engaged simultaneously; the Internal Revenue Service and you cannot both be right. Such differences in demands often lead to a hostile or antagonistic relationship between two or more parties. A conflict can also be considered a dispute, feud, controversy, or private war!

The intent of this chapter is to describe ways of resolving conflict so that both parties can live with each other after the conflict is settled. Both sides should leave the conflict feeling that their needs have been satisfied without having to resort to extreme behavior. You want to get what you deserve but at the same time preserve the dignity and self-respect of the other party.

WHY SO MUCH CONFLICT EXISTS

Many reasons exist for the widespread presence of conflict in all aspects of life. We shall discuss seven of the most common sources of conflict here. All these reasons for conflict stem directly or indirectly from the same underlying cause—two incompatible motives, demands, or events. To be incompatible, motives may be the same or they may differ. That is, conflict can arise when two people want the same thing at the same time, or when they want different things at the same time.

Competition for Limited Resources

Have you seen any old movies on TV in which two cowboys duel with guns or two knights duel with swords over the love of a woman? The combatants compete for a limited resource, one woman they both desire. Similarly, a fundamental reason that you might experience conflict with another person is that not everyone can get all the money, material, supplies, or human help he or she wants. In some families, two or more children are pitted in conflict over the limited resources of money available for higher education.

When time becomes a scarce resource, this, too, can lead to conflict. You might have an important idea that you want to present to your boss before he or she leaves for a business trip. When you ask to see the boss before she leaves, she says, "I'm sorry but I have already agreed to meet with Len. Why don't you catch me first thing after vacation?" At that moment you will probably feel frustrated because your goal of presenting your idea to the boss is blocked. You might also be in conflict with Len who has monopolized your boss's time for the balance of the day. The limited resource in this situation is the boss's time.

Personal Differences

You may encounter conflict with another person simply because the two of you are radically different types of people. This source of conflict is one of the main reasons college dormitory officials use questionnaires to try to match strangers who will be assigned as roommates. One roommate who places a high premium on loud music, beer-drinking, gum-chewing, and late-morning sleeping would come into conflict with a person of different inclinations.

Various personality and cultural differences among people contribute to job conflict. Difference in age is one such factor. The generation gap can lead to conflict because members of one generation may not accept values of another. Cooperation is sometimes difficult to achieve between older and younger members of a department because older employees question the seriousness of purpose of the younger employees. Simultaneously, the younger workers may believe that the older workers are resistant to change and blindly loyal to the company.

Dependency on Others

If two people are dependent on each other, the very nature of that dependency usually breeds some conflict. Imagine being stuck in a lifeboat with two other people for a week! Marriage partners, couples living together, and roommates often enter into conflict simply because so much of what they can or cannot do depends on what the other person does.

In the same way that people sharing the same living quarters can come into conflict, so the departments of an organization requiring the cooperation of each other tend to find reasons for conflict. The operations and maintenance units of an airline are thus frequently in conflict with each other because they are interdependent. Without an airplane to service, the maintenance department is out of business. Without a properly serviced airplane, the operations department can quickly go out of business.

Differences in Goals

One middle-aged man is embroiled in frequent conflict with his daughter. Her goal is to "take life easy" by working at odd jobs and spending as much time as possible at the beach or at ski resorts. His goal is to have a daughter who will "make something of herself." Until they both modify their goals in each other's directions, they will stay in conflict over this issue. In general, when two groups differ considerably in their goals, the potential for conflict is high.

Conflict between instructor and students sometimes reflects a difference in goals. An instructor might look upon his or her course as a valuable contribution to each student's career. The instructor's goal is that students maximize their effort in study and classroom participation. The goal of some of the students may be to receive the maximum grade for the minimum amount of study and participation. When an examination question is based on a minor point made in supplementary reading, conflict occurs. If the students shared the goal of maximizing learning, they would not object to the question. If the instructor shared the goal of maximum grade for minimum effort, he or she might not have asked the question.

Different Methods for Reaching a Common Goal

Alternative approaches can be used to achieve almost any goal. Individuals and groups often enter into conflict over the best method of accomplishing a goal. A continuing conflict of this nature took place in one company between Alice, the head of the secretarial pool, and her boss Jack, the manager of office services.

> Jack believed strongly that the secretarial pool should produce high-quality work but also be run as economically as feasible. His strategy was to urge Alice to hire mostly student and part-time help. He reasoned that their low wages would reduce operating costs. Jack thought that with close supervision these young typists could produce high-quality work. Alice shared Jack's goal of running a department with high-quality work at low cost. Her solution was to pay good wages to experienced typists and secretaries. She reasoned that by paying high wages to mature women a stable work force could be established. Alice thought that the savings on turnover costs would more than compensate for high wages.
>
> Alice and Jack frequently argued about which strategy would best achieve their shared goal. Jack finally imposed his formal authority and basically or-

dered Alice to use a compromise strategy; an attempt was made to strike a balance between hiring trainees and experienced workers.

Unclear Boundaries and Tasks

"You fool, the picnic is supposed to start in twenty minutes, and the franks and hamburgers aren't here," shouted Jeff. "Don't yell at

me," said Luke. "Nobody told me I was supposed to get the franks and hamburgers." The cause of the conflict between Jeff and Luke is a common one—someone has failed to define clearly the nature of an assignment.

Closely related to unclear tasks, is the problem of not knowing where your responsibilities end and someone else's begin. Sometimes this is referred to as a jurisdictional dispute.[2] Imagine that you are

designated the truck salesperson and another individual the car salesperson during one shift at a car and truck dealership. A prospective
customer walks in wanting to purchase a van to use for commercial
purposes. Instead of flipping a coin to see who takes care of this customer, the two of you argue it out. Your boss should have clarified who
is to sell vans for commercial, rather than personal, use. Without such
clarification, a situation has arisen that placed you two in a jurisdictional dispute (conflict).

Conflict-prone Job Duties

If you were a collection agent for a finance company, an investiga-
tor of welfare fraud, or an auditor for the Internal Revenue Service, you
could expect to enter into frequent job-related conflict. Some conflict is
thus more related to the roles that people occupy than to their basic
personality. (A role is a set of behaviors a person is supposed to engage
in because of his or her job, occupation, or situation in life. Role-playing exercises ask you to place yourself in a particular role.) Certain
jobs have built-in conflict in the sense that people tend to resent the
activities performed by the holder of that job (his or her role).

An extreme example of a conflict-prone role is that of a hatchet
man. Such an individual is sent to do the dirty work of a high-ranking
official who wants to be liked by an many people as possible. The
hatchet man personally delivers notices of firings and demotions to
executives, as well as reprimands from the top boss.

THE GOOD AND BAD SIDE OF CONFLICT

Conflict over significant things is a source of stress. We usually do not
suffer stress over minor conflicts such as having to choose between one
color sweater and another. Since conflict is a source of stress, it can
have both positive and negative consequences to the individual. Like
stress in general, we need an optimum amount of conflict to keep us
mentally and physically energetic.

You can probably recall an incident in your life when conflict
proved to be beneficial in the long run. Perhaps you and your friend or
spouse hammered out an agreement over how much freedom each one
has in the relationship. Handled properly, moderate doses of conflict
can be beneficial. Some of the benefits that might arise from conflict
can be summarized around these key points:

1. Talents and abilities may emerge in response to conflict. When faced
   with a conflict, people often become more creative than they are in a

tranquil situation. Assume that your employers told you that they would no longer pay for your advanced education unless you used the courses to improve your job performance. You would probably find ways to accomplish such an end.

2. Conflict can help you feel better because it satisfies a number of psychological needs. By nature, many people like a good fight. As a socially acceptable substitute for attacking others, you might be content to argue over a dispute on the job or at home.

3. Conflict can lead to beneficial innovation and change. The history of the labor movement contains numerous examples of conflict over such matters as reducing the work week from six to five days and demanding safety devices on machines and in mines. You might be in conflict with a roommate or spouse about dividing up household responsibilities. The net result might be a more equitable sharing of tasks.

4. Many individuals are bored with their jobs and evenings at home. Thus they find squabbles with co-workers or family members to be a refreshing pause in their routine. Office conflicts add sparkle to coffee break chatter, even if the participants are not personally involved in the dispute.

5. As an aftermath of conflict, the parties in conflict may become united. Two adolescents engaged in a fistfight may emerge bloodied but good friends after the battle. And two warring supervisors may become more cooperative toward each other as an aftermath of confrontation.

Despite the glowing picture of conflict just painted, it can also have some detrimental consequences to the individual, the organization, and society. War, sabotage, homicide, suicide, alcoholism, and drug abuse are among the harmful consequences of conflict between people. These harmful consequences of conflict make it important for people to learn how to resolve conflict:

1. Prolonged conflict can be detrimental to some people's emotional and physical well-being. As a type of stress, prolonged conflict can lead to such problems as heart disease and chronic intestinal disorders. U.S. President Lyndon B. Johnson suffered his first heart attack after an intense argument with a young newspaper reporter.

2. People in conflict with each other often waste time and energy that could be put to useful purposes. Instead of fighting all evening with someone, the two of you might fix up your place. Instead of writing angry memos back and forth, two department heads might better invest that time in thinking up ideas to save the company money.

3. The aftermath of extreme conflict may have high financial and emotional costs. Sabotage—such as ruining machinery—might be the financial consequence. At the same time, management may develop a permanent distrust of many people in the work force, although only a few of them are saboteurs.

4. Too much conflict is fatiguing, even if it does not cause symptoms of emotional illness. People who work in high-conflict jobs often feel spent when they return home from work. When the battle-worn individual has limited energy left over for family responsibilities, the result is more conflict. (For instance, "What do you mean you are too tired to go to the movies?" or "If your job is killing your appetite, find another job.")

5. People in conflict will often be much more concerned with their own interests than with the good of the family, organization, or society. A married couple in conflict might disregard the welfare of their children. An employee in the shipping department who is in conflict with his supervisor, might neglect to ship an order. And a gang in conflict with another might leave a park or beach strewn with broken glass.

DEALING WITH ANGER

Conflict typically leads to **frustration,** a blocking of need or motive satisfaction. You experience a sense of frustration when something stands in the way between you and the goal you want to achieve. Frustration, in turn, leads to anger. And even if you did not experience frustration when in conflict, you would still feel some anger. Learning how to handle anger is therefore an important part of dealing with conflict. Here we are concerned with how anger affects people, and how anger can be handled constructively.

The Nature of Anger

Anger is a feeling of extreme hostility, indignation, or exasperation. The feeling of anger or hostility triggers a stress reaction, including its physiological changes. For instance, during anger the normal movements of the stomach and intestines associated with digestion usually stop. Other physiological changes accompanying anger include increased muscle tension, heart rate, diastolic blood pressure, and body metabolism. Food in the blood stream and the body tissues are burned off at a faster rate, giving the angry person additional energy.

The physiological changes associated with anger are part of the body's built-in biological response to prepare for either fight or flight— to stand and face the enemy or flee if necessary. This mechanism is quite useful when a person is threatened by a mugger or an enraged animal. As described below, when anger is properly channeled it can also help us deal with psychologically threatening relationships.

One notable physical indicator of anger is that the pupils may enlarge, causing the wide-eyed look typical of people in a rage. An unfortunate byproduct of anger is that one's judgment may become clouded. People often act impulsively and violently when experiencing anger or rage. One punch or invective hurled at a supervisor can do serious damage to a person's career.

How to Best Handle Anger

Experts go back and forth on how much free expression should be given to anger. Mental health professionals have always agreed that anger and frustration should not be entirely suppressed. Bottled emotions are said to be harmful—they lead to psychosomatic disorders and sudden bursts of uncontrollable emotion. During the permissive 1960s people were urged to "tell it like it is" and "let it all hang out." Some psychotherapists even suggested that venting all anger would get rid of it.[3] Managers and employees were urged to be candid in expressing anger toward each other.

In recent years, more emphasis has been placed on controlling anger so that it does not lead to destructive consequences. For example a research report for executives recommends, "Avoid anger. Getting angry is a waste of time. If there is an open display of hostility between junior and senior, the junior staff member always loses."[4]

Despite these conflicting views about expressing anger, here are several suggestions that may prove helpful in managing anger in work and social situations:

1. *Recognize that anger is an energizer, and is therefore potentially useful.* When angry, for example, it is a good time to get through laborious tasks that do not require heavy judgment and concentration. Use the energy derived from anger to clean out your files, wash and wax a car, clean out a basement, or conduct an inventory. But stay away from operating potentially dangerous machinery like a power tool or automobile.

2. *Use anger to remind you to share your feelings with an important person in your life.* You might say to a close friend, "I'm angry that you didn't invite me to that dinner party." On the job you might say, "I'm angry that I was passed over for promotion to supervisor. I wanted the job and I think I deserve it." (Notice that you have not flown into a rage by making these statements.)

3. *When angry at another person, first express those feelings to yourself and then share the less destructive feelings with him of her.* The old idea of counting to ten when angry has merit. Or you can write down all your angry feelings and then sort out the useful ideas in your anger letter. Assume your instructor gave you a D on a paper you thought deserved an A. Compose a letter to yourself explaining how angry you are at the instructor. Then return to the instructor with your legitimate concerns and rational feelings.

4. *Don't carry grudges.* A **grudge** is the unresolved or unexpressed anger we feel against someone whom we believe has wronged us. Freudenberger

warns us that "Consistent grudges can lead to stress, and everything from backaches to chest pains. And they can be very damaging with friends, family, and at work."[5] Exhibit 9–1 presents some useful ideas on how to get rid of grudges.

EXHIBIT 9–1   HOW TO EXORCISE A GRUDGE

Do you often carry a grudge? Since you recognize the problem, you have already taken an important step toward overcoming grudges. In addition to recognizing the problem, choose from among these suggestions:

☐ Express your hurt, disappointment, or anger to the person you believe has slighted you. You must communicate in order to clear the air.

☐ See the situation from the other person's perspective. There may be a very good reason for his or her behavior.

☐ Weigh the seriousness of the offense.

☐ Consider your options. List even the ridiculous ones to help you vent your anger.

☐ Confront the person you have a grudge against in a way that minimizes the consequences.

☐ Express your anger in a letter you never send if the risks are too great. This is a good way to vent anger against people who are no longer present, including an ex-spouse or a deceased parent.

☐ Work on acceptance. Let the anger go, and move on to positive life events.

SOURCE: Adapted with permission from Karen S. Peterson, "Holding Grudges Can Hold You Back," *USA Weekend,* October 18–20, p. 29.

STRATEGIES FOR RESOLVING CONFLICTS WITH OTHERS

The information presented so far is designed to help you understand the nature of conflict. Such background information is useful for resolving conflict because it helps you understand what is happening in a conflict situation. In this and the following section we present some specific strategies for resolving conflict between yourself and another person. In addition, Exhibit 9–2 offers a brief review of some common personal approaches to resolving conflict.

Compromise

Almost any resolution of conflict—from a hostage situation to a neighborhood dispute over garbage collection—involves some element of compromise. One party agrees to do something if the other party

---

EXHIBIT 9–2   WHAT IS YOUR CONFLICT RESOLUTION STYLE?

The next sections of this chapter are concerned with a variety of methods for resolving conflict. A related topic is your basic style or approach to resolving conflict with others. Five of them will be described in this box.[6] A person's general style of resolving conflict might be used in carrying out different methods. For example, your style might be that of a problem solver. You would approach different methods of resolving conflict such as gentle confrontation and appeal to a third party, in a productive, problem-solving style.

Tough Battler. These people are tough to battle with because they "think conflict occurs only when others are too stupid, stubborn, or misinformed to see that their position is the right one."[7] Abrasive persons typically use the tough battler style of resolving conflict. They attack viciously to win their point. Winning a conflict gives the tough battler a temporary feeling of elation. Because winning is so important to them, tough battlers frequently show signs of anger, frustration, and outrage during a conflict.

Friendly Helper. Winning the acceptance, friendship, and affection of others is a dominant need of friendly helpers. Faced with conflict, they are likely to say, "If that's what you really want and it will make you happy, I'll go along with it." Friendly helpers would prefer to avoid conflict and live in perpetual harmony. They will sometimes interject humor when feelings become too intense. Friendly helpers usually give in to their opponents and lose rather than take the chance of hurting another person's feelings.

Runaway. Persons using this style of conflict resolution have little hope that they can win a conflict. Runaways, therefore, flee conflict situations both mentally and physically. Mentally, runaways ignore the presence of conflict and avoid taking sides in a disagreement even if the outcome influences their well-being. Physically, they flee by not showing up at a meeting where the battle is to be fought. Their escape behavior sometimes takes the form of quitting a job rather than facing a conflict with a co-worker or superior.

Compromiser. Compromisers are good office politicians. They seek a middle ground that will satisfy all the parties involved in the conflict. Compromisers value the quick settlement of a dispute, and are willing to grant concessions to bring things to a close. (In real life, most conflicts are settled by compromise, so compromisers cannot be chastised too heavily.)

Problem Solver. People of this type believe that conflict is natural and that conflicts can be resolved in a mutually satisfactory manner, without frustrating either side's needs. True problem solvers represent the ideal and are rare birds. In a conflict situation, problem solvers create trust by being honest and open. At the same time they are sensitive to people's feelings thus being assertive, not aggressive. In addition, they encourage relevant parties to participate in resolving the conflict and to express their true thoughts, feelings, and positions. Problem solvers seek to satisfy their own needs without frustrating the needs of others.

Which one of the five styles described above best fits you? How do you know?

agrees to do something else: "I'll bring you the output from the computer earlier if you will stop changing directions on me after the information is already set for the computer." Compromise is at the heart of negotiation, and is so central to the resolution of everyday conflict that it receives separate mention later.

Practice Gentle Confrontation

Gentle confrontation is a method of resolving conflict in which you make a candid statement of the problem facing you without hinting at any form of counterattack or aggression. Nevertheless, you lay the problem out on the table as you see it. Gentle confrontation is particularly recommended when the other party has more power than you. Here is how the technique works:

Suppose you find out that a co-worker is being assigned overtime work (at premium pay) each week. Yet he has the same experience and education as you. To your knowledge, you are considered to be an equally good worker. Using gentle confrontation, you would tactfully discuss this problem with your boss, asking if the inequity could be resolved. One statement you might make would be, "I wonder if there has been a mistake in assigning me overtime. The fellow who works next to me works overtime regularly, but I haven't had an overtime assignment in three months." Most bosses will respond positively to a logical appeal of this type. If, instead, you came storming into the office to try and resolve the inequity, your boss might have no sympathy for your problem.

Allow the Other Person to Simmer Down

Listening can be a powerful method of resolving conflict, particularly when the opposing side is fired up with anger. Today many police workers are trained in this simple technique. It is almost like letting a raging bull kick and snort until he is calmed down enough to be corralled. Similarly, if your personal or job conflict with another person is so intense that he or she is verbally violent, play it cool. Let most of your opponent's anger dissipate before you return with a counterargument. Until the other party has expressed most of his or her angry feelings, he or she won't listen to your side of the story. Have you ever heard of a raging bull or bucking bronco who listened to instructions? Once the person has ventilated his or her feelings, you can begin the process of effectively working out your problem.

Disarm the Opposition

The armament your criticizer has is valid negative criticism of you. The criticizer is figuratively clobbering you with knowledge of what you did wrong. If you deny that you have made a mistake, the criticism intensifies. A simple technique has been developed to help you deal with this type of manipulative criticism. **Disarm the opposition** is a method of conflict resolution in which you disarm the criticizer by agreeing with his or her criticism of you. The technique assumes that you have done something wrong.

Disarm the opposition capitalizes on the same principle that children often use in handling conflict or potential conflict with their par-

ents. A child might say, "I spilled my drink on the sofa by mistake. Go ahead and beat me. I deserve it." Disarm the opposition works more effectively than counterattacking a person with whom you are in conflict.

Agreeing with criticism made of you by a superior is effective because by doing so you are then in a position to ask for that superior's help in improving your performance. Most managers realize that it is their responsibility to help employees overcome problems, not merely to criticize them. Imagine that you have been chronically late in submitting reports during the last six months. It is time for a performance review and you know you will be reprimanded for your tardiness. You also hope that your boss will not downgrade all other aspects of your performance because of your tardy reports. Here is how disarming the situation would work in this situation:

YOUR BOSS: Have a seat. It's time for your performance review and we have a lot to talk about. I'm concerned about some things.

YOU: So am I. It appears that I'm having a difficult time getting my reports in on time. I wonder if I'm being a perfectionist. Do you have any suggestions?

YOUR BOSS: I like your attitude. I think you can improve in getting your reports in on time. Maybe you are trying to make your reports perfect before you turn them in. Try not to figure out everything to four decimal places. We need thoroughness around here, but we don't want to overdo it.

Use the DESC Scripts

Disarm the opposition is a technique of assertiveness training, and so is the technique called DESC Scripts. DESC stands for Describe, Express, Specify, and Consequences.

> DESCRIBE. You begin your script by factually describing the behavior that is troubling you, such as "Twice this week you criticized me when we were in front of friends."
>
> EXPRESS. Express your feelings about this behavior: "This makes me feel humiliated and embarrassed. I'm also concerned that other people will think we have a bad relationship."
>
> SPECIFY. Request a different, specific behavior: "I want you to stop criticizing me in front of others. If you must criticize me, do it when we are alone."
>
> CONSEQUENCES. Specify what the reward will be if the person changes his or her behavior. You might also specify what your punishment will be if the person does not change: "If you stop criticizing me in public, I'll be more willing to go places, sailing and camping with you." Or, "If you criticize me in public once more, I'll refuse to go camping or sailing with you."[8]

To make these scripts effective, write them out ahead of time and rehearse them in front of a mirror. After doing this a few times, you will become adept at making up these scripts on the spot.

Appeal to a Third Party

Now and then you may be placed in a conflict situation in which the other party either holds most of the power or simply won't budge. Perhaps you have tried techniques such as gentle confrontation or disarming the opposition, yet you cannot resolve your conflict. In these situations you may have to enlist the help of a third party with power—more power than you or your adversary has. Among such third parties are your common boss, union stewards, personnel managers, or a highly placed relative in your company. Taking your opponent to court is another application of the third party technique.

In some situations, just implying that you will bring in a third party to help resolve the conflict situation is sufficient for you to gain advantage. One woman felt she was repeatedly passed over for promotion because of her gender. She hinted that if she were not given fairer consideration she would speak to the Equal Employment Opportunity Commission (EEOC). She was given a small promotion shortly thereafter.

Do Not Overemphasize Winning

Too many people overvalue winning when facing a conflict. Public relations executive Henry Rogers observes, "You may lose more when you win than you lose when you lose." If keeping a good working relationship with another person is important, it may be necessary to sacrifice a few arguments. A good relationship between co-workers, friends, or spouses is damaged when one person tries to win every dispute. To take this approach of winning the war, not just the battle, Rogers advises that these questions be kept in mind:

> How important is my relationship with this person?
> How truly important is the issue we are discussing? Is it one of my priorities?
> How much am I going to gain and what am I going to get out of it if I "win" this battle?
> How much am I going to "lose" if I lose this battle?[9]

When you consider these four questions, you will probably decide not to bother arguing in most instances. Do you agree with Rogers that winning isn't everything?

The role plays at the end of this chapter give you a chance to practice some of the techniques of conflict resolution we just discussed.

NEGOTIATING AND BARGAINING YOUR WAY OUT OF CONFLICT

Another way of defining conflicts is to say they are situations calling for **negotiation** or bargaining. When you are trying to negotiate a fair price for a used automobile, you are also trying to resolve a conflict. At first the demands of both parties seem incompatible: The asking price is $5,500; your offering price is $4,200. After haggling a while (a form of negotiation), you will probably reach a price that is satisfactory to both sides. Negotiating and bargaining might then be considered a general strategy for resolving conflict. Learning to become a good negotiator takes time. Following are some strategies for negotiation, or tips that might be used in conjunction with ideas already described in this chapter.[10]

Allow Room for Negotiation

The basic strategy of negotiation is to begin with a demand that allows you room for compromise and concession. Anyone who has ever negotiated the price of an automobile, bicycle, house, or used furniture recognizes this vital strategy. If you are a buyer, begin with a low bid. (You say, "I'll give you $35 for that painting" when you are prepared to pay $70.) If you are the seller, begin with a high demand. (You say, "You can have this painting for $100," when you are ready to sell it for as low as $70.) As negotiations proceed, the two of you will probably arrive at a mutually satisfactory price. This negotiating strategy can also be used for such purposes as obtaining a higher starting salary, or dividing property after a divorce or legal separation.

Begin with a Plausible Demand or Offer

Common sense propels many negotiators to allow *too much* room for negotiation. They begin negotiations by asking way beyond what they expect to receive, or offering far less than they expect to give. As a result of these implausible demands, the other side may become hostile, antagonistic, or walk away from the negotiations. Assume you spotted a VCR in a retail store that you really wanted. The asking price was $298.95. In an attempt to negotiate the price, you offered the store manager $98.95 for the VCR. Most likely the store owner would move on to the next customer. However, if you began with a plausible offer such as $240, the store manager would take you seriously.

Raise Your Level of Expectation

Set a high demand for yourself in resolving conflict, stick firmly to your demands, and you will fare well. People who set low goals for themselves in a negotiating or bargaining session do not fare as well. Part of the underlying psychology is that by setting such high goals (but not preposterous ones) for yourself, you project an air of self-confidence. And the other side is usually impressed by a self-confident individual.

Make Small Concessions Gradually

This strategy has been described as the soft approach to bargaining. Research suggests that making steady concessions leads to more mutually satisfactory agreements in most situations. Gradually you concede little things to the other side. ("Okay, if you agree to let me move in with you folks, I'll bring along my new set of table lamps.")

The hard-line approach to bargaining is to make your total concession early in the negotiation and grant no further concession. ("If you folks agree to have me as your third roommate I'll bring along my wall component, my portable color TV, and my new set of table lamps. I have nothing else to offer.")

Reveal All the Money You Have to Deal With

"What's the nicest set of snow tires you can sell me for $125. That's all the money I have in my budget for snow tires." The potential purchaser of snow tires who made this statement will probably return home with a set of tires well worth $125. So effective is this negotiating technique that the federal government uses it to encourage vendors to redesign their proposal to make the cost fit the government money available for the purchase.

Revealing the full amount of money you have allocated for the purchase has another built-in advantage. It usually does not bring about hostility from the other side. You are only asking the other side if they might be able to accommodate you for the funds you have available. No hard feelings will surface on either side if they are unable to accommodate you.

Use Deadlines

Giving the other side a deadline is often helpful in winning a negotiation. Deadlines often force people into action. Among these effective deadlines are "No more tickets will be sold for this concert after September 14," or "Have your job application in by May 20." Here are examples of types of deadlines you might be able to impose in order to gain advantage in your negotiation:

> "Will I be receiving a promotion from associate programmer to programmer by December 31? If not, I will feel impelled to act on this job offer from another company. It has become a matter of pride."

> "After June 30, the price of all goods in our catalog will be going up by 15

percent. If you make your purchase before June 30, I can guarantee you the old price."

Give Yourself Time to Think

A hasty decision made while negotiating is often a poor one. Although it may seem that you are pressed to make a fast decision, there are usually several legitimate stalling tactics available. Suppose the person you are seeing says, "Give me your answer by tomorrow. We either get married before the year is out or the relationship is off." You might point out that you would like at least two weeks to make a decision that will obviously affect the rest of your life. Or you might ask, "Why would our marriage be any less valuable if we decided to get married a couple of years from now?"

Maintain Emotional Control

A good general rule for success in business is to be cool under pressure. Negotiating sessions are a source of pressure in which this rule is particularly applicable. You might pound the table or speak loudly to demonstrate enthusiasm and sincerity, but try to avoid becoming so emotional that you make an irrational decision. Suppose you run a lawn care business as a supplement to school or full-time employment. An estate owner that you are negotiating with makes you such a low offer that you do not want to take on the business. You are so insulted by the low bid that you shout indignantly, "Nobody can insult me like that and get away with it. Go find somebody else to do your job." It would have been preferable to retain emotional control and negotiate for a higher price for your services.

Play Hard to Get

A commonsense negotiating strategy is to make it appear that you will not readily grant concessions to the other side or immediately accept their offer. The overeager job applicant may meet with less success than the applicant who is somewhat reticent. To say, "I might be interested if the conditions are right," is a more effective tactic than, "Please let me have the job. I can begin this afternoon.

Make a Last and Final Offer

In many circumstances, presenting a final offer will break a deadlock. You might frame your message something like this, "All I can possibly pay for your guitar is $250. You have my number. Call me when it is available at that price." Sometimes the strategy will be countered by a last and final offer from the other side: "Thanks for your interest. My absolute minimum price for this guitar is $300. Call us if that should seem OK to you." One of you will probably give in and accept the other person's last and final offer.

Allow for Face Saving

We have saved one of the most important negotiating and conflict resolution strategies for last. Negotiating does not mean that you should try to squash the other side. You try to create circumstances that will enable you to continue working with that person if it is necessary. People prefer to avoid looking weak, foolish, or incompetent during negotiation or when the process is completed. If you do not give your opponent an opportunity to save face, you will probably create a long-term enemy. A unique example of face saving occurred between a tenant and his landlords:

> Parker rented a small upstairs apartment in a large private home. The owners of the building planned to be away one Memorial Day weekend. Parker took the occasion to throw a party for his friends in his apartment. Somehow things got out of control and substantial damage was done throughout the building, which included broken windows, handrail, and porch furniture. When the owners returned they were horrified. Parker wanted to make amends because apartments were in scarce supply in this particular town.
>
> Since Parker had been a good tenant up to that point, the owners were willing to negotiate with him about which items needed repair and replacement. Parker and the owners worked over an hour on a settlement plan. It involved a combination of repairing and replacing damaged items. At the end of the session the owners said to Parker, "You really don't have to replace that porch couch that you finished off. We had planned to buy one soon anyway. If you complete the other chores we have agreed upon, you will have more than compensated us for the damages."
>
> This face-saving maneuver on the landlord's part, allowed Parker to live comfortably and peacefully in his apartment.

SEXUAL HARASSMENT: A SPECIAL KIND OF JOB CONFLICT

Sexual harassment is any unwanted attention of a sexual nature from someone in the workplace that creates discomfort or interferes with the job.[11] It includes such actions as:

> Telling sexually oriented jokes to people who do not want to hear such jokes
> Sex-oriented verbal "kidding" or abuse

Subtle pressure for sexual activity

Physical contact such as patting, pinching, or constant brushing against another's body

Demands for sexual favors, accompanied by implied or overt promises of preferential treatment or threats concerning an individual's employment status

Conflict results from sexual harassment because the harasser and the victim have incompatible motives. The harasser wants the victim (or potential victim) to submit to certain demands, while the victim wants to avoid such involvement. The potential victim may also suffer from a conflict in values. He or she says, "I want to get ahead, but submitting to this person's demands would be morally wrong."

Legal Aspects of Sexual Harassment

According to the Equal Employment Opportunity Commission (EEOC) of the United States government, there are two types of sexual harassment. These two types encompass the definition of sexual harassment presented above:[12]

1. Superior-subordinate relationships where the employee suffers a job loss or other unfavorable employment action for refusing the sexual advances of a superior.

2. An offensive or hostile work environment where no tangible employment loss is directly involved, but verbal or physical conduct of a sexual nature unreasonably interferes with an employee's worth or performance.

Sexual harassment is considered to be a form of job discrimination and therefore illegal under Title VII of the Civil Rights Act. It is discriminatory for at least two reasons. For one, if a subordinate submits to the boss's sexual demands, that subordinate is likely to be treated more favorably than other subordinates who are not involved with the boss. Another problem is that the boss is usually picking on members of one only sex—and therefore discriminating.

Since sexual harassment is a threat to employee welfare, and illegal, most large companies have policies forbidding harassment. Therefore, if a harassed person reports the actual or potential harasser to management, the harassed person will be supported by the firm. As one executive told us, "The days of having to sleep your way to higher pay and more exciting jobs has come to a close. The law is now on the side of human dignity."

How to Handle Sexual Harassment or Its Threat

The employee who feels intimidated by sexual harassment should try to resolve the conflict through any of the methods discussed in this chapter. In the past such conflicts were almost always between female subordinates and male bosses. In recent years cases have been reported of male bosses harassing male subordinates, and female bosses harassing male subordinates. If the softer conflict resolution approaches do not work, call in a powerful third party such as the company president or the Equal Employment Opportunity Commission representative.

Exhibit 9–3 presents additional information about handling actual or potential sexual harassment, and how it may sometimes be prevented.

EXHIBIT 9–3   HOW TO HANDLE OR PREVENT SEXUAL HARASSMENT

The potential or actual victim of sexual harassment is advised to use the methods and tactics described below to deal with the problem.

Formal Complaint Procedure

Organizations that have formal policies against sexual harassment typically use a complaint procedure that follows this format:

Whenever an employee believes that he or she has encountered sexual harassment, or if an employee is suspected to be the perpetrator of sexual harassment, the complainant should:[13]

Report the incident to his or her immediate superior (if that person is not the harasser) or to the next higher level of management if the supervisor *is* the harasser. The supervisor contacted is responsible for contacting the Affirmative Action officer immediately regarding each complaint.

The Affirmative Action officer will explain the investigative procedures (both informal and formal inquiries) to the complainant and any supervisor involved. All matters will be kept strictly confidential including private conversations with all parties.

Dealing with the Problem on Your Own

The easiest way to deal with sexual harassment is to nip it in the bud. The first time it happens, respond with a statement of this type: "I won't tolerate this kind of talk." "I dislike sexually oriented jokes." "Keep your hands off me."

Tell the actual or potential harasser, "You're practicing sexual harassment. If you don't stop I'm going to exercise my right to report you to management." Similarly, "I think I heard you right. Would you like to accompany me to the boss's office and repeat what you said to me?"

Choosing a Conflict Resolution or Negotiating Tactic

How do you know which strategy to pick for any given problem? The best answer is consider both your personal style and the situation. With respect to your personal style, pick a conflict resolution or negotiating strategy that you think you would feel comfortable using. One person might say, "I like gentle confrontation because I'm an open and up-front kind of person." Another person might say, "I'll avoid disarming the opposition for now. I don't yet have enough finesse to carry out this technique.

In fitting the strategy to the situation, it is important to assess the gravity of the conflict or topic for negotiation. A woman might say to herself. "My boss has committed such a blatant act of sexual harassment that I had best take this up with a higher authority immediately" (appeal to a powerful third party). Sizing up your opponent can also help you choose the best strategy. If he or she appears reasonably flexible, you might try to compromise.

SUMMARY

Conflict occurs when two sets of demands, goals, or motives are incompatible. Such differences often lead to a hostile or antagonistic relationship between people. A conflict can also be considered a dispute, feud, or controversy.

Conflict is inevitable in most aspects of life. Among the reasons for the widespread presence of conflict are: (1) competition for limited resources, (2) personal differences among people, (3) dependency on other people, (4) differences in goals, (5) different methods proposed to reach a common goal, (6) unclear boundaries and tasks (definitions of who should be doing what), (7) conflict-prone jobs.

Conflict has both beneficial and detrimental consequences. Among the benefits are: the emergence of talents and abilities, constructive innovation and change, and increased unity after the conflict is settled.

Conflict can have consequences detrimental to a person's mental and physical health. It can result in wasted resources, fatigue, and self-interest.

Conflict typically leads to frustration and anger. Frustration is a blocking of need or motive satisfaction. Anger is a feeling of extreme hostility, indignation, or exasperation, thus leading to stress. Anger and frustration should be expressed but not so they lead to destructive consequences. Suggestions for handling anger include: (1) use it as an energizer; (2) use it to remind you to share your feelings with an important person; (3) express anger to yourself and then share the less destructive feelings with another person; (4) don't carry grudges.

Strategies for resolving conflicts with others include:

1. Compromise—each side gives a little

2. Gentle confrontation—lay out the problem accurately but tactfully
3. Allow the other person to simmer down
4. Disarm the opposition—agree with the criticizer
5. DESC Scripts—rehearse the technique of describe, express, specify, and mention consequences
6. Appeal to a third party
7. Do not overemphasize winning.

Negotiating or bargaining is a general strategy for resolving conflict. Most conflict is resolved through some form of negotiation. The negotiating tactics described here are:

1. Allow room for negotiation.
2. Begin with a plausible demand or offer.
3. Raise your level of expectation.
4. Make small concessions gradually.
5. Reveal all the money you have to deal with.
6. Use deadlines.
7. Give yourself time to think.
8. Maintain emotional control.
9. Play hard to get.
10. Make a last and final offer.
11. Allow for face saving (the win-win philosophy).

Sexual harassment is any unwanted attention of a sexual nature from someone in the workplace that creates discomfort or interferes with the job. Conflict results from harassment because the harasser and the victim have incompatible motives. Sexual harassment is considered to be a form of job discrimination and therefore illegal under Title VII of the Civil Rights Act. Harassment can be handled through formal complaint procedures or by dealing with it informally by oneself. The various methods of conflict resolution can also be used to deal with harassment.

In choosing a conflict resolution or negotiating strategy, consider both your personal style and the nature of the situation facing you. The situation includes such factors as the gravity of the conflict and the type of person you are facing.

QUESTIONS AND ACTIVITIES

1. Behavioral scientists have pointed out that compromise has a built-in disadvantage as an approach to resolving conflict. What do you think it is?

2. Explain why conflict usually leads to frustration.

3. How can a display of anger help you when you are negotiating?

4. Suppose you are caught speeding by a police officer. Which conflict resolution method do you think would be best suited to handling the conflict with the officer? Explain your reasoning.

5. Some people contend that if you "make enough noise" you will get your way in a dispute. How does this belief fit any of the tactics described in this chapter?

6. What are some personal characteristics a good negotiator should have?

7. Identify five situations in life that can be classified as negotiations.

8. A clerk taped a large photograph of a nude woman on the side of his desk. A co-worker demanded that he remove the photograph because it was a form of sexual harassment. Explain whether or not you agree with the co-worker.

9. What have you learned in this chapter that you will probably use in your next attempt at resolving conflict or negotiating?

10. Suppose you worry that you are becoming lethargic because there is not enough conflict in your life. What can you do to introduce the right amount of conflict into your life?

A HUMAN RELATIONS CASE PROBLEM: THE LITTER BUG

Barton, Osburne, and Jones (BOJ) is a growing financial services firm with six locations at present. At the heart of their operation are financial consultants, the individuals who sell financial products. (Financial consultants were previously referred to as stockbrokers.) These "products" include stocks, bonds, mutual funds, and real estate investment trusts. Most consultants work out of a small office shared with several other consultants. Only experienced consultants, or those with outstanding records, have their own offices.

Tracy Rivera, who has been with the firm five months, was recently assigned a new office mate, Jerry Farrel. Tracy's previous office mate left because she was promoted to senior financial consultant and assigned her own office. When Tracy first met Jerry, she was mildly concerned that he looked too disheveled to be a financial consultant. She thought, however, that once Jerry became more accustomed to serving in the brokerage business, he would appear more businesslike.

During Jerry's first week he kept cartons loaded with books and papers around and on top of his desk. His wastebasket stayed overflowing with discarded magazines, memos, and food wrappers. Similar debris was piled on the top of his desk. Tracy thought that Jerry would straighten out his work area once he was fully unpacked, and oriented to the firm.

By the end of thirty days, Jerry's work area looked even worse. As Jerry acquired more information about the business an increasing number of reports were piled on his desk. Tracy became concerned that Jerry's littered work area would detract from her clients' confidence in BOJ. Consequently, they would be less willing to invest their money through BOJ even if her desk were orderly.

When Jerry's clutter became a preoccupation of hers, Tracy decided to delicately approach him about the problem. On her way out to lunch one morning, Tracy said to Jerry, "Aren't you afraid that those magazines you have piled on top of your computer will block the vent? That could result in permanent damage to your monitor."

"Thanks for the tip," said Jerry. He then removed the magazines from the top of the computer and placed them alongside his desk.

Tracy decided to approach the problem from another direction. This time she said to Jerry, "Oh, by the way, what do you think your clients will think of all the magazines and reports you have on your desk?"

"It sounds like you think I keep too much information at my fingertips. Don't worry about it. I should be seeing actual clients next week. I know they will be very impressed to see that I read all this financial information. I want to look informed."

Tracy thought to herself as she left for lunch, "I guess my next step would be to speak to our boss about getting him to order Jerry to clean up. But if I do that, and Jerry knows I prompted the boss to get after him, Jerry and I will be in a constant battle. Yet if something isn't done, working here will be very uncomfortable for me."

Questions

1. What conflict is Tracy facing?
2. How effective is Tracy's approach to dealing with this problem?
3. Is Jerry in conflict with Tracy about the condition of his desk?
4. Would Tracy be taking the right step by going to the boss?
5. What method of conflict resolution or negotiation should Tracy use to resolve her dilemma?

A HUMAN RELATIONS ROLE PLAY: RESOLVING CONFLICT

Most of the methods of resolving conflict described in this chapter lend themselves well to role playing. Three conditions seem necessary to role-play methods of conflict resolution. First, the participants have to feel as if they are really in conflict about something. Second, they have to clearly understand the conflict resolution techniques to avoid simply having an ordinary argument. Third, the issue chosen has to have some substance. It's difficult for some people to put much energy into resolving a trivial issue. (Yet others relish fighting over minor matters.)

Following are several conflict incidents that can be role-played using the techniques of compromise, gentle confrontation, or disarm the opposition. The role players decide in advance which of these three techniques they will use to resolve the conflict. The dialogue should continue for about ten minutes. As usual, the observers will provide feedback.

A. The boss gives the subordinate a 5 percent salary increase, while the subordinate believes that at least a 10 percent increase was deserved.

B. A good friend of yours has borrowed your car with your permission. After it is returned you notice that a fender is dented and there is a new tear in the upholstery.

C. The librarian at your school tells you she is sending the bursar a note to fine you $97.50 in overdue charges for a book you have misplaced. You contend that the book can be purchased new for $14.95, and you would prefer that alternative.

Have you noticed that assertion skills as taught in AT are also very useful in resolving a conflict with another person?

REFERENCES

[1] H. Kent Baker and Philip I. Morgan, "Building a Professional Image: Handling Conflict," *Supervisory Management,* February 1986, p. 24.

[2] Ramon J. Aldag and Arthur P. Brief, *Managing Organizational Behavior* (St. Paul, MN: West Publishing Company, 1981), p. 394.

[3] Michael Unger, "Is Anger a Hazard to Your Health?" *Newsday* story syndicated May 4, 1985.

[4] "How to Buck Your Boss," *Research Institute Personal Report for the Executive,* March 1, 1986, p. 1.

[5] Karen S. Peterson, "Holding Grudges Can Hold You Back," *USA Weekend,* October 18–20, 1985, p. 28.

[6] Based on information synthesized by Aldag and Brief, *Managing Organizational Behavior,* pp. 398–400.

[7] Ibid., p. 398.

[8] Sharon Bower and Gordon Bower, *Asserting Yourself: A Practical Guide for Positive Change* (Reading, MA: Addison-Wesley, 1976), pp. 222–223.

[9] Priscilla Petty, "In An Argument, Winning May Not Be Your Most Productive Priority," Gannett News Service article syndicated September 25, 1984.

[10] Most of these tactics were originally reported in Chester L. Karass, *Give & Take: The Complete Guide to Negotiating Strategies and Tactics* (New York: Thomas Y. Crowell, 1974).

[11] Kay Bartlett, "Is Sexual Harassment in the Work Place the 1980s Glamour Cause," Associated Press story, Febuary 28, 1982.

[12] Curtiss K. Behrens, "Co-Worker Sexual Harassment: The Employer's Liability," *Personnel Journal,* May 1984, p. 12.

[13] Rochester Institute of Technology, *News & Events,* March 22, 1984, p. 4.

SOME ADDITIONAL READING

BENFIELD, CLIFFORD J.   "Problem Performers: The Third-Party Solution." *Personnel Journal,* August 1985, pp. 96–101.

DALTON, DAN R., and WILLIAM D. TODOR.   "Gender and Workplace Justice: A Field Assessment." *Personnel Psychology,* Spring 1985, pp. 133–151.

FRAYNE, COLETTE A., and HUNSAKER, PHILIP L.   "Strategies for Successful Negotiating." *Personnel,* May–June 1984, pp. 70–76.

JOHNSTON, ROBERT W.   "Negotiation Strategies: Different Strokes for Different Folks." *Personnel,* January–February, 1981, pp. 13–22.

KING, DENNIS.   "Three Cheers for Conflict." *Personnel,* January–February 1981, pp. 13–22.

RAIFFA, HOWARD.   *The Art and Science of Negotiation.* Cambridge, MA: Harvard University Press, 1983.

STIMAC, MICHELE.   "Strategies for Resolving Conflict: Their Functional and Dysfunctional Side." *Personnel,* November–December 1982, pp. 54–64.

WALL, JAMES A., JR.   *Negotiation: Theory and Practice.* Glenview, IL: Scott Foresman, 1985.

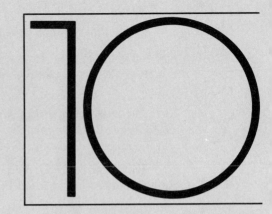

Choosing a Career and Career Switching

Learning Objectives

After studying the information and doing the exercises in this chapter you should be able to:

- Make a few tentative career choices if you haven't already selected a first career
- Appreciate the complexity of choosing a career
- Understand how jobs differ in the emphasis they place on data, persons, or things
- Identify several growth fields for the balance of the century
- Pinpoint major considerations in career switching

If you have not already chosen a career, or are beginning to tire of your present one, this chapter is especially important. If you are content with your career, this chapter can be read with the intention of learning more about that vital part of your life. What a person does for a living is one of the key influences on his or her life. Its impact rivals such things as your marital status, religion, or physical strength. Your career is also a prime source of your self-esteem and your identity.

The next time you converse with a stranger at a social gathering, notice how quickly that person informs you of his or her occupation or main career interest. If you ask "What do you do?" you will almost always get a job-related answer such as "I'm a beautician," or "I work at the assembly plant." Few people will say, "I play my VCR," or "I eat dinner with my family regularly."

A **career** is a series of related job experiences that fit into some meaningful pattern. If you have a series of odd jobs all your working life, that is hardly a career. But if each job builds carefully on the previous one, we say you are building a career. We assume that by making a sound initial choice of occupation, you will be on the first step toward building a real career. The other four chapters in this part of the book provide information to help you advance in whatever career you have chosen.

HOW MOST PEOPLE FIND A CAREER FIELD

Finding a career field that holds the promise of bringing you personal satisfaction and material rewards is usually done unsystematically. Few people are even aware that this major life choice can be done systematically. Among the more frequent ways in which people find a career to pursue are these:

1. *Influence of parent, relative, or friend:* "My aunt owned a children's clothing store, so I went into the retail business."
2. *Reading and study:* "While in high school I read a lot about airplanes, so I decided to become an air traffic controller."
3. *Natural opportunity:* "I was born into the business. Who would give up the chance to be a vice-president by the time he was 28? Our family has always been in the office supplies business."
4. *Forced opportunity:* "I had never heard about electronics until I joined the army. They told me I had aptitude for the field. I enjoyed working as an electronics technician. After the army I applied for a job with a business machines company as a field service engineer. It has worked out well."
5. *Matching yourself with a compatible person.* A novel way of finding a career is first to locate a person with whom you have similar interests.

You then choose that person's field of work for yourself, using this reasoning: "I seem to like what that person likes in most things. All things being equal, I would probably like the kind of work he or she does."

6. *Discovery through counseling and testing.* "I took an interest test in high school. My guidance counselor told me I had interests similar to those of a business manager. Not knowing what else to do I entered the field of restaurant management." (This is the most systematic of the six methods mentioned here.)

If you have not already found satisfaction using one of these or another method, it might be to your advantage to proceed systematically in finding a career.

LEARN ABOUT YOURSELF FIRST

A general strategy for making a sound career choice is to understand first the inner you, including what you have to offer. You then match that information with opportunities in the outside world. The Self-Knowledge Questionnaire presented in Chapter 1 asks many questions that are relevant for making a career choice. Almost any of the information provided by candid answers to those questions could help you make a sound career choice. Several specific illustrations are in order.

Question 9 asks, "What aspect of these jobs did I enjoy?" Suppose you answered, "Anytime I was left alone to do some figuring, or report writing I was happy. Thinking made me happy." Your answer could mean that you should search for a field in which working with ideas and data is more important than working with people or things. What about investigating laboratory work or financial analysis?

Question 1 asks, "How far have I gone in school?" If you answered, "Three years of high school," or "Four years of high school and two years of business school," you will need additional education for many fields. Among them are management, teaching, counseling, or social work.

Question 31 asks, "What gives me satisfaction in life?" Suppose you answered, "Playing with my children, going fishing, and getting involved with my friends almost every day." However good for your mental health this answer might be, it certainly does limit the level of responsibility you can aspire toward in most careers. A busy executive or professional person often comes out on the short end with respect to having ample time for family, fishing, and friends.

Some additional questions useful in clarifying the type of work you would prefer, are presented in Exhibit 10–1.

EXHIBIT 10–1   LEARNING MORE ABOUT YOURSELF

By candidly answering the questions that follow, you may be able to develop some new understanding about your career preferences. Try to write at least twenty-five words in response to each question, even if your answer is uncertain.

A.   What kind of work would make me proud?

_____

_____

B.   What would be a horrible way for me to make a living?

_____

_____

C.   How important is a high income to me? Why?

_____

_____

D.   How do I really feel about what other people think of the kind of work I do?

_____

_____

E.   What kind of work would really be fun for me to do?

_____

_____

F.   What kind of work would I be willing to do for ten consecutive years?

_____

_____

G.   What kind of work would make me smile almost every day?

_____

_____

H.   What is my attitude toward doing the same thing every workday?

_____

_____

I.   How do I really feel about being held responsible when things go wrong?

_____

_____

Your answers to these questions and the Self-knowledge Questionnaire should be kept in mind as you read the section "Twenty-four Groups of Jobs" presented later in this chapter. Another suggestion is to discuss your answers with a counselor, instructor, or good friend.

Getting Help from a Career Counselor

In choosing a career or switching careers, an excellent method of learning more about yourself in relation to the world of work is to obtain help from a professional **career counselor.** A counselor usually relies on a wide variety of tests plus an interview to assist you in making a sound career choice. It is untrue that any single test will tell you what occupation you should enter. Tests are designed to provide useful clues, not to give you definite answers. Nor is it true that a career counselor will tell you what occupation you should enter. Using tests and human judgment, the counselor assists you to become more aware of yourself and the alternatives that might suit your circumstances. This chapter emphasizes choosing a career by yourself. It is recommended, however, that you seek the help of a guidance counselor, career counselor, or counseling psychologist.

MATCHING YOUR CAREER TO YOUR LIFESTYLE

Ideally, you should pursue a career that provides you with the right balance between work, leisure, and interaction with people.[1] Some degree of compromise is usually necessary. If your preferred lifestyle was to take two-hour lunch breaks each workday, it would be difficult to attain a high level of responsibility. Executives, public relations specialists, and sales representatives who seem to spend considerable time at lunch are usually conducting business over their meal. They are not taking time out during the workday. If a cornerstone of your lifestyle is to remain in top physical and mental shape, you should probably avoid some of the high pressure careers, such as ambulance paramedic or securities sales representative. On the other hand, you would want to avoid a career that provided too little challenge.

As just hinted, the term lifestyle can refer to many different key aspects of your life. In terms of making a career choice, it is helpful to regard **lifestyle** as the pattern by which a person invests energy into work and nonwork. Being the proverbial beach bum or ski bum is one lifestyle. So is being the ninety-hour-a-week government executive.

Today, an increasing number of people at different stages in their careers are making career choices that improve their chances of leading their preferred lifestyle. The general manager of a plant in a small town makes a revealing comment about modern lifestyles: "A number of years ago we couldn't get nearly the number of skilled people we needed to work here. The people who had a choice wanted to live in an area near a big city. Now we get loads of unsolicited résumés. It seems that a lot of people want access to camping and fishing. I think they're also worried about crime and pollution in the cities."

The move toward a healthy balance between work and nonwork might also be considered part of the movement toward a higher quality of life. For some people living in a $1,300-a-month studio apartment in New York or Washington, D.C., represents a high quality of life. Such city dwellers would, of course, have to aspire toward a very high-paying occupation in order to support their preference. How will your preferred lifestyle influence your career decision making?

FINDING OCCUPATIONAL FACTS

Whether or not you have already made a career choice, you should follow a fundamental rule of plotting your career—get the facts. Few people have valid information about careers they wish to pursue. A glaring example of occupational misinformation relates to the legal field. Many young people say, "I would like to be a lawyer. I'm good at convincing people. And I know I could sway a jury." Similarly, "I want to be a paralegal assistant. I have the mind of a detective. I know I could break most of the tough cases given me to research."

In reality, the work of a lawyer or paralegal assistant includes the processing of much nonglamorous information. One example is figuring out how much money a bankrupt bakery owes to twenty-seven different suppliers. Three general sources of occupational information are printed material, spoken information, and firsthand experience. Without this information it is difficult to find a good fit between yourself and existing opportunities.

Printed Information

Few people take advantage of the voluminous information available on careers or career planning. Most libraries and bookstores are well supplied with this type of information. (See the suggested reading section of this chapter.) The most comprehensive source document of occupational information is the *Occupational Outlook Handbook,* published every two years by the U.S. Department of Labor. Each occupation listed is described in terms of (1) nature of the work, (2) places of employment, (3) training, (4) other qualifications and advancement, and (5) employment outlook. Using this handbook, one can find answers to such questions as "What do zoologists do and how much do they earn?" The Bureau of Labor Statistics also publishes the *Occupational Outlook Quarterly,* which supplements the Department of Labor's handbook with articles on current occupational developments.

Other highly useful general source books include:

Encyclopedia of Careers and Vocational Guidance
What Can I Be? A Guide to 525 Liberal Arts and Business Careers
Occupational Briefs
A Guide to Careers through College Majors

BusinessWeek's Guide to Careers is a periodical that features career information. Published every several months, it contains current information on job opportunities in business and related fields. The Job Market section of the magazine describes job opportunities in specific fields. Representative titles of these articles are "Library Management," "Air Traffic Controller," "Telemarketing," and "Restaurant Management." *BusinessWeek's Guide* also reports on working conditions and job opportunities at specific firms such as Xerox, Federal Express, and IBM.

Computer-Assisted Career Guidance

Several career guidance information systems have been developed for access by computer. The information contained in these systems is designed to help users plan their careers. Guidance information systems go one step beyond printed information because you can ask questions (interact with) the computer. For instance when you are keyed in on a specific occupation, you can ask "What is the promotion outlook?" and "What effect will technology have?"

The most widely used of these systems are *Guidance Information System,* DISCOVER, and SIGI PLUS (System for Interactive Guidance and Instruction). Hundreds of counseling centers and guidance departments use one of these software packages. Prior knowledge of computers is not necessary to use them. Here we will describe the basic version of SIGI.[2]

The purpose of SIGI is to help people seeking career information learn three things: (1) which values are important to them, (2) factual information about various occupations, and (3) how to make better career decisions. SIGI has five subsystems, each contributing to learning about occupations.

You begin with the *Values* subsystem, which rates how much you like each value such as independence and leadership. The second subsystem is *Locate,* which shows you the occupations listed in SIGI that match your values. The third subsystem, *Compare,* gives the user a chance to ask up to twenty-eight questions about the listed occupations. One such question is, "What is the income potential?"

Planning is the fourth subsystem. It provides information about the type of education and the special skills and abilities required for the occupation. Planning takes into account both interest in a particular field and an individual's willingness to prepare for the occupation in terms of education and training.

Strategy is the fifth subsystem. It helps you evaluate the advantages and disadvantages of an occupation for you in terms of rewards, risks, and values. Ideally, Strategy helps you combine reward and risk to make a sound occupational choice.

Speaking to People

An invaluable supplement to reading about occupations is to speak to people engaged in them. No matter what occupation interests you, search out a person actually employed in that kind of work. Most people welcome the opportunity to talk about themselves and the type of work they do. If you do not know anyone engaged in the career field that interests you, do some digging. A few inquiries will usually lead to a person you can contact. It is best to interview that person in his or

her actual work setting in order to obtain a sense of the working conditions people face in that field.

Remember, however, that many people will probably say that although they are very happy in their work, there are better ways to
make a living. Ask your dentist, doctor, lawyer, or plumber about his
or her field, and you will likely be told, "Don't believe all those stories
about people in this field being wealthy. We work long and hard for our
money. And there's always the problem of people not paying their
bills. I don't recommend that you enter this field."

Suppose you want to learn about the field of occupational safety
and health. Yet you do not know anyone who knows any person doing

this kind of work. Try the cold-canvas method. Call one or two large
companies and ask to speak to someone in the occupational health and
safety department. When you reach that department, indicate that you
are trying to make a sound career choice and then proceed with your
inquiry. The success ratio of this approach is remarkably high.

Firsthand Experience

One career manual suggests that if you really want to explore an
occupation, you should get some firsthand experience in that occupa-

tion.[3] Part-time and temporary employment is particularly useful. One young man who is a self-employed landscape consultant first tried out the field by working two summers for an established business. Some schools offer cooperative, or work-study, programs. However modest your cooperative employment, it can provide you with much valuable information. For instance, it is surprisingly helpful to observe whether or not people engaged in that type of work ever smile or laugh. If not, the work might be intense and dreary.

Temporary work in a field you might wish to enter could lead to a job offer. It is standard practice for employers to use part-time and temporary jobs as a way of screening prospective employees. A young woman who is now a sales representative for a well-known business corporation presents this anecdote: "I took the most menial clerical position in the marketing department. My supervisor told her boss that I was a good worker. Somebody who would give a fair shake to the company. Now I'm making more money and having more fun than I thought possible at my age."

CHOOSING A GROWTH OCCUPATION AND FIELD

An advantageous way of choosing a career is to pursue an occupation that appears to have growth potential. The career seeker searches for a match between his or her capabilities and interests, and a growth occupation in a growth field. For instance, a person who likes dealing directly with people and computers might choose a career as a travel agent. The reasoning here is that travel agents deal with people and have a computer at hand to book travel and hotel reservations. Also, the travel agency business is a growth field.

Be aware that every position in a growth field is not a growth occupation. For instance, there is a decreasing demand for middle managers in both growth and declining fields. You can also be in a growth occupation in a declining field. The best example is robotics work. Although manufacturing is declining in the United States and Canada, robotics specialists (including engineers and repair workers) are in heavy demand.

How do I identify growth fields? One way is to use the career-information sources described above. For example, *BusinessWeek's Guide to Careers* periodically publishes surveys about expanding fields and occupations. Exhibits 10–2 and 10–3 summarize information from such surveys. Exhibit 10–2 lists growth occupations that already exist, while Exhibit 10–3 lists many occupations that do not yet exist. Ca-

EXHIBIT 10–2   GOOD JOB OPPORTUNITIES FOR THE NEXT TEN YEARS

Technical, Semiprofessional, and Professional Jobs

Business Workers
- Accountant and auditor
- Advertising specialist
- Architect
- Bank officer
- Personnel (human resources) specialist
- Stocks, bonds, and financial services sales rep
- Manufacturer's representative
- Telemarketing specialist
- Real estate agent, broker
- Retail store buyer
- Purchasing agent, buyer (industrial company)

Computer Specialists
- Operator
- Programmer
- Service and repair technician
- Systems analyst
- Robotics engineer, technician, service technician
- Computer-aided manufacturing technician

Engineering
- Civil engineer
- Electronic and electrical engineer, technician
- Mechanical engineer
- Industrial engineer
- Laser engineer and technician
- Hazardous waste technician

Personal and Professional Services
- Lawyer
- Dietician
- Travel agent
- Flight attendant
- Child-care worker
- Energy auditor
- Energy conservation technician
- Counseling psychologist
- Housing rehabilitation technician
- Geriatric social worker
- High school teacher
- Urban planner

Secretarial, Clerical
- Medical secretary
- Legal secretary, paralegal assistant
- Office automation equipment operator

Health-Care Providers
- Dental assistant
- Dental hygienist
- Registered nurse
- Practical nurse, nurse's aide
- Physician assistant
- CAT scan technician
- Physical therapist

Managerial Jobs

Sales
- National account manager
- Brand manager (person who oversees a particular product such as a Conair hair dryer)
- International sales coordinator

Finance
- Security investments manager
- General accounting
- Financial planning director
- Bank manager
- Chief internal auditor

Personnel and Human Resources
- Management training director
- Personnel/human resources manager
- Labor relations director
- Employee training and development manager

Manufacturing
- Plant manager
- Quality assurance manager
- Materials handling manager (includes purchasing)
- Purchasing manager

Computer and Information Systems
- Service and repair manager
- Management information systems director
- Computer operations supervisor
- Robotics supervisor

Engineering and Research
- Research and development director
- Corporate construction director

Protective and Service
  Firefighter
  Police and detective
  Correction officer, jailer

Chief industrial engineer
Public Service
  City manager
  Urban planning manager

SOURCES: John Stodden, "Jobs With a Future," *BusinessWeek's Guide to Careers How to Get a Job Guide,* 1986 edition, p. 40; Otis Port, "Where the Jobs Will Be," *BusinessWeek's Guide to Careers,* Spring/Summer, 1985, p. 62; Steven S. Ross, "The 12 Top Money-Making Careers of the '80s," *BusinessWeek's Guide to Careers,* Spring 1983, p. 9.

EXHIBIT 10–3   A SAMPLE OF EMERGING CAREERS FOR THE TWENTY-FIRST CENTURY

PROFESSIONAL

Cable TV auditor
Career counselor
Career change counselor
Certified alcohol counselor
Certified financial planner
Child advocate
Communications specialist
Computer designer
Computer scientist
Computer security specialist
Computer systems analyst
Data base designer
Data base engineer
Divorce mediator
Documentation specialist
Ecologist
EDP auditor
Energy auditor
Engineering geologist
Environmental engineer
Ethicist
Family mediator
Forecaster
Forensic scientist
Fusion engineer
Gene splicing worker
Geneticist
Genetic counselor
Geriatric nurse
Health physicist
Hibernation specialist
Human services expert
Image consultant

Information broker
Information research scientist
Lead system analyst
Licensed therapeutic recreation specialist
Marine geologist
Mineral economist
Molecular biologist
Neutrino astronomer
Ombudsman
Oncology nutritionist
Phobia therapist
Planetary engineer
Planetary scientist
Professional ethnicist
Public affairs psychologist
Robot engineer
Robotic scientist
Security engineer
Selenologist
Sex therapist
Software writer
Solar architect
Solar designer
Solar energy consultant
Space colonist
Space botanist
Sports psychologist
Strategic planner
Thanatologist
Theoretical chemist
Underwater archeologist
Volcanologist
Wind prospector

PARAPROFESSIONAL

Exercise technician
Family planning and midwife
Home health aide
Hotline counselor
Lawyer's aide
Library aide

Licensed psychiatric technician
Medical aide
Sex counselor
Social work aide
Teacher's aide
Veterinary aide

MANAGERIAL AND SUPERVISORY

Complaints manager
Data base administrator
Data base manager
Director of human resources
Director of software developments
EDP audit systems manager
Employee relocation services director
Executive VIP for international product
  planning
Halfway house manager
Information coordinator
Information manager

International sales and marketing
  manager
International systems director
New product manager
Site selector specialist
Space launch director
Systems analysis manager
Technical services manager
Telecommunications marketing director
Transplant coordinator
Underwater hotel, pavilion or
  observatory director

SALES

Cable TV salesperson
Computer salesperson
Digital radiography sales representative
Distributor of new business equipment
Phonovision salesperson
Robot salesperson

Salesperson for talking encyclopedias
Sales trainer
Software salesperson
Telecommunication salesperson
Telephone salesperson

SMALL BUSINESS

Aquaculture
Artist (graphic)
Book club sales
Catering and fast food
Child daycare service
Computer games developer
Consultant
Electric car service station
Financial consultant
Financial planner
Fish farmer
Freelance writer
Home correspondence courses
Information salesperson
Inventor

Manufacturer of talking signs
Music store
New health foods
Orthotist
Picture framer
Plant and pet service
Publishing
Self-employment
Shrimp and trout fish farming
Specialized food services
Telephone answering service
Training services
Truffle nursery
Tutor
Videodating services

SKILLED

Asteroid miner
Bioconversion technologist
Biomedical technician
Bionic medical technician
Computer assisted design (CAD)
  technician
Computer assisted manufacturing (CAM)
  specialist
Computer axial tomographer (CAT)
  technologist
Computer programmer
Computer service technician
Cryogenic technician
Cyborg technician
Diagnostic medical sonographer
Dialysis technician
Exotic welder
Fiber optic technician
Hazardous waste technician
Hibernation technician

Holographic inspection specialist
House husband and house wife
Industrial robot technician
Laser technician
Lunar miner
Materials utilization technician
Mechanic for hydrogen powered
  automobiles
Medicine aid technician
Microbiological mining technician
Nuclear fuel technician
Nuclear reactor technician
Positron emission tomograph (PET)
  technician
Rehabilitation housing technician
Space mechanic
Solar engineering technician
Telecommunications technician
Underwater culture technician

SEMISKILLED

Battery technician
Bio-gas technician
Computer graphics assistant
Paramedics
Courier

UNSKILLED

Home companion
House pet and plant sitter
TV monitor (guard)

SOURCE: S. Norman Fiengold, "Tracking New Career Categories Will Become a Preoccupation for Job Seekers and Managers," *Personnel Administrator*, December 1983, p. 90.

reer advancement is likely to be more rapid in the occupations listed in these two exhibits than in stable or declining occupations such as steel-foundry supervisor.

DATA, PEOPLE, OR THINGS?

A helpful way of looking at the world of work is to characterize jobs according to the amount of time you would devote to working with data (or ideas), people, or things.[4] Your responses to the Self-knowledge Questionnaire plus your intuition should help you determine your preference. Even more important is to understand your preference for the right balance among these three elements. Despite how much you might enjoy working with people, it is difficult to avoid working with data in any responsible job today.

One or two examples will illustrate this critical aspect of understanding jobs and careers. Computer programmers and statisticians have a high involvement with data and a low involvement with people and things. In contrast, machine operators and truck drivers have a high involvement with things and a low involvement with data and people. How would you rate an airplane pilot on these three dimensions?

Most jobs involve a combination of dealing with data, people, and things. It is usually a question of the relative proportion of each dimension. Managers, for example, have high involvement with data and people and a low involvement with things. Registered nurses have an average involvement with all three.

LEVELS OF RESPONSIBILITY

Another useful way of understanding occupations, and therefore helping to plan your career, is to think about the level of responsibility you are seeking. In general, the higher the level, the more education is required, and the harder you will have to work. But, the higher the level, the more the pay and personal satisfaction. Thus, if work is important to you, you will find greater fulfillment in performing high-level work. Work can be conveniently and logically divided into the following six levels.[5]

1. *Unskilled work* is simple and routine, requiring little independent decision making or creativity. Beginners in the work force are usually assigned such jobs. Among them are floor sweeper, dishwashing machine attendant, and delivery person.

2. *Semiskilled jobs* require some skill and knowledge or a high degree of manual skill in a limited number of tasks. A general clerk in an office or a drill press operator in a factory fits here.

3. *Skilled occupations* require specialized skills, expert knowledge, and sound judgment in carrying out assigned tasks. Included here would be tool-and-die maker, administrative assistant, or X-ray machine technician.

4. *Semiprofessional and managerial positions* involve tasks requiring independent judgment and the making of nonprogrammed decisions. An insurance claims adjuster or a first level supervisor both fit this category.

5. *Professional positions* require considerable knowledge, judgment, and information that is carried from job to job. Computer scientists, accountants, and engineers fit here. Debate often exists as to whether a given occupation at this level belongs in the next higher category.

6. *Higher professional and managerial positions* require a high level of knowledge, judgment, and ability to work independently. Physicians, psychologists, research scientists, and business executives fit here. If you want to earn a six-figure income you will probably need to reach this occupational level. People at lesser occupational levels reach six figure incomes occasionally. Among them are *some* entertainers, professional athletes, and sales representatives.

The higher the occupational level, the higher the amount of formal education required. Level six usually requires a degree beyond a bachelor's degree such as an M.D., Ph.D., or M.B.A. Level 5 usually requires a college degree. Levels 3 and 4 usually demand high school, college, or other specialized training. Levels 1 and 2 can be attained with on-the-job training, or no training at all in many instances.

You Need to Be Realistic

In planning a career, you must realize that there are proportionally fewer positions available as you move up the occupational ladder. Each firm needs only a handful of top executives, and middle-manager jobs are becoming scarcer. In order to speed up decision making and decrease costs, many middle-manager positions have been eliminated. As a result, supervisors (first-level) managers are often given more responsibility.

Another aspect of realism in career planning is awareness that not everybody can earn an above-average income. Furthermore, many newcomers to the job market will not earn as much as their counterparts of the past. The economy is now generating fewer and fewer permanent jobs that pay middle-class wages, while churning out more and more lower-wage jobs.[6] The reason is that service jobs, such as food service and child-care work, pay less than manufacturing jobs. A dominant trend in our economy is a decline in domestic manufacturing and an increase in services.

Each person starting a first, or later career should ponder this question: At what point will my demand for occupational status coincide with the demand for people of my talents and education? Or, "Considering who I am and what I can do, how low on the occupational ladder can I rest and still be happy?" Whoever can answer these questions will be on the road to job satisfaction.

TWENTY-FOUR GROUPS OF JOBS

The U.S. Department of Labor estimates that there are about 24,000 different kinds of jobs. It is not surprising, therefore, that many different methods have been used to organize these jobs into manageable categories. These categories or job groups are useful in familiarizing people with the world of work and careers. The developers of the Ohio Vocational Interest Survey (OVIS) have divided jobs into twenty-four groups.[7] The jobs in each group have relatively similar ratings for the emphasis they place on data, people, and things. If you take the OVIS, you will find out which of these twenty-four job groups are most closely related to your occupational interests. For a preliminary survey of your interest in these groups, turn to Exhibit 10–4.

EXHIBIT 10–4   CHOOSING A CAREER FOR MYSELF

Assume that right now you have to narrow down your career choices to the five most probable job groups. From the list below, choose the five fields that seem the most attractive to you. For information about these job groups, refer to the chapter appendix. The most attractive will be ranked, 1; the next most attractive will be ranked 2; and so on. As part of your decision making, include reality factors such as your intended level of education, and your talents (as best you can judge them).

Job Group (Fields)	*Ranks (1 to 5)*
1. Manual work	——
2. Machine work	——
3. Personal services	——
4. Caring for people or animals	——
5. Clerical work	——
6. Inspecting and testing	——
7. Crafts and precise operations	——
8. Customer services	——
9. Nursing and related technical services	——
10. Skilled personal service	——
11. Training	——
12. Literary	——
13. Numerical	——
14. Appraisal	——
15. Agriculture	——
16. Applied technology	——
17. Promotion and communication	——
18. Management and supervision	——
19. Artistic	——
20. Sales representative	——
21. Music	——

22. Entertainment and performing arts   ____
23. Teaching, counseling, and social work   ____
24. Medical   ____

On a separate sheet of paper jot down the reasons you chose each of the five fields. For example, one young woman wrote, "Sales representative is for me. All my life people have told me I can sell anybody anything. I also enjoy solving problems. So it sounds like a natural. I'm also sold on the idea of unlimited income." Perhaps you can discuss your choices with a friend, relative, teacher, or counselor.

The appendix to this chapter summarizes these twenty-four job groups along with their rating on data-people-things. These ratings are described as high (2), average (1), or low (0). The rating is placed next to the job group title—for example, Literary (200). This means high on data, and low on people and things. Additional brief information is presented about each job group that may prove helpful for career decision making. As you read each job group, relate it to yourself. A question you should always ask is, "Would I find satisfaction doing this kind of work?"

CAREER SWITCHING

It is becoming increasingly common for people to change careers (enter a new field) after achieving success in another. One such person held a prestigious government job, then resigned to open a grocery store. Her explanation was, "My job in Washington was intellectually exciting and stimulating but it wasn't me at all." At age thirty she bought a grocery store on Long Island. After three years the little store blossomed into an impressive gourmet food and catering business.

She further explains: "I was sitting at my desk in Washington trying to figure out what I was going to do when I grew up and I came across an ad for this business for sale in Westhampton. I drove up that weekend, looked it over and said I'd take it."[8] At last report, she works from 7 A.M. to midnight six days a week from May through September. Her husband, who works in New York City, joins her on weekends. During the winter, when she moves back to the city, she continues the catering part of her business.

People switch careers for many valid reasons, including growing discontent with their present careers, or the desire to do something more exciting with their lives. (Exhibit 10–5 illustrates one reason for a career switch and how the switch was handled.) Many people who

EXHIBIT 10–5   VERETTA MAKES AN EARLY CAREER SWITCH

As a teenager Veretta invested much time and energy in photography as a hobby. Recognizing that few people can make a living as photographers, she chose to pursue a career in biomedical photography. After successfully completing a degree in this field, Veretta found employment. Three years later she decided to make a career switch. Her reasoning followed this line:

"Biomedical photography is more of a laboratory job than one dealing with people. I think the real reason I enjoy photography is that it puts me in contact with people. I enjoy doing some technical work, but I dislike the total emphasis. Besides, a job in biomedical photography gives me the feeling of being confined in one place. It would be very difficult to switch jobs.

"I would like to do something else for a living that's at a comparable level to my present job, but I don't want to go through an extensive, costly period of retraining. But no specific field comes to mind."

At the advice of her former technical school counselor, Veretta decided to scan the entire *Occupational Handbook* to search for a new field that might capture her interest. On the basis of her genuine desire to help people and her positive attitudes toward the medical field, Veretta concentrated on medical service occupations. One hour into the project, she hit upon the occupation of audiometrist.

Immediately Veretta conjured up images of herself administering hearing tests to private patients in a busy, aesthetically pleasing private medical office. After reading several articles about audiometry and glancing through one textbook on the subject, she tried to find out firsthand what a typical workweek is like for an audiometrist.

Veretta arranged to speak to Rick, an audiometrist who worked in the office of an ear, nose, and throat specialist she had visited within the previous year. Rick enlisted the help of Wilma, another audiometrist in the same office. As Veretta learned more about audiometry, she became more intrigued. Particularly pleasing to her was the fact that she would not have to go through an extensive training program to work as an audiometrist. Her two years of technical training combined with a few courses and some on-the-job training were all that were required to qualify as an audiometrist in the state where she lived.

Veretta had little difficulty finding employment in her new field as an audiometrist. Working in a large group practice, Veretta seems to have found a satisfying career.

Faced with dissatisfaction in her original field, Veretta implemented successfully two important methods of selecting a field: gathering valid occupational information and speaking to knowledgeable people. Consulting with the counselor from her school might even be considered her most basic strategy. The approaches Veretta took can be applied to finding a first, second, or later career.

make a career change later switch back to their original careers. Sometimes the change is not carefully thought through. It is sufficient for our purposes here to make three passing suggestions about finding a second (or beyond) career: be thorough, build a new career gradually, and consider self-employment.

Be Thorough

When you feel it is necessary to find a new career, go through the same kind of thinking and planning that is recommended for finding a first career. Everything said in this chapter about choosing a first career is also relevant for choosing a later career. The advantage for the career switcher, however, is that the experienced person often has a better understanding of the type of work he or she does not want to do. As a licensed practical nurse commented, "I have to find a new line of work. My back can't take lifting people anymore. From now on, the only people I want to touch are those close to me. I've also had it with taking care of the physical problems of strangers."

Build a New Career Gradually

Few people are able to leave one career abruptly and step into another. For most people who switch careers successfully, the switch is more of a transition than an abrupt change. Business executives who become college professors are a case in point. During the last two decades a number of successful people in business and government have been able to find faculty or administrative positions for themselves at universities and colleges. Most of these career switchers taught courses part-time for several years in order to qualify for a full-time position.

Similarly, many people who enter real estate selling as a full-time occupation have been devoting weekends and evenings to this type of work for many years. The principle remains the same: If you find a part-time occupation satisfying and rewarding, you might consider expanding it into a full-time career. A valid illustration of this principle is the experience of Eric, a former industrial buyer. He summarized his success story:

> I worked for the company as a buyer for close to ten years. No complaints. I had received three promotions and I was earning a good living. But somehow it wasn't enough for me. I wanted a little more excitement out of life than the company was providing me. A neighbor of mine owned a thriving, but small, car dealership. As we got to talking, he sensed that my big company experience might help his dealership. So I began to help him out a little part-time. I helped him get some efficient new office procedures going. Then I sketched out a program of computerizing his car and parts inventory. Soon I got caught up in the

excitement of making a major impact on an employer. Since the company had 85,000 employees, it was hard for me to believe that I was making a major impact. The punch line is that I became vice-president of administration at the dealership. I took a 20 per cent reduction in pay, but I would be participating in the profits of the dealership. If I helped them save money, I would be getting a piece of the action.

Consider Self-employment

A major reason that many employees consider a new career is that they crave more independence. For those people a logical path to self-fulfillment is **self-employment.** A typical pattern is for a future entrepreneur (a person who founds and operates an innovative type of business) to first gain business experience as an employee. Soon that person develops an idea of the type of self-employment that would be sensible for him or her.

Despite all the glamor of self-employment, it has two well-documented problems. For one, self-employed people work very hard and long; work weeks of sixty, eighty, or even one hundred hours are not uncommon. Second, about 50 percent of new businesses fail the first year. If you are skeptical, walk through a few shopping malls. Take note of the small businesses there, and check back twelve months later. Or simply go through the yellow pages, calling a number of small businesses at random. You will receive many recorded messages saying "Sorry, the number you have dialed is no longer in service."

One indication of the allure of self-employment is reflected by the American Entrepreneurs Association (AEA).[9] The basic business of this association is to sell manuals to show you how to set up your own business. Our purpose in mentioning AEA is to illustrate the world of possibilities in self-employment. A sampling of the association's offerings in several categories is presented in Exhibit 10–6.

EXHIBIT 10–6   A SAMPLING OF OPPORTUNITIES FOR SELF-EMPLOYMENT, AS SUGGESTED BY THE AMERICAN ENTREPRENEURS ASSOCIATION

UNUSUAL-TYPE BUSINESSES	AUTOMOTIVE-TYPE BUSINESSES
Art-show promoting	Auto painting shop
Bartender trade school	Auto valet parking
Firewood dealer	Propane conversion center
Gold mining	Sheepskin seat covers
Mobile locksmithing	Thirty-minute tune-up shop
Pet cemetery	
Weight control clinic	

MANUFACTURING-TYPE BUSINESSES	FOOD-TYPE BUSINESSES
Burglar alarm manufacturing	Churro snack shop
Customized rug making	Gourmet coffee & tea shop
Hot tub manufacturing	Health-food store
Sculptured candle manufacturing	Low-calorie baker
Stained glass manufacturing	No-alcohol bar
TOURIST-TYPE BUSINESSES	**SERVICE-TYPE BUSINESS**
Antique photo shop	Chimney sweeps
Balloon vending	Coin-op TVs
Dive-for-a-pearl shop	Dating service
Stuffed toy-animal vending	Energy loss prevention
	Roommate-finding service
SPORTS/RECREATION-TYPE BUSINESSES	**RETAIL-TYPE BUSINESSES**
Athletic-shoe store	Antique ceiling fan store
Backpacking shop	Day-care center
Candid keychain photos	Do-it-yourself cosmetic shop
Physical fitness center	Intimate apparel shop
Windsurfing school	Vitamin store

SUMMARY

Your career is one of the key influences in your life. Aside from being a way of making a living, your career is a major contributor to your level of self-esteem and identity. Nevertheless, many people choose first careers for themselves in a casual, nonsystematic manner.

A good starting point in choosing a career is to understand yourself in terms of such things as values, preferences, and skills. In turn, this information is matched against career opportunities. Ideally you should choose a career that meshes well with your preferred lifestyle—the pattern of how you invest energy into work and nonwork.

A recommended strategy for making a sound career choice is to gather valid occupational facts. The four sources to be consulted are printed information (such *BusinessWeek's Guide to Careers*), computer-assisted guidance, knowledgeable people, and firsthand experience. The last category covers information gained from visiting places of work or from part-time or temporary employment. An advantageous way of choosing a career is to pursue an occupation that appears to have growth potential. You search for a match between your capabilities and interests, and a growth occupation in a growth field (see Exhibits 10–2 and 10–3).

A helpful way of looking at occupations is to characterize every job by the proportion of time you devote to working with data, people, or things. It is best to choose an occupation or field that fits your preferences in these three work dimensions.

Another useful way of planning your career is to consider the level of responsibility you are seeking. Occupations have been classified into six levels in terms of increasing responsibility (and sometimes income and prestige): unskilled work, semiskilled jobs, skilled occupations, semiprofessional and managerial positions. It is important to be realistic about the occupational level to which you aspire. Statistically, it is impossible for everyone to reach the top. Also, it helps to be candid about your true level of ambition.

Twenty-four groups of jobs have been identified according to the relative emphasis they place on data, people, and things. Jobs in the same group (such as inspecting and testing or personal services) place about the same emphasis on data, people, and things. Studying these twenty-four job groups (or fields of work) might help you with your selection of a first or new career. A tabular summary of these job groups is found on pages 257–258.

Switching careers follows many of the same principles as choosing a first career. You must be thorough in investigating career possibilities. In addition you might consider building a new career gradually and you might investigate self-employment.

QUESTIONS AND ACTIVITIES

1. Now that you have read this chapter, what do you think you will do differently if you should be choosing a career?
2. Why do you think it is helpful to be successful in your first career before choosing another one?
3. To what extent is it still possible for a person to enter a career at level 1 (unskilled work) and rise to level 6 (higher professional and managerial positions)?
4. How would you describe your present lifestyle?
5. How would you describe your ideal lifestyle?
6. What are the pros and cons of using fate as a primary method of choosing a career?

7. What flaw do you detect in the strategy of choosing a career based on whether the field you are selecting is a growth field?

8. How are you going to cope with the fact that it is becoming increasing difficult for people to earn a middle-class wage?

9. What makes it so difficult for some people to find a career?

10. Interview a person who you think has a worthwhile career to find out how that person chose his or her career. Be ready to discuss your findings in class.

A HUMAN RELATIONS CASE PROBLEM: THE DISILLUSIONED ACCOUNTANT

Amy Dong glanced out the window while her dentist completed polishing a filling he inserted into a chipped tooth. After the syringe was removed from her mouth, Amy asked the dentist, "Why do you think my tooth chipped? I don't recall biting a walnut or getting hit in the mouth."

"The problem you have is not an unusual one," replied the dentist. "The chip comes from grinding your teeth. I'll bet you are experiencing a lot of stress. I can tell which of my patients are under the most pressure simply by looking at their teeth. The more pressure a person faces, the more the person grinds his or her teeth. Most of my patients do not even realize they grind their teeth."

"Thanks for repairing my chip, and for the tip about stress. When you see me in six months, I hope to have stopped grinding my teeth."

Amy thought to herself as she headed back home on the bus, "I guess my dissatisfaction with accounting has finally gotten to me. If my teeth are being ground down, who knows what stress symptom I'll develop next? I'm going to speak to Debbie Hendrix (Amy's boss) tomorrow."

Amy was able to see Ms. Hendrix the next day. "Sit down, Amy," said Debbie. "What is it you wanted to speak to me about?"

"I'll have to be candid," said Amy. "I like working for the state, and I like working for you. But working as an accountant is not for me. I've done it for two years now, and it's getting to me."

"What is it that you don't like about accounting? It's the field you were trained for."

"I can't take sitting in my cubicle and crunching numbers all day long. I keep getting fed data to analyze as if I were a computer. I'm beginning to get headaches toward the end of every working day. I want a job with more of a human touch."

"Maybe you should take a vacation. Or maybe you should take a ten-minute break each afternoon. That should cure your headaches."

"The problem is bigger than that, Debbie. I'm afraid I'm in the wrong field, but I don't know what else to do. I've invested too much time already into becoming an accountant. It's tough to learn a new field when you're twenty-two years old."

"I think you're overreacting to your problem," said Debbie. "Nobody's career is perfect. Just get yourself a good rest this weekend."

Questions

1. What should Amy do about her career dissatisfaction?
2. How sound is the advice offered by Debbie Hendrix?
3. Do you think the dentist had the right to diagnose Amy's problem?
4. What is your opinion of Amy's contention that "It's tough to learn a new field when you're twenty-two?"

A HUMAN RELATIONS ROLE PLAY: THE CAREER SWITCHER

The scenario in the case just presented serves as background information for this role play. One student plays the role of Amy Dong, the disgruntled accountant. She visits a career counselor to explain her tale of woe, and to get good advice on switching to a field that will bring her more contentment. The other person plays the role of a career counselor who will try and persuade Dong to think through carefully her tentative career switch. The counselor deals with the situation in a highly professional way by not looking for a quick fix to Dong's problem.

APPENDIX: TWENTY-FOUR JOB GROUPS[10]

1. Manual Work (001). If you enjoy working with your hands, with small tools, or with machinery, you might enjoy jobs calling for manual work. To be successful, you must be strong, have good balance, and good eye-hand coordination. These jobs tend to be low paying, and do not command much prestige. Typical job titles are meat cutter, cannery worker, cement mason helper, and furniture mover. Career-minded people usually do not aspire toward manual work.

2. Machine Work (002). Should your interests be in operating machinery or heavy equipment, or in driving vehicles, the field of machine work might be for you. People who can perform machine work well are in much demand. Machine work includes operating complex production equipment or driving bulldozers. You often need to attend trade school or an apprentice program to work in this field. Typical job titles in this cluster are lens grinder, structural steel worker, well-drill operator, and bulldozer operator. Good workers in this field often earn higher income than people in semiprofessional jobs.

3. *Personal Services (010)*. If you enjoy working with people and helping them directly, jobs in this expanding area might appeal to you. Job titles in this category include private detective, chauffeur, restaurant hostess, and flight attendant. Extensive formal education is not required for this field, but you should have: (a) an interest in working closely with people, (b) self-confidence in dealing with people, and (c) a pleasant appearance and personality.

4. *Caring for People or Animals (011)*. If you like getting close to people and taking care of their physical and emotional needs, fields to explore are practical nurse, companion, or hospital attendant. Among the duties involved are providing people with bedside care, bathing them, preparing their food, taking messages for them, reading to them, or taking them on walks. Animal keepers, veterinarian's assistants, and animal trainers also fit into this job group. (Job groups 23 and 24 contain higher-level occupations that also involve caring for people.)

The training required for these fields varies. Special courses are usually required to become a practical nurse, while on-the-job training is usually sufficient for becoming a hospital attendant. Pay and prestige are usually not high in this job group, but a practical nurse usually enjoys the prestige associated with the nursing field.

5. *Clerical Work (100)*. Jobs in the clerical field will appeal to you if you would enjoy working in an office environment handling records, using office machines, or performing miscellaneous chores. No firm can survive without an ample supply of clerks. In general, you should have an interest in routine, organized work to enjoy being a clerk. Completion of commercial (business), keyboarding, or shorthand courses is very helpful in obtaining a clerical job. Income and prestige, as well as opportunities for advancement, are limited in most clerical jobs. Clerks are often referred to as office assistants.

Representative job titles in the clerical job group include file clerk, inventory clerk, mail carrier (fairly good pay), bookkeeper, typist, and data-entry clerk. Secretaries are at the top of the clerical work job group.

6. *Inspecting and Testing (101)*. As the world is becoming more concerned about the quality of goods produced, jobs in this group will become more important. Such work might appeal to you if you would enjoy checking prod-

ucts against standards, or performing scientific tests to check them out. You can choose from three types of jobs. A stock clerk receives, examines, stores, and issues supplies, and keeps records. A quality control inspector examines various products to grade or check them against specifications. The demand for quality control inspectors is very high. Another possibility is to work as an assistant to a scientist or technician.

Inspecting and testing jobs are at the semiskilled level. As such the amount of formal schooling required is not extensive, nor is the pay or occupational prestige very high.

7. Craft and Precise Operations (102). People who like to fix things or have "craft instincts" find satisfaction in this field. Many different jobs exist in this field, some involving the use of hands, others placing more emphasis on the use of machinery. Sample job titles include computer operator, dental technician, optician, electrician, carpenter, airline pilot, machinist, and photographer.

For most of these jobs, vocational technical or trade school training is very important. On-the-job training can be very specialized, such as that for a commercial airline pilot. This category cuts across skilled workers, semiprofessional, and professional workers. Pay can be very high ($90,000 a year for some pilots) and so can the prestige. It appears that a high demand will exist for craft workers indefinitely.

8. Customer Services (110). If you would enjoy frequent contact with people during the work day, this field might be worth exploring. The basic task is to take care of the customer's needs. Among the many job titles included here are receptionist, sightseeing guide, reservation agent, teller, telephone operator, appliance salesperson, and taxi driver. Educational preparation for these types of jobs is modest, and so is the income. On the positive side, you would deal directly with people.

9. Nursing and Related Technical Services (111). People who find satisfaction in this field enjoy both helping ill people and working as part of a medical team. Among the jobs in this field are hospital, office, and private duty nurse; X-ray technician; physical therapist; and dental hygienist. The nursing field continues to move toward higher professional status. Some nurses, called nurse practitioners, are now in private practice. The opinion is often expressed that nurses are underpaid. Most registered nurses (RN) today are college graduates, while dental hygienists and X-ray technicians are often graduates of two-year schools.

10. Skilled Personal Services (112). A person who enjoys sewing, styling other people's hair, or cooking might enjoy working as a dressmaker, beautician, barber, or cook. The training and education you will need to work in this field depends on the particular job you choose (the same could be said for every job group). Dressmakers, cooks, and tailors usually learn their trades performing lesser tasks under the supervision of an experienced worker. An encouraging aspect of this field is that although the average income may be modest, the income potential is virtually unlimited. Dressmakers and cooks sometimes reach celebrity status.

11. Training (120). If you enjoy working with people or animals and you also find pleasure in teaching them how to do things, you might want to investigate training jobs. They can be divided into: (a) business or industrial training, (b) sports-hobby training, and (c) animal training. Instructors in industry teach employees how to operate machines or equipment and how to perform tasks. Instructors in a business setting would teach employees about company policies, regulations, and how to deal with customers. Sports-hobby trainers might teach people how to drive a car or ski. Animal trainers sometimes work in conjunction with veterinarians, or independently, to teach house pets discipline.

To qualify for training jobs, you usually have to have a strong background in the particular specialty. Sometimes a college degree in education combined with additional training can be a useful entry to this field. Jobs in this field often fall into the semiprofessional and professional level.

12. Literary (200). If you enjoy writing and have high ability, you might want to explore jobs in the literary field. People in this field are usually knowledgeable specialists in one particular discipline, and in addition develop writing skills. Among the diverse jobs in this field are creative writing, technical writing, translating, and editing. Technical writers are in more demand that other types of writers. One task performed by technical writers is preparing instruction manuals for complicated equipment. A college degree, or beyond, is required for most positions in this field.

Most people who call themselves authors or writers do their writing part-time in conjunction with their regular occupations. The average income from writing alone is about $6,500 a year. However, some creative writers make over a million dollars a year. Do you have a good idea for a novel?

13. Numerical (200). At this point in your life, you probably know whether or not you are interested in mathematics and science. Occupations in this job group include accountants, mathematicians, computer programmers, and physical scientists such as physicists and meteorologists. In addition to having a flair for mathematics, workers in this field must have extreme patience, good organizing ability, and must be able to keep track of details.

Most jobs in this category fall into the professional and higher professional job levels. Success in this kind of work often leads to high-level managerial positions. College degrees, often a master of business administration, are required today to advance in this field. The demand for people in the numerical field is outstanding, particularly in the computer area.

14. Appraisal (201). This relatively nonpublicized job group includes engineers who inspect and evaluate equipment and buildings, and food and drug inspectors. The work is similar to that of a quality-control inspector, except at a higher job level. If you like to examine and inspect things, and you enjoy mathematics, this field could be of interest.

Jobs in this field are at several levels. You need an engineering degree for a position as an engineer in the appraisal field. For surveying and prospecting jobs, a high school education with course work in map reading, freehand and mechanical drawing, mathematics, geography, and earth science is required.

15. Agriculture (202). People who enjoy this field generally have had exposure to farming or gardening in early life. There are two general types of jobs in this job group—those relating to farming, gardening, and animal breeding, and those dealing with agricultural and biological science.

Firsthand experience with farm life, combined with special courses, is good preparation for a career in farming. Agricultural and biological scientists usually have four-year college degrees, and many have doctoral degrees. The income of farmers shows about the same variation as that of movie stars or prize fighters. Scientists in this field make about the same income as most salaried professional-level workers.

16. Applied Technology (202). If you enjoy mathematics and science from a practical standpoint, you might look into this field. To work in this area you must have the talent and interest to learn and apply the basic principles and methods of your particular field such as engineering or drafting. Scientific and engineering research calls for creativity. Drafting calls for the skilled use of hands and figures.

The training and education depend on the job you choose. Technician jobs require a high school diploma, and usually some additional technical training. To be a full-fledged architect, chemist, or similar worker you need a college degree, and sometimes a master's or doctoral degree. Among the exciting job titles in this field are nuclear engineer, photographic engineer, autobody designer, and oceanographer.

17. Promotion and Communication (210). If you enjoy working with people and are skilled at explaining things to them and giving them information, you might be interested in the field of promotion and communication. Included in this job group are publicist (publicity work), TV broadcaster, newspaper reporter, lawyer, or some secretarial positions. Jobs in this field call for vastly different kinds of educational preparation. Some are ordinarily considered skilled occupations (such as secretary) while some are higher professional (such as lawyer).

The income and prestige associated with positions in the promotion and communication field also differ greatly. The top handful of TV reporters are wealthy people known to millions. A challenging aspect of the promotion and communication field is the competitiveness in attaining an above-average job. Competent secretaries, however, are always in demand.

18. Management and Supervision (210). If you think you would enjoy (or do enjoy) responsibility, and you like to plan, organize, and be in charge of projects, you might want to explore management and supervision jobs. The usual route to these positions is to demonstrate competence in a speciality, and also to show promise of being able to lead others and do administrative work. About one-tenth of the work force is classified as a manager or supervisor. Among the representative job titles are department head, superintendent, supervisor, store manager, vice-president of finance, chief engineer, and president. Management is a field with virtually no limit to income, prestige, and work load. Top-level managers in big business earn seven-figure incomes.

The education you need includes your field of specialty, plus courses or a degree in a field like business administration. Today many top executives have MBA degrees, but on-the-job accomplishment is still the number-one requirement for advancement into management.

19. Artistic (212). By now you already know if you have artistic talent and interests. Among the job titles in this field are art director, set decorator, commercial photographer, advertising lay-out specialist, clothes designer, painter, sculptor, and paintings restorer. There are countless talented people competing for very few openings in this field. Many work their way into full-time positions in this field by performing chores for an established professional. Others pursue artistic jobs part-time until they find a full-time position.

20. Sales Representative (212). If you are persuasive, enjoy working with people, and can accept rejection and criticism, the sales field might be worth exploring. The modern sales representative often serves as a technical adviser to customers and prospective customers. Personal charm is important but not sufficient for today's sales representative. Note carefully that as a sales representative you might be responsible for a variety of administrative duties such as answering sales correspondence and preparing sales reports, completion reports, expense accounts, mailing lists, and work schedules.

Educational and training requirements depend on the nature of the service or product you will be selling. More complex products require college degrees, sometimes in a technical field such as engineering. For many other sales positions, a high school diploma, some additional course work, and a willingness to learn are sufficient. Sales representatives work hard, but in many positions you are paid a combination of salary and commission. You can therefore earn as much income as professionals and executives.

21. Music (220). Only people with specialized talents can hope to make a living in the music field. Furthermore, you will rarely ever see a classified ad of this nature: "Wanted: top-forty recording artist. Heavy travel required, work with glamorous celebrities. Starting salary, $975,000 per year." Nor will you find ads posted for symphony conductors. Many people in the music field work more conventional jobs full-time, and pursue music part-time until they achieve their big break.

22. Entertainment and Performing Arts (220). Positions in this job group include actor, actress, comedian, dancer, professional athlete, and magician. Only a relative handful of the thousands of people trying to earn a living as entertainers actually accomplish such a feat. Entertainment and performing arts, aside from being an exciting field itself, serves as an excellent start for a second career. Many sales representatives, business owners, and public officials were formerly entertainers. Who else can you think of besides Ronald Reagan?

23. Teaching, Counseling, and Social Work (220). If you enjoy working with people, and you also like to help them learn things and cope with problems, this field might be worth exploring. Jobs within this field are at many different levels. Many college teachers spend relatively little time teaching in comparison with the time they devote to research and writing. Some social workers work under austere conditions, while some others maintain thriving private practices of marriage counseling. You would need at least a four-year college degree for almost any position in this field. People at the top of this field—such as astronomer-professor-author-TV personality Carl Sagan—have extraordinary incomes and vast exposure to the public. But most workers, teachers, counselors, or social workers lead much more conservative careers.

24. Medical (222). If you are interested in helping people, are an excellent student, and enjoy direct contact with others, medicine could be your field. Many more people apply to medical, dental, and veterinary school than can be accommodated. You might find, however, that more opportunities exist in occupational therapy, or audiology. Most positions in the medical field have strict educational requirements and you will be required to pass a licensing exam.

Physicians and dentists devote many years to preparing themselves for their careers but their income and prestige reach very high levels. Other medical specialists who are not physicians, such as podiatrists (foot doctors) and optometrists (eye doctors), also lead satisfying and financially rewarding careers.

REFERENCES

[1] A full discussion of this topic is found in Clarke G. Carney, Cinda Field Wells, and Don Streufert, *Career Planning: Skills to Build Your Future* (New York: D. Van Nostrand, 1981), pp. 104–107.

[2] *System of Interactive Guidance and Information* (SIGI PLUS), Educational Testing Service, Princeton, NJ 08540-9885; DISCOVER, American College Testing, 230 Schilling Circle, Hunt Valley, MD 21301; Peggy Schmidt, "Computerized Career Planning," *BusinessWeek's Guide to Careers,* December 1985, pp. 28–32.

[3] Carney, Wells, and Streufert, *Career Planning,* p. 115.

[4] Ayres G. D'Costa and others, *Ohio Vocational Interest Survey: Guide to Career Exploration* (New York: Harcourt Brace Jovanovich, 1972), p. 1.

[5] Carney, Wells, and Streufert, *Career Planning,* pp. 87–89.

[6] Kathy Sawyer, "Job Market Warnings: It's Harder to Get Middle-Class Wage," *Washington Post* reprint, May 19, 1984.

[7] "Twenty-four Groups of Jobs," is based on the *Ohio Vocational Interest Survey.*

[8] Both quotes are from Enid Nemy, "Rebels: A Few Executives Are Trading Presidencies for Happiness," *New York Times* reprint, August 14, 1981.

[9] American Entrepreneurs Association, 2311 Pontius Avenue, Los Angeles, CA 90064.

[10] This appendix is based on the *Ohio Vocational Interest Survey.* All the quotes in this section are from the same source.

SOME ADDITIONAL READING

BOLLES, RICHARD N. *The Three Boxes of Life and How to Get Out of Them.* Berkeley, CA: Ten Speed Press, revised regularly.

CETRON, MARVIN, with MARCIA APPEL. *Jobs of the Future.* New York: McGraw-Hill, 1985.

CETRON, MARVIN, with THOMAS O'TOOLE. *Encounters With the Future.* New York: McGraw-Hill, 1985.

KELLEY, ROBERT E.   *The Gold Collar Worker.* Reading, MA: Addison-Wesley, 1985.

O'BRIEN, MARK.   "How to Pick a Growth Company." *BusinessWeek's Guide to Careers,* October 1984, pp. 75–76.

STUMPF, STEPHEN A., with CELESTE KENNON ROGERS.   *Choosing a Career in Business.* New York: Simon & Schuster, 1985.

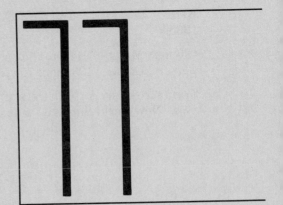

Finding a
Suitable Job

Learning Objectives

After studying the information and doing the exercises in this chapter you should be able to:

- Understand the steps involved in conducting a job campaign
- Prepare an effective cover letter, job résumé, and follow-up letter
- Handle yourself more effectively when being interviewed for a job
- Cope with a stress interview
- Improve greatly your chances of finding a suitable job

People need to find a job for many reasons. You may be starting your career; you may be tired of your present job; you may want to boost your career; and you might be laid off, or fired. Finding a new job does not always mean that you will be leaving your present firm. People who work for large employers often seek new employment in another unit (division, department, agency, and so forth) within the same organization.

If you have already identified a field for yourself, the job-finding process will be somewhat narrowed—you will conduct your job campaign for a position related to your primary field of interest. If you have not already selected a field, the job-finding process itself might help you identify a field. A twenty-seven-year-old hotel manager was asked how she got into the hotel management field. She replied, "Pure luck. I graduated from business school without any idea of what to do. I found out that a hotel chain was interviewing graduates from our school. After two interviews, I was offered a job as a management trainee. Here I am today, a real manager, and loving every minute of it."

For many readers, finding a job is the exciting payoff to years of attending school. It is safe to say that many people would not even enroll in a post–high school program unless they thought graduation would lead to a job.

WHAT KIND OF WORK ARE YOU LOOKING FOR?

A job search begins with a reasonably flexible description of the type of job or jobs you are looking for. Flexibility is called for because with so many different jobs available, it is difficult to be too specific. A reasonable objective might be something of this nature: "I am searching for a job in the numerical field, with a large employer, located within thirty miles of here. I prefer bookkeeping work. My minimum salary would be $350 per week."

Most people can more readily identify the jobs they don't want than those they do want. Your chances of finding suitable employment are directly proportional to the number of positions that will satisfy your job objectives. One person with an interest in the literary field might be willing to accept only a job as a newspaper reporter—always a difficult position to find. Another person with the same background is seeking a job as (1) a newspaper reporter, (2) a magazine staff writer, (3) a copywriter in an advertising agency, (4) a communications specialist in a firm, or (5) a copywriter in a public relations firm. The second person has a better chance than the first of finding a job.

What Kind of Organization?

Closely tied in with the type of work you are seeking is the type of organization in which you would prefer to work. Unless you have had exposure to different types of organizations, you may have only tentative answers to this question. Questioning people who work at different places can provide you with some useful clues. As well, plant tours open to the public can provide valuable tips about what it is like to work

in that particular firm. Visits to stores, restaurants, and government agencies will provide informal information about the general nature of working conditions in those places. As you begin your job search, ask yourself these questions to help you identify the type of organization that *might* be right for you:

> Would I feel more comfortable working in an office with hundreds of other people? Or would I prefer just a handful of co-workers?

Would I prefer working in a place where people went out of their way to dress in a stylish manner? Or would I prefer an informal place where not so much emphasis was placed on appearance?

Would I prefer to work in a small town or in a busy metropolitan area? How important is access to stores and restaurants?

Would it be best for me to work where I could rely on public transportation?

Would I really prefer an easygoing atmosphere or a highly competitive, "rat race" environment?

How important are the social aspects of work to me? Would I only be happy in a place where I could meet prospective dates and make new friends?

WHAT ARE EMPLOYERS LOOKING FOR?

What you are looking for in an employer must be matched against what an employer is looking for in an employee. Job interviewers do not all agree on the qualifications they seek in employees. Nevertheless, a number of traits, characteristics, skills, and accomplishments are important to many employers.[1] Exhibit 11–1 summarizes these qualifications sought for in job applications.

Several important conclusions can be drawn from the list of qualifications in Exhibit 11–1. One is that these qualifications are success factors in most lines of work. For instance, to achieve success in most fields you must have the appropriate education, be a good problem solver, and be well motivated. Another conclusion is that most of these qualifications can be developed or acquired. To illustrate, if you have not yet demonstrated leadership ability, you can actively seek leadership experience.

A third implication of this list is that employers set high expectations when they attempt to fill job openings. A bank personnel officer explained, "We seen no sense in hiring an applicant who does not have a professional outlook. It does less damage to the bank to let a position go unfilled than to hire someone we are not proud to have as an employee."

GO WHERE THE OPPORTUNITIES ARE

Finding a job involves an element of risk. You want to take some risks, but you also want to engage in activities that will improve your chances of getting the payoff you want—a suitable job. A key strategy here is

EXHIBIT 11–1   QUALIFICATIONS SOUGHT BY EMPLOYERS

Qualifications a substantial number of employment interviewers and hiring managers looking for in job applicants including the following:

Appropriate education and satisfactory grades. Your education should be a reasonable fit with the demands of the job. Satisfactory grades are important because they may be an indicator of intelligence and hard work. Large, successful employers place the most emphasis on grades.

Relevant work experience. Although a career beginner may have limited job experience, some job experience may be helpful. Part-time and temporary work related to your job objective may be sufficient.

Communication and interpersonal skills. The ability to communicate with people and get along with different types of people are two of the most desirable qualities in job candidates. Job interviewers attempt to judge these qualities during the interview.

Motivation and energy. Well-motivated and energetic employees are needed to increase productivity and keep employers from becoming insolvent. Your past record of achievements will be used to judge your motivation and energy. It also helps to *look* energetic and well-motivated. One way to do this is by speaking enthusiastically about the prospective job and employer.

Problem-solving ability. Employers seek bright employees except when hiring for routine, repetitive jobs. Your problem-solving ability is reflected in how you handled problems in the past, your grades, your interests, and how intelligently you respond to the interviewer's questions.

Judgment and common sense. Good judgment and common sense are important supplements to job knowledge in every position. An applicant's description of how he or she handled problems in the past is often used to assess judgment and common sense. Behavior during the interview can also be an indicator. For example, if a phone call came through for the interviewer, good judgment would be to say, "Would you like me to step out of the room for a moment?"

Flexibility. Since job demands change so frequently, flexible employees are considered valuable. One indicator of flexibility is whether an applicant responds well to the prospects of taking a job different than the one originally planned.

Emotional maturity. Maturity is valued because it helps an employee behave professionally and responsibly. What constitutes maturity is a subjective evaluation. However, a candidate who does such things as engage in excessive small talk, chew gum, ask for change to use the vending machine, or bring a friend to the waiting room will be considered immature.

Leadership. Employers seeking potential supervisors and managers look for applicants to have past leadership accomplishments. Formal leadership positions, such as a team or club captain, are significant. So are experiences such as having organized a charity collection.

SOURCE: Based on Bob Weinstein, "What Employers Look For," *The Honda How to Get a Job Guide* (Special Edition of *BusinessWeek's Guide to Careers*), 1985, pp. 10–13; William T. Leonard, "What the Recruiter Looks For," *BusinessWeek's Guide to Careers*, Fall/Winter, 1983, pp. 22–23.

to search for a job in a prospering field or industry. Or the expansion might be related to a particular technology, such as office automation or robotics.

Another aspect of expansion is the occupation itself, such as paralegal assistant or bank manager. It is important to remember that a prospering field, industry, or occupation might be limited in time. Much more important is the general principle of carefully researching job opportunities at any specific time.

Some opportunities will come looking for you. Expanding firms often seek out school placement offices. Firms actively seeking to expand their work forces will typically place classified ads in newspapers. At other times, you may have to gather information to uncover where opportunities lie. Exhibits 10–2 and 10–3 presented in the last chapter are useful guides to growth opportunities as conditions presently exist.

The business section of your local newspaper is another source of information about expanding businesses. Bank officials may be aware of expansion plans because firms that are expanding often borrow money from banks. Local chambers of commerce may also have current information on prospering enterprises in the area.

If you are several months away from looking for a job in your area, you might inquire if any new malls or buildings are being constructed. Then find out who the tenants will be. Inevitably when a business starts anew, or relocates within a community, new employees are needed. Many employees are not interested in being transferred, even into a new location within the same town. Vacancies are thus created.

EXPLORE MULTIPLE JOB-FINDING TECHNIQUES

Some methods of finding a job are better than others, but any technique will pay off now and then. A wise job seeker thus pursues job-finding methods of high, low, and medium probability. Believing in this multiple approach, one advertising agency executive tried hard to land an account. In a sense, he was looking for a job. His approach was to hang a flag outside the fortieth floor of a window directly across from the office of the executive he wanted to impress. His novel approach paid off. The enterprising advertising agency executive did get a chance to make a presentation to the executive's firm. Ultimately he landed the account. For an exercise in exploring some creative job-finding techniques, turn to Exhibit 11–2.

Many a job seeker has claimed, "I've tried everything," when he or she has only pursued a few job-finding approaches. For convenience,

---

EXHIBIT 11–2   CREATIVE JOB-FINDING TECHNIQUES

Job seekers often make the mistake of not exploring enough different methods for finding a job. After exploring a few conventional techniques, such as making a trip to the placement office, they sit back and wait for job offers to pour in. A better approach is to search for creative alternatives to finding a job. Think of every possibility, then sort out the workable from the unworkable later on. To accomplish this task, the class will be organized into brainstorming groups. The goal is to specify as large a number of job-finding techniques as possible. Here are seven rules to serve as guidelines for having a productive brainstorming session:

1. Group size should be about five to seven people. Too few people, and not enough suggestions are generated; too many people, and the session becomes uncontrolled.

2. No criticism allowed. All suggestions should be welcome; it is particularly important not to use derisive laughter. As the old cliché states, "They laughed at Thomas Edison."

3. Freewheeling is encouraged. "The more outlandish the idea, the better. It's always easier to tame down an idea than think it up."

4. Quantity and variety are very important. The greater the number of ideas put forth, the greater the likelihood of a breakthrough idea.

5. Combinations and improvements are encouraged. Building upon the ideas of others, including combining them, is very productive. Piggybacking is an essential part of brainstorming.

6. Notes must be taken during the sessions either manually or with a mechanical device. One person usually serves as recording secretary.

7. Do not overstructure by following any of the above six rules too rigidly. Brainstorming is a spontaneous activity.

---

these approaches or channels can be divided into three general types: networking, a prospective employer list, and placement office/employment agency.

Networking

By far the most effective method of finding a job is through personal contacts. **Networking** is the process of establishing a group of contacts who can help you in your career. Networking is particularly helpful because it taps you into the "insider system" or "internal job market." The internal job market is the large array of jobs that haven't been advertised and are usually filled by word of mouth or through friends and acquaintances of employees.

About 85 percent of job openings are found in the hidden job market. The other 15 percent of jobs are advertised or registered with employment agencies and placement offices. The best way to reach the jobs in the hidden market is by getting someone to recommend you for one. When looking for a job it is therefore important to tell every potential contact of your job search. The more influential the person the better. Be specific about the type of job you are seeking.

To use networking effectively, it may be necessary to create contacts aside from those you already have. Potential sources of contacts include:

Friends
Parents and other family members
Faculty and staff
Former or present employer (assuming you hold a temporary job)
Former graduates of your school
Athletic teams
Community groups, churches, temples, and mosques
Trade and professional associations
Career fairs[2]

Prospective Employer List

Another way to tap the internal job market is to write dozens of letters to prospective employers. Although this method of finding a job is part of the insider system, it is unique enough to warrant a category of its own. The plan is to come up with a master list of firms you might want to work for. The more comprehensive and thorough the list, the better your chances of finding employment. You make up the list according to the category or categories that make the most sense in your particular situation.

Assume that you are intent on finding a job in the San Francisco Bay area. For you geography is more important than the nature of the business. You might then purchase a business and industry list from the San Francisco Chamber of Commerce. Using a cover letter (described later in this chapter) you would write to specific individuals in as many firms as possible, including the federal, state, county, and city governments. Another term for this technique is the **unsolicited letter campaign**. The approach often works well for a newcomer to the work force because that person is flexible and does not require the salary of a more experienced employee.

Another meaningful way of organizing your list is by type of enterprise. Suppose your long-term career goal was to become a bank executive. To get started in banking, write to as many banks in the areas of the country in which you would be willing to work. Most business and central libraries have directories that provide such information. Two useful business directories are those published by Dun and Bradstreet and by Standard and Poors. Both provide full addresses and names of key people in the firms listed. The information is organized by such factors as size of the firm, location, or type of business (for example, banks or petroleum companies). Again, use a person's name; not Dear Sir, Madam, or Ms. Even if the person you write to is deceased, or has moved, your letter will be referred to someone else who might be able to help you.

How effective is the prospective employer list as a method of obtaining a job interview or a job? In general, think of writing about one hundred letters to get several interviews and one job. Your postage, stationery, and printing costs will be covered by your first two paychecks.

School Placement Office/Employment Agency

It would be wasteful of tuition dollars and human energy not to regard your placement office as a primary method of finding a job. Even if you do not find a job through the placement office, you will still gain valuable experience there. The job interviews you do have will move you one step closer toward acquiring the job-getting skills you need. You will probably also receive some helpful tips, including how to prepare a résumé and write a cover letter.

The thought of using an employment agency crosses the mind of every job seeker, be that person a clerk or an executive. My general advice is, Why not? so long as the employer pays the fee. Or, if you pay the fee, it is still worthwhile if the agency helps you find an outstanding position. If the agency does not help you find the job you want, you are under no obligation. Employment agencies, both those operated by the state and those privately owned, are one more legitimate method of helping you find a job.

Employment agencies are more valuable for people with about five to ten years of job experience than for newcomers or people at the top of their professions. On the one hand, employers who use agencies are generally looking for experienced people, not beginners. On the other hand, top jobs are usually found through personal referrals or through ads in newspapers and special magazines.

When should you begin looking for a job? The answer to this question depends somewhat on the type of job you are seeking. In general, the bigger the job, the longer the job campaign. Job-hunting advisers generally agree that it will take about six months to find a full-time position in your field.[3] You will need this much time to prepare your résumé and cover letter, and to pursue all the methods described in this section. Another factor is that most prospective employers take at least thirty days to notify you of their employment decision.

PREPARE AN ATTENTION-GETTING COVER LETTER

When people talk of finding a job, their reflex is to prepare a résumé. A résumé is necessary but not sufficient, however, for conducting an intelligent job campaign. You also need an attention-getting cover letter to accompany your résumé. The cover letter multiplies the effectiveness of the résumé because it enables you to prepare a tailor-made, individual approach to each job situation you are pursuing. The most important purpose of the cover letter is to explain why you are applying for the position in question. Simultaneously, you try to convince the prospective employer to take you seriously.

The cover letter is particularly suited to responding to a want ad or an announcement posted in a placement office, or when writing unsolicited job-seeking letters. Most job applicants use the conventional (and somewhat ineffective) approach of writing a letter attempting to impress the prospective employer with their background. A more effective approach is to capture the reader's attention with a direct statement of what you might be able to do for the firm in question. Keep this "what I can do for you" strategy paramount in your mind at every stage of finding a job. It works wonders in the job interview, as it will in the rest of your career.

Once you have stated how you can help the employer, you should present a one-page summary of your education and the highlights of your job and educational experience. A sample cover letter is presented in Exhibit 11–3. Here are two examples of opening lines (a portion of the cover letter) geared to two different types of jobs:

1. Person seeking employment in credit department of garment maker: "Everybody has debt-collection problems these days. Let me help you gather in some of the past-due cash that you rightfully deserve."

2. Person looking for position as administrative assistant in hospital where vacancy may or may not exist: "Is your hospital drowning in paperwork? Let me jump in with both feet and clear up some of the confusion. This will give you much more time for taking care of patients."

A general rule is to try to be positive and forceful without appearing flippant or brash. A case in point is a young man looking for a job as a financial analyst (someone who helps a firm determine how to make the best use of its money). The cover letter he wrote began in this

EXHIBIT 11–3   SAMPLE COVER LETTER

> 27 Buttercup Lane
> Little Rock, Arkansas 72203
> Date

Mr. Bart Bertrand
President
South View Dodge
258 Princess Boulevard
Little Rock, Arkansas 72201

Dear Mr. Bertrand:

Without a good service department, a new-car dealership is in big trouble. An efficiency-minded person like myself who loves autos, and likes to help customers, can do wonders for your service department. Give me a chance, and I will help you maintain the high quality of after-sales service demanded by your customers.

The position you advertised in the Dispatch is an ideal fit for my background. Shortly, I will be graduating from Pine Valley Community College with an associate's degree in automotive technology. In addition, I was an automotive mechanics major at Monroe Vocational High.

My job experience includes three years of part-time general work at a Mobil Service Station, and two years of clerical work at Brandon's Chrysler. Besides this relevant experience, I'm the proud owner of a mint condition 1975 sports coupe I maintain myself.

As a single parent who lives with her mother, I'm very stable in this community. A well-paying, secure job where I can make a contribution is important to me.

My enclosed résumé contains additional information about me. When might I have the opportunity to be interviewed?

> Sincerely yours,
>
> Rita Mae Jenkins

manner: "Need help in getting off your assets? I'm the person who can show you how." What do you think of his opening line?

PREPARE AN EFFECTIVE RÉSUMÉ

No matter what method of job hunting you use, inevitably somebody will ask for a résumé. Most companies require a résumé before seriously considering a job candidate from the outside. You might also be asked for your résumé if you are being considered for transfer to a new position within your firm. The purpose of a résumé is to help you obtain a job interview, not a job. Very few people are hired without a personal interview.

Countless suggestions have been offered to the résumé writer. An important point to remember is that there is no one best way to prepare a job résumé. Different people reading résumés have different ideas about what constitutes an effective résumé. Nevertheless, a few general guidelines can be offered which, if followed, will help you avoid making a serious mistake.

Effective résumés are straightforward, factual presentations of a person's experience and accomplishments. They are neither too lengthy nor too sketchy. A general rule is that one or two pages in length is best. One page may seem too brief to many people. Yet you will find some people who think anyone should be able to condense his or her life experience into one page. A résumé that is three pages or longer may irritate an impatient employment official. Most of the facts you need to complete your résumé are contained in your Self-Knowledge Questionnaire (Chapter 1).

Three Types of Résumés

The three most commonly used résumé formats are the chronological, functional, and target.[4] You might consider using one of these types, or a blend of them, based on what information about yourself you are trying to highlight. Whichever format you choose, you must include essential information.

The **chronological résumé** presents your work experience, education, and interests, along with your accomplishments, in reverse chronological order. A chronological résumé is basically the traditional résumé with the addition of accomplishments and achievements. Some people say the chronological résumé is too bland. However, it contains precisely the information that most employers demand and it is easy to prepare.

The **functional résumé** organizes your skills and accomplishments into the functions or tasks that support the job you are seeking. A section of a functional résumé might read:

SUPERVISION: Organized the activities of five park employees to create a smooth-running recreation program. Trained and supervised four roofing specialists to help produce a successful roofing business.

The functional résumé is useful because it highlights the things you have accomplished and the skills you have developed. In this way, an ordinary work experience might seem more impressive. For instance, the tasks listed above under "supervision" may appear more impressive than listing the jobs "Playground supervisor" and "Roofing crew chief." One problem with the functional résumé is that it omits the factual information many employers demand.

The **targeted résumé** focuses on a specific job target, or position and presents only information about you that supports that target. Using a target format, an applicant for a sales position would only list sales jobs. Under education, the applicant would focus on sales-related courses such as communication skills and marketing. A targeted résumé is helpful in dramatizing your suitability for the position you are seeking. However, this résumé format omits other relevant information about you, and a new résumé must be prepared for each target position.

A general purpose résumé, following a chronological format, is presented in Exhibit 11–4. A large number of people who have followed this format report good results. A more detailed résumé format is presented in Exhibit 11–5. Personnel managers and prospective bosses often demand the details presented in this type of résumé. To prepare such a résumé and cover letter, follow the work sheets presented in Exhibits 11–5 and 11–6.

How to Handle the Job Objective Section

On the résumé, a **job objective** is the position you are applying for now or intend to hold in the future. A job objective is also referred to as a job target or a position objective. Although stating a job objective seems easy, it is a trouble spot for many résumé writers. Early in their careers many people feel compelled to state their long-range career objectives in the job objective section. A twenty-one year old might state, "To become president of an international corporation." Certainly this is a worthy objective, but it is better to be more modest at the outset.

EXHIBIT 11–4   A GENERAL-PURPOSE RÉSUMÉ

RÉSUMÉ

Rita Mae Jenkins
27 Buttercup Lane
Little Rock, Arkansas 72203

Born August 8, 1963
Single parent; one child
(501) 385-3986

Job Objective	Management position in service department of new-car dealership.
Job Experience 1986–present	Senior clerk, Brandon Chrysler-Plymouth, Little Rock; about 30 hours per week. Responsible for receiving customer payments for service performed; preparing customer invoices; miscellaneous tasks as requested by service manager. KEY ACCOMPLISHMENT: Set up filing system that saved space and reduced file-searching time.
1983–1986	Service station attendant, Manny's Mobil Service. Performed wide variety of light mechanical tasks such as assisting in brake relinings, replacing mufflers and tail pipes, tune-ups. Independent responsibility for lubrication and oil changes. KEY ACCOMPLISHMENT: Increased sales of tires, batteries, and accessories by 18 percent during time periods I was on duty.
Formal Education 1985–1987	Pine Valley Community College, Associate Degree, automotive technology, May 1987. Studied all phases auto repair including computerized diagnostics, service department management. Attended school while working about 30 hours per week. B$^+$ average.
1981–1985	Harrison Vocational Technical High School, Little Rock. Graduated 10th in class of 137. Majored in automotive repair and maintenance. Also studied commercial subjects such as bookkeeping, business machines, and business systems and procedures.
Job-Related Skills	Able to handle paperwork systems in office. Practical knowledge of bookkeeping. Able to handle customer concerns and complaints in person or by phone. Able to diagnose and repair wide range of automotive problems (domestic and foreign cars).
Personal Interests and Hobbies	Most spare time now devoted to parenting. Enjoy

automobile restoration and maintenance. Physical fitness enthusiast. Read self-improvement books and current fiction; daily newspaper.

References   On file with placement office at Pine Valley Community College. Permissible to contact present or former employers.

EXHIBIT 11–5   WORK SHEET FOR JOB RÉSUMÉ DEVELOPED BY JOHN F. HITCHCOCK

Résumé Format

PERSONAL DATA
Name
Home address, zip code
Area code, phone number
Social Security No.:

Birthdate, place of birth
Height and weight:
Condition of health:
Marital status:

EDUCATION (in reverse order)
Postsecondary
Somerset County Technical
  Institute
P.O. Box 6350
North Bridge St. & Vogt Drive
Bridgewater, N.J. 08807
(201) 526-8900, Ext. 33
Dates of Attendance

Graduate: Use date
Major/diploma:

Average:
Honors:
Activities:

Describe your major and courses successfully completed.
Modify description from current catalogue.
If you have attended other community colleges or schools, place information here in the same sequence as above. If required, make a request for a catalogue.
Warning: DO NOT SPLIT ANY INFORMATION ON TWO PAGES.

Secondary
Name of high school
Address, zip code
Area code, phone number
Dates of attendance

Graduate: date
Diploma: type
Average:
Honors:
Activities:

EMPLOYMENT (in reverse order)
Name of firm
Stress address
Town, zip code
Area code, phone number
Person to contact, title
Dates: 1/2/3–4/5/6

Job title:
Describe in concise English what
  you do (did) along with your major
  accomplishments
Do not write long sentences:
  keep it choppy.

Next previous employer
Street address
Town, zip code
Area code, phone number
Dates: 1/2/3–4/5/6

Job title:
Same as previous description.
Continue with jobs from your
  junior-senior summer in
  high school.

VOLUNTEER WORK (fire, hospital, charity, etc. Use only if applicable.)
  Fire department
  Street address
  Town, zip code
  Person to contact, title
  Dates: Same as previous

Job title:
Rank, describe job;
  your qualifications

MILITARY EXPERIENCE (Use only if applicable.)
  Last military address
  Active service dates
  Reserve dates

Rank, title
Describe what you did
Honors, decorations

LEISURE INTERESTS
  List items such as reading, furniture refinishing, hobbies, sports, Do *not* list
  women, men, beer, and so forth!

REFERENCES
  You will need at least six persons who have known you for a long time. They
  include business contacts, instructors, friends (not classmates) who are older
  than you, ministers and members of the clergy, and so forth.

MISCELLANEOUS
  Items such as copies of your work, prints, projects, etc., are mandatory.

Employers will tend to interpret the job objective as a statement of your short-term plans. If you think your long-term objective should be stated, you might divide the section into "immediate objective" and "long-term objective." Current practice is to use the position under consideration as a job objective. Longer-term objectives can then be discussed during the job interview.

Another problem with the job objective section is that your objective will often have to be tailored to the specific job under consideration. In other words, the job objective you have printed on your résumé may not fit exactly the job you are applying for. You might be considering a sales career. You find two good leads, one for selling an industrial product, and one for a consumer product. You would want your objective on one résumé to mention industrial sales and on the other, consumer sales.

EXHIBIT 11–6   COVER LETTER FORMAT DEVELOPED BY JOHN F. HITCHCOCK

Work Sheet to Cover Letter

Your address
Town, street, zip code
Date

Name of person, Title (e.g., Personnel Manager)
Name of firm
Address
Town, street, zip code

Dear Mr., Mrs., or Ms. Smith:
    Paragraph 1: State the type of job that you want.
    Paragraph 2: Summarize your qualifications.
    Paragraph 3: Ask for interview. State your availability.
    Paragraph 4: Do not forget "Thank you."

Yours truly,
Signature
Name typed out
Alternative address
location

One approach to this problem is to keep your résumé filed in a word processor. You can then modify the job objective section for a given job lead. Another approach is to omit the job objective section. Your cover letter can describe the link between you and the job under consideration. Notice how the cover letter in Exhibit 11–3 made this link. (The same person, however, did include a job objective on her résumé.)

What About the Creative-Style Résumé?

Since so many résumés are sent to employers, it is difficult to attract an employer's attention. The solution offered to this problem is a creatively prepared résumé. A **creative-style résumé** is one with a novel format and design. Do not confuse this idea with the "created résumé" in which one "creates" facts to make a favorable impression.

One creative approach is to print your résumé in the format of a menu. One job seeker went so far as calling his education the "appetizer," his work experience the "entrée," and his hobbies and interests the "dessert." Others try to make their résumés distinctive by printing them on tinted paper or oversized paper.

If done in a way to attract positive attention to yourself, these approaches have merit. If you are applying for a position in which creative talent is a primary factor, the creative-style résumé is helpful. A more conventional job requires a more conventional résumé. Several human resources managers have said they detest oversized résumés because they are difficult to fit into standard files.

Résumé Errors to Avoid

Another way to distinguish your résumé from others is to prepare one that is neat, well organized, and professional in appearance. The positive advice offered so far should help you attain this goal. Despite all the help available to job seekers, many applicants still mail out careless, poorly organized, and unprofessional-looking résumés. Avoid the following mistakes commonly found in résumés:

- Too lengthy, containing much useless information; or written in narrative, rather than short, punchy statements
- Disorganized, including the same type of information presented under different headings
- Poorly typed or word-processed, with narrow margins and writing in the margins, excessive spacing between lines and words, and typed or printed using a faded ribbon
- Skimpy or insufficient information (only dates, titles, and incomplete addresses)
- Excessive information, including general information (such as a listing of the product line of an employer like Procter and Gamble)
- No listing of accomplishments or skills
- Misspellings, typographical and input errors, errors corrected by pen, poor grammar, and frequent abbreviations
- Starting sentences with phrases such as "I did," "I was," "I am," instead of action verbs like initiated, created, supervised, managed, and so on
- Overly elaborate résumé, for example, using calligraphy, fancy typesetting, or plastic binder
- So much emphasis on nontraditional résumé that basic facts are missing (if company officials cannot verify facts such as work experience and addresses of schools attended or assess qualifications, the résumé is discarded)
- Inflating experience or distorting information (if discovered when references are checked, this usually leads to immediate disqualification or, if candidate has already been hired, to dismissal)[5]

HOW TO HANDLE YOURSELF IN A JOB INTERVIEW

A successful job campaign results in one or more employment interviews. The one exception is that you could conceivably be hired for an out-of-town position without being interviewed. Becoming a skillful interviewee requires practice. You can acquire this practice as you go through the process of finding a job. In addition, you can rehearse simulated job interviews with friends and other students. Practice answering the questions posed in Exhibit 11–7.

Video-taping these interviews is especially helpful because it provides you with feedback on how you handled yourself. In watching the replay, pay particular attention to your spoken and nonverbal communication skills. Then make adjustments as needed.

A sound general strategy is to present yourself favorably but accurately in the interview. Job hunters typically look upon the employment interview as a game in which they must outguess the interviewer. A sounder approach is to do your best to present a positive, but accurate picture of yourself.

EXHIBIT 11–7   QUESTIONS FREQUENTLY ASKED OF JOB CANDIDATES

A useful way of preparing for job interviews is to rehearse answers to the kinds of questions you will most likely be asked by the interviewer. The following fifteen questions are of the same basic type and content encountered in most employment interviews. Practice answers to them in front of a mirror or with a friend.

1. What are your short-term and long-term goals?
2. What do you expect to be doing five years from now?
3. How much money do you expect to be earning five years from now?
4. What are your strengths? Weaknesses?
5. Why did you prepare for the career you did?
6. How would you describe yourself? (Or, Who are you?)
7. How would other people describe you?
8. What did you think of school?
9. Why do you want to work for this company?
10. Why should we hire you?
11. If hired, how long would you be working for us?
12. What makes you think you will be successful in business?
13. Where else are you interviewing?
14. What has been your biggest accomplishment on the job?
15. What do you know about computers?

Outright deception in the interview, if discovered, will lead to your rejection. If the facts you present (such as attendance at a particular school) are later discovered to be untrue, you might be dismissed from the job for which you have been hired. The suggestions presented next will help you appear to be a sincere and responsible jobseeker.

1. Prepare in advance. Be familiar with pertinent details about your background including your social security number and names and addresses of references. Do your homework regarding your potential employer. It is important to know some important facts about the firm in which you are seeking employment. Annual reports, brochures about the company, and sometimes newspaper and magazine articles should provide valuable information. A brief conversation with one or two current employees might provide some basic knowledge about the firm. One man seeking employment as a caseworker in a welfare agency used a tactic that helped create a favorable impression during an interview. He asked two welfare recipients he knew how they perceived the job of a caseworker. Talking about these perceptions helped the young man establish a good communications bridge with the employment interviewer.

2. Arrive on time for the interview. Although employers will often keep you waiting, they truly resent late applicants.[6] To avoid being late, leave yourself ample time to handle such emergencies as clogged traffic, car problems, or getting lost. Plan to be at the interview location about forty-five minutes before the interview. Take a walk outside the building or wait in the main lobby. Ten minutes before the interview, coolly and confidently stride into the reception area for your interview.

3. Dress appropriately. So much emphasis is placed on dressing well for job interviews that some people overdress. Instead of looking businesslike, they appear to be dressed for a wedding or a funeral. The safest tactic is to wear moderately conservative business attire when applying for almost any position. Do not be misled by dress consultants who advise you to avoid certain colors or never to wear short sleeves. The dean of the Harvard Business School wears short-sleeved shirts year-round.

4. Have reasons to justify your plans. Sometimes it is important to defend your reasons for seeking a particular position or for trying to gain entrance into a particular field. Many people with education in different fields, for example, aspire toward personnel work. It is crucial to give a reason other than the often-mentioned, "I like people." Perhaps you believe that the proper utilization of people leads to improved profits. If so, use that reason to justify your plans.

5. Focus on important things about the job. Inexperienced job candidates often relieve their tension by asking questions about noncontroversial topics such as the cafeteria, company-sponsored athletic facilities, or the number of paid holidays. All of these topics may be important to you, but discuss them after the basic issue—the nature of the job—has been discussed.

6. Do not worry too much about hidden meanings. Few interview questions are as revealing as you might think. Respond in a straightforward and nondefensive way to even the most absurd-sounding question. If you believe that your privacy is being invaded or that the question is discriminatory, you may choose not to answer. (One extreme example, "Do you have to work, or is this job just for spending money?") Even professional interviewers do not necessarily have a wrong answer in mind to an unusual question. One such example is, "If you had to choose one, which animal would you prefer to be?" Any sane answer, given in a nondefensive way, will suffice. One woman impressed an interviewer with her answer to this question. She said, "An eagle, so I could soar to new heights in my career. And people would look up to me."

7. *Be ready for a frank discussion of your strengths and weaknesses.* Almost every personnel interviewer and many hiring supervisors will ask you to discuss your strengths and weaknesses. (Some other frequently asked questions are presented in Exhibit 11–7.) Everyone has weaknesses or at least needs to improve in certain areas. To deny them is to appear uninsightful or defensive. However, you may not want to reveal weaknesses that are unrelated to the job (such as recurring nightmares or fear of swimming). A mildly evasive approach is to emphasize weaknesses that could be interpreted as strengths. A case in point: "Sometimes I'm too impatient to get things done."

8. *Allow the interviewer to talk.* Under the pressure of trying to impress the interviewer, you may neglect to give that person a chance to talk. Although a skilled interviewer lets the interviewee do most of the talking, there are times when the person across the desk wants to communicate something to you, for example, information about the firm, or an analysis of how you would fit into the firm. Use your intuition to determine when the interviewer has finished talking and wants you to carry the conversation.

9. *Ask a few good questions.* An intelligent interviewee asks a few good questions. Authenticity is important. Ask only questions of interest to you. Here are a few questions worth considering:

a. If hired, what kind of work would I actually be doing?
b. What would I have to accomplish on this job in order to be considered an outstanding performer?
c. What kind of advancement opportunities are there in your company for outstanding performers?
d. What have I said so far that requires further explanation?

10. *Show how you can help the employer.* To repeat, an effective job-getting strategy is to explain to a prospective employer what you think you can do to help the company. This gains more for you than telling the prospective employer of your good qualities and characteristics. If you were applying for the position of billing specialist in a small company that you knew was having trouble billing customers correctly, you might try this thrust: "Here is what I would do to work with experienced employees to help develop a billing system with as few bugs as possible:—————.''

HANDLING YOURSELF IN A STRESS INTERVIEW

A **stress interview** is a deliberate method of placing a job applicant under considerable pressure and then observing his or her reactions. The purpose of the stress interview is to see how well the applicant handles pressure.[7] It is difficult not to become defensive, distraught, or angry when the interviewer does such things as:

Sits across from you and says nothing, waiting for you to begin talking about yourself.

Comments that "Most other people from your school have been a big disappointment to our firm. What's so special about you?"
Yawns when you describe your strengths.
Says, "I have the impression that others see you as kind of a punk."
Glares at you and says, "You've been lying to me and I know it."
Spills a glass of water on you, pretending it was an accident.

The best way to handle a stress interview is to try to relax, perhaps by exhaling or saying to yourself, "I won't let this get to me." After you have relaxed, answer the questions the best you can. Remember, there is really no one best answer to any of these off-the-wall questions. Also, there is no one best response to these off-the-wall comments and antics.

Another approach is to handle the pressure by expressing your feelings in an assertive manner. State how you feel but avoid being abrasive or hostile—even if such a response is deserved. Two possible comments are: "I feel as if I'm being placed under pressure. I don't mind because I work well under pressure." "Is this what is called a stress interview? It makes me tense, but I'm willing to cooperate." Expressing your feelings helps relieve tension and enables you to think more clearly.

Industrial psychologist Sandra Davis also recommends that you keep in mind anecdotes to illustrate your strengths.[8] In this way if an interviewer tries to create stress for you by challenging your positive points, you can back up what you say. Suppose an interviewer says, "I doubt you can get your way with people," you respond by saying, "Let me give you an example of how I negotiated a better price on a tractor for our family farm."

THE FOLLOW-UP LETTER

Your responsibilities in job hunting do not end with the employment interview. The vital next step is to mail a courteous follow-up letter several days after the interview. Even if you decide not to take the job, a brief thank-you letter is advisable. You may conceivably have contact with that firm in the future.

If you want the position, state your attitudes toward the position and the company, and summarize any conclusions reached about your discussion. A follow-up letter is a tip-off that you are truly interested in the position. Sending such a letter may therefore give you an edge over other applicants for the position. A sample follow-up letter is shown in Exhibit 11–8.

KEEPING PRESSURE ON YOURSELF
WHEN JOB HUNTING

For some people, finding a job is an easy task, particularly if they happen to be in a field in which the number of positions available are far greater than the number of job applicants. For many other people, the job search can be a mixed experience; some joy and some frustration. Much rejection can be expected. Few people are wanted by every

EXHIBIT 11-8   A SAMPLE FOLLOW-UP LETTER

27 Buttercup Lane
Little Rock, Arkansas 72203
Date

Mr. Bart Bertrand
President
South View Dodge
258 Princess Boulevard
Little Rock, Arkansas 72201

Dear Mr. Bertrand:

Thank you for my recent chance to discuss the assistant service manager position with you and Mr. Ralph Alexander. It was illuminating to see what a busy, successful operation you have.

I was impressed with the amount of responsibility the assistant service manager would have at your dealership. The job sounds exciting and I would like to be part of the growth of the dealership. I realize the work would be hard and the hours would be long, but that's the kind of challenge I want and can handle.

My understanding is that my background is generally favorable for the position, but that you would prefer more direct experience in managing a service operation. Since the car repair and service business is in my blood, I know I will be a fast learner.

You said that about two weeks would be needed to interview additional candidates. Count on me to start work on July 1, should you extend me a job offer.

Sincerely yours,

Rita Mae Jenkins

employer. You have to learn to accept such rejection in stride, remembering that a good deal of personal chemistry is involved in being hired. Suppose the person doing the hiring likes you personally. You then have a much greater chance of being hired for the position than does another individual of comparable merit. If the interviewer dislikes you, the reverse is true.

Since rejection is frequent in job hunting, it is easy to become discouraged. An important strategy is to keep pressure on yourself to avoid slowing down because you are discouraged. Remember, you have to perform dozens of tasks in finding a job. Many of them have already been described, such as preparing a statement of your job objective, a cover letter, and a résumé. You also have to line up your references and take care of every job lead that comes your way. When you do not have a job, almost no sensible lead should be ignored. Each lead processed takes you one step closer to finding a job. And all you are looking for is one job.

SUMMARY

Job-finding skills may be used at different stages in your career. The process of finding a job sometimes facilitates choosing a career. The job search begins with a reasonably flexible statement of the type of job you are seeking (your job objective). A job objective can also include the type of place you would like to work.

Qualifications frequently sought by employers include: appropriate education and satisfactory grades, relevant work experience, communication and interpersonal skills, motivation, problem-solving ability, flexibility, emotional maturity, and leadership. Your chances of finding a suitable job increase if you investigate occupations, fields, and industries in which opportunities are expanding.

A systematic job search relies on a wide variety of job-finding techniques including: networking (developing contacts), sending letters to the prospective employer list, and using placement offices and employment agencies. Be creative in thinking of job-finding alternatives and begin your job search about six months in advance.

An attention-getting cover letter should accompany your job résumé. The letter should explain why you are applying for a particular position and should identify your potential contribution to the employer. Be positive and forceful without being brash.

An effective job résumé is the core of the job campaign. Most firms require a résumé before seriously considering an external or internal job candidate. There is no one best way to prepare a résumé. Effective résumés are straightforward, factual presentations of a person's experience and accomplishments.

The chronological résumé presents your work experience, education, and interests, along with your accomplishments, in reverse chronological order. The functional résumé organizes your skills and accomplishments into the functions or tasks that support the job you are seeking. The targeted résumé focuses on a specific job target, or position, and presents only information that supports that target.

The job objective on your résumé should describe the position you are seeking now or in the short-term future. Creative-style résumés bring favorable attention to your credentials, but should be used with discretion.

A résumé should be neat, well organized, and professional in appearance. Common résumé mistakes to avoid include: excessive length, disorganization, poor typing or word processing, insufficient or excessive information, no listing of accomplishments, spelling and input errors, missing facts, and inflated facts.

It is helpful to rehearse being interviewed, and then present yourself favorably but accurately in the interview. Specific interview tips include: (1) prepare in advance, (2) arrive on time, (3) dress appropriately, (4) have reasons to justify your plans, (5) focus on important things about the job, (6) do not worry too much about hidden meanings, (7) be ready to discuss your strengths and weaknesses, (8) allow the interviewer to talk, (9) ask good questions, and (10) show how you can help the employer.

A stress interview is a deliberate method of placing a job applicant under considerable pressure and then observing his or her reactions. When placed under this type of pressure use a relaxation technique or express your feelings. Also, be prepared for a stress interview by having anecdotes to support your statements.

Finding a job can be a demanding task with some joys and many frustrations. It is therefore important to keep pressure on yourself to perform the many chores required of a successful job-hunting campaign. Process every lead and try not to take rejection personally.

QUESTIONS AND ACTIVITIES

1. Which technique of job finding is used most frequently by people you know? What accounts for the popularity of this technique?

2. What do you think is the main reason that production and clerical workers rarely use a job résumé?

3. What do you think of the practice of sending a prospective employer a tape cassette with information about yourself, instead of using a résumé and cover letter?

4. What are the advantages and disadvantages of asking a parent or spouse to help you find a job?

5. Why do you think that top-paying jobs in most fields are rarely advertised or listed with employment agencies?

6. What should you do if it appears the job interviewer and you have negative chemistry, or "bad vibes"?

7. It has been said that some interviewers use stress interviews just to relieve the boredom of interviewing job candidates. How can this observation help you deal with a stress interview?

8. Ask an experienced career person what he or she thinks is the best method of finding a job. Be prepared to discuss your findings in class.

9. What can you do today to help you develop a contact that could someday lead to a job?

A HUMAN RELATIONS CASE PROBLEM: THE NEGATIVE REFERENCE CHECK

As Kevin concluded his interview with Peggy Samson of Ramco Enterprises, he was quite pleased. Ms. Samson gave him reason to feel good as she said, "Kevin, you appear to be just the type of person we want in our sales force. You have some work experience, your education is fine, and you make a good first impression. However, before we can make you a firm job offer, we have to check out a few routine details. You'll be hearing from us quite soon."

The smile of Kevin's face quickly turned into a frown, reflecting his inner concern. He thought as he walked out the door of the Ramco office, "I hope this lady isn't going to check my references. That darn amusement park incident will pop up again. On the other hand, maybe she'll let things go with my reference at the restaurant. I know that one to be real good."

Later that day, Peggy Samson did call Olympic Amusement Park and spoke to the owner. "Hello there, Mr. Gordon, this is Peggy Samson from Ramco Enterprises. We've interviewed a young man, Kevin Yates, who apparently worked for you several summers."

"Yeah, I know the guy well. What do you want to know about him?"

"Kevin has applied for a sales position with us," answered Peggy. "How well does he handle people?"

Gordon paused for a moment and then answered, "If this is confidential, I'll tell you the whole story. The guy can be a real hothead. He got into two fights while working for us. The first time he floored another park employee who he claimed insulted him. We told him that one more fight and he would be out. Later that summer he punched out a customer. Kevin claimed the customer knocked him down while running to get a good set on the carousel.

"Kevin's a nice kid. But I wouldn't trust him with customers. One of them might rub him the wrong way."

One week later, Kevin received a letter from Ramco Enterprises thanking him for his interest in the job, but also explaining that another candidate was chosen. Discouraged, Kevin telephoned Peggy Samson to learn more about why he wasn't hired.

"Ms. Samson, this is Kevin Yates. I really wanted to work for Ramco. I know I could do a good job for you, but I respect your decision. As a personal favor to me, could you please tell me why I wasn't hired?"

"Kevin, all I'm at liberty to say, is that your reference checks were not quite as strong as we would like. Otherwise everything was fine. Good luck in finding the right job for yourself."

Kevin thought to himself, "Foiled again by those darn amusement park fights. Neither of them was my fault, but nobody wants to hear my side of the story. I wonder if I'll ever get a job?"

Questions

1. What strategy should Kevin use to overcome his negative reference check given out by the amusement park?
2. In what way would you criticize Peggy Samson?
3. Should Kevin have brought up the topic of the amusement park incidents before Peggy checked his references?

A HUMAN RELATIONS ROLE PLAY: THE STRESSFUL AND THE SUPPORTIVE JOB INTERVIEWS

The interviewee role players in the situation described below play themselves. The interviewee thus tries to act as he or she would under real circumstances. Your own work and educational background, attitudes, and preferences can be used as the basis for your answers. Both interviewees should assume that they want the job in question—a high-paying position as assistant to the marketing vice-president of a major airline. As a fringe benefit, the person hired will have free air travel to many places in the world.

One person plays the role of the stress interviewer. After a pleasant warm-up, your intention is to place the interviewee under a good deal of pressure. You firmly believe that a person who cracks under pressure is unsuited for this job.

Another person plays the role of the supportive (warm and reassuring) interviewer. You want to encourage the person to talk freely and to feel respected.

Both interviewers should prepare some questions in advance. After the interview samples (about fifteen minutes) have been conducted, other class members will provide feedback on the behavior of both interviewer and interviewee.

REFERENCES

[1] Bob Weinstein, "What Employers Look For," in *The Honda How to Get a Job Guide* (*BusinessWeek's Guide to Careers,* 1985), pp. 10–13; William T. Leonard, "What the Recruiter Looks For," *BusinessWeek's Guide to Careers,* Fall/Winter 1983, pp. 22–23.

[2] Karen O. Dowd, "The Art of Making Contacts," in *The Honda How to Get a Job Guide* (*BusinessWeek's Guide to Careers,* 1985), p. 24.

[3] Peggy Schmidt, "When to Start Looking for a Job," *BusinessWeek's Guide to Careers,* February 1986, p. 71.

[4] Tom Jackson, "Writing the Targeted Resume," *BusinessWeek's Guide to Careers,* Spring 1983, p. 24; Sandra Grundfest, "A Cover Letter and Resume Guide," *Honda's How to Get A Job Guide* Published by *BusinessWeek's Guide to Careers,* 1986 edition, p. 9.

[5] Jackson, "Writing the Targeted Resume," pp. 26–27; and John W. Zehring, "18 Rules for Résumé Writers," in Bill Repp, *Why Give It Away When You Can Sell It?* (Rochester, NY: Creative Communications, 1982), pp. 121–124.

[6] Marcia Fox, "Interview Do's and Don'ts," *BusinessWeek's Guide to Careers,* Spring/Summer 1984, p. 52.

[7] Sandra L. Davis, "How to Handle the Stress Interview," *BusinessWeek's Guide to Careers,* March/April 1985, p. 28.

[8] Ibid., p. 29.

SOME ADDITIONAL READING

ARTHUR, DIANE. "Preparing for the Interview." *Personnel,* February 1986, pp. 37–49.

FADER, SHIRLEY SLOAN. "Those Intimidating Interview Questions." *BusinessWeek's Guide to Careers,* October 1984, pp. 26–29.

LEVITT, JULIE GRIFFIN. *Your Career: How to Make It Happen.* Cincinnati, OH: South-Western Publishing Co., 1985.

MEDLEY, H. ANTHONY. *Sweaty Palms: The Neglected Art of Being Interviewed.* New York: Lifetime Learning, 1985.

ROGERS, EDWARD J. *Getting Hired.* Englewood Cliffs, NJ: Prentice-Hall, 1984.

SALKIND, BONNIE LYONS. "Diary of a Job Search." *Personal Journal,* February 1985, pp. 44–48.

12

Developing Good Work Habits

Learning Objectives

After studying the information and doing the exercises in this chapter, you should be able to:

- Appreciate the importance of good work habits and time management
- Cut down on your procrastination
- Develop attitudes and values that will help you become more productive
- Develop skills and techniques that will help you become more productive

THE IMPORTANCE OF GOOD WORK HABITS AND
TIME MANAGEMENT

A person is more likely to be fired from a job or flunk out of school because of poor **work habits** rather than poor aptitude. Furthermore, many people impair their personal lives because they are disorganized in setting up social appointments. In contrast, people with good work habits tend to be more successful in their careers than poorly organized individuals, and they tend to have more time to spend on personal life. They also enjoy their personal lives more because they are not preoccupied with unfinished tasks.

Good work habits and time management are more important than ever because of today's emphasis on productivity. **Personal productivity** refers to your level of efficiency and effectiveness. Efficiency means that you accomplish tasks with a minimum of wasted time and fanfare. Effectiveness refers to accomplishing important results while maintaining high quality. Being efficient often clears the way for being effective. If you are on top of your job, it gives you the time to work on important tasks and strive for quality.

The goal of this chapter is to help you become a more productive person who is still flexible. Someone who develops good work habits is not someone who becomes so obsessed with time and so rigid that he or she makes other people feel uncomfortable. Ideally, you should become well organized but still be flexible.

We have organized information about becoming more productive into three main categories that show some overlap. One is overcoming procrastination, a problem that plagues everybody to some extent. The second is developing attitudes and values that foster efficiency and effectiveness. The third category is the lengthiest: developing the skills and techniques that lead to personal productivity.

DEALING WITH PROCRASTINATION

Procrastination is putting off doing a task for no valid reason. It is the major work habit problem for most employees and students. Exhibit 12–1 will help you recognize when you are procrastinating. Unproductive people are the biggest procrastinators, but even highly productive people have some problems with procrastination. A reporter for *People* magazine had this to say about procrastinators: "Some of the most talented writers are practically starving. Magazine editors respect their talents, but they know that if these writers are given an

306

EXHIBIT 12–1   HOW DO YOU KNOW WHEN YOU ARE PROCRASTINATING?

Obviously, when you are not getting things done that should be done you are procrastinating. Procrastination can also be much more subtle. You might be procrastinating if one or more of the following symptoms apply to you:

- You overorganize a project by such rituals as sharpening every pencil, meticulously straightening out your desk, and discarding bent paper clips.
- You overresearch something before taking action, such as getting five different estimates on replacing a defective auto radiator.
- You keep waiting for the "right time" to do something, such as getting started on an important report.
- You underestimate the time needed to do a project, and say to yourself, "This won't take much time, so I can do it next week."

SOURCE: Based on information in "Procrastination Can Get in Your Way," *Research Institute Personal Report for the Executive,* December 24, 1985, pp. 3–4.

---

assignment, it will not be completed on time. The writers I'm talking about just can't get it together to meet deadlines."[1]

Why People Procrastinate

People procrastinate for many different reasons. One is that we perceive the task to be done, such as quitting a job, as unpleasant. Another reason we procrastinate is that we find the job facing us to be overwhelming, such as painting a house. Another major cause of procrastination is a fear of the consequences of our actions.[2]

One possible negative consequence is a negative evaluation of your work. For example, if you delay preparing a report for your boss or instructor, that person cannot criticize its quality. Bad news is another negative consequence that procrastination can sometimes delay. If you think your personal computer needs a new disk drive, delaying a trip to the computer store means you will not have to hear the diagnosis: "Your disk drive needs replacement. We can do the job for about three hundred and seventy-five dollars."

Another reason some people procrastinate is that they fear success. People sometimes believe that if they succeed at an important task, they will be asked to take on more responsibility in the future. They dread this possibility. Some students have been known to procrastinate completing their degree requirements in order to avoid taking on the responsibility of a full-time position.

Techniques for Reducing Procrastination

To overcome, or at least minimize, procrastination we recommend a number of specific tactics. A general approach, however, is simply to be aware that procrastination is a major drain on productivity. Being aware of the problem will remind you to take corrective action in many situations. When your accomplishment level is low, you might ask yourself, "Am I procrastinating on anything of significance?"

Calculate the Cost of Procrastination. You can reduce procrastination by calculating its cost.[3] One example is that you might lose out on obtaining a high-paying job you really want by not having your résumé and cover letter ready on time. Your cost of procrastination would include the difference in salary between the job you do find and the one you really wanted. Another cost would be the loss of potential job satisfaction.

Create Some Momentum to Get You Moving. One way to get momentum going on an unpleasant or overwhelming task is to set aside a specific time to work on it. If you have to write a report on a subject you dislike, you might set aside Saturday from 3 P.M. to 5 P.M. as your time to first attack the project. Another way to create some momentum is to find a leading task to perform. A **leading task** is an easy, warm-up activity.[4] If you were procrastinating about painting your apartment, you might purchase the brush and paint as a way of getting started.

Peck Away at an Overwhelming Task. Assume that you have a major project to do that does not have to be accomplished in a hurry. A good way of minimizing procrastination is to peck away at the project in fifteen- to thirty-minute bits of time. Bit by bit the project will get down to manageable size and therefore not seem so overwhelming. "Pecking away" is also referred to as the **Swiss-cheese method** because you eat holes in the total task.

A related way of pecking away at an overwhelming task is to subdivide it into smaller units. For instance, you might break moving down into a series of tasks such as filing change-of-address notices, locating a mover, and packing books.

Motivate Yourself with Rewards and Punishments. Give yourself a pleasant reward soon after you accomplish a task you would ordinarily procrastinate about. You might, for example, jog through the woods after having completed a tough take-home exam. The second part of this tactic is to punish yourself if you have engaged in serious procrastination. How about eating only oatmeal for five days?

Make a Commitment to Other People. Put pressure on yourself to get something done on time by making it a commitment to one or more other people. You might announce to co-workers that you are going to get a project of mutual concern completed by a certain date. If you fail to meet this date you may feel embarrassed. One administrative assistant told his co-workers, "I will get the new coffee system in our office by March thirty-first, or I will buy everybody's coffee for a week."

DEVELOPING THE PROPER ATTITUDES AND VALUES

Developing good work habits and time-management practices is often a matter of developing proper attitudes toward work and time. For instance, if you think that your job is important and that time is valuable, you will be on your way toward developing good work habits. In this section we describe a group of attitudes and values that can help improve your productivity through better use of time and improved work habits.

Value Your Time

Successful people believe that their time is valuable. It is therefore difficult to engage them in idle conversation during working hours. Successful people also minimize wasting their own time by such means as daydreaming on the job or taking a two-hour lunch break unrelated to business. As you proceed further into your career, the value of your time will usually increase.

Become a Goal-Oriented Person

Being committed to a goal propels you toward good use of time. Imagine how efficient most employees would be if they were told, "Here is five days' worth of work facing you. If you get it finished in less than five days, you can have all that saved time to yourself." One negative side effect, however, is that many employees might sacrifice quality for speed.

Having goals, and thus becoming a goal-oriented person, is perhaps the first step in any serious program of improving work habits and time management.

Value Good Attendance and Punctuality

On the job, in school, or in personal life, good attendance and punctuality are essential for developing a good reputation. Also, you can't accomplish much if you're not there. Has a friend ever failed to show up when he or she promised to drive you to the airport? Or has a co-worker ever not showed up when the two of you were supposed to handle an assignment?

Two important myths about attendance and punctuality should be challenged early in your career. One is that a certain number of sick days are owed an employee. Some employees who have not used up their sick days will find reasons to be sick at the end of the year. Another myth is that absence is preferred to lateness. Some employees believe, for example, that it is more honorable to be absent because of illness than late because of oversleeping. Consequently, the employee who oversleeps calls in sick rather than face the embarrassment of arriving to work late.

Value Neatness and Orderliness

An orderly desk, file cabinet, or work area does not inevitably signify an orderly mind. Yet orderliness does help most people become more productive. Less time is wasted and less energy is expended if you do not have to hunt for missing information. Knowing where information is and what information you have available is a way of being in control of your job. When your job gets out of control, you are probably working at less than peak efficiency. The best approach to maintaining a neat work area is to convince yourself that neatness is valuable.

Strive for Both Quantity and Quality

"Tell me," said the new employee to the supervisor, "are you looking for quantity or quality on this job?" The wise supervisor replied, "Both." Most employees want a great deal of work accomplished but they also need high-quality work. Anyone who has had an auto recalled knows firsthand the costs (including human time and irritation) associated with low quality.

As a first principle, work as rapidly as you can just before the point at which you are committing an unacceptable number of errors. Striving for perfection is usually not worth the price, but achieving high-quality goods and services is valued in most firms today.

Avoid Perfectionism

Thoroughness on most jobs is a virtue until it reaches the point of diminishing returns. Perfectionists devote so much attention to detail that they have difficulty ever completing a project. They continue to work toward perfection past the project's due date. Another key problem of **perfectionism** is that perfectionists often fail to see the "big picture." They want to stay on top of every detail and be in control of the outcome of situations. Since the overall picture is uncertain, the perfectionist focuses on the more certain details.[5]

To become more productive, the perfectionist must admit that he or she is striving too hard to reach an impossible goal. Only by making this admission can perfectionists become less harsh with themselves and others and learn to tolerate mistakes more readily.

Appreciate the Importance of Rest and Relaxation

A valid attitude to maintain is that overwork can be counterproductive and lead to negative stress and burnout. Proper physical rest contributes to mental alertness and improved ability to cope with frustration. Constant attention to work or study is often inefficient. It is a normal human requirement to take enough rest breaks to allow oneself to approach work or study with a fresh perspective. Each person has to establish the right balance between work and leisure within the bounds of freedom granted by the situation.

DEVELOPING THE PROPER SKILLS AND TECHNIQUES

So far we have discussed improving productivity from standpoints of dealing with procrastination and developing the right attitudes and values. Skills and techniques are also important for becoming more efficient and effective. Here we describe some well-established methods of work-habit improvement, along with several new ones.

Prepare a List and Set Priorities

Almost every successful person in any field composes a list of important and less-important tasks that need doing. Some executives and professional people delegate their list making and errand running to a subordinate. These lists are similar to the daily goals described in Chapter 2. Before you can compose a useful list, you need to set aside a few moments a day to sort out the tasks at hand. Such activity is the most basic aspect of planning. A list used by a working parent is presented in Figure 12–1.

Where Do You Put Your Lists? Some people dislike having small "To Do" lists stuck in different places. One reason is that these lists are readily lost among other papers. Many people therefore put lists on

FIGURE 12–1. A SAMPLE "TO DO" LIST

From the Desk of Jennifer Bartow

JOB

Make ten calls to prospects for new listings.
Have "For Sale" signs put outside Hanover Blvd. house.
Set up mortgage appointment at 1st Federal for the Calhouns.
Get old file cabinets replaced.
Order new memo pads.
Meet with the Goldsteins at 5 PM.
Set up time to show house to the Bowens.

HOME

Buy running shoes for Todd.
Buy Jeans for Linda.
Get defroster fixed on freezer.
Write and send out monthly bills.
Clip cat's nails.
Check out problem with septic tank.
Make appt. with dentist to have chipped filling replaced.

FIRST REALTY CORPORATION
Jacksonville, Florida

---

desk calendars or printed forms called daily planners. Software is also available to help you keep track of your activities.[6]

A time-management consultant recommends another useful approach. Use a notebook (either spiral or loose-leaf) that is small enough to carry around with you. The notebook becomes your master list to keep track of errands, things to do or buy, and general notes to yourself about anything requiring action.[7]

Setting Priorities. Because everything on a "To Do" list is not of equal importance, priorities should be attached to each item. A typical system is to use A to signify critical or essential items, B to signify important items, and C for the least important ones. Although an item might be regarded as a C (for example, refilling your stapler), it still has a contribution to make to your productivity and sense of well-being. Many people report that they obtain a sense of satisfaction from crossing an item however trivial, off their list. Second, if you are at all conscientious, small undone items will come back to interfere with your concentration.

Concentrate on One Task at a Time

Effective people have a well-developed capacity to concentrate on the problem or person facing them, however surrounded they are with potential distractions. The best results from concentration are achieved when you are so absorbed in your work that you are aware of virtually nothing else at the moment. Another useful by-product of concentration is that it helps reduce absentmindedness. If you really concentrate on what you are doing, the chances that you will forget what you intended to do diminish.

Researchers have discovered that conscious effort and self-discipline can strengthen concentration skills. "There are two types of concentration: passive and active," explains psychologist Auke Tellegen. "The former is used when you are drawn into something riveting, such as a good novel. The latter demands self-constraint." The best way to sharpen your concentration skills is to set aside fifteen minutes a day and focus on something repetitive, such as your breathing or a small word. This is the same approach that is used in mediation to relieve stress.[8]

Concentrate on Important Tasks

To become more effective in your job, or at home, you have to concentrate on tasks in which superior performance could have a large payoff. No matter how quickly you took care of making sure that your store paid its bills on time, for example, this effort would not make your store an outstanding success. If, however, you concentrated your efforts on bringing unique and desirable merchandise into the store, this action could greatly affect your business success. At home, cleaning out a child's toy box might be constructive. But a greater payoff would come from helping that child learn a skill like riding a tricycle.

In following the A-B-C system, you should devote ample time to the essential tasks. You should not pay more attention than absolutely necessary to the C (trivial) items. Many people respond to this suggestion by saying, "I don't think concentrating on important tasks applies to me. My job is so filled with routine, I have no chance to work on the big breakthrough ideas." True, most jobs are filled with routine requirements. What a person can do is spend some time, perhaps even one hour a week, concentrating on tasks of potentially major significance.

Exhibit 12–2 presents a case history of a man who capitalized on the technique of concentrating on important tasks.

EXHIBIT 12–2   RAY MAKES AN IMPACT ON HIS SKI SHOP

Several years ago Ray worked as the manager of the repair department in a thriving ski shop. During the nonskiing season Ray helped with the sale and repair of bicycles and performed miscellaneous maintenance chores around the store. Ray became preoccupied with the idea that somehow the ski shop where he worked should become truly a year-round store. He saw a good future for the store and himself if it became a more profitable enterprise. Ray asked his boss, the store owner, to allow him to devote one hour a work day to planning for an all-season store. His proposal met with skepticism. Ray saw several alternatives. He could: (1) quite the store and look for an employer who was more receptive to his forward thinking; (2) use his nonwork hours for planning to make the store into a busy year-round enterprise; (3) drop the idea; or (4) continue to prod the boss to give him a chance to develop and implement a plan for store diversification.

Ray chose alternative (4). He tactfully and assertively pestered the store owner until he was granted the opportunity to develop a plan to move the skip shop toward an all-season venture.

Ray devoted one hour a day to developing ideas and collecting information about additional merchandise lines for his store. After six months of investigation, Ray shocked his boss in a positive way with a detailed marketing report on the diversification of the ski shop into a two-season (winter and spring-summer-fall) store. Ray comments:

"My boss was particularly impressed with the logic of my ideas. I wrote and phoned other ski shops that had achieved success with diversification. I did the same for the failures. At my suggestion, we basically turned to a ski, tennis, racquetball, and bicycle shop. But we also threw in a very important addition. We called this the "hot sport" department. Whatever fad came along that seemed to hold promise of at least a two-year run became a candidate for that department.

"Skateboards are a perfect example. We had the most solidly stocked skateboard department in town. A promotional stunt I invented was to have a group of fellow and gals clad in bathing suits skate outside the store. We set up a small ramp on which they could perform tricks. We sold hundreds of skateboards that way."

Ray's persistence and imaginative thinking paid off. The store prospered, and his boss developed trust in Ray's business judgment. Because of this, Ray was offered a chance to buy into the business. His focus on important tasks—instead of on sorting inventory and tending to store maintenance during the off-season—represented a breakthrough in his career.

Work at a Steady Pace

In most jobs, working at a steady clip pays dividends in efficiency. The spurt worker creates many problems for management. Some employees take pride in working rapidly, even when the result is a high error rate. At home, too, a steady pace is better than spurting. A spurt houseworker is one who goes into a flurry of activity every so often. An easier person to live with is someone who does his or her share of housework at an even pace throughout the year.

Another advantage of the steady pace approach is that you accomplish much more than someone who puts out extra effort just once in a while. The completely steady worker would accomplish just as much the day before a holiday as on a given Monday. That extra hour or so of productivity adds up substantially by the end of the year. Despite the advantages of maintaining a steady pace, some peaks and valleys in your work may be inevitable.

Schedule Similar Tasks Together

An efficient method of accomplishing small tasks is to group them together and perform them in one block of time. To illustrate, you might make most of your telephone calls in relation to your job from 11:00 to 11:30 each workday morning. Or you might reserve the last hour of every workday for correspondence. When you go downtown or to a shopping mall, think of all the errands that can be run while you are in that location. Over a period of time, you will save a large number of wasted trips.

By using this method you develop the necessary pace and mental set to go through chores in short order. In contrast, when you jump from one type of task to another, your efficiency may suffer.

Identify and Plug Time Leaks

A useful way of accomplishing more work each day and therefore developing better work habits is to plug time leaks. A time leak is anything you are doing or not doing that allows time to get away from you. One time leak found in many school and work settings is gathering people together for lunch. Have you ever noticed that the luncheon gang starts collecting people at 11:45 A.M? By the time they start lunch, it is 12:15 P.M. Often the crowd does not return until 1:15 P.M. Or have you seen the "chain coffee break" in the cafeteria? As you are about to get up from your coffee break, another person comes to join you. So you stay an extra ten minutes. As you are about to get up again, someone else joins you. And so on, until a third of the morning has leaked away.

A major time leak for many workers is **schmoozing**, informal socializing on the job including small talk and telephone conversations with friends. Other notable time leaks include excessive time spent warming up to get started working, too much time spent winding down to stop working, and visiting other employees instead of phoning them to discuss a work problem. Or what about standing in the halls before class starts?

Make Use of Bits of Time

A truly productive person makes good use of miscellaneous bits of time, both on and off the job. While waiting in line at a post office, you might update your "To Do" list; while waiting for an elevator, you might be able to read a brief report; and if you have finished your day's work ten minutes before quitting time, you can use that time to clean out a file. By the end of the year your productivity will have increased much more than if you had squandered these bits of time.[9]

The new craze referred to as "grazing" is a variation of making good use of bits of time. **Grazing** is eating meals on the run in order to make good use of time ordinarily spent on sitting down for meals. Many ambitious young people today nibble at snacks rather than disrupt their work by visiting a restaurant.[10] Grazing does have its disadvantages: you cannot network while grazing, eating while working can be bad for digestion and it may deprive you of a needed rest break.

Harness Your Natural Energy Cycles

The old beliefs, "I'm a morning person," or "I'm a night person," are backed up by scientific findings. According to studies of biorhythms, people vary somewhat in their hours of peak efficiency. A week of charting should help you to determine the hours at which your mental and physical energy is apt to be highest or lowest.

After you have determined your **energy cycles**, that is, your strong and weak energy periods, you should be able to arrange your work or study schedule accordingly. Tackle your most intellectually demanding assignments during your energy peaks. Avoid creative work or making major decisions when fatigue has set in.

What do you do if you're a night person but your job demands a morning person or at least an afternoon person? Gradually shift your internal time clock to the point at which you can do your most demanding work during normal working hours. Perhaps a one-hour shift each week over a few months will be enough for the conversion. Shifting eating and sleeping times should help. Specifically, go to bed earlier and eat a larger breakfast in order to become a morning person.

Stay in Control of Paperwork

The federal government once made a $168 million mistake because someone forgot to compare two sets of blueprints on a large plumbing and heating job. Other examples of failure to pay attention to necessary paperwork are failure to answer a memo or failure to renew a registration sticker. Paperwork essentially involves taking care of minor administrative details such as correspondence, expense account forms, and inventory forms. If it is argued that the widespread use of computers and copying machines has increased, rather than decreased paperwork in the office, then managing paperwork has actually become more important in our daily lives.

Unless you handle paperwork efficiently, you may lose control of

your job or home life. Once that happens, a stress reaction may take place. Ideally, a small amount of time should be invested in paperwork every day. Nonprime time (when you are at less than your peak of efficiency, but not overly fatigued) is the best time to take care of paperwork.

Set a Time Limit for Certain Tasks

As workers become experienced with certain projects, they are able to make accurate estimates of how long a project will take to complete. A paralegal assistant might say, for example, "Getting this will drawn up for the lawyer's approval should take about two hours." A good work habit to develop is to estimate how long a job should take and then strive to complete the job within the estimated time.

A productive variation of this technique is to decide that some B and C items are only worth so much of your time. Invest that much time on the project, but no more. Preparing a file on advertisements that cross your desk is one example.

Ask "What is the Best Use of My Time Right Now?"

A major technique for improving your productivity is to ask, "What is the best use of my time right now?"[11] This question helps you to justify your every action. A particularly good time to ask this question is when you have been interrupted by a visitor or phone call. When the interruption has been completed, check whether you should go back to what you were doing or on to something new. Asking this question helps you to justify the productive value of many of your routines and rituals. For instance, "Is it really a good use of my time to search for a cigarette machine?"

Your answer to the best-use-of-time question may be different in comparable situations. One day you are waiting for an elevator in your office building. You ask, "What is the best possible use of my time right now?" Your answer is "Certainly not waiting for an elevator. I'll run up the stairs and get some needed exercise."

One week later you are again waiting for the elevator. You ask the same question. This time your answer is, "Waiting for the elevator is a good use of my time right now. It's about time I touched base with a few employees from different departments in the company. I would like to know what's going on."

Be Decisive and Finish Things

An often overlooked way of improving your personal productivity is to be decisive. Move quickly, but not impulsively, through the problem-solving and decision-making steps outlined in Chapter 3 when you are faced with a nonroutine decision. Once you have evaluated the alternatives to the problem, choose and implement one of them.

Another aspect of being decisive is to make the decision to finish tasks you have begun. Incompleted projects lower your productivity. Marge Baxter puts it this way: "It's better to complete a few things than to have seventeen things half done."[12] Another point to remember is that nobody gives you credit for an unfinished project.

HOW TO BEGIN IMPROVING YOUR WORK HABITS

Assume you were able to implement every suggestion in this chapter along with the suggestions made in Chapter 3 about solving problems and making decisions. You would now be on the road toward becoming one of the most productive people in your field. The flaw in the statement just made is that almost no one is equipped to implement immediately every suggestion. The best way to begin improving your work habits is to start small. Select one or two strategies that appear feasible and practical to you. Try out the strategy. Monitor your progress and move on to another strategy.

A good starting point for anyone wanting to become more productive is to sort out things and make up a list. Another useful approach is to review the tactics mentioned in this chapter in a checklist manner. Then implement several tactics of the most relevance for your particular circumstances. Exhibit 12–3 can be used for this purpose. The same exhibit also suggests a classroom activity that will help you gain momentum in becoming more productive.

EXHIBIT 12–3   THE PERSONAL PRODUCTIVITY CHECKLIST

	Especially applicable to me
OVERCOMING PROCRASTINATION	
1. Increase general awareness of the problem.	____
2. Calculate cost of procrastination.	____
3. Create some momentum to get going.	____
4. Peck away at overwhelming task.	____
5. Motivate self with rewards and punishments.	____
6. Make commitment to other people.	____
DEVELOPING PROPER ATTITUDES AND VALUES	
1. Value your time.	____
2. Become a goal-oriented person.	____
3. Value good attendance and punctuality.	____
4. Value neatness and orderliness.	____
5. Strive for both quantity and quality.	____
6. Avoid perfectionism.	____
7. Appreciate the importance of rest and relaxation.	____

DEVELOPING THE PROPER SKILLS AND TECHNIQUES

	Especially applicable to me
1. Prepare a list and set priorities.	____
2. Concentrate on one task at a time.	____
3. Concentrate on important tasks.	____
4. Work at a steady pace.	____
5. Schedule similar tasks together.	____
6. Identify and plug time leaks.	____
7. Make use of bits of time.	____
8. Harness your natural energy cycles.	____
9. Stay in control of paperwork.	____
10. Set a time limit for certain tasks.	____
11. Ask "What is the best use of my time right now?"	____
12. Be decisive and finish things.	____

CLASS PROJECT

Each class member will use the above checklist to identify the two biggest mistakes he or she is making in work habits and time management. The mistakes could apply to work, school, or personal life. In addition to identifying the problem, each student will develop a brief action plan about how to overcome it. For instance, "One of my biggest problems is that I tend to start a lot of projects but finish very few of them. Now that I am aware of this problem, I am going to post a sign over my desk that reads, 'St. Peter won't give me credit for things I never completed.'"

Students then present their problems and action plans in front of the class. After each student has made his or her presentation, a class discussion is held to reach conclusions and interpretations about the problems revealed. For instance, it might be that one or two time management problems are quite frequent.

How Personal Characteristics Influence Your Ability to Improve Your Work Habits

Some people will find it easier than others to improve their productivity. Above all, you need the right talent and motivation to make much improvement feasible. Another factor is that certain personality characteristics are related to work habits and time management. At the top of the list is **compulsiveness**, a tendency to pay careful attention to detail and to be meticulous. A compulsive person takes naturally to being well organized and neat. If you are less concerned about detail and meticulousness by nature, it will be more difficult for you to develop exceptional work habits.

People who are highly spontaneous and emotional also tend to be naturally inclined toward casual work habits. Being overly compulsive can also be a detriment to personal productivity. The compulsive person may have a difficult time concentrating on important tasks, but get hung up on details and fail to see the "big picture." The truly productive person finds an optimum balance between concern for detail and the larger perspective.

SUMMARY

People with good work habits tend to be more successful in their careers than poorly organized individuals, and they tend to have more time to spend on personal life. Good work habits are more important than ever because of today's emphasis on productivity. Personal productivity refers to your level of efficiency and effectiveness.

Procrastination is the major work habit problem for most employees and students. People procrastinate for many reasons, including their perception that a task is unpleasant, overwhelming, or may lead to negative consequences. Fear of success can also lead to procrastination. Awareness of procrastination may lead to its control. Five other techniques for reducing procrastination are: (1) calculate the cost of procrastination, (2) create some momentum to get you moving, (3) peck away at an overwhelming task, (4) motivate yourself with rewards and punishments, and (5) make a commitment to other people.

Developing good work habits and time management practices is often a matter of developing proper attitudes toward work and time. Seven such attitudes, values, and beliefs are: (1) value your time, (2) become a goal-oriented person, (3) value good attendance and punctuality, (4) value neatness and orderliness, (5) strive for quantity and quality, (6) avoid perfectionism, (7) appreciate the importance of rest and relaxation.

Twelve skills and techniques to help you become more efficient and effective, and therefore more productive, are as follows: (1) prepare a list and set priorities, (2) concentrate on one task at a time, (3) concentrate on important tasks, (4) work at a steady pace, (5) schedule similar tasks together, (6) identify and plug time leaks, (7) make use of bits of time, (8) harness your natural energy cycles, (9) stay in control of paper work, (10) set a time limit for certain tasks, (11) ask "What is the best use of my time right now?" and (12) be decisive and finish things.

The best way to begin improving your work habits is to start small. Select one or two tactics that appear particularly relevant to your circumstances and give them a try. Monitor your progress and then move on to another tactic.

QUESTIONS AND ACTIVITIES

1. Why are good work habits and time management practices essential for the self-employed person?

2. What is your reaction to the statement, "People who are very well organized are usually not creative"?

3. To what extent do athletes practice good work habits and time management practices during a game?

4. How can you estimate how well organized a person is upon first meeting him or her?

5. Give an example for your own life in which striving for perfection was not worth the effort.

6. What is your reaction to the statement, "A clear and orderly desk reflects a clear and orderly mind"?

7. What is the best use of your time right now?

8. Ask an experienced career person what steps he or she takes to stay well organized under pressure. Be prepared to discuss your findings in class.

A HUMAN RELATIONS CASE PROBLEM: THE OVERWHELMED ORDERLY

Hank looked into the mirror of the hospital locker room and thought to himself, "You're looking bad, kid. Somehow, you've got to get your life straightened out. You're on a treadmill and you don't know how to get off. But no time for thinking about myself now; it's time for my meeting with my boss, Nurse Simpson. I wonder what she wants?"

Anne Simpson began the meeting with Hank in her usual candid manner: "Hank, I'm concerned about you. For a long time you were one of the best orderlies on the floor. You received compliments from nurses, doctors, and patients. Now you're hardly making it. You've become so irritable, so lacking in enthusiasm. We've talked about this in the past. The reason I'm bringing the subject up again is that things have gotten worse. What's the problem?"

"I wish it were only one problem, Nurse Simpson. I feel like the world is caving in on me. I work here about forty hours a week. I'm trying to upgrade myself in life. As you know I'm taking two courses in an engineering technology program. If I can keep up the pace, I'll qualify for an engineering technician job in one year. But it's getting to be a grind."

"How are things at home, Hank?"

"Much worse than they are here. My wife works, too, and she's getting fed up with never seeing me when she comes home. It seems that when she's home, I'm either at the hospital, in class, or studying at the library.

"Our daughter, Heather, isn't too happy either. She's only five but the other day she asked me if her Mommy and I were getting divorced. She doesn't see us together much. When she does see us, we're fighting."

"So you're under pressure at the hospital and at home," said Anne.

"Add school to that list. I'm having a devil of a time getting through the electronics course I'm taking. If I flunk, my program goes down the tubes."

"Do the best you can, Hank. I'm sympathetic, but I need better performance from you."

As Hank left Nurse Simpson's office, he said, "Thanks for being honest with me. My problem is that my boss, my wife, my child, and my professors all want better performance from me. I wish I knew how to give it."

Questions

1. What suggestions can you offer Hank for working his way out of his problems?
2. Why is this case included in a chapter about improving your work habits?
3. How well do you think Anne Simpson handled the interview?

A HUMAN RELATIONS ROLE PLAY: HELPING AN OVERWHELMED ORDERLY

The above case gives you the background information for this role play. One person plays the role of Nurse Simpson, who has decided to meet with Hank again to help him deal with his problems. Simpson will listen to Hank discuss his problems and then give him some good advice about working his way out of his predicament.

Another person plays the role of Hank, who is so anxious about his predicament that he doubts Nurse Simpson can be of much help. Nevertheless, he wants to be helped because he feels that his life is getting out of control.

REFERENCES

[1] Personal communication from Cable Neuhaus, January 1983.

[2] Henry C. Everett, M.D., "Conquering Procrastination," *Success!,* June 1981, p. 26.

[3] Alan Lakein, *How to Gain Control of Your Time and Your Life* (New York: Wyden Books, 1973), pp. 141–151.

[4] Michael LeBoeuf quoted in Priscilla Petty, "Saying No to Unproductive Jobs Frees Time for High-Priority Goals," Rochester *Democrat and Chronicle,* June 21, 1983, p. 10D.

[5] Robert M. Meier and Susan Sheffler, "The Perils of Perfectionism," *Success!,* September 1984, p. 14.

[6] "The 'Get Organized' Boom," *Research Institute Personal Report for the Executive,* March 1, 1986, p. 5.

[7] Stephanie Winston, *Getting Organized* (New York: Warner Books, 1979), p. 28.

[8] "Increase Your Powers of Concentration," *Research Institute Personal Report for the Executive,* January 7, 1986, p. 7.

[9] Warren Keith Schilit, "A Manager's Guide to Efficient Time Management," *Personnel Journal,* September 1983, p. 740; Winston, *Getting Organized,* p. 43.

[10] Nancy Jenkins, "Taking Meals on the Hoof," *New York Times* reprint, February 9, 1985.

[11] Lakein, *How to Gain Control,* p. 99.

[12] Quoted in Beth Brophy and Diane Cole, "10 Timely Tips," *USA Weekend,* October 25–27, 1985, p. 22.

SOME ADDITIONAL READING

BAKER, H. KENT, and PHILLIP I. MORGAN. "Building a Professional Image: Dealing with Time Problems." *Supervisory Management,* October 1985, pp. 36–42.

BERNARDO, STEPHANIE. "Time Is Money." *Success!,* September 1985, pp. 50–53.

"Don't Procrastinate." *Practical Supervision,* January 1986, p. 3.

JANUZ, LAUREN R., and SUSAN K. JONES. *Time Management for Executives.* New York: Scribner's, 1981.

TURLA, PETER A., and KATHLEEN L. HAWKINS. "How to Stay Charged Up All Day Long." *Success!,* June 1984, pp. 50, 52.

TURLA, PETER A., and KATHLEEN L. HAWKINS. *Time Management Made Easy.* New York: Dutton, 1984.

WEBBER, ROSS. *Time Is Money: The Key to Managerial Success.* New York: Free Press, 1980.

13

Getting Ahead in Your Career

Learning Objectives

After studying the information and doing the exercises in this chapter you should be able to:

- Recognize the importance of good interpersonal skills for getting ahead in your career
- Select several strategies and tactics for advancing your career by taking control of your own behavior
- Select several strategies and tactics for advancing your career by exerting control over your environment
- Think through how you would handle being unemployed

A central theme of this book is that certain skills and behaviors will help you succeed in your career and personal life. In this chapter we focus on a sampling of strategies, tactics, and attitudes that are specifically related to climbing the organizational ladder. For those people not interested in climbing the ladder, some of the same information can be used to keep yourself perched on the rung that fits your needs.

Since the information about how to succeed in business is so vast, we have divided it into three categories, each having a somewhat different slant: the first section deals with the need for **interpersonal** (or human relations) skills for getting ahead; the next section deals with approaches to managing or taking control of your own behavior in order to get ahead; and the third section deals with approaches to exerting control over your environment in order to improve your chances for success.

Since the word success has many subjective meanings, it requires some clarification. Success as used here means attaining the twin goals of organizational rewards and personal satisfaction. Organizational rewards include such things as higher ranking positions, more money, and challenging assignments. Personal satisfaction refers to enjoying, or liking, what you are doing. If your employer thinks you're terrific and therefore rewards you, and you're happy, you're a success from the viewpoint expressed here.

THE IMPORTANCE OF INTERPERSONAL SKILLS

It is exceedingly difficult to get ahead in business or any other work environment unless you can relate effectively to other people. People are bypassed for promotion generally because someone thought they could not effectively handle being responsible for the work of others. People are more likely to be fired for poor interpersonal skills than for poor technical skills. As one expert has put it, *"The most important skills for the success of your career are the interpersonal skills needed for cooperating with other employees."*[1]

Effective interpersonal or human relations skills can refer to many specific practices. At a meeting, if you crack a joke that relieves tension and serves as an ice-breaker, you are showing good interpersonal skill. Suppose someone borrows your dictating machine without asking permission and you retrieve it without destroying your working relationship with that individual. You have shown good human relations skills. And if, as company president, you inspire most of the employees in your firm to strive harder for high quality, you have shown good interpersonal skills.

Chapters 5 through 9 of this book focus on important interpersonal skills such as communicating, being assertive, and managing conflict. At the same time, human relations or interpersonal skills include other topics in this book, such as developing self-confidence and exerting leadership (Chapter 14). Next we will examine some specific strategies and tactics for getting ahead in your career.

TAKING CONTROL OF YOURSELF

One unifying thread to the strategies, tactics, and attitudes described in this section is that you must attempt to control your own behavior. You advance your career by trying to harness the forces under your control. The following section concentrates on getting ahead in your career by trying to control your external environment in some small way. Do not be concerned about any overlap between the general categories of controlling yourself versus controlling your environment, but do be concerned about the meaning and application of the strategies and tactics themselves.

Develop Expertise

A logical starting point in getting ahead in your career is to develop a useful job **skill**. This tactic is obvious if you are working as a specialist such as a home-improvement cost estimator. Being technically competent is also one of many requirements for being promoted to a supervisory position. After being promoted to a supervisor or other managerial job, expertise is still important for further advancement. It helps a manager's reputation to be skilled in such things as memo writing, using computer applications, troubleshooting equipment, preparing a budget, or interviewing job candidates.

Perform Well on All Your Assignments

Common sense and research support the idea that you have to perform well on your present assignment in order to move ahead.[2] Good job performance is the bedrock of a person's career. In rare instances a person is promoted on the basis of favoritism alone. In all other situations an employee must have received a favorable performance appraisal in order to be promoted. Before an employee is promoted, the prospective new boss asks, "How well did this person perform for you?"

Make an Accurate Self-analysis

To effectively plan your career and to advance in it, you need an accurate picture of your strengths, areas for improvement, and preferences. The exercises in Chapters 1 and 2, combined with the job-finding material called for in Chapter 11, will provide much of the information needed for self-evaluation. In addition, listen attentively to feedback you receive from growth groups, superiors, and co-workers.

Here is an example of how this strategy might be used. Jimmy, an engineering technician, carefully fills out the Self-Knowledge Questionnaire. He notices that his self-evaluation is weakest in the area of dealing with people. Jimmy then requests a conference with his boss to discuss his development in this area. The verdict comes back, "Much improvement needed. You tend to be too abrupt with people, and you finish people's sentences for them." Jimmy then requests an assignment that emphasizes dealing with people. His boss is generous enough to allow Jimmy to risk a few mistakes in order to improve his human relations skills. While on this new assignment Jimmy concentrates on not being too abrupt with people. In addition, he plans some community activities that give him a chance to practice human relations skills such as being toastmaster or assuming a leadership position in a technical society.

Document Your Accomplishments

Keeping an accurate record of what you have accomplished on the job can be valuable when you are being considered for promotion or transfer. A record of this type is also useful when your performance is being evaluated. You can then show your boss what you have done for the organization lately. Here are two examples of documented accomplishments from different types of jobs:

1. As bank teller, suggested one side door be modified to accommodate customers in wheelchairs. Number of physically handicapped customers jumped 324 percent in two years.
2. As maintenance technician, decreased fuel costs in office by 27 percent in one year by installing ceiling fans.

Be Conventional in Your Behavior

Although this book does not emphasize conformity to conventional norms of behavior, they are of value in getting ahead. More precisely, by flaunting tradition you could hurt your career. Areas in which conventional behavior is expected by most employers include good attendance and punctuality, careful grooming, courtesy to superiors, appropriate amount of smiling, good posture, adherence to company safety rules, and obeying authority. Employees who insist on being nonconformists in these areas do so at considerable risk to their career advancement. The chairman of the board of the world's largest manufacturer of photographic supplies once commented:

"The biggest problem with young people today, is that they spend so much time fighting the system. After about five years of fighting the system, some of them finally come around and are ready to work with the firm rather than against it. Those are the people we need." In what way do you fight the system?

Look Successful

Your clothing, your desk and office, and your speech should project the image of a successful but not necessarily flamboyant person—at least in most places of work. Your standard of dress should be appropriate to your particular career stage and work environment. Appropriate dress for an inventory specialist is not the same as for a vice-president. Wearing wing-tip shoes and rings seems more appropriate for a management trainee in a bank than for his counterpart in a lumber mill. Size up the situation before deciding on the success look for your particular work situation.

Appearing physically fit is also part of a success image. Man or woman, a person with a well-rested, trim, and muscular appearance has a slight edge over the competition—all things being equal. Discrimination against overweight people is widely practiced in business. The rationalization offered is that overweight people are high health risks. Being too underweight can also detract from your success look.

Take a Creative Approach to Your Job

As emphasized in Chapter 3, being creative helps you get ahead in business. Your ideas must be backed up with concrete plans for their implementation. If you are associated with an innovative idea, and that idea pays dividends, your career might receive a big boost. By age 27, Garth was the regional manager of a chain of hotels. He explained his success in these terms:

> Several years ago I was working as the assistant manager at one of our big hotels. As I was reviewing the room rates one day, it hit me that the public really needed inexpensive, clean lodgings. There must be thousands of people who simply can't afford $90 a night and up for a room. If they don't want to pay that much, they often have to stay at third-rate places.
>
> My solution was to propose the construction of a no-frills motel on the outskirts of town in one sample location. We would use the least expensive, safe

construction available. The rooms would be clean but modest. Our prices would be about the lowest in the area except for really run-down hotels in the most undesirable section of town. Much to my surprise, the hotel executives agreed with my plan. From the beginning, we have had almost 100 percent occupancy at the first location. We're now looking for more locations where these inexpensive units can be built. I would never be where I am today in my career if it weren't for that one simple, but important idea.

Toot Your Own Horn (Softly)

Ideally, good performance should be recognized. The most competent people in any organization should be offered the most responsible jobs. Since most organizations do not have a perfect system for identifying the good performers, you may need to find a subtle way of letting others know how good you are. Documenting your accomplishments, as described above, is one method of self-merchandising, or tooting your own horn.

Another method is to request a formal audience for discussing your ideas and accomplishments. You might request an opportunity to make a formal presentation to your boss (and perhaps his or her boss) to review the status of a project to which you have been assigned. Your thrust might be something of this nature, "Here is what *we* have accomplished so far in computerizing these files. And here are some ideas I have for creating even more storage space. . . ."

Accept Reality

Many newcomers to the work force have a difficult time accepting the reality of full-time employment.[3] You are expected to learn a job very well and stay with it for several years before you are promoted or transferred. Much of the glamor that appears on the surface soon wears off once you are settled into a job. Even detective work, which in the popular stereotypes seems filled with change and excitement, involves a heavy dose of routine work. One detective said that he could spend as much as two days going through telephone directories tracking down leads.

Another aspect of job reality that causes problems for many people who were recently students is the resistance to the application of current knowledge they encounter on the job. Many courses emphasize the way business should be run, rather than how it is run. A person taking an office systems course might learn about ideal methods for filing and retrieving information. Once on the job you might suggest revamping the present filing system. Your boss may say, "Why bother? We haven't had any complaints." In situations like these you must learn to accept the reality that it takes time to bring about constructive change. An idea that may seem technically sound to you will still have to be sold to the right people—again, this will require interpersonal skill.

Another reality ambitious people must learn to accept is that career advancement for most people today will be less rapid than for their counterparts of the recent past. Too many baby boomers are chasing too few jobs. Many companies and government agencies have stabilized in growth, and tend to avoid overstaffing. The Bureau of Labor Statistics reports that the prime age group for middle managers (the baby boomers) will grow by 42 percent by 1990. Yet the number of available management jobs will probably remain the same or actually decline.[4]

Display Loyalty and Integrity

Being loyal and honest is a good way to impress your boss. It is also a good way to advance your career, or prevent your career from being short-circuited. Loyalty has many different meanings. On the job it means such things as keeping in mind the best interests of your boss, department, and firm. A loyal employee would not participate in a cafeteria gripe session about his or her boss, department, or firm. A loyal employee would emphasize the good aspects of his or her employer to people in the community. A loyal employee would also try to use products manufactured or sold by his or her employer. Also, loyal employees do what they can to attend company functions such as picnics and holiday parties.

Being loyal should not mean, however, that you surrender your ability to make constructive criticism about things that need change. An assistant buyer at a discount department store overhead a few people talking about the incompetent help at her store. She brought this problem to the attention of the store management. After further investigation, they discovered that the complaints were not unfounded. A new training program for new employees was instituted that helped remedy the situation of employees having such limited ability to help customers.

Keep Growing Through Self-development

One of the major contributions of a formal education is that it equips you to keep on learning. You also have to help the process along by being willing to engage in self-development. Without a keen interest in self-development, you stand a good chance of being held back in your career. Although most firms offer courses of their own, or encourage you to take courses outside the company, self-development and self-improvement are still your responsibility. You should also keep in mind that much of the self-development you need to get ahead occurs outside of a formal course. Reading newspapers, books, and articles can be an important source of job-related self-development. Len describes how a simple form of self-development led to his promotion to supervisor:

> I knew we were having quality problems in our department. I heard a friend of mine talk about a great film showing how the Japanese have kept their manufacturing quality so high. I went to a library showing of this film. One segment described quality circles. This involves ordinary workers making suggestions for improving product quality. I then read an article on the same topic. The procedure is much like brainstorming. A group of employees and their supervisor, or a supervisor from another department, try to figure out how to improve the quality of a product. The employees take turns offering suggestions. Quality circles are based on the idea that the fellow or gal who actually makes the product is in the best position to make suggestions for its improvement. Employees take pride in being able to make suggestions about improving the quality of the products made by the company.
>
> Next, I wrote a memo to my boss suggesting that we try quality circles in our company. One thing led to another and I was appointed head of a quality

circle project. It led logically to my being appointed supervisor of a small department.

Practice Office Etiquette and Business Manners

A subtle aspect of advancing in your career is to practice office etiquette and display business manners. **Etiquette** is a special code of behavior required in certain situations. **Business manners** are polite social behavior especially appropriate to work settings. Figuring out what constitutes proper etiquette and manners is not always easy. One approach is to ask for tips and suggestions from successful career people. Another is to watch and emulate polished people who know the score.[5]

A third approach is to consult a current book about business etiquette such as *Letitia Baldridge's Complete Guide to Executive Manners* or *The New Office Etiquette*. Many of the suggestions offered in these books follow common sense, but many others would not be obvious to an inexperienced career person. The overall principle of etiquette and manners offered by these guides is to be considerate of other people. Specific guidelines stem from this key principle. Exhibit 13–1 presents a sampling of the specific suggestions recommended by such sources.

EXHIBIT 13–1   BUSINESS ETIQUETTE AND MANNERS

Below are fourteen specific suggestions about office etiquette and business manners that should be considered in the context of a specific job situation. For example, the suggestion, "Shouting is out" would not apply to traders on the floor of the New York Stock Exchange where shouting is routine.

1. *Names should be remembered.* It is both good manners and good human relations to remember the names of work associates, even if you see them only occasionally.

2. *Respect other people's senses.* Any assault on other people's senses—sight, sound, smell, or touch—should be avoided. Thus strong cologne or perfume are unwelcome, as are grotesque color combinations in your clothing, pinching co-workers, and making loud noises with chewing gum.

3. *Avoid vulgarities.* As George Mazzei says, "It is rude to use what we still call four-letter words in any business context. If you are tough, you don't have to prove it by falling back on the 'F' or 'S' word."

4. *Males and females should receive equal treatment.* Amenities extended to females by males in a social setting are minimized in business settings today. During a meeting, a male is not expected to hold a chair or a door for a woman, nor does he jump to walk on the outside when the two of them are walking down the street. Many women workers resent being treated differently than males with respect to minor social customs.

5. *Shouting is out.* Emotional control is an important way of impressing superiors. Following the same principle, shouting in most work situations is said to detract from your image.

6. *Coats can be removed in the office.* Today it is considered appropriate to take off your coat, and keep it off, not only in your own work area, but when moving to other parts of the building.

7. *The host or hostess pays the bill.* An area of considerable confusion about etiquette surrounds business lunches and who should pay the check, the man or the woman. The new rule of etiquette is that the person who extends the invitation pays the bill. (Do you think this same rule should be extended to social life?)

8. *Introduce the higher-ranking person to the lower-ranking person.* Your boss's name will be mentioned before a co-worker's; you introduce the older person to the younger person; and a client is introduced first to co-workers.

9. *Address superiors and visitors in their preferred way.* As the modern business world has become more informal, a natural tendency has developed to address people at all levels by their first names. It is safer to first address people by a title and their last name and then wait for them to correct you if they desire.

10. *Respect the chain of command.* Organizations value the **chain of command,** the official statement of who reports to whom. It is therefore inadvisable for you to initiate contact with your boss's boss without your boss's permission.

11. *Make appointments with high-ranking people rather than dropping in.* Related to the above principle, it is taboo in most firms for lower-ranking employees to casually drop in to the office of an executive.

12. *Stand up only for infrequent visitors.* It is still considered polite to stand up when an infrequent visitor of either sex enters the office. However, if another worker enters your work area frequently, such as a file clerk who needs regular access to your files, standing up is not required.

13. *Sexiness in the office should be muted.* Women are strongly advised to avoid looking overly sexy or glamorous in the office. Thus waist-length hair should be avoided and so should dangling jewelry, five-inch high heels, and heavy eye makeup. Men, too, should not appear too sexy, and thus tight pants and shirts are to be avoided.

14. *Watch out for smoking on the job.* Smokers are beginning to believe increasingly that their civil rights are being violated in many public places. Nevertheless, good business etiquette these days is to avoid smoking in meetings and in the work areas of other people. In some firms smoking is outlawed completely, or restricted to limited areas such as locker rooms and the parking lot.

Caution: Although all the above points could have some bearing on the image you project, violation of any one of them would not necessarily have a negative impact on your career. It is the overall image you project that counts the most. Therefore, the general principle of being considerate of work associates is much more important than any one act of etiquette or manners.

SOURCE: Based on information from: George Mazzei, *The New Office Etiquette* (New York: Simon & Schuster, 1983); Richard Michaels, "Manners," *Success!,* August 1982, pp. 40–43; Marilyn Moats Kennedy, "Executive Etiquette," *BusinessWeek's Guide to Careers,* December 1984/January 1985, pp. 65–66.

Take Sensible Risks

An element of risk taking is necessary to advance very far in your career. Almost all successful people have taken at least one moderate risk in their careers. These risks include starting a new business with mostly borrowed money, joining a fledgling firm, or submitting a ground-breaking idea to management. Consultant Robert Wendover sizes up the importance of risk taking in this way: "Non–risk takers not only inhibit their careers, but may also impede the progress of an organization. Progress requires risks."[6]

Hitch Your Wagon to Yourself

The ultimate strategy for developing career thrust is to have faith in what you are doing and to persist in doing it well. If you hitch your wagon to yourself you will not be bothered by your critics. Eventually your contributions will be recognized because what you are doing is worthwhile and of value to your employer or employers. Hitching your wagon to yourself is your career foundation. Other strategies for getting ahead are designed to supplement this basic strategy. If you lack skill in dealing with people, data, or things and lack ideas of your own, you are lacking the basis for a successful career.

EXERTING CONTROL OVER THE OUTSIDE WORLD

Here we emphasize strategies and tactics requiring you to exert some control over the outside environment. If you do not fully control it, at least you can try to juggle it to your advantage. For instance, "Find a sponsor," suggests that you search out a powerful person who can help you advance in your career.

Stay Tuned to the Outside World

Organizations must adapt to their external environment in order to survive and so must individuals. Since the outside world is more unstable than stable, suggestions for what you should do right now to cope with the environment are of temporary value. Many fields and occupations have their ups and downs in demand. Two examples are high school teaching and engineering. As described in Chapter 10, it is important to know which fields are currently expanding and which are shrinking.

Geographic shifts in areas of economic prosperity are another key factor to consider in career planning. You have a greater chance for career advancement in a growing industry in a prosperous geographic area. Only by carefully studying information sources such as government reports and the *Wall Street Journal* can external forces be understood and your moves planned accordingly.

Develop a Career Path

Planning your career inevitably involves some form of goal setting. If your goals are laid out systematically to lead you to your ultimate career goal, you have established a career path. A **career path** is thus a sequence of positions necessary to achieve a goal. The ultimate goal you are seeking is called a **target position.**[7]

If a career path is laid out in one firm, it must be related to the present and future demands of that firm. If you aspire toward a high-level manufacturing job, it would be vital to know the future of manufacturing in that company. Many U.S. firms, for example, plan to conduct more of their manufacturing in the Far East or Mexico. If you were really determined, you might study the appropriate language and ready yourself for a global position. Computerization is another factor that should be considered in developing a career path. How much computer knowledge will you need in the future to be successful in your line of work?

While sketching out a career path you should list your personal goals. They should mesh with your work plans to help avoid major conflicts in your life. Some lifestyles, for example, are incompatible with some career paths. It would be difficult to develop a stable home life (spouse, children, friends, community activities, garden) if a person aspired toward holding field positions within the Central Intelligence Agency.

Contingency ("what if?") plans should also be incorporated into a well-designed career path. For instance, "If I don't become an agency supervisor by age thirty-five, I will seek employment in the private sector." Or, "If I am not promoted within two years, I will enroll in a business school program."

Lisa Irving, an ambitious twenty year old, formulated the career path shown below prior to receiving an associate's degree in business administration. After she presented her tentative career path to her classmates, several accused Lisa of shooting for the moon. Lisa's career goals are high, but she has established contingency plans. Presented as an example, not an ideal model, here is Lisa's career plan path:

WORK

1. Purchasing trainee for two years
2. Assistant purchasing agent for three years
3. Purchasing agent for five years (will join Purchasing Manager's Association)
4. Purchasing supervisor for five years
5. Purchasing manager for six years
6. Manager, materials handling for five years
7. Vice-president, procurement, until retirement

PERSONAL LIFE

1. Rent own apartment after one year of working.
2. Attend college evenings until receive B.S. in business administration.
3. Marriage by age twenty-seven (plan only one marriage).
4. One child by age thirty.
5. Live in private home with husband and children by age thirty-three.
6. Volunteer work for Downs Syndrome children.
7. Travel to India before age fifty.

CONTINGENCY PLANS

1. Will seek new employment by stage 3 if not promoted to purchasing agent.
2. If not promoted to vice-president by stage 6, will consider opening small retail business.
3. If I encounter sex discrimination at any stage, will look for employment with firm that has large government contracts (where discrimination is much less likely).
4. If develop stress disorder at any point, will seek nonsupervisory position in purchasing field.

Career paths can also be laid out graphically, as shown in Figure 13–1. One benefit of a career path laid out in chart form is that it gives a clear perception of climbing steps toward your target position. As each position is attained, the corresponding step can be shaded in color or cross hatched.

Most of the goals just mentioned include a time element, which is crucial to sound career management. Your long-range goal might be clearly established in your mind (such as owner and operator of a health salon). At the same time you must establish short-range (get any kind of job in health salon) and intermediate-range (manager of a health salon by age thirty) goals. Goals set too far in the future that are not supported with more immediate goals may lose their motivational value. A class exercise to help you develop a career path is presented in Exhibit 13–2.

FIGURE 13-1. A CAREER PATH

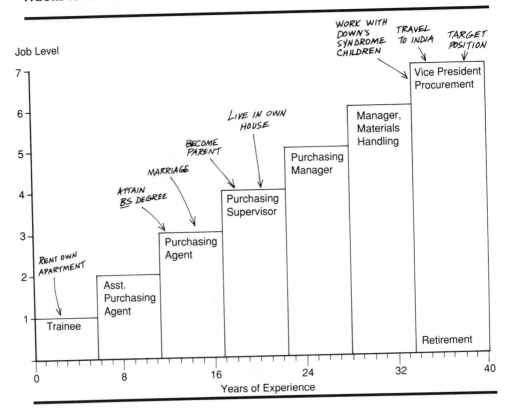

Have an Action Plan to Reach Your Goals

As described in Chapter 2, a useful goal is backed up by a logical plan for its attainment. A recommended practice is to supplement your career path with a description of your action plans. Lisa Irving, the woman who wants to succeed in the purchasing field, might have one or two action plans of this nature:

In order to be promoted from purchasing agent to supervisor I will: (1) perform in an outstanding manner on my job, (2) have completed my B.S. degree, and (3) ask to attend company-sponsored supervisory training programs.

In order to become manager of materials handling, I will need to: (1) perform in an outstanding manner as purchasing manager, (2) engage in continuous self-study about the entire materials handling field, (3) be active in the local purchasing association group, and (4) make sure that top management is aware of my talent and ambition.

Action plans can be drawn up in minute detail. As with any other aspect of career planning, however, avoid becoming too rigid in your thinking. Career paths and career plans are only tentative. A different path to your goal might fall right in your lap. Ten years from now, for instance, Lisa might receive a telephone call from an executive employment agency. The caller might say, "My client has engaged me to find a materials manager who is female. Your name was given to us. Could you possibly meet me for lunch to discuss this exciting career opportunity?"

EXHIBIT 13–2   CAREER PATHING

1.   Each class member will develop a tentative career path, perhaps as an outside assignment. About six volunteers will then share their paths with the rest of the class. Feedback of any type will be welcomed. Class members studying the career paths of others should keep in mind issues as such,

   a.   How logical does it appear?
   b.   Is this something the person really wants or simply an exercise in putting down on paper what the ambitious person is supposed to want?
   c.   How well do the individual's work plans mesh with personal plans?

2.   Each class member will interview an experienced working person outside of class about his or her career path. Most of the people interviewed will have already completed a portion of their path. They will therefore have less flexibility (and perhaps less idealism) than people just getting started in their careers. The conclusions reached about these interviews will make a fruitful class discussion. Among the issues raised might be:

   a.   How familiar were these people with the idea of a career path?
   b.   How willing were they to talk about themselves?
   c.   Were many actual "paths" discovered, or simply a series of jobs that came about by luck or fate?

Practice Networking

Developing a network of contacts was recommended in Chapter 11 as a method of finding a job. Currently the most popular career-advancement tactic, networking has several purposes. The contacts you establish can help you find a better position, offer you a new position, become customers, valuable suppliers, or help you solve difficult problems. People in your network can also offer you emotional support during periods of adversity.

The starting point in networking is to obtain an ample supply of business cards. You then give a card to any person you meet who might be able to help you now or in the future. People in your network can include relatives; people you meet while traveling, camping, or attending trade shows; and classmates. Many cities have networking clubs that meet periodically after work at a cocktail lounge. In some clubs only nonalcoholic beverages are served. These clubs operate much like singles bars except that contacts are developed primarily for business. Community activities and religious organizations can also be a source of contacts. Golf is still considered the number-one sport for networking because of the high-level contacts the sport generates.[8]

A recent trend is for career-minded people to develop work and social contacts by computer networks. Most days and every night, people are communicating by computer and modem with each other and information centers. (A modem is an instrument that allows computers to communicate over phone lines.) The essence of this form of networking is that people establish and develop contacts via electronic mail—sending messages by computer. Some computer networks are even used for dating services. Computer networking systems sometimes used for career networking include *The Source, CompuServe,* and *Delphi.*[9]

Swim Against the Tide

Risk taking was mentioned previously as a strategy for taking control of your own behavior. A form of risk taking can also be applied to taking control of the environment. According to the tactic of **swim against the tide,** you advance your career by taking an unconventional path to career success. An unconventional path can be considered riskier. The key element to swimming against the tide (SWAT) is that you place yourself in an environment where the competition might not be so overwhelming.

Some men swim against the tide by entering the secretarial field. Since males in secretarial work are still relatively rare, they apparently stand out as potential supervisors. (The reader should note that about sixty-five years ago, few secretaries were female.)

Another way to swim against the tide is to capitalize on your personal characteristics. Suppose you are outgoing and personable. Many well-intended relatives and friends will say to you, "Go into sales. You're a natural." If you prefer to SWAT, enter the numerical or applied technology field. In this way, you can use your strong people skills to help you rise into management. You might have the edge over the many people in these fields who work better with data and things than with people.

A disadvantage of swimming against the tide is that you might drown. You might place yourself in an environment in which your talents or credentials are not appreciated. Suppose you are seeking a career in business administration. You decide to work in the front office of a professional football team because so few people of your background have thought of this path. Ultimately you find out that your background can take you only so far. The good jobs go to former football players, no professionally trained administrators.

Achieve Broad Experience

Most people who land high-ranking positions are people of broad experience. Therefore, a widely accepted strategy for advancing in responsibility is to strengthen your credentials by broadening your experience. It is best to achieve this breadth early in your career. Since your salary demands are low at the early stages of your career, it is not so difficult to be transferred from one area of the business to another. Broadening can come about by performing a variety of jobs, or sometimes by performing essentially the same job in different organizations. You can also achieve breadth by working on committees and special assignments.

If you work for a boss who the firm thinks is unpromotable, try to move out from under that boss. He or she is probably not a good model and will block your upward progress. Tactfully ask for a transfer, or look around the organization for an opening for which you might qualify. If these tactics fail, your career progress may depend on your finding a job in another company.

Self Nomination

A more general strategy for achieving breadth is to practice self nomination. Have the courage and aggressiveness to ask for a promotion or a transfer. Your boss may not believe that you are actually seeking more responsibility. An effective method of convincing him or her is to volunteer yourself for specific job openings or for challenging assignments. A boss may need convincing, because many more people will be seeking advancement than who are actually willing to handle more responsibility.

Be Visible

A big career booster for many people is to call favorable attention to themselves and their accomplishments. Ways of gaining visibility include: performing well on committee assignments, winning a suggestion award, performing well in a company-sponsored athletic event, getting an article published in a trade magazine, getting your name in the firm's newspaper, or distinguishing yourself in a community activity. Once you achieve visibility, you have a better chance of being noticed by an important person in the firm.

Find a Sponsor

A well-traveled route to career progress is to find someone at a high place in the firm who is impressed with your capabilities. A **sponsor** is a higher-ranking individual who is favorably impressed with you and therefore recommends you for promotion and choice assignments. A sponsor of this type can even be a blood relative or one by marriage. One reason that project and committee assignments are helpful to career progress is that they provide the opportunity to be seen by influential people. Many people who have performed well in an activity such as the United Way have landed a promotion in the process.

Find a Mentor

Mentors are bosses who take subordinates under their wings and guide, teach, and coach them. Mentorship is an important development process in many occupations: master-apprentice, physician-intern, teacher-student, and executive-junior executive.[10] An emotional tie exists between the less-experienced person (protégé) and the mentor. The mentor therefore serves as a positive model. A relationship with a sponsor involves much less teaching, coaching, and formation of emotional ties. It is possible to have more than one mentor at a given point in one's career. Bob, a thirty-year-old sales manager, describes how finding a mentor helped him in his career:

> My career had its first big boost when I was noticed by Walt Brainbridge, our regional manager. He personally complimented me for my showing in a sales contest. From that point on he would ask to see me when he visited our office. He gave me lots of encouragement and told me what a good future I had with the firm. Without asking for credit, Walt was the one who assigned me to some of the best accounts. He set me up to succeed. He taught me a lot of good tricks including how to fight the feeling of being rejected. I don't think I would have advanced nearly as far as I have today without Mr. Brainbridge.

Grab a Shooting Star

Obviously, everyone does not have access to a sponsor. There are only so many influential people around to take a personal interest in a lower-ranking employee. Besides, if you are typing invoices it will be difficult for the vice-president of finance to discover you. It might be possible, however, to cultivate someone who does have a sponsor. "Grab a shooting star" has also been labeled as "cling to somebody's shirttails" or "become a protégé of a protégé." The strategy is to find someone who appears to be rising in his or her career and to develop a good relationship with that person. As he or she moves up the organization, you will follow. Val provides an apt illustration:

> I work for the city. In my department, the head of the internal audit section of the finance division was the protégé of the director of finance. An employee in the internal audit section, because of family ties, became the protégé of the internal auditor. When the position of assistant to the director of finance opened up, the internal auditor's protégé was chosen over five senior members of the department. A lot of people were surprised when this young man from another department was selected for the assistant position.[11]

Capitalize on Luck

Few people do well in their careers without a good break along the way. Lucky events include your company suddenly expanding and therefore needing people to promote into key jobs; your boss quitting on short notice and you being asked to take over his or her job; or the business field in which you are working suddenly experiencing a boom, similar to the home security business today.

A good strategy is not to simply wait for luck to come your way. Instead, manage luck to some extent by recognizing opportunities and taking advantage of them. The unlucky person is often the individual who, out of timidity, lets a good opportunity slip by. Suppose the boss says, "We need a volunteer to work on a special audit in the home office next month." The employee who manages luck will sense the opportunity to be noticed by influential people. The unlucky person will say, "Why bother doing all that extra work when there's no mention of extra money?"

Another way of managing luck is to be ready to take advantage of opportunities when they come along. If you maintain a record of excellent work performance, and you strive to complete your program of studies, you will position yourself to take advantage of opportunities.

Now that we have looked at a number of strategies for advancing your career, turn to the exercise in Exhibit 13–3 to help you to analyze the strategies you might choose to fit your personality and work situation.

COPING WITH BEING UNEMPLOYED

So far this chapter has been optimistic in tone. We have dealt with developing forward thrust in your career. Yet there are times in many people's careers when they have to face the grim reality of trying to merely survive. Three such crisis situations are being laid off, being fired, or being forced to quit because you find your job insufferable. The techniques for finding a career or a job described in chapters 10 and 11 are directly relevant for coping with unemployment. The primary goal of most people is to rejoin the ranks of the employed. In this section we will describe briefly some coping strategies that deal more with attitudes and emotions than with the mechanics of job finding.

EXHIBIT 13–3   SELECTING A SUITABLE CAREER ADVANCEMENT STRATEGY

As with most suggestions for self-improvement, some of the suggestions in this chapter will have more relevance for you than others. Among the factors influencing which strategy is best suited to you is your personality, the stage of your career, and the place you work. One person might say, "I think the tactic, display loyalty and integrity is a good one for me. I'm loyal by nature. I'm just getting started so the company would look for those qualities. Also, our company generally promotes from the inside. They want to see loyalty before you get a big promotion."

Each class member will write down the two strategies described in this chapter that he or she will most probably put into action (or is already using). Also, provide a brief explanation of why this strategy is particularly relevant. Once these analyses are completed, each person will share his or her answers with the rest of the class.

It will be interesting to note if any strategy or tactic for getting ahead is mentioned by virtually all class members.

Try Not to Panic

The most important strategy for regaining employment is not to panic. Although you may perceive your job loss as a catastrophe, many other people have experienced the same problem. Immediately begin talking over your situation with your family. They may have to find ways to earn extra income while you are unemployed.

Work Out a Deal with Your Creditors

A positive, sincere approach to creditors often results in a workable compromise that will help you manage some of the emotional discomfort associated with not being able to meet all of your current financial obligations. It is sometimes possible, for example, to make only interest payments until you get back on your feet financially.

Share Your Burden with Your Friends. Coping with unemployment is a lonely enterprise. Each day turns up its own joys and disappointments. A phone call to a friend to update him or her on your job search can be a useful way of dealing with your feelings. A particularly invaluable friend is someone who has successfully handled being fired.

Job Hunting

Admit You Were Fired. Admitting that you were fired will not automatically remove you from further consideration in a job interview. On the contrary, not admitting you were fired will lead people to think of you as a fabricator. A reference check will usually reveal that you were dismissed involuntarily. It is recommended that you take the initiative to explain the circumstances of your dismissal without being self-abasing or unduly critical of your past employer.

Capitalize on the Hidden Opportunity. Being fired often represents a positive turning point in a career. Many people take being fired as an opportunity to step off the treadmill and ponder what they would really like to do for a living. When few companies in the area are hiring, some people without jobs enter family businesses or start businesses of their own. Others relocate to a section of the country that has more job opportunities.

Keep Pressure on Yourself. Before being fired, many people have been in a job situation that didn't leave enough time to accomplish all the necessary job and personal chores. When you are between jobs, you will naturally be less busy. Such a slowing down of your work pace can greatly delay finding a new job. Above all, take seriously all the job-finding strategies described in Chapter 11. Also, follow up every lead, however insignificant it may seem at the time. One woman found a job by pursuing a lead that turned up while she was waiting in line for food stamps.

SUMMARY

Career success, as defined here, means that you attain organizational rewards and personal satisfaction. The strategies, tactics, and attitudes described in this chapter are generally accepted ways of advancing your career.

Good interpersonal skills are vital for getting ahead. The most important skills of this nature relate to cooperating with co-workers. Interpersonal skills also include the actions and practices described in Chapters 5 through 9 of this book.

One set of strategies and tactics for getting ahead can be placed in the category of taking control of your own behavior. Included here are:

1. Develop expertise.
2. Perform well on all your assignments.
3. Make an accurate self-analysis.
4. Document your accomplishments.
5. Be conventional in your behavior.
6. Look successful.
7. Take a creative approach to your job.
8. Toot your own horn (softly).
9. Accept reality.
10. Display loyalty and integrity.
11. Practice office etiquette and business manners.
12. Take sensible risks.
13. Hitch your wagon to yourself.

Another set of strategies and tactics for getting ahead center around taking control of your environment, or at least adapting it to your advantage. Included here are:

1. Stay tuned to the outside world.
2. Develop a career path.
3. Have an action plan to reach your goals.
4. Practice networking.
5. Swim against the tide.
6. Achieve broad experience.
7. Be visible.
8. Find a sponsor.
9. Find a mentor.
10. Grab a shooting star.
11. Capitalize on luck.

Coping with being unemployed is sometimes a necessary part of managing your career. The strategies recommended here are: try not to panic, work out a deal with your creditors, share your burden with your friends, admit you were fired, capitalize on the hidden opportunity, keep pressure on yourself. In addition, you must use recommended job-finding techniques.

QUESTIONS AND ACTIVITIES

1. Why is it that new books and articles about career advancement are published regularly?
2. To what extent do you think successful people make a deliberate attempt to use some of the strategies and tactics described in this chapter?
3. Aside from choosing the appropriate clothing, what can a person do to "look successful"?
4. How can you document your accomplishments if you have a routine job?
5. What could you do in your career to SWAT?
6. What would happen to an organization, and to society, if virtually every employee tried to implement most of the strategies and tactics described in this chapter?
7. Which of the tactics described in this chapter seem to be used by the head of state (president or prime minister) in your country.

8. What is the theme of this chapter?

9. Interview any person you consider successful. Ask that person to check the tactics and strategies in this chapter he or she believes are the most important for getting ahead. Be prepared to discuss your findings in class.

A HUMAN RELATIONS CASE PROBLEM: THE SQUEEZED-OUT SPONSOR

Tony Chavez joined his firm as a sales representative several years ago. During his second year on the job, Tony led the Midwestern region in total sales. No sales representative with less than five years experience had ever led any region in sales in the past. Tony received a $2,000 bonus for his accomplishment, along with a personal letter of congratulations from Mike Calabash, the vice president of marketing.

Three months after receiving the letter, Calabash made arrangements to speak to Chavez in person during Calabash's annual visit to regional headquarters. Calabash invited Chavez to lunch. During much of their lunch, Calabash asked Chavez questions about his career plans and hopes for the future. Toward the end of the lunch, the marketing vice president said:

"Tony, the real reasons I asked you to lunch were to get to know you better and verify my hunches about your capabilities. Now that I've met you in person, I'm convinced you're the person we need to manage the new Fort Wayne office. You have the talent and the drive to make that office a winner."

One week later, Tony's immediate boss presented him with the formal offer to become the branch manager of the new Fort Wayne office. Tony enthusiastically accepted the offer. Under Tony's leadership, the Fort Wayne office exceeded expectations. Within three years, Tony was offered a position as the assistant vice president of marketing, reporting directly to Calabash at company headquarters. Although Tony enjoyed his position and made many good friends in Fort Wayne, he decided it would be to his advantage to accept the new job offer.

Tony found himself an apartment ten miles from the downtown Chicago headquarters of the firm. The increase in housing, commuting, and luncheon expenses consumed Tony's new salary adjustment. Nevertheless, he felt this new position was worth it because it would give him the home-office experience he needed to become a marketing executive.

Ten days into the new job, Calabash told Chavez he had some unfortunate news for him. With an apologetic facial expression, Calabash said: "What has happened to me is the ugly side of corporate life we executives don't like to admit. The president is holding me responsible for the failure of our new copying machine. I'm not being fired, but I'm being put on a shelf. My new title will be vice president of special projects.

"This means that I'll be sitting in a corner doing odds and ends that nobody else wants to do. The strategy is to make me feel so bad about myself that I'll resign."

"This is terrible, Mike," said Tony. "Who will be my new boss?"

"That's part of the bad news. I recommended that you stay in your position as the assistant vice president of marketing. The president says that he couldn't allow it because you think too much like me. He even implied that you were partially responsible for introducing the copying machine that bombed. It looks like my falling out of power has dragged you down with me.

"You may be reassigned as a sales representative. In the meantime, I'm going to start looking for a new marketing executive position. If I do find something, maybe you could join me in the new company.

"The company should be giving you official word about your fate within the week."

"I'm sorry this has happened to you, Mike," said Tony. "You've done so much for me. I have to say, though, I'm also feeling sorry for myself. I'm really in a bind."

Questions

1. What theme does this case illustrate about the potential disadvantages of being closely identified with a sponsor?
2. What actions should Tony take about his job situation?
3. How do you think this incident will affect Tony's career?
4. What suggestions can you offer Mike Calabash?

REFERENCES

[1] David W. Johnson, *Human Relations and Your Career: A Guide to Interpersonal Skills* (Englewood Cliffs, NJ: Prentice-Hall, 1978), p. 336.

[2] Joseph A. Raelin, "First-job Effects on Career Development," *Personnel Administrator,* August 1983, pp. 71–76.

[3] Clarke G. Carney, Cinda Field Wells, and Don Streufert, *Career Planning: Skills to Build Your Future* (New York: D. Van Nostrand, 1981), p. 168.

[4] This trend is valid today, although originally predicted by the Bureau of Labor Statistics in 1981.

[5] Marilyn Moats Kennedy, "Executive Etiquette," *BusinessWeek's Guide to Careers,* December 1984/January 1985, pp. 66.

[6] Robert Wendover, "The Importance of Risk-Taking," *BusinessWeek's Guide to Careers,* October 1985, p. 75.

[7] Lester R. Bittel, *What Every Supervisor Should Know About Supervisory Management,* 5th ed. (New York: McGraw-Hill, 1985), p. 609.

[8] Donald H. Dunn, "The Business Sport," *BusinessWeek's Guide to Careers,* Spring/Summer 1985, pp. 57–58.

[9] Chrys Goyens, "Yuppies Go On Line With Computer Networks," *The Gazette, Montreal,* April 27, 1985, pp. 1–9.

[10] David Marshall Hunt and Carol Michael, "Mentorship: A Career Training and Development Tool," *Academy of Management Review,* July 1983, p. 475.

[11] Researched by Mark Kindig.

SOME ADDITIONAL READING

DAVIS, GEORGE, and GLEGG WATSON. *Black Life in Corporate America.* New York: Anchor/Doubleday, 1984.

FISHMAN, STEVE. "The Art of Networking." *Success!,* July/August 1985, pp. 36–43.

HARRAGAN, BETTY LEHAN. *Knowing the Score.* New York: St. Martin's Press, 1984.

MIRABILE, RICHARD J. "A Model for Competency-Based Career Development." *Personnel,* April 1985, pp. 30–38.

NEWMAN, JAMES A. *Climbing the Corporate Matterhorn.* New York: John Wiley & Sons, 1984.

ROSENBAUM, JAMES E. *Career Mobility in a Corporate Hierarchy.* Orlando, FL: Academic Press, 1984.

SORCHER, MELVIN. *Predicting Executive Success: What It Takes to Make It Into Senior Management.* New York: John Wiley & Sons, 1985.

STEWART, MARJABELLE YOUNG, and MARIAN FAUX. *Executive Etiquette: How to Make Your Way to the Top with Grace and Style.* New York: St. Martin's Press, 1985.

14

Developing Self-Confidence and Becoming a Leader

Learning Objectives

After studying the information and doing the exercises in this chapter, you should be able to:

- Develop a strategy for increasing your self-confidence if you think it is desirable to do so
- Understand the relationship of self-confidence to leadership
- Identify a number of personal traits and characteristics of effective leaders
- Identify a number of behaviors of effective leaders
- Map out a tentative program for developing your leadership potential and skills

If your efforts at developing career thrust are successful, you will eventually become a leader. Rising to leadership can happen when people come to respect your opinion and personal characteristics, and thus are influenced by you. Another way of becoming a leader is to be appointed to a formal position, such as supervisor, in which it is natural to exert leadership. Your greatest opportunity for exerting leadership, however, will come about from a combination of these methods of influence. As a result, an individual with appealing personal characteristics who is placed in a position of authority will find it relatively easy to exert leadership.

Before most people can exert personal or positional leadership, or both, they have to develop the right amount of self-confidence. **Self-confidence** is a belief in your own capabilities, or a positive self-regard.[1]

WHAT IS THE RIGHT AMOUNT OF SELF-CONFIDENCE?

Surprisingly enough, people who have worked their way into prominent positions know they do not have all the answers and they welcome the advice and opinions of other people. We are not implying that no famous and influential people are pompous and arrogant. In general, however, effective leaders tend to be highly, but not overwhelmingly self-confident.

Self-confidence is necessary for leadership because it helps assure followers that things are under control. Assume you are an airplane passenger. Turbulence occurs and the airplane begins to dip up and down. As you look around, you see children crying, adults gripping the arm rests, and the flight attendants urging everyone to fasten their seat belts. Suddenly the chief pilot (your leader) makes an announcement in a sobbing, weeping voice: "I'm sorry, I'm just no good at flying in a storm. I don't think I can get us out of this mess. I'm turning the controls over to my co-pilot. Let's pray that he can save us."

In this circumstance, the passengers and crew would probably suffer a stress reaction. You would want the pilot to behave in a confident, assured manner. Yet if the pilot were too arrogant about things, if he dismissed the problem too lightly, you might not feel safe, either. In less extraordinary leadership situations as well, the leader who functions best is self-confident enough to assure others and to appear in control. But if the leader is so self-confident that he or she will not admit errors, listen to criticism, or ask for advice, that, too, creates a problem.

In short, a leader who is self-assured without being bombastic or overbearing instills confidence in his or her subordinates. Aside from being a psychological trait, self-confidence or self-assurance refers to the behavior shown by the person in various situations. It might be concluded that Jeanne is a confident supervisor if (1) she retains her composure when an employee threatens to file a grievance, and (2) she calmly helps an employee fix a machine when the department is behind schedule. Exhibit 14–1 provides some tentative insight into whether or not you have the right amount of self-confidence.

EXHIBIT 14–1   JUST HOW HUMBLE ARE YOU?

A Purdue University social scientist has conducted a series of studies on the relationship of self-confidence to problem solving.[2] One of his major findings is that people who do not have a particularly high level of self-confidence may do better at solving problems than people who are highly self-assured. The same finding about self-confidence apparently applies to leadership. Answer the research instrument below to obtain some tentative insight into your level of self-confidence (or humility).

Which category do you fit into? Do you have self-confidence to spare, a satisfactory level, a fair share of the characteristic, or do you score low in self-esteem? Take this quiz and find out (check the answers that best apply to you).

A. You are assigned a task involving an entire area that is unfamiliar to you. You would:
- ☐ 1. Delegate someone else to do it.
- ☐ 2. Get someone to help you do it.
- ☐ 3. Study the procedure carefully, and then do it yourself.
- ☐ 4. Plunge right into the work without giving it much thought.

B. You solicit the advice of others before making a decision:
- ☐ 1. Almost always.
- ☐ 2. Sometimes.
- ☐ 3. Rarely.
- ☐ 4. Never.

C. You offer advice to others:
- ☐ 1. Never.
- ☐ 2. Hardly ever.
- ☐ 3. Willingly, if you are asked to do so.
- ☐ 4. Often (even when no one asks for it).

D. At business meetings you come up with ideas for projects:
- ☐ 1. Never.
- ☐ 2. Sometimes.
- ☐ 3. Frequently.
- ☐ 4. Always (to let the bosses know you've got a million ideas).

E. When meeting with your superiors, you acknowledge the ideas you've received from others rather than passing them off as your own:
- ☐ 1. Never.
- ☐ 2. Rarely.
- ☐ 3. Often.
- ☐ 4. Always.

F. Your boss expresses an opinion that is contrary to your strong beliefs or convictions. You would:
- ☐ 1. Remain silent.
- ☐ 2. Attempt to disagree only if you felt it wouldn't jeopardize your job.
- ☐ 3. Explain your feelings about the issue.

☐ 4. Become incensed and speak up about your views.

G. If there were a job opening that you would like in a higher classification at work, you would:

☐ 1. Wait until a superior asked if you were interested in it.

☐ 2. Drop hints to your boss that you just might be interested in it.

☐ 3. Go through the regular channels to apply for it.

☐ 4. Do everything you can to persuade your boss that he or she should recommend you for the position.

H. You feel your work is inadequate:

☐ 1. Always.

☐ 2. Frequently.

☐ 3. Hardly ever.

☐ 4. Never.

I. You feel that you deserve a position of leadership in an organization or in your job:

☐ 1. No.

☐ 2. Perhaps.

☐ 3. Yes (and hope others recognize your leadership qualities).

☐ 4. Without a doubt.

J. You believe you are brighter than many of your colleagues at work:

☐ 1. Never.

☐ 2. At times.

☐ 3. Usually.

☐ 4. Of course.

K. In response to criticism, you:

☐ 1. Feel devastated and say nothing to the person who made the comment.

☐ 2. Become angry at first but later try to analyze the criticism.

☐ 3. Discuss the matter with the person who made the comment and try to resolve it.

☐ 4. Tell the person to buzz off.

L. At a party, you introduce yourself to people you don't know and begin conversations:

☐ 1. Never.

☐ 2. Hardly ever.

☐ 3. Usually.

☐ 4. Always.

M. In a restaurant, you will complain about improper service or bad food:

☐ 1. Never.

☐ 2. Sometimes.

☐ 3. Usually, and in a calm, constructive way.

☐ 4. Always and loudly.

N. While waiting in long line for a bus, or at the movies or supermarket:

☐ 1. You let others get ahead of you.

☐ 2. You wait patiently wherever you may be.

☐ 3. You try to speed up the line.

☐ 4. You push ahead of others.

O. When someone compliments you about something you've done:

☐ 1. You are embarrassed and don't know what to day.

☐ 2. You say, "Oh, it was nothing, really."

☐ 3. You smile and say, "Thank you."

☐ 4. You say, "Thanks," and add, "Yes, I know I'm talented and wonderful."

Score yourself by adding up the numbers you checked.

If you scored 16 to 25, you are eating too much humble pie.

If you scored 26 to 35, your SC (self-confidence) quotient is not low, but you could work a little on raising your self-esteem.

If you scored 36 to 50, you are brimming with self-confidence.

If you scored 51 to 60, you are an overconfident type who should give some thought to tempering your arrogance.

DEVELOPING SELF-CONFIDENCE

People interested in elevating their level of self-confidence have tried various do-it-yourself, professional, and commercial approaches. Many a person who does not feel confident enough to meet daily challenges has undergone psychotherapy or counseling—often with good results. Millions of people have achieved some temporary or long-term boost in self-confidence from attending a Dale Carnegie training program. Perhaps one of the real reasons people enter any kind of personal improvement program is to achieve a boost in self-confidence.

Boosting your self-confidence can be achieved if you experience success in a variety of situations. A confident guitarist may not be generally self-confident unless that same guitarist also achieves success in activities such as taking exams, forming good relationships, parallel parking a car, typing a letter, and balancing a checkbook. First you establish some goals, achieve them, set some more difficult goals, achieve them, and continue the process.

Although this general approach to building self-confidence appears to make sense, it does not work for everyone. Some people who seem to succeed at everything still have lingering feelings of self-doubt. Low self-confidence is so deeply ingrained in this type of personality that success in later life is not sufficient to change things. Following are some specific strategies for elevating self-confidence, assuming a person does not have deep-rooted feelings of inferiority.

Obtain a Few Easy Victories

Since self-confidence accumulates as you achieve success, start with small tasks. Suppose you are studying statistics, a subject that seems to lower your self-confidence. Before tackling a large assignment, conquer the easiest problems in the earliest chapters of your text. If downhill skiing is important to you, use it to help you develop self-confidence. Obtain a few easy victories by skiing down hills labeled easiest. Later, as your self-confidence develops, move on to the more difficult slopes.

Enter a Less Competitive Environment

An extension of the easy victory strategy is to place yourself in a less competitive environment when you find that you are over your head in your present environment. A less competitive environment might be just what you need to establish a satisfactory level of self-confidence. A recent graduate of a business school used this strategy to help him develop his self-confidence as a sales representative:

Right out of school, I took a job selling a line of home-improvement services. It included painting, siding, and insulation. After getting dozens of doors slammed in my face, and very few sales, my confidence was shaken. If selling was this bad, I didn't know how I could ever work my way up to become a marketing executive. After talking over the problem with one of my former business teachers, I decided the problem was the service I was selling, not my sales ability.

I looked for a line of selling that wasn't quite as competitive, one where people weren't bombarded with so many people offering a similar product or service. I found a job selling low-priced desk top copiers. Although we had a healthy amount of competition, there was at least a real market for what I was selling. Although I wasn't getting rich, I was meeting my quota. All the while I was becoming confident in my ability to sell a product.

Attack Situations Assertively

If your self-confidence is at a low level, one way to elevate it is to start taking a positive, assertive approach to the problem situation. If you are demoted, and are upset and disappointed over this problem, plunge into your lesser responsibilities with aggressiveness and determination. As your positive approach begins to pay dividends, your self-confidence will inch back up to its former level.

The strategy of attacking situations assertively applies equally well to your social life. A loss in self-confidence often takes place after a person has been "dumped" by a boyfriend or girlfriend. After some of the initial hurt wears away, you can start to build confidence assertively by attacking the challenge of meeting new people. Among the positive techniques to use are joining clubs, asking for referrals from friends, taking up new recreational interests, and joining a singles club. As you begin to achieve some success in finding dates you enjoy, your self-confidence will elevate.

Achieve Something that Stretches Your Capability

This strategy is similar to the general strategy of building self-confidence by attaining a series of increasingly difficult goals. If you do achieve something that stretches your capability, that achievement serves as objective evidence that you are a capable (and therefore confident) individual. Perhaps you might implement this strategy after you have gained a few easy victories, as described earlier.

Large numbers of people use running as a confidence builder. As one middle manager put it, "Today is one of the most important days in my life. It's my fortieth birthday and I ran ten miles for the first time in my life. I feel great." This man took several years to work his way up to running ten miles. His mental and physical efforts have paid off in self-confidence. Achieving the ten-mile breakthrough has boosted his self-confidence. It appears that his renewed self-confidence has spread over to some extent to his work and personal life. Another example of this strategy is presented in Exhibit 14–2, which illustrates a slightly different variation of stretching your capability.

EXHIBIT 14–2   RICK BUILDS HIS SELF-CONFIDENCE

Throughout his childhood and early adulthood, Rick believed that he had a self-confidence problem. As he explains, "I don't know why, but I never had much faith in myself. I did not think I was incompetent, but I never believed I was as capable as some of my friends. My lack of total confidence showed up even in my social life. I usually hesitated to ask a woman for a date who was my first choice. I figured she would reject me. Instead, I tended to ask out women who I thought would most likely not refuse me. The same tendency is with me today.

"Despite my low self-confidence, I was able to successfully complete a degree program in electronics technology, a field that has always interested me. I was hired by an importer of Japanese business machines to work as a customer service representative. The job is also referred to as a troubleshooter. The company put me through an extensive training program designed to teach me how to repair disabled machines located on customer premises. Although I was receiving good training and good support from my boss, I still had some concerns about how well I could perform under field conditions. It was the old self-confidence problem surfacing again.

"To phase me into my job the firm sent me out on repair assignments with my boss. Soon it was my turn to troubleshoot customer problems on my own. One Friday morning I was sent out on my first solo assignment. A customer was having problems with one of our biggest copiers. The machine seemed to chew up paper and create a jam that the customer could not fix.

"Trembling somewhat inside, I arrived at the customer office to lend my expertise. I poked around inside the machine but I couldn't locate the cause of the problem. By the end of an hour I had made no progress and I was becoming uptight. My armpits were soaked and I developed an uneasy feeling in my stomach. Much to my embarrassment, I had to call my boss to help me locate the root of the problem. What a blow to my self-confidence! However, my boss was very helpful. He patiently explained to me where I went wrong.

"If I had had confidence in my own abilities, I would have located the problem on my own. I vowed from that moment on I would be calmer in a crisis. What future is there for a troubleshooter who panics in an emergency? My plan for building my confidence in my troubleshooting skills was to properly handle the next customer problem of the same kind. I told my boss that I knew where I went wrong and that I wanted another try. He told me he had no intention of dumping me as a troubleshooter.

"One week later I was called out on a similar problem with another machine leased by the same customer. Within forty minutes I had diagnosed and remedied the problem creating the paper jam. My rising to the occasion in that second chance was a turning point in building my self-confidence. Once the copying machine was back in operation I believed that I was on my way to becoming a first-class troubleshooter. Unless you believe in your abilities to repair a machine when the stakes are high, you'll never make it as a customer service representative."

Rick's successful strategy for boosting his self-confidence is a variation of achieving something that stretches your capability. It is called return to the harassing situation. Overcoming a problem that threw you in the past will tend to bolster your self-confidence in that and comparable situations. Rick, of course, must develop a similar strategy for bolstering his self-confidence in his relationships with women.

Take an Inventory of Your Personal Assets

A fundamental reason that many people suffer from low self-confidence is that they don't appreciate their own good points. To bolster your self-confidence you might therefore take an inventory of your assets as a person. Concentrate on personal characteristics rather than tangible assets such as "about $6,000 in inherited stock." In preparing your list of assets, try not to be modest. You are looking for any confidence-booster you can find. Asking the help of a good friend can be useful.

Two lists, one prepared by a man, the other by a woman, should suffice to give you an idea of the kinds of assets that might be included on such a list.

Lillian	*Angelo*
Good listener; most people like me; good handwriting; good posture; inquisitive mind; good at solving problems; good sense of humor; patient with people who make mistakes; better than average appearance.	Good mechanical skills; work well under pressure; good dancer; friendly with strangers; strong as an ox; good cook; can laugh at my own mistakes; great looking guy; humble and modest.

The value of these asset lists is that they add to your self-appreciation. Most people who lay out their good points on paper come away from the activity with at least a temporary boost in self-confidence. The temporary boost, combined with a few success experiences, may lead to a long-term gain in self-confidence.

Ask Others About Your Good Points

An important supplement to listing your own assets is hearing the opinion of others on your good points. This tactic has to be used sparingly, however, and mainly with people who are personal-growth minded. A good ice-breaker is to tell your source of feedback that you have to prepare a list of your assets for a human relations exercise (the one you are reading about right now!). Since that person knows of your work on your capabilities, you hope that he or she can spare a few minutes for this important exercise.

For many people, positive feedback from others does more for building self-confidence than does feedback from oneself. The reason is that self-esteem depends to a large extent on what we think others think about us. Consequently, if other people—whose judgment you trust—think highly of you, your self-image will be positive.

Dress to Feel Confident

Dressing in a manner that makes you feel good about yourself can sometimes give you a slight boost in self-confidence. But be careful not to choose a wardrobe that makes you think more about your clothing than the situation you are facing. To find a confidence-building outfit, you may have to try on different outfits that you already own or purchase new clothing.

Your best outfit can be a confidence builder. For some people, best might be casual attire purchased from a discount clothing store. For other people, best might be conservatively tailored and expensive suits bearing a label with snob appeal. To many an adolescent, a confidence builder might be jeans and an inscribed T-shirt. For still others, any clean, recently purchased outfit in their wardrobe enhances their self-confidence. What kind of clothing makes you feel confident?

The point of all this is that if your clothing makes you feel inwardly confident, you will be better able to project a confident image to the outside world. However mystical it seems, projecting outer confidence begins a process that makes you feel confident. As others respond to you positively because of the confidence that you project, you will in fact become more self-confident. In the same way, raising your self expectations becomes a self-fulfilling prophecy.

Raise Your Self Expectations

Perhaps the ultimate solution to developing self-confidence is to convince yourself that you expect to be a confident person. The same process is referred to as developing a **positive mental attitude,** a strong belief that things will work out in your favor. A skeptic might comment here, "If I had a positive mental attitude I would already be self-confident."

Fortunately, the skeptic is only partly right. If you assume a role long enough, you begin to take on characteristics of a person who occupies that role. An effective coaching technique is to have the learner visualize an expert executing a particular shot or making a particular maneuver. Horse riders are urged to visualize themselves jumping flawlessly over a fence; tennis players are urged to visualize themselves hitting thunderous serves deep to the opponent's backhand. And students of public speaking are told to visualize themselves making a captivating, confident presentation in front of an audience.

Avoid Saying Negative Things about Yourself

A lack of self-confidence is reflected in statements such as, "I may be stupid but," "Nobody asked my opinion," "I know I'm usually wrong, but . . . ," "I know I don't have as much education as some people, but . . ." Self-effacing statements like these serve to reinforce low self-confidence.

It is also important not to attribute to yourself negative, irreversible traits such as "idiotic," "ugly," "dull," "a loser," and "hopeless."[3] Instead look upon your weak points as areas for possible self-improvement. Negative self-labeling can do long-term damage to your self-confidence. If a person stops the practice today, his or her self-confidence may begin to climb upward.

WHAT IS LEADERSHIP AND WHO IS A LEADER?

So far we have emphasized the importance of developing self-confidence so that you can eventually provide leadership to others. One reason self-confidence is important is that **leadership** *is the process of influencing others in order to achieve certain objectives.* People tend to be influenced most by a person of high—but not unreasonable—self-confidence.

The key word in understanding the concept of leadership is influence. If influence is not exerted, leadership, strictly speaking, has not been performed. A night manager of a hotel might work her designated five nights a week and perform her chores in a highly satisfactory manner. Guests, employees, and the hotel owner are all kept happy. Her boss checks with her from time to time to see how things are going, but the two of them have little contact with each other. She performs well without the benefit of another's influence on her performance. She therefore does not require leadership.

Not every method of influencing others should be considered a form of leadership. If you were mugged, your assailant would not be considered a leader. Someone who drugged you against your will would not be considered a leader. If you were taken hostage and brainwashed, your captor would not ordinarily be considered your leader. On the positive side, here are several examples of situations in which leadership *is* exercised:

> A coach takes over a soccer team that has lost eight straight games. Under her leadership, they win six and lose two of their remaining games.
>
> Your little brother is failing in school. You decide to spend about three hours with him each week discussing his problems and coaching human study habits. By the next marking period he achieves no grade lower than a C.
>
> You are appointed supervisor of a crew of night computer operators. For the past year their error rate has been 20 percent below standard. Within six months under your supervision, the error rate is only 2 percent below standard.

A **leader** then, is a person who exerts influence over others to achieve certain objectives. As implied earlier, not everyone holding an administrative, supervisory, or managerial position is truly a leader. You are only a leader if you influence or inspire people to do something that they wouldn't ordinarily do in just following their jobs.

Leaders Are at Every Level

Many people think that the term leader refers to someone who exerts leadership at a top executive or nationally prominent level. To them a leader is a Nobel prize winner, the chief executive officer of a large corporation, the governor of California, or the prime minister of England. In reality, a leader can be the manager of a well-run ice cream store, the captain of a little league softball team, or the captain of the high school band. So long as you are influencing people in order to achieve objectives they might not have achieved if you weren't around, you're a leader.

TRAITS AND CHARACTERISTICS OF EFFECTIVE LEADERS

About 10,000 studies have been conducted on the characteristics that contribute to the effectiveness of a leader. One conclusion reached by numerous researchers is that the answer depends upon the situation. A supervisor in a logging camp and a supervisor in a beauty parlor will probably need a different set of personal characteristics. A rock band leader may need a different personality style from that of a hockey team coach. The situation includes such factors as the people to be supervised, the job to be performed, the company, and the cultural background of the people.

Despite these vast differences in situations, some generalizations can be drawn about the inner qualities that are important for **leadership effectiveness** in a wide variety of situations. **Effectiveness** in the sense used here means that the leader helps the group accomplish its objectives. Simultaneously, the leader achieves these results without ignoring the welfare, morale, or satisfaction of subordinates. Another way of stating the same idea is to say that in order to be an effective leader, certain traits and characteristics are particularly important.

Self-confidence

To repeat, an effective leader is usually a self-confident individual. Research has shown this to be true in a wide variety of situations from the shop floor to the executive suite. A self-confident leader helps group members overcome their feelings of concern about being able to accomplish the tough requirements of a job. A confident leader also conveys the impression of knowing how to handle the task of supervising the group.

Again, a distinction must be drawn between self-confidence and arrogance or cockiness. A person too high in self-confidence may give subordinates the impression of being brash and unfeeling or, worse, covering up feelings of insecurity. A national study of ninety prominent achievers revealed "no trace of self-worship or cockiness in our leaders."[4]

One factor contributing to the self-confidence of leaders is their **internal locus of control,** a belief that one is the primary cause of events happening to oneself. People with an external locus of control attribute cause to external events such a bad luck and office politics. Supervisory leaders with an internal locus of control are seen by their subordinates as more effective than those with an external locus.[5]

Sound Human Relations Skills

An effective leader must work well with people. Working well with people does not necessarily mean a leader is particularly easygoing with them. It means that a leader relates to people in such a way as to capture their trust and cooperation. A leadership researcher observed that human relations skills involve:

> Accepting responsibility for your own ideas and feelings
>
> Being open to your own and other's sentiments
>
> Experimenting with new ideas and feelings
>
> Helping others accept, be open to, and experiment with their own ideas and attitudes[6]

Insight Into People and Situations

Good insight helps you develop human relations skills. **Insight** is a depth of understanding that requires considerable intuition and common sense. Insight into people and situations involving people is an essential leadership characteristic. A leader with good insights is able to make better work assignments and do a better job of training and developing subordinates.

An example of an insightful leader would be one who looks at the expression on subordinates' faces to see if they really understand a new procedure. If not, the leader would provide more explanation. An example of poor insight would be to hold a departmental meeting late in the afternoon before a major religious or national holiday. Why try to capture employees' attention when they are thinking about something else? A meeting about an emergency, however, would be an exception to this principle of poor insight.

Sensitivity to People

Having insight leads to **sensitivity**—taking people's needs and feelings into account when dealing with them. Sensitivity also implies that the leader minimizes hurting the feelings of people and frustrating their needs. Being sensitive to people is therefore needed for leadership effectiveness.

Insensitivity to others prevents many up-and-coming managers from realizing their full potential. In a study of executive leadership, psychologists compared "derailed" executives with those who had progressed to senior management positions. The leading category of fatal flaws was insensitivity to others, characterized by an abrasive, intimidating, bullying style.[7]

Technical Competence

The closer a leader is to working with the technical aspects of an organization, the more technically competent he or she must be. **Technical competence** refers to understanding the actual details of the operation you are leading—for example, the head of a bakery must know how to bake. Supervisors and middle managers who are not technically competent run the risk of not establishing rapport with their subordinates. To be effective, the manager of the word-processing department should know something about word processing.

The widely held belief that once you are a top-level leader you can leave technical details behind, is greatly exaggerated. Most successful people are still quite knowledgeable about the details of the field in which they found success. A recently appointed top executive of a major architectural and engineering firm had this to say about his new position: "I'm not going to be doing any design work on the boards and that's been true for a long time. But having a design sensibility is something you bring to the job every day, both in dealing with clients and trying to help the people in the office do their work."[8]

Strong Work Motivation and High Energy

Leadership positions tend to be demanding both physically and mentally. A successful holder of a leadership position must be willing to work hard and long in order to achieve success. Many leaders appear to be driven by a need for self-fulfillment. Another fundamental reason strong work motivation is required for effectiveness is that a person has to be willing to accept the heavy responsibility that being a supervisor entails. As one department manager said, "Whoever thought being a manager would mean that I would have to fire a woman who has three children to feed and clothe?"

Good Problem-Solving Ability

Leaders in most situations should be equal to or more adept at solving problems than their subordinates. Effective leaders anticipate problems before they occur and diligently stay with them until solved. By so doing a leader demonstrates creative problem solving. Effective leaders also are not afraid to experiment with untried methods and approaches.

Good Work Habits

A disorganized, unplanned, impulsive leader is an ineffective leader. With the increasing paperwork requirements of most leadership positions, he or she has to be all the more organized, goal oriented, and attentive to details. Personal efficiencies or good work habits are so important for success that an entire chapter was devoted to them as part of developing career thrust.

Sense of Humor

"Appropriate use of humor in the workplace enhances communication, motivation, creativity, and ultimately productivity," says David Baum, a humor consultant.[9] Whether or not you take Baum's balm seriously, humor is a contributor to leadership effectiveness. Humor helps leaders influence people by reducing tension, relieving boredom, and defusing anger.[10] Another advantage is that an appropriate use of humor helps the leader appear warm and human.

The most effective form of humor by a leader is tied to the leadership situation. It is much less effective for the leader to tell rehearsed jokes. A key advantage of a witty work-related comment is that it indicates mental alertness. A canned joke is much more likely to fall flat.

Here is an example of effective humor by a managerial leader. Marie had just learned that because of a cost-reduction program, no employee would receive more than a 3 percent salary increase. She called her employees together and announced, "I have some good news and bad news. On the good side, we all have our jobs if we want them; and we will all have a chance to fight inflation by controlling wage increases. The bad news is that we will have to live with a maximum of a 3 percent raise this time around." Marie's humor helped the group put the small salary increase in proper perspective.

The Ability to Inspire and Motivate Others

Not every effective leader has a magnetic personality, or has the charm referred to as **charisma.** Yet to be effective as a leader you need some degree of this intangible personal quality.[11] Famous and well-loved leaders have this type of personal charm in large doses. No leader can hope to appeal to everyone. It's a question of inspiring many more people than those you do not inspire or on whom you have a neutral impact. Even a well-liked U.S. president can hope to gain little more than 70 percent of the popular vote.

Vision and Foresight

Top-level leaders need a visual image of where the organization is headed, and how it can get there. The progress of the organization is dependent on the top executive having this vision. Effective leaders project ideas and images that excite people, and therefore inspire employees to do their best.[12] Leadership positions of lesser responsibility also call for some **foresight,** a positive idea about where the leader is going and what to do about it.[13]

Enthusiasm

In almost all leadership situations it is desirable for the leader to be enthusiastic. Subordinates respond positively to enthusiasm, partially because enthusiasm may be perceived as a reward for constructive behavior. Enthusiasm is also effective because it helps build good relationships with subordinates. Verbal expressions of enthusiasm include such statements as "Great job," and I love it." The leader can express enthusiasm nonverbally through gestures, touching, and so forth.

BEHAVIORS OF EFFECTIVE LEADERS

The personal traits and characteristics just discussed help create the potential for effective leadership. A leader also has to do things that influence followers to do the job. Numerous books have been written about what a manager (or other type of leader) should do. The conclusions they reach about leadership effectiveness, however, must be interpreted with caution. Leadership depends to a large extent on the specific situation as described earlier. With this caution in mind, turn now to the following summary of activities carried out by effective leaders—those who maintain high productivity and morale.

Share Decision Making

A good leader is willing to share some of his or her power. He or she doesn't insist on making all the major decisions. Instead, the leader solicits the group's opinion on many matters of significance to them. In some circumstances, the manager must make the decision without consulting the group. One example would be to ask a noncontributing member to leave. A leader who shares decision making is described as a **participative leader.**

Help Subordinates Reach Goals

Effective leaders help subordinates in their efforts to achieve goals. In a sense, he or she smoothes out the path to reaching goals. One important way to do this is to provide the necessary resources to subordinates. An important aspect of a leader's job is to ensure that subordinates have the proper tools, equipment, and personnel to accomplish their objectives.

Reduce Frustrating Barriers

An important psychological part of a leader's job is to help reduce some of the barriers that prevent followers from reaching their goals. A leader who helps subordinates cut their way through red tape (minor rules and regulations) would be engaging in such behavior. In the factory, a supervisory leader has a responsibility to replace faulty equipment, to see to it that unsafe conditions are corrected, and to see that troublesome employees are either rehabilitated or replaced.

Create Opportunities for Personal Satisfaction

Another important general set of actions characteristic of an effective leader is looking out for the satisfaction of the group. Small things sometimes mean a lot in terms of personal satisfaction. One office manager fought for better coffee facilities for her subordinates. Her thoughtfulness contributed immensely to job satisfaction among them.

Exert Influence Throughout the Organization

Good leaders have some clout in terms of getting things done for group members. Employees respond positively to supervisors who are able to influence higher-level managers and other key personnel. Supervisors with such influence are able to fight for the demands of their subordinates. Would you want your boss to stand behind your requests?

Provide Emotional Support and Consideration

Having good human relations skills of this nature is often more important for improving morale than producing work. It is an important leadership behavior. An emotionally supportive leader would engage in activities such as listening to subordinates' problems and offering them encouragement.

Differentiate Themselves from Subordinates

If you walk into an office or other leadership situation you should be able to tell which person is the leader. An effective leader is not simply another member of the department. He or she plans, regulates, and coordinates but does not become directly involved in performing the work. The effective leader does some personal work, however, like making plans for the future, recruiting new members, or figuring out a budget.

Exercise Flexible Rather than Tight Supervision

With some exceptions, most employees feel better and work better when they have breathing room in which to carry out their chores. As one experienced executive put it, "A good manager begins with a tight rope around a subordinate's neck. He or she gradually loosens the rope as the subordinate shows that he or she can handle freedom." It must be added that the effective leader tries to avoid suppressing the subordinate, even at the outset of their relationship.

Establish Realistic Goals

An effective leader helps group members set goals that will raise both individual and group productivity. At the same time, these goals are not so lofty that frustration from not reaching them will be inevitable. Goal setting helps the group determine its purpose. Some leaders therefore see goal setting as one of the most important functions of a leader. Goal setting ties in closely with the ability of a leader to inspire and motivate people. Specifically, if you raise your goals and reach them, you will inspire your subordinates.

Make Their Expectations Known

People function better when they know what they have to do to achieve work goals. Each person needs to know what is expected of him or her in order to make a contribution to the mission of the department. The leader provides answers to such questions as, "What am I as an individual supposed to do to help the company build this ocean liner?" Or, "What can I do to help get this budget completed today?"

Hold Others to High Standards of Performance

Another leadership behavior of note is to hold subordinates to high standards of performance. If you as a leader expect others to succeed, they are likely to live up to your expectations. Management professor Burt K. Scanlon puts it this way, "Low expectations breed low performance and apathy, while high expectations lead to high performance and a more demanding performance tone."[14]

Give Frequent Feedback on Performance

Employees are told how they can improve and are given encouragement for the things they are doing right. Ineffective leaders, in contrast, often avoid confrontation and give limited positive feedback. An exception is that some ineffective leaders become involved in many confrontations—they are masters at reprimanding people!

Delegate Assignments to the Right People

Delegation is the leadership act of letting go, that is, passing authority down to subordinates. As a supervisor you might authorize an employee to represent your department in an important meeting. By delegating such authority, you do not escape accountability for the manager in which the task is performed. If the person you send to the meeting makes no contribution, you have done a poor job (as well as the person you sent). It is therefore important to delegate assignments to people who are capable of performing them now, or are willing to learn. The ability to judge people is an important attribute of a good delegator.

Manage a Crisis Effectively

When a crisis strikes, that's the time to have an effective leader around. When things are running very smoothing, you may not always notice whether your leader is around. Effectively managing a crisis means giving reassurance to the group that things will soon be under control, specifying the alternative paths for getting out of the crisis, and choosing one of the paths.

Another aspect of managing a crisis is the ability to bounce back from adversity. Prominent leaders in any field are known for their ability to work their way out of difficult times. They are not discouraged by obstacles or turned aside by roadblocks. A telltale fact is that effective leaders rarely use the term "failure" in reference to things that did not go well. Instead, they prefer terms such as "bungle," "false start," and "setback."[15]

DEVELOPING YOUR LEADERSHIP POTENTIAL

How to improve your potential for becoming a leader is a topic without limits. Almost anything you do to improve your individual effectiveness will have some impact on your ability to lead others. If you strengthen your self-confidence, improve your memory for names, study this book carefully, read studies about leadership, or improve your physical fitness, you stand a good chance of improving your leadership potential. Four general strategies might be kept in mind if you are seeking to improve your leadership potential.

General Education and Specific Training

Almost any program of business training or education can be considered a program of leadership development. Courses in human relations, management, or business psychology have obvious relevance for someone currently occupying or aspiring toward a leadership position. Many of today's leaders in profit and nonprofit organizations hold formal degrees in business. Specific training programs will also help you improve your leadership potential. Among them might be skill development programs in interviewing, employee selection, listening, assertiveness training, budgeting, planning, improving work habits, resolving conflict, and communication skills.

Leadership Development Programs

Some programs are designed specifically to improve your ability to influence or lead other people. An excellent program of this nature is offered by the Center for Creative Leadership in Greensboro, North Carolina. Such programs are often one week in length and cost about $2,000 in tuition and expenses. Leadership programs of this nature have two important features in common. First, you are given feedback from other people and from questionnaires about your current leadership style (or leadership tendencies if you are not now a leader). Second, you interact with other group members in an organized way in addition to hearing lectures about leadership.

Leadership Experience

No program of leadership improvement can be a substitute for leadership experience. Because leadership effectiveness depends somewhat on the situation, a sound approach is to attempt to gain leadership experience in different settings. A person who wants to become an executive is well advised to gain supervisory experience in at least two different organizational functions (such as marketing and manufacturing).

First-level supervisory jobs are an invaluable starting point for developing your leadership potential. It takes considerable skill to manage a fast-food restaurant effectively or to direct a public playground during the summer. A first-line supervisor frequently faces a situation in which subordinates are poorly trained, poorly paid, and not well motivated to achieve company objectives.

Modeling Effective Leaders

Are you committed to improving your leadership skill and potential? If so, carefully observe a capable leader in action and incorporate some of his or her approaches into your own behavior. You may not be able to or want to become that person's clone, but you can model (imitate) what the person does. For instance, most inexperienced leaders have a difficult time confronting others with bad news. Observe a good confronter handle the situation, and try that person's approach the next time you have some unfavorable news to deliver to another person.

SUMMARY

Before most people can exert leadership, they need to develop an appropriate amount of self-confidence. It is necessary for leadership because it helps assure followers that things are under control. A leader who is too self-confident, however, may not admit to errors, listen to criticism, or ask for advice. Also, you may appear insecure if you are too self-confident.

A general principle of boosting your self-confidence is to experience success (goal accomplishment) in a variety of situations. As you achieve one set of goals, you establish slightly more difficult goals, thus entering a success cycle. The specific strategies for building self-confidence described here are:

1. Obtain a few easy victories.
2. Enter a less competitive environment (if you were in over your head previously).
3. Attack situations aggressively.
4. Achieve something that stretches your capability.
5. Take an inventory of your personal assets.
6. Ask others about your good points.
7. Dress to feel confident.
8. Raise your self expectations (the self-fulfilling prophecy).
9. Avoid saying negative things about yourself.

Leadership is the process of influencing others in order to achieve certain objectives. A leader is a person who exerts influence over others in order to achieve certain objectives.

Although leadership is situational, some traits and characteristics contribute to leadership effectiveness in many situations. These include self-confidence, sound human relations skills, sensitivity to people, insight into people and situations, technical competence, strong work motivation and high energy, good problem-solving ability, good work habits, sense of humor, the ability to inspire and motivate others, vision and foresight, and enthusiasm.

The behaviors engaged in by effective leaders (those who maintain high productivity and morale) include the following:

1. Share decision making.
2. Help subordinates reach goals.
3. Reduce frustrating barriers.
4. Create opportunities for personal satisfaction.
5. Exert influence throughout the organization.
6. Provide emotional support and consideration.
7. Differentiate themselves from subordinates.
8. Exercise flexible rather than tight supervision.
9. Establish realistic goals.
10. Make their expectations known.
11. Hold others to high standards of performance.
12. Give frequent feedback on performance.
13. Delegate assignments to the right people.
14. Manage a crisis effectively.

Many activities in life can in some way contribute to the development of a person's leadership potential. Four recommended strategies for improving your leadership potential or leadership skills are: (1) general education and specific training, (2) participation in leadership development programs, (3) acquisition of leadership experience, and (4) modeling experienced leaders.

QUESTIONS AND ACTIVITIES

1. When you first meet a person, how can you tell whether that person is self-confident?
2. Name two occupations for which you think self-confidence is especially important. Explain your reasoning.
3. Name two occupations for which you think self-confidence is *not* especially important. Explain your reasoning.
4. Identify several negative things people often say about themselves in addition to those mentioned on page 364.
5. How can having an "internal locus of control" help you in your career and personal life?
6. What is your opinion of the importance of a leader having a good sense of humor?
7. How will your current program of study contribute to your development as a leader?

8. Which leadership traits and characteristics do you already possess? How do you know?

A HUMAN RELATIONS CASE PROBLEM:
"MY LEADERSHIP ISN'T WORKING"

Sherry Gabrielli had worked as the security supervisor at the regional office of Affiliated Department Stores for six months. She was appointed supervisor after four years of good performance as a security officer. Sherry looked forward with some apprehension to her performance review with boss, Al Badway. Sherry felt she was not accomplishing anywhere near what she wanted to accomplish.

Badway greeted Sherry with a smile and said, "May I get you a cup of coffee, tea, or soft drink? I want you to relax."

"I will take you up on a decaffeinated, diet cola drink. Despite this job, I haven't slipped back to trying to cure my tension with coffee."

"Your health kick must be working, Sherry, because you appear quite relaxed on the job to me. One of your strong points as a security supervisor is that you are cool and calm under pressure. In fact, my overall performance rating of you is well above average. Both my boss, the operations chief, and I think you're doing a bang-up job. You can expect an above-average salary increase this next paycheck.

"How do you think you are doing Sherry? Any problems we may have missed? Anything we can help you with?"

"I'm glad you asked," replied Sherry. "I am experiencing one difficulty as a supervisor that may not be showing up in my job performance. My leadership isn't working as well as I would like. The way I see it, our department still isn't acting professional enough. The fellows and gals are doing a good job, but they are lacking that professional image."

"Sounds like a real concern," said Al with a pensive look on his face. "Could you be more specific, though?"

"I can give you a couple for instances," replied Sherry." Mona, one of the security officers, sits in the office with her feet on the desk. And she's forever munching apples. Gordie, our newest security officer, tells about one gross joke each workday. Eduardo, the senior officer who should know better, whistles whenever he's trying to relax."

"What have you done so far about the problems?" asked Al.

"I talk about the need for professionalism in security work, but nothing happens. I once even told Eduardo to stop whistling because it gave me a headache. He just gave me a funny look."

"Maybe you and I can talk about this again at a later date. I'll have to give this problem some more thought. In the meantime, we still think you're a gem of a security supervisor."

Questions

1. Is Sherry justified in being concerned about the professional image of security officers?
2. What can Sherry do to exert more influence about professional behavior among the security officers?
3. What should Al's role be in helping Sherry?
4. What specific leadership behaviors should Sherry be emphasizing in order to increase professionalism in the group?

A HUMAN RELATIONS ROLE PLAY: INFLUENCING PROFESSIONAL BEHAVIOR

One person plays the role of Sherry Gabrielli, the security supervisor who wants to influence her group to act more professionally in the office. Three other people play the role of security officers (Mona, Gordie, and Eduardo) who lack enthusiasm for her influence attempts. Conduct a role play, in which a group acts out a brief departmental meeting on the subject of professionalism.

REFERENCES

[1] Warren Bennis and Burt Nanus, "The Leading Edge," *Success!,* April 1985, p. 58.

[2] Barbara Varro, "Let's Hear It for Humility," *Chicago Sun Times* story reprinted June 23, 1981. Reprinted here with permission.

[3] Philip G. Zimbardo, *Shyness: What It Is. What To Do About It.* (New York: A Jove/HBJ Book, 1977), p. 209.

[4] Bennis and Nanus, "The Leading Edge," p. 58.

[5] Avis L. Johnson, Fred Luthans, and Harry W. Hennessey, "The Role of Locus of Control in Leader Influence Behavior," *Personnel Psychology,* Spring 1984, p. 70.

[6] Jay Hall, "What Makes a Manager Good, Bad, or Average?" *Psychology Today,* August 1976, p. 53.

[7] Morgan W. McCall, Jr., and Michael M. Lombardo, "What Makes a Top Executive?" *Psychology Today,* February 1983, p. 28.

[8] "Architectural Firm Picks New President," *New York Times,* May 22, 1981, p. D2.

[9] Dan Oldenburg, "Corporate Man 1986?" *Washington Post* story, March 17, 1986.

[10] W. Jack Duncan, "Humor in Management: Prospects for Administrative Practice and Research," *Academy of Management Review,* January 1982, pp. 136–140.

[11] David L. Sudhalter, *The Management Option: Nine Strategies for Leadership* (New York: Human Sciences Press, 1980), p. 12.

[12] Richard I. Lester, "Leadership: Some Principles and Concepts," *Personnel Journal,* November 1981, p. 870.

[13] J. Robert Connor, "The Qualities of Leadership," *BusinessWeek's Guide to Careers,* December 1985, p. 9.

[14] Burt K. Scanlon, "Managerial Leadership in Perspective: Getting Back to Basics," *Personnel Journal,* March 1979, p. 169.

[15] Warren Bennis and Burt Nanus, "The Leadership Tightrope," *Success!,* March 1985, p. 63.

SOME ADDITIONAL READING

ADAIR, JOHN. *Effective Leadership: A Self-Development Manual.* Brookfield, VT: Gower Publishing, 1983.

ADAMS, JEROME, and JANICE D. YODER. *Effective Leadership for Women and Men.* Norwood, NJ: Ablex, 1985.

BLAKE, ROBERT R., and JANE S. MOUTON. *The Managerial Grid III: The Key to Leadership Excellence,* 3rd ed. Houston, TX: Gulf Publishing, 1985.

COX, ALLAN. "Using Your Unique Leadership Strengths." *Success!,* February 1985, pp. 18–19.

CRIBBIN, JAMES J. *Leadership, Your Competitive Edge.* New York: American Management Associations Publications Group, 1985.

HOWELL, JON P., PETER W. DORFMAN, and STEVE KERR. "Moderator Variables in Leadership Research." *Academy of Management Review,* January 1986, pp. 88–102.

SARGENT, ALICE G. *The Androgynous Manager: Blending Male & Female Management Styles for Today's Organization.* New York: AMACOM, 1984.

SCHEIN, EDGAR H. *Organizational Culture and Leadership: A Dynamic View.* San Francisco: Jossey-Bass, 1985.

15

Managing Your Personal Finances

Learning Objectives

After studying the information and doing the exercises in this chapter you should be able to:

- Do a better job of managing your personal finances
- Establish a tentative budget for yourself or family
- Identify several widely used forms of savings and investment
- Recognize that overborrowing can be both a financial and a psychological problem
- Begin the practice of giving yourself a yearly financial checkup

*I*t is important to manage your personal finances in such a way that money is not a major worry and concern in your life. Financial problems lead to other problems. A major source of ineffective job performance is poor concentration stemming from financial worries. Many disputes between marital partners or roommates stem from conflict about financial problems. Financial problems can also drain you of energy that could be used to further your career or enrich your personal life.

In this chapter we discuss key ideas that should enable a person to start on the road to financial comfort or escape financial discomfort. If you are intent upon becoming a millionaire in a hurry, or an expert in personal finance, pursue the references at the end of this chapter.

ESTABLISHING FINANCIAL GOALS

Personal finances is yet another area in which goal setting generally improves performance. A common approach to setting financial goals is to specify amounts of money you would like to earn at certain points in time. One individual might set yearly financial goals, adjusted for inflation. Many ambitious people in business hope to double their income every seven years. Although this goal sounds fanciful, it is realistic if you take into account inflation and the fact that your income increases are compounded. That is, the income base upon which you get a raise keeps increasing. One year you earn $20,000. The next year you receive a 10 percent increase, thus earning $22,000; the next year with another 10 percent increase, you will receive $24,200, and so forth.

Assume that a person reading this book earns a salary of $25,000 in 1988, and then doubles his or her salary every seven years. By the year 2009 he or she will be earning $200,000. What color Rolls Royce will you buy for yourself?

One expert offers these suggestions for financial planning:[1]

1. Set your goals down in writing.
2. Keep the goals high but realistic (not out of reach).
3. Set a period of time, or time frame, in which to accomplish each financial goal.
4. Establish mini goals as stepping stones to major goals. Also set up an action plan for achieving them.
5. Change your goals when your life circumstances change.
6. Once you've set your goals, take immediate action to turn them into reality. Avoid procrastination.

A Nonmonetary Way of Setting Financial Goals

Financial goals expressed in dollar figures have several disadvantages. First of all, it is difficult to accurately predict the effects of inflation. You must therefore use a standard such as, "By 1995 I would like to earn $40,000 a year expressed in 1988 dollars." Secondly, financial goals may seem too mercenary and crass to some people. For those people it is preferable to plan to earn enough money to support a particular lifestyle. Here are three examples:

> By the year 2005, I want to earn enough money to own my own home, plus a summer home near a lake, and take a winter vacation each year.
>
> By 1992 I want to earn enough money to have my own apartment and car, and buy nice gifts for my family and relatives.
>
> By 1990, I want to earn enough money to be able to attend business school part-time and travel out-of-town one weekend a month.

SPENDING LESS THAN YOUR NET INCOME

The key to lifelong financial security and peace of mind is to spend less money than you earn. By so doing you will avoid the stresses of being in debt and worrying about money. If you wanted to become wealthy, you might not follow this strategy. Books that tell you how to become a millionaire usually emphasize borrowing as much money as you can. You then invest that borrowed money into something that yields a high enough return to enable you to pay off your debt.

Suppose you borrowed $20,000 to buy into an apartment building operated by someone else. Your loan repayments would be $500 per month, while your rate of return from the apartment building would be $600 per month. Your monthly cash profit would be $100. In addition, you would be acquiring equity (cash value) in the building, and would also be receiving some tax advantages. Unless you are a particularly shrewd investor, it is better for your peace of mind to invest money that you have saved, not borrowed.

People at all income levels have difficulty spending less than their **net income.** Many people who find themselves in deep financial trouble earn substantial incomes but have gradually allowed their expenses to creep up higher than their income. A case in point is Fred, a highly paid public relations specialist. One part of the story he brought to a debt counselor centered around spending more than his net income:

> My boss told me I would be getting a $500 a month raise. I was so excited that I went out and bought a Lincoln Continental for $25,000 and sold my old car. I figured I could easily handle the new payments with another $250 per month. I

was wrong. My net increase in pay was only $200 after taxes, social security, and profit sharing were deducted from my pay. Besides, some of my other expenses increased so my raise really didn't put me ahead.

Two months after receiving my increase I was spending $110 more per month than I was making. I started to borrow to make up the difference. Then things really got nasty. It became necessary to eat away at my small savings.

Fred ultimately salvaged his situation by selling his luxury car for a price that barely exceeded the money he owed on the car. The family's second car has become the only car, at least until Fred can rebuild his financial situation.

USING A BUDGET TO PLAN YOUR SPENDING

When most people hear the word budget they think of a low-priced item or of miserly spending habits. Their perception is only partly correct. A **budget** is a plan for spending money to improve your chances of using your money wisely and not spending more than your net income. The basic idea is to estimate your expenses over a period of time and allocate the money you have available to cover those expenses. In addition, you set something aside for reserves or savings. The budgeting process can be divided into a series of logical steps.[2]

Step 1: Establishing goals. It is important to decide what you or your family really need and want. If you are establishing a family budget, it is best to involve the entire family. For the sake of simplicity, we will assume here that the reader is preparing an individual budget. Individual budgets can be combined to form the family budget. Goal setting should be done for the short, intermediate, and long term. A short-term goal might be "replace hot water heater this February." A long-term goal might be "accumulate enough money for a mobile home within ten years."

Step 2: Estimating income. People whose entire income is derived from a salary can readily estimate their income. If you anticipate a salary increase, include some reasonable figures such as a 10 percent additional gross (not net) income. Nonsalary sources of income include inheritance, stock dividends, interest from savings accounts, and money from part-time employment. A simple chart can be used, as follows on page 387.

Step 3: Estimating expenses. After you have determined how much your income will be for the planning period, it is time for the difficult part—estimating your expenses. If you have any records of previous spending habits and patterns, they can serve as a basis for your budget. For instance, "How much a month do I spend for newspapers, magazines, and books? How much for records and movies?" List the item of expense, followed by the actual or

Estimated income for _____

ITEM	AMOUNT
Wage or salary	$_____
Net profit from part-time business or job	_____
Interest, dividends	_____
Inheritance, gifts	_____
Other	_____
Total	$_____

estimated amount you spend a week or month on that item. For most people a monthly budget makes the most sense, since so many expenses are once-a-month items. Included here are rent, mortgage payments, car payments, and bank credit card payments.

All your expense categories should come to mind in about twenty minutes of concentrated thinking. List them separately and later lump some of them together. If you listed "get-well gifts," and "meals out while visiting friends and relatives in hospital" separately, you might later lump these together under "emergency expenditures."

Use your records and your recollections to help you decide whether to continue your present pattern of spending or to make changes. For instance, estimating your expenses might reveal that you are spending far too much on gasoline. An antidote might be to consolidate errand-running trips or make some trips by foot or on bicycle.

An important part of estimating future expenditures is to plan for new situations and changing conditions. As a case in point, assume you will be joining a health club. Estimate your dues, cost of transportation, and extra meals out to accommodate the new demands on your time.

Try to plan your large expenses so they are spaced at intervals over several years. If you plan to purchase a car one year, plan to remodel your kitchen another year. If you buy an overcoat one season, you might have to delay buying a suit until the next year. Many of the specific items in a budget depend on your income level. One person might consider an electronic type-writer to be a major expenditure, whereas a person earning twice as much money might consider that to be a petty cash expenditure. One person might set aside $60 per month for hair styling. To a person of lower income, this might seem like a frivolous expense. Instead that person has a friend cut his or her hair.

A straightforward worksheet for preparing your spending plan is presented in Exhibit 15-1. Modify the specific items to suit your particular spending patterns. For instance, record collecting might be so important to you that it deserves a separate category.

EXHIBIT 15–1   A SPENDING PLAN

Income, set-asides, and expenses	Amount per month
Total income	$_____
Set-asides:	
Emergencies and future goals......................	$_____
Seasonal expenses	_____
Debt payments...........................	_____
Regular monthly expenses:	
Rent or mortgage payment............. $_____	
Utilities................................ _____	
House and car repairs .... _____	
Installment payments .... _____	
Other .... _____	
Total .... _____	_____
Day-to-day expenses:	
Food and beverages.................. $_____	
Household operation, nonfood .... _____	
Furnishings and equipment .... _____	
Entertainment....................... _____	
Clothing .... _____	
Personal (including lunches) .... _____	
Transportation .... _____	
Gifts and contributions............... _____	
Miscellaneous .... _____	
Total	_____
Total set-asides and expenses	$_____
Profit (Total income—set-asides and expenses)..........	$_____

Remember that the true profit from your labor is the difference between your net income and your total expenses. Set-asides are considered an expense, since you will inevitably use up that money to meet future goals or pay for seasonal expenses. Without a miscellaneous category, many budgets will project a profit that never materializes. Any household budget has some miscellaneous or unpredictable items each month. After working with your budget several months you should be able to make an accurate estimate of miscellaneous expenses. Here is a sampling of the type of miscellaneous items that often work their way into monthly expenditures:

Somebody steals your lawnmower, which has to be replaced immediately.
Your best piece of clothing is caught on a nail and requires a $35 mending job by the tailor.
A poor relative begs you for money to put some food on the table. It costs you $60 to avoid feeling guilty about refusing your relative.

Step 4: Comparing expenses and income. Add the figures in your spending plan. Now compare the total with your estimate of income for the planning period. If the two figures balance, at least you are in neutral financial condition. If your income exceeds your estimate of expenses, you have made a profit. You may decide to satisfy more of your immediate wants, set aside more money for future goals, or put the balance into savings or investment.

If your income is below your estimated expenses, you will have to embark on a cost-cutting campaign in your own household. It may be necessary to see old movies instead of first-run movies; you may have to eat more soybeans and less beef; or you can make gifts for friends instead of purchasing them. If you brainstorm the problem by yourself or with friends, you will come up with dozens of valid expense-reducing suggestions.

Step 5: Carrying out the budget. After you have done your best job of putting your spending plan on paper, try it out for one, two, or three months. See how close it comes to reality. Keep accurate records to find out where your money is being spent. It is helpful to make a notation of expenditures at the end of every day. Did you forget about that $23 you spent on party snacks Sunday afternoon? It is a good idea to keep all financial records together. You may find it helpful to set aside a desk drawer, a large box, or other convenient place to put your record book, bills, receipts, and other financial papers.

Step 6: Evaluating the plan. Compare what you spent with what you planned to spend for three consecutive months. If your spending was quite different from your plan, find out why. If your plan did not provide for your needs, it must be revised. You simply cannot live with a budget that allows for no food the last four days of the month. If the plan fitted your needs but you had trouble sticking to it, the solution to your problem may be to practice more self-discipline.

A budget usually needs reworking until it fits your needs. Each succeeding budget should work better. As circumstances change, your budget will need revision. A budget is a changing, living document that serves as a guide to the proper management of your personal finances.

ESTIMATE THE VALUE OF YOUR TIME

How many people do you know who spend at least two evenings a week clipping and sorting grocery coupons? Often one of these coupon-clippers will say, "I saved six dollars this week by taking my coupons to a store that gives double coupon discounts." True, this person saved six dollars, that is, if his or her time was worth very little. The person probably invested six hours in time to save six dollars.

The person just described has struck a good bargain if coupon-clipping can be considered a form of entertainment. If the person placed no value on his or her time, the six dollars was a real savings. From another standpoint, coupon-clipping can be said to bring negative returns. Six hours a week invested in self-development, or earning a second income, would probably pay much greater returns than the same amount of time invested in coupon-clipping. Exhibit 15–2 presents a useful perspective on the value of one's time.

Another expensive saving is to spend two hours going to and from a library to save the price of purchasing a paperback book. Some executives think that flying coach is more expensive than flying first class, even though the coach ticket price is lower. The reasoning offered is that it is easier to work, and therefore saves time and money, in first class than in coach. Can you think of any expensive saving in your life?

EXHIBIT 15–2   THE WORLD'S BEST INVESTMENT

This is the one that will always pay the best dividends and the one best calculated to help you most when the others might not be doing so well. Investing in the long-term growth of American industry has always proved to be an excellent idea, but responsible for its growth are men and women who had the wisdom and foresight to invest in themselves.

We know, for example, that the youngster who invests his time and effort in getting a high-school diploma will earn tens of thousands of dollars more, on the average, than the person who does not. But what about the sixty years or so after graduation? Here's where systematic investment in yourself really pays big dividends.

It's impossible to put a price tag on knowledge, because it's so much more far-reaching than the extra money involved. It also pays off in satisfaction, enjoyment, peace of mind, interest, and stature as a person. The average working person generally puts in a forty-hour week. This leaves the person about seventy-two hours a week neither working nor sleeping, or about twice the time spent on the job. More than ample time to follow programs designed to increase self-knowledge and knowledge of the world, knowledge of one's business and all the people one deals with, and methods for improving communication with them. If the person only devoted one hour a day to this kind of self-investment, it would still leave about sixty hours a week for leisure activities.

The business in which the person works would soon go broke if it failed to plow back a certain percentage of its profits into research and development—ways and means of making it a better company. But does the person do the same thing? As a general rule, the person does not.

How much of your income do you plow back into your own research-and-development department? Or do you take the common attitude that you already know all you need to know? If you do, don't feel that you're different, because you're not. You belong, in fact, to the largest club in the country. You've got all kinds of company. If a convention were ever held for your group to have a get-together, we would have to completely empty the major cities of the country just to accommodate you.

If a person earns, say, $20,000 a year and makes it a practice to invest even 1 percent of the sum in personal growth, that $20 could result in a return greater than the return on the 99 percent of income spent and invested in other ways.

If what I've said here gets under your skin a little, why don't you do something about it? As I said in the beginning, it's the world's best investment.

SOURCE: Adapted and updated from Earl Nightingale, "The World's Best Investment," *Success!*, October 1981, p. 60. Reprinted with permission.

CHOOSING A SAVINGS OR INVESTMENT PLAN

A serious plan for managing your personal finances must include some method of either increasing the value of your money or preventing it from eroding rapidly as it would in a safe-deposit box or hidden in the attic. You should obtain information about investing your money from the numerous available publications on the subject, or you should seek professional counsel. Most newspapers run features or columns written by experts about investing your money. Here we will define and comment on many common methods of saving or investing.[3]

Interest-Bearing Checking Accounts

Keeping your monthly money in a checking account is a necessary practice for most people. It allows you to write checks at a modest cost, or sometimes for free if you keep a monthly balance of around $750; banks vary considerably in the details of their plan. Canceled checks are your most reliable receipt. Also, they eliminate the risk of losing or being robbed of cash. The interest paid on these accounts is usually about half the inflation rate, but you must expect to pay something for this important service. Brokerage firms now offer attractive alternatives to checking accounts for people wealthy enough to maintain a $25,000 minimum balance.

Passbook Savings Accounts

Under this arrangement, you can deposit and withdraw money from the account as often as you wish. This type of account pays about one-quarter percent more than a regular checking account. Most sophisticated investors have abandoned this type of savings account. Your money is insured, as it is in virtually all bank accounts, but otherwise receives no benefit whatever from this account. Although banks and savings and loan associations still offer these accounts, they rarely recommend that you open one.

Term Savings Accounts and Certificates of Deposit (CDs)

Banks and savings and loan associations offering these accounts require that you deposit a reasonably large sum of money for a specified period of time. Often the minimum investment is $500. The popular CDs are offered in $10,000 units and pay a rate of interest above the rate of inflation. Currently, a rate of about 9 percent is typical. Term savings accounts are usually for eighteen- or twenty-four-month periods while CDs represent a six-month agreement.

If you have a considerable amount of cash and are not worried about having your money tied up for a specific time period, term savings accounts and certificates of deposit are ideal. If you close one of these accounts before its due date, the amount of penalty lowers your interest rate to approximately that of an interest-bearing checking account.

Money-Market Mutual Funds

The fastest-growing savings and investment instrument of the early 1980s has been money market funds. Many people who formerly kept their money in banks have shifted their money to these high-yielding, but uninsured funds. Paying well above the inflation rate, many of these funds can be used almost like checking accounts. Usually you need to invest an initial $2,500 in these funds. An important feature is that you have easy access to your money. Most funds allow you to write checks for amounts of $500 or more. The funds themselves charge a small, almost unnoticed, management fee. They invest your money in high-yield, short-term investments such as loans to the federal government or top-quality business corporations.

Treasury Notes and Bonds

Offered by the U.S. government, treasury notes are medium term. Your principal is returned within one to ten years. You can purchase a treasury note in $1,000 denominations and greater. Treasury bonds, which have maturities of five to thirty years, are for the more patient investor. Some are available in $500 denominations. T-notes and T-bonds have much to recommend them. Interest is paid semiannually at a pace that matches inflation, and it is exempt from state tax.

Corporate Bonds

Large corporations sell bonds to the public in order to raise money to further invest in their business. Many of these bonds are twenty- to thirty-year loans. They pay a fixed rate of return such as 8 or 10 percent. If you want to cash in your bond early, you may not be able to sell it for the original value. You would thus take a loss. You can, however, purchase a bond for less than its face value. You might be able to buy a $1,000 bond for $920, collect interest on it, and eventually redeem it for its face value. Trading bonds—buying and selling them for speculation—is a risky activity that should be reserved for knowledgeable investors.

Two types of bonds gaining attention lately are "zero-coupon bonds," and "junk bonds." *Zero-coupon bonds* are well suited to the patient investor. Unlike traditional bonds, which carry coupons that you cash in for dividends periodically, zero-coupon bonds incorporate yields into their price. They sell at much less than their face value. For instance, you might purchase a $1,000 bond for $103.75 and cash it in for $1000 in twenty years. (The yield here is 10.375 percent.)

Junk bonds are bonds offering a high yield because they are rated as having a high risk. One reason could be that the firm offering them is facing financial trouble. Junk bonds are best suited to big investors but some mutual funds invest in them, making them accessible to smaller investors. The default rate on junk bonds is actually quite low.

U.S. Savings Bonds

Many people still purchase these bonds out of patriotism. Essentially you lend the federal government money at a rate well below the rate of inflation but higher than a passbook savings account. U.S. savings bonds are often sold through a payroll deduction plan. The new series EE bonds are sold for $25, pay 9 percent interest, and can be redeemed in eight years. Savings bonds achieved their height of popularity during World War II, and are currently in demand because of their attractive yields.

Common Stocks

Every reader of this book has heard of the stock market, a place where you can purchase shares of public corporations. On a given business day it is not unusual for over 150 million shares of stocks to be bought and sold on the American and Canadian stock exchanges. Common stocks are actually shares of ownership in the corporations issuing them. Stocks pay dividends, but the hope of most investors is that the stock will rise in value. The majority of buying and selling of stocks today is done by institutions rather than by small investors. These institutions include union pension funds, banks, or mutual funds.

Stock prices rise and fall over such tangible factors as the price of oil and fluctuations in interest rates. They also rise and fall over people's perception of events such as national elections. Good news elevates stock prices and bad news brings them down. To cope with these price fluctuations, investors are advised to use dollar-cost averaging. Using **dollar-cost averaging,** you invest the same amount of money in a stock or mutual fund at regular intervals over a long period of time. This eliminates the need for trying to time the highs and lows. Since you are investing a constant amount, you buy less when the price is high and more when the price is low. Over a long period of time, you pay a satisfactory price for your stock (or mutual fund).

Mutual Funds

Since most people lack the time, energy, and knowledge to manage their own stock portfolio, mutual funds are increasingly relied on. The concept of mutual funds is straightforward. For a modest management fee, a small group of professional money managers invest your money, along with that of thousands of other people, into a broad group of common stocks. Numerous mutual funds exist to suit many different purposes and risk-taking attitudes. You can find mutual funds that invest in conservative low-risk stocks or high-risk stocks. The latter tend to have a larger payoff if the company succeeds. Some funds specialize in particular industries such as energy or food. In general, mutual funds have provided excellent rates of return to their investors. Some mutual funds report ten-year rates of return of 200 percent. Many other mutual funds perform about as well as a randomly selected group of common stocks.

Gold and Silver

Gold and silver are widely recognized as sound investments, gold being the more favored. Financial experts note that gold and silver are helpful in fighting both depression and inflation. The most popular form of gold and silver ownership these days is gold coins. Despite all the amazing tales about wealth acquired through investment in gold and silver, these commodities have some disadvantages. Because it is risky to keep gold and silver at home, you have to pay to have them stored. Also, gold and silver pay no dividends. Your yield is zero until you convert them to cash.

Coins, Antiques, Paintings, and Other Collectibles

An enjoyable way of investing is to purchase coins and objects of art that you think will escalate in value. Almost anything could become a collectible, including stamps, old advertising items, or even today's push-button telephone. You have to be both patient and lucky to cash in on collectibles. You should have a sound diversified investment program before you invest your money in collectibles. If you are looking for an expensive hobby that might pay off financially, however, collectibles are ideal.

A word of caution to the person looking for collectibles. Although it has been said that the limited edition merchandise offered by commercial mints are attractive items, they are unlikely to escalate in value. Among these instant collectibles are ceramic plates and coins commemorating famous people.

Income Property and Other Side Businesses

All the investment methods (or instruments) described so far are passive. After making your initial purchase, you put little effort into managing your investment. An exception is collectibles that you have to polish weekly. **Income property,** real estate that you rent to tenants, and other side businesses are different. Owning a building is a business that requires substantial human effort to maintain. There are rents to collect, broken water pipes to repair, porches to rebuild, rooms to be painted, and conflicts to settle. If you have a large sum to invest, it is possible to hire a manager to take care of these types of problems. Otherwise, you will have to play an active role in managing the business. Many people who own real estate work up to thirty hours a month to earn about $100 in actual cash. Most forms of real estate do not even generate cash. They provide a tax write-off and the excellent prospects of the property increasing in value over the years.

The discussion of self-employment in Chapter 10 provides a good sampling of side businesses. All are active rather than passive investments.

Real Estate Investment Trust (REIT)

A modern investment vehicle makes it possible for you to invest in real estate without actually managing property. The real estate investment trust (REIT) is a method of pooling the money of many people in order to make substantial investments in real estate. REITs are designed like mutual funds since they sell shares and these shares fluctuate in value. When real estate prices are rising, REITs can pay returns as high as 25 percent. An added inducement is that by investing in a REIT you attain some of the tax advantages of owning real estate, such as depreciation allowances and gains in equity.

Some REITs invest mostly in properties, while others invest in mortgages, and some do both.[4] REITs are mainly for advanced investors, since they often sell shares, or "units," in multiples of $5,000.

IRAs (Individual Retirement Accounts) and Keogh Plans

Retirement accounts held by individuals, rather than offered by employers, can be used to invest in most of the instruments described so far. Both IRAs and Keogh plans are popular because they allow you to save money for retirement and offer generous tax savings. By beginning an IRA or Keogh plan early in your career you can amass an enormous nest egg.

An **IRA** is an investment plan that supplements other retirement plans such as Social Security and employer benefit programs. Anyone with earned income, including government employees, may open an IRA. Single workers may contribute up to $2,000 per year. One-paycheck couples may invest up to $2,250 annually. Two-paycheck couples may contribute $4,000 a year if both work and each earns at least $2,000. Distributions from your IRA may begin as early as age fifty-nine and a half, but must begin by seventy and a half. Early withdrawal is subject to a 10 percent penalty plus payment of taxes on the amount withdrawn.

The amount of your IRA contributions is no longer deducted from taxable income, even if you itemize. Dividends and interest from your IRA are not taxed as long as they are not withdrawn. When you begin withdrawals, your IRA distributions are taxed as ordinary income. Almost any investment vehicle qualifies for an IRA except for gold bullion and collectibles.[5]

Keogh Plans are retirement plans for individuals who are self-employed, or who earn part of their income from self-employment. They follow the basic idea of IRAs but differ in several respects. First, to qualify, you must earn some self-employment income. Second, you can invest up to 15 percent of your net self-employment income in a Keogh, up to a maximum of $30,000 under some plans. Third, they involve substantially more government-generated paperwork than do IRAs. An individual can hold both an IRA and a Keogh plan.

The only possible disadvantage of an IRA or Keogh plan is that your money is tied up until age fifty-nine and a half unless you pay a stiff penalty. Pending legislation, however, would allow borrowing from an IRA if the money is used to purchase a first home. The dramatic financial returns from an IRA is shown in Exhibit 15–3. Remember that you do not have to invest the full $2,000 each year. How can any employed person ignore thinking about opening an IRA account?

EXHIBIT 15–3   HOW IRAS CAN GROW

Years of Contribution	Rate of Return		
	8%	10%	12%
5	$11,733	$12,210	$12,705
10	$28,973	$31,875	$35,097
15	$54,304	$63,544	$74,559
20	$91,524	$114,550	$144,104
25	$146,212	$196,694	$266,667
30	$226,566	$328,998	$482,665
35	$344,634	$542,048	$863,326

Note: This chart assumes a $2,000 yearly contribution at year end. The same figures would apply for a Keogh plan if the same amount were invested annually.

WORKING YOUR WAY OUT OF DEBT

Saving and investing money is a cheerful aspect of financial planning. A less cheerful, but equally important aspect, is working your way out of debt. Heavy debt forces you to postpone savings and investments and can also create adverse amounts of stress. You must therefore assertively attack your debts in order to improve your general well-being. How do you know when you are too far in debt? The following checklist helps provide an answer:

1. Do you use credit today to buy many of the things you bought in the past for cash?
2. Have you taken out loans to consolidate your debts, or asked for extensions on existing loans to reduce monthly payments?
3. Does your checkbook balance get lower by the month?
4. Do you pay the minimum amount due on your charge accounts each month?
5. Do you get repeated dunning notices (letters demanding payments) from your creditors?
6. Have you been drawing on your savings to pay regular bills that you used to pay out of your paycheck?
7. Do you depend on extra income, such as overtime and part-time work, to get to the end of the month?
8. Do you take out new installment loans before old ones are paid off?
9. Is your total savings less than three months' take-home pay?
10. Is your total installment credit (not counting mortgage) more than 20 percent of your take-home pay?[6]

If your answer is yes to two or more of the above questions, financial counselors would advise you to declare war on some of your debts. A recommended strategy of reducing debt is to **concentrate on one bill at a time**. According to this technique, you first pay off your smallest debt with a variable payment and then concentrate on your next smallest variable-payment debt. You keep concentrating on one bill at a time until the last debt is eliminated. The technique is illustrated and described in Exhibit 15–4.

EXHIBIT 15–4   HEATH AND JUDY CONCENTRATE ON ONE BILL AT A TIME

After seventeen years of marriage, Heath and Judy had acquired an upsetting level of debt. Part of their problem was the debt they had accumulated in the process of acquiring two 2-family houses that they used as income property. At the urging of a financial counselor, Heath and Judy scrutinized both their debts and their spending habits. Their debt picture looked like this:

Type of Loan	Balance on Loan	Approximate Monthly Payment
Auto	$1850	$185
Home improvement	975	49
Visa	428	35
MasterCard	859	45
Furnaces for income properties	2562	185
Tuition	500	90
Orthodontist	750	75
	$7924	$664

In today's economy an indebtedness of $664 may not seem extreme. Nevertheless, in terms of their other living expenses, including the support of three children, $664 a month of debts was creating stress for Heath and Judy. The couple might have taken the traditional debt-reduction program of spreading out their monthly debt reduction fund over all their bills. In so doing, they would have tried to make approximately equal payments to all creditors. Instead, Heath and Judy chose to reduce their debts by concentrating first on the variable-payment debt with the smallest balance. In other words, they concentrated first on the debt that they were capable of eliminating first.

Following this strategy, Heath and Judy began their debt-reduction program by first working down the Visa debt. Each month they would put as much money as they could spare into their Visa payment even though they had previously paid only $35 monthly for that particular bill. The couple also made minimum payments to MasterCard until their Visa balance was reduced to zero. Then came a thrust against the loan when they were able to make one or two double payments. (The general principle is to eliminate, one by one, each of the loans for which variable (rather than fixed) payments are possible. In addition, take on new debts for emergency purposes only.)

The above case history indicates that an effective program of debt reduction involves both financial and emotional issues. Getting rid of debts one by one provides an important emotional boost to the debtor. As the debts are peeled off, tension is reduced. The one-debt-at-a-time strategy is also tied in with goal theory. You experience a feeling of accomplishment as each debt is eliminated. Simultaneously, you are motivated to tackle the next variable debt.

A financial specialist might rightfully contend that some loans are uneconomic to discharge more quickly than required. The interest rate you pay on such loans might be less than the return you would earn by investing your extra payments elsewhere such as growth stocks. Although this is true from a financial standpoint, the biggest return on your investment from a mental health standpoint is getting out of debt.

STAYING OUT OF DEBT

Some people believe we are on the way to a cashless society. They contend that electronic transfer of funds, credit cards, and **bank debit cards** (one that instantly transfers money from your bank account to the account of a merchant) will eliminate the need for cash. High technology may soon make the cashless society a reality. In the meantime, do not dismiss the value of cash in helping you recover from sloppy financial habits.

No one ever went bankrupt who bought things for cash only. Cash also refers to money orders and checks drawn against funds that you legitimately have on hand. If you only buy things that you can actually pay for at the moment of purchase, you will suffer some hardships. It is no fun riding the bus or walking until you save enough money to have another transmission put in your car. It would be agonizing if you needed dental treatment but had to wait until payday to have a broken tooth repaired. On balance, these are small miseries to endure in comparison with the misery of being overburdened with debt. For many people, preoccupation with debt interferes with work concentration and sleep.

Staying out of debt is often difficult because the debtor has deep-rooted problems that prompt him or her to use credit. For instance, the debtor may regard material objects as a way of gaining status. Exhibit 15–5 presents a psychological analysis of excessive borrowing.

EXHIBIT 15–5   CREDIT CARD SPLURGING IS A PSYCHOLOGICAL PROBLEM

When those credit card bills come pouring in, do you wonder how it all happened? Why *did* you buy three VCRs and a dozen pair of shoes you'll never use? Experts say your credit card splurging may be more than whimsical overindulgence. Psychiatrists and credit counselors are finding credit card abuse often reflects deeper psychological problems and it is a growing problem in today's society. Credit card abuse is often associated with drug abuse, alcohol problems, delinquency, unconscious anger, revenge, or passivity.

More and more people are pushing their credit cards to the limit—and beyond. It is resulting in serious emotional and financial problems for the abusers and their families. One psychiatrist says, "The situation is explosive. The nation has gone crazy with credit, and it is a ticking plastic bomb." One problem is that this society emphasizes accumulation of material possessions as a mark of success. Credit card abuse cuts across all economic and social levels. Likely credit card offenders are found among:

- Insecure people trying to win acceptance from peers. One man stole his grandmother's credit card and treated his friends to an all-expenses-paid trip to the Bahamas.
- A spouse in the middle of a bitter divorce. Credit cards offer a last chance to "get even."
- Parents who had to disappoint children because of economic restraints. They try to make up for the past by charging items they cannot afford.
- People who are depressed and think the cards can buy them a little happiness.
- People who have trouble dealing with rules and regulations. They feel life has shortchanged them and the cards give them a chance to catch up.
- Uncontrollable impulse buyers.
- People who think that accumulation of possessions will make them feel better about themselves.

Once people realize their borrowing problem, recovery comes slowly because underlying problems must also be solved. It is as difficult to discontinue credit card abuse as smoking or fingernail biting. Treating the underlying problem is a slow process of learning to substitute more adaptive coping techniques and building self-esteem.

SOURCE: Adapted with permission from Susan Bennett, "Credit Card Splurging is Psychological Problem," *USA Weekend*, March 7–9, 1986, p. 14.

THE PERSONAL ANNUAL REPORT

A potentially uplifting strategy of managing your finances is to chart your yearly financial status. You can accomplish this by constructing a **personal annual report**—a yearly summary of your assets and liabilities. The uplift comes from discovering that you are making progress. Progress here means that your net worth is increasing. (Net worth is the difference between your assets and liabilities.)

EXHIBIT 15–6   A PERSONAL ANNUAL REPORT

	December 31, Year 1	December 31, Year 4
ASSETS		
House equity (based on market value)	$18,000	$28,000
Cash in checking account	141	392
Cash on hand	75	315
Savings account	118	792
Mutual fund	—	896
Car resale value	3,600	1,800
Jewelry resale value	850	2,000
	$22,784	$34,195
LIABILITIES		
Auto payments	$ 2,500	—
Visa	1,215	$ 350
MasterCharge	1,150	400
American Express	850	80
Sears charge	550	128
Home improvement loan	3,975	—
Loan from uncle	895	—
Property tax due	850	350
School tax due	650	400
Plumber	275	—
	$12,910	$ 1,708

You include in your personal annual report only **liquid assets—** those you can convert into cash relatively quickly. Even if the equity in your home is not very liquid, it is worth including. Without house equity, most home owners would have modest liquid assets.

Personal annual reports for two years are presented in Exhibit 15–6. The person who prepared both reports was in financial difficulty when the first report was prepared. Notice the progress this individual has made over the four-year period. In the first year, his liquid assets aside from his home equity and car resale value totaled $1,184. Including house and car, his assets were $22,784. Thanks in part to both self-discipline and modest inflation, his assets jumped to $34,195 four years later. Without the house equity and car resale value, his liquid assets were $4,395.

The liability picture is even more impressive. In the first year, the man had outstanding debts of $12,910. Four years later, his debts had shrunk to $1,708. His liability position had improved an enviable $11,202. Over the same period his asset picture had improved $11,411. Adding both improvements together, we are able to give the individual a financial improvement score of $22,613 for the four-year period. Recognize, however, that the $10,000 growth in house equity was a major contributing factor to his financial improvement.

LIFE INSURANCE AS PART OF YOUR FINANCIAL PLAN

No financial plan would be complete without some life insurance. If you are employed full-time, life insurance is almost always included among your benefits. The real issue is not whether you should carry life insurance, but how much to carry. Here we briefly review guidelines for choosing the right amount of coverage, and the basic types of life insurance policies.[7]

Choosing the Right Amount of Coverage

An old rule of thumb was that your life insurance should equal about six times your annual income. This rule no longer applies because of several factors. One is the growth of corporate pension and profit-sharing plans that supplement Social Security. Another is the spread of assets into numerous other investments such as IRAs and mutual funds. The two-income family also lessens the need for heavy insurance coverage for either partner.

To figure out how much life insurance is necessary, calculate what, in addition to your family's other assets, would be required to support your spouse and children until they can take care of themselves without your income. If you are single, consider the financial help you are providing loved ones.

Circumstances, and thus the proper amount of insurance, vary from family to family. Still, some general guidelines are useful:

☐ If you are unmarried and have no children, or have a two-income family with no children, you probably need just enough life insurance to cover your debts and funeral expenses.

☐ If you have a spouse and children who are dependent on your income, you will typically need a large amount of life insurance during your twenties and thirties.

☐ In your middle years, your needs for life insurance should decline sharply, especially as your children finish college. Money that was formerly placed in life insurance should be diverted into other higher-yielding assets that can be used for retirement.

☐ In your preretirement years, if you have built up sufficient assets you may need very little life insurance. However, if you have built up a huge estate you may need enough insurance to cover estate taxes.

Basic Types of Life Insurance

The two traditional types of life insurance are whole life and term. *Whole life insurance* combines insurance with forced savings to provide a cash value that you can borrow against later. You pay a fixed premium for a long period of time, and these premiums earn dividends. Whole life policies were the dominant form of life insurance for many years, but have declined in popularity. One adverse factor is their cost. A whole life policy of $100,000 for a thirty-year old male would cost around $1,000 annually. Many people are also dissatisfied with the small dividends paid by these policies. A major advantage of whole life insurance is that it represents forced savings for people who lack self-discipline to make other investments.

Term insurance is a form of life insurance that insures you for the period of the designated time on the policy, but does not accumulate cash value. Term insurance is much like automobile insurance. Its key advantage is that it provides coverage at a lower price than whole life. The average cost for a term policy of $100,000 is $184 per year for a 30-year-old nonsmoking male, $258 for a 40 year old, and $566 for a 50 year old. Life insurance offered by your employer is almost always term insurance.

Two innovations in life insurance are universal-life policies and variable-life policies. *Universal life insurance* divides premiums into insurance and savings segments and allows policyholders to vary premium payments as well as the amount of coverage. An attraction of universal life is that it is a better investment than whole life. *Variable-life insurance* offers a guaranteed death benefit plus whatever can be earned on a separate investment account. Unlike universal policies, the premium is a fixed amount, but investments are more flexible.

SUMMARY

An important part of managing your personal life is to manage your personal finances in such a way that money is not a major source of worry and concern in your life. Financial problems often lead to marital problems, for example.

Setting financial goals is an important starting point in managing your personal finances. Such goals can be expressed in dollars, or in the type of things you would like to accomplish with money, or the type of lifestyle you would like to lead.

The key to lifelong financial security and peace of mind is to spend less money than you earn. Nevertheless, in order to become wealthy it may be necessary to invest borrowed money.

A vital aspect of financial management is to follow a budget or a spending plan. Establishing a budget can be divided into six steps: (1) establishing goals, (2) estimating income, (3) estimating expenses, (4) comparing expenses and income, (5) carrying out the budget, (6) evaluating the plan.

When looking for cost-saving measures, it is important to attach some value to your time or labor. For example, it is sometimes more profitable in the long run to invest a unit of time in self-development than to look for a relatively trivial money-saving measure.

To manage your finances properly, you need some kind of savings or investment plan. Among the many ways of investing or saving money are: interest-bearing checking accounts, passbook savings accounts, term savings accounts and certificates of deposit (CDs), money-market mutual funds, treasury notes and bonds, corporate bonds, U.S. savings bonds, common stocks, mutual funds, gold and silver, coins and other collectibles, income property and other side businesses, and real estate investment trusts.

Individual retirement accounts (IRAs) and Keogh Plans (retirement accounts for self-employment income) have achieved substantial popularity because contributions are tax deductible. Almost any investment vehicle qualifies for an IRA or Keogh except for gold bullion and collectibles.

Heavy debt has adverse financial and personal consequences. A general rule is that you are too far in debt when more than 20 percent of your take-home pay is needed to cover installment debts. One way of working your way out of debt is to concentrate on one bill at a time—try to pay off first your variable payment with the smallest balance. Another way of rebuilding yourself financially is to pay for goods and services with cash and therefore stop borrowing money.

We recommend giving yourself a yearly financial checkup by preparing a personal annual report, a list of your liquid assets and liabilities. Progress is measured in terms of the difference between assets and liabilities. The bigger the difference, the better your financial health.

Life insurance is an important part of your financial plan. To calculate how much coverage you need, estimate what would be required to support your spouse and children until they can take care of themselves without your income. If you are single, consider the financial help you are providing loved ones. Whole life insurance builds up cash values; term life insurance is less expensive but does not have a cash value. Universal life and variable life policies are combinations of life insurance and other investments.

QUESTIONS AND ACTIVITIES

1. Why is it difficult to convince most people under age twenty-five to open an IRA?
2. Why do you think so few people prepare a personal annual report?
3. How would you estimate the cost a particular lifestyle you want to lead?
4. What relevance does this chapter have for a full-time student?
5. Why does preparing a budget sometimes help people reduce their worry about money?
6. If you think you will live at least one hundred years, how will it affect your savings and investment strategy?
7. Describe at least one form of investment that was not included in this chapter.
8. Which investment vehicle would be the most fun for you? Why?
9. If life insurance is so important, why do so few people actively seek the services of life insurance companies?

A HUMAN RELATIONS CASE PROBLEM:
THE PROBLEM BUDGET

The spending plan presented below was submitted by a twenty-eight-year-old man with a good job. He says that owning a home and entertaining his friends are important parts of his lifestyle. Yet he also contends. "I'm committing slow-motion financial suicide. Each month I go further into debt. Right now I don't see a good way out unless I give up a lot of things that are important to me. You've got to have fun in life, don't you?"

Review this man's budget and make some specific recommendations to him for improving his financial health. Also, what flaws do you find in his logic?

Spending plan for Greg Walters

INCOME, SET-ASIDES, AND EXPENSES		AMOUNT PER MONTH
TOTAL INCOME		$ 2,000
Set-asides:		
Emergencies and future goals		$ 0
Seasonal expenses		50
Debt payments		275
Regular monthly expenses:		
Rent or mortgage payment	$ 650	
Utilities	105	
House and car repairs	55	
Installment payments	225	
Tennis and swim club dues	88	
Total		1,123
Day-to-day expenses:		
Food and beverages	$ 280	
Household operation, nonfood	35	
Furnishings and equipment	100	
Clothing	50	
Personal (including lunches)	150	
Transportation	95	
Gifts and contributions	5	
Miscellaneous	55	
Total		795
Total set-asides and expenses		$ 2,243
Profit (total income—set-asides and expenses)		$ 243 (loss)

A HUMAN RELATIONS ROLE PLAY:
COUNSELING A CREDIT-CARD JUNKIE

One person plays the role of a "credit-card junkie." This person owns five credit cards and often uses cash advances from one to make minimum monthly payments on another. The person's boss observes that he or she is having difficulty concentrating on the job. The boss refers the employee to the company Employee Assistance Program which includes credit counseling for people in financial trouble. The employee shows up for the first appointment with the credit counselor still thinking that extensive use of credit is a good idea. The employee contends that "our country runs on credit" and everyone "deserves a few luxuries in life."

The other person plays the role of the credit counselor who will try to get the credit-card junkie to take constructive action about his or her problem. The counselor thinks he or she is committing slow-motion financial suicide.

REFERENCES

[1] Robert Goldsborough, "The Joy of Winning," *Success!*, December 1980, p. 42. The goal statement is quoted from Paula Nelson, the financial adviser.

[2] The six steps are based on and paraphrased from U.S. Department of Agriculture, *A Guide to Budgeting for the Family*, Home and Garden Bulletin 108 (Washington, DC: Government Printing Office, revised 1976).

[3] Based in part on two sources: Joseph Wiltsee, "Investing in Your Future," *BusinessWeek's Guide to Careers*, February/March 1985, pp. 53–56, and "Getting There: Your Money, A Financial Planning Guide," *Success!*, June 1981, pp. A1–A16.

[4] "It May Be Time to Rediscover REITs," *BusinessWeek*, October 14, 1985, p. 162.

[5] "Investing Now in Your IRA," *AIDE*, Winter 1986, p. 22.

[6] "Are Your Debts Too Great?" United Press International story, March 28, 1982; Susan Bennett, "Credit Card Splurging is Psychological Problem," *USA Weekend*, March 7–9, 1986, p. 14.

[7] This section of the chapter is based on "Today's World of Financial Services: Strategies for Your Personal Assets." Brochure prepared by IDS, Minneapolis, MN.

SOME ADDITIONAL READING

Amling, Frederick, and William G. Droms. *The Dow Jones-Irwin Guide to Personal Planning.* Homewood, IL: Dow-Jones Irwin, 1982.

Hardy, C. Colburn. *Dun & Bradstreet's Guide to Your Investments.* New York: Harper & Row, revised regularly.

Loeb, Marshall. *Marshall Loeb's Money Guide.* Boston: Little, Brown, 1983.

Money magazine, any issue.

Wiltsee, Joseph L. "Setting Up a Realistic Budget." *BusinessWeek's Guide to Careers.* Spring/Summer 1984, pp. 83–85.

Wiltsee, Joseph L. "How to Establish a Credit Rating." *BusinessWeek's Guide to Careers,* February/March 1984, pp. 66–68.

16

Enhancing Your Personal Life

Learning Objectives

After studying the information and doing the exercises in this chapter you should be able to:

- Specify several key factors that contribute to personal happiness
- Understand that finding companionship often requires planning
- Develop several strategies for enhancing your personal life
- Pinpoint several useful principles in resolving conflict with your partner
- Identify the challenges in making a dual-career family run smoothly

A satisfying and rewarding personal life is an important end in itself. It also helps you to have a satisfying and rewarding career. If your personal life is miserable, you will have difficulty concentrating on your work. Also, a barren personal life leads one to question the meaning of his or her work. As a lonely securities sales representative said to a bartender he had never met before, "What's this all about? Why am I working sixty-five hours a week, fifty weeks a year? I have no wife and no close friends. Nobody cares about me. What's my purpose?"

In this final chapter, we look at some of the major issues involved in leading an enriched personal life. In addition, a number of concrete suggestions will be offered that may help some people enhance their personal lives. We begin by summarizing some modern ideas about happiness.

TEN KEYS TO HAPPINESS

A group of former presidents of the American Psychiatric Association outlined the habits and traits of happy people. Based on their observations, the psychiatrists recommend ten keys to happiness. These keys are simple but effective ways of improving your personal life.

1. Experience love and friendship. A happy person is one who is successful in personal relationships, who exchanges care and concern with loved ones. Happy people are able to love and be loved.

2. Develop a sense of self-esteem. One must love oneself in order to love others: High **self-esteem,** a sense of being worthwhile, enables one to love and be loved. Developing a good self-image leads to the self-esteem required for love relationships. A feeling of self-worth is important also because it helps prevent a person's being overwhelmed by criticism from others.

3. Seek accomplishments and the ability to enjoy them. A fundamental secret of happiness is accomplishing things and savoring what you have accomplished. A contributor to unhappiness is comparing one's successes, or lack of them, to those of other people. To be happy you must be happy with what you yourself achieve.

4. Develop an attitude of openness and trust. Trusting other people leads to happiness, but distrusting others leads to unhappiness. Happy people have open, warm, and friendly attitudes.

5. Appreciate the joys of day-to-day living. Another key to happiness is the ability to live in the present without undue worry about the future or dwelling on past mistakes. Be on guard against becoming so preoccupied with planning your life that you neglect to enjoy the happiness of the moment. The essence of being a happy person is to savor what you have right now.

6. Be fair and kind to others. The Golden Rule is a true contributor to happiness: "Do unto others as you would have them do to you." It is also important to practice charity and forgiveness.

7. Contribute to the well-being of others. Helping others brings personal happiness. Knowing that you are able to make a contribution to the welfare of others gives you a sense of continuing satisfaction and happiness.

8. Have fun in your life. A happy life is characterized by fun, zest, joy, and delight. When you create the time for fun, you add immensely to your personal happiness. However, if you devote too much time in play, you will lose out on the fun of work accomplishment.

9. Learn to cope with anxiety, stress, grief, and disappointment. To be happy one must learn how to face problems that occur in life without being overwhelmed or running away. Once you learn to cope with problems you will be more able to appreciate the day-to-day joys of life.

10. Develop a philosophy or system of belief. Another key contributor to happiness is to believe in something besides oneself. Happy people have some system of belief—whether it be religion, philosophy or science—which comforts them and gives them a reason for being.[1]

The balance of this chapter describes some challenges in personal life that need to be dealt with properly in order to accomplish the above ideal states. For example, you need to find a companion in order to have somebody to love.

A PLANNED APPROACH TO FINDING COMPANIONSHIP

How many people have you heard complain about a poor social life because of circumstances beyond their control? Such complaints take various forms: "The women in this school are all nerds," "The men at my school are all out after one thing," "There's absolutely nobody to meet at work," or "This is the worst town for meeting people."

Some of the people expressing these attitudes can be scientifically minded when it comes to handling work or mechanical problems. In those circumstances they use the problem-solving method (review Chapter 3 briefly). But when it comes to their social lives, they rely exclusively on chance, fate, or luck.

The approach we recommend here is to use your problem-solving skills to improve your personal life. Whatever the problem, try to attack it in a logical, step-by-step manner. We are not ruling out the influence of emotion and feeling in personal life. We are simply stating that personal life is too important to be left to fate alone. Fate can bring you happiness such as a kitten left on your doorstep or a wonderful new friend you meet while waiting in line at registration. But you have to take a hand in this matter, too.

Dating is one area of life that too many people leave to chance or to a few relatively ineffective alternatives. Too many young adults lament, "Either you go to a singles bar or you sit at home." In reality, both men and women can find new dates in dozens of constructive ways. It is a matter of identifying some of these alternatives and trying out a few that fit your personality and preferences. See Exhibit 16–1 for more details.

The consequences of finding or not finding someone to date are substantial. Positive dating experiences elevate the self-confidence of people, while negative dating experiences and having no dates at all tend to lower a person's self-confidence.[2]

EXHIBIT 16–1   IN SEARCH OF A DATE?

Every relationship begins with one person meeting another. In order to find one good relationship you may need to date more than a dozen people. Next is a sampling of potentially effective methods for making a social contact.

HIGHLY RECOMMENDED

1. Participate in an activity that you do well and enjoy. For example, if you are a good frisbee player, use frisbee playing as a vehicle for meeting people.
2. Get involved in your work or other activity not logically related to dating. People of the opposite sex* naturally gravitate toward a busy, serious-minded person.
3. Take courses in which the man-to-woman ratio is in your favor, such as automotive technology for women and interior decorating for males.
4. Ask your friends for introductions and explain the type of person you are trying to meet—but don't be too restrictive.
5. Get involved in a community or political activity in which many single people participate. A good example is to become a political-party worker.
6. For men, join almost any formal single group such as Parents Without Partners. The membership of these clubs is overwhelmingly female.
7. For women, join a national guard reserve unit. The membership of these units is overwhelmingly male.
8. Take advantage of every social invitation to a party, picnic, breakfast, or brunch. Social occasions are natural meeting places.
9. Place a personal ad in a local newspaper or magazine stating the qualifications you are seeking in a companion and how you can be reached. Personal ads have achieved such popularity that several national magazines now accept them.

THE SINGLE LIFESTYLE

An increasing number of people in this country live alone. About a fourth of the households in these countries are headed by unmarried people.[3] Many of these single people are romantically involved with another person to the extent that they do not consider themselves single. Many of these single heads-of-households are not dating anyone in particular at a given point in time. Thus they are truly making their way in the world by themselves. Many people who are married will someday become single again and add to the number of households headed by single people.

Going it alone is thus one of the many possible lifestyles open to young people. A large number of widows and widowers, of course, have traditionally lived by themselves. Some people prefer to live alone for a substantial part of their lives. Some find many satisfactions in living alone and do not regard their lifestyle as a temporary arrangement until they are able to find a spouse or companion to live with.

Some people find that living alone enhances their lives. A major attraction of the single lifestyle is the freedom it offers. Freedom in this sense can have several meanings. Some singles think it means freedom from regular hours for meals, rising, and visiting relatives. Other singles think it means freedom from the responsibility of having to care for or worry about other people. One single woman admitted, "Not having responsibility suits my needs. I don't even have a pet." Many others consider responsibilities to be a valued part of life. How much responsibility would make you happy?

A drawback to the single lifestyle is the inevitable loneliness that arises when a person is between relationships. Often this loneliness is the force that drives a person to form an exclusive relationship with the next compatible person he or she finds. Subsequently, the same person who wanted to escape loneliness may soon begin to think about the advantages of freedom. Many people never find that right balance between responsibility and freedom. Freedom is potentially exciting but lonely, while responsibility is sometimes dull but emotionally close. This dilemma has been referred to as the ineluctable conflict.

FIND ADEQUATE LIVING ACCOMMODATIONS

Whether you are married, living with someone, or single, a major source of satisfaction or dissatisfaction in life is your basic living accommodations. Having a place to come home to that you take pride in can be a source of comfort. Coming home to a place you regard as a stressor can contribute to a depressed mood. It is therefore essential to give housing high priority in your budget.

What people define as adequate living arrangements varies enormously. Some young people enjoy the congestion, noise, and camaraderie provided by a fraternity or sorority house. Some people can only find contentment living on a farm. Others regard as paradise a studio apartment located in the downtown section of a large city. Some people prefer to live as one member of a large family unit. It may take a young person several years to define adequate living accommodations. Also, your definition will change at different stages of your life.

A New Trend in Modern Living

The latest trend in finding adequate accommodations is in reality an old custom, now referred to as flying back to the nest. Many young adults are choosing to move back with their parents upon completion of schooling or after divorce. The high cost of housing and the problems of locating high-quality, low-cost child care have contributed to this trend. Increasing numbers of parents are refurbishing basements, garages, spare bedrooms, and attics for returning children. In one suburban community, a large number of homeowners even violated zoning laws to renovate their houses to accommodate two families. Rather than try to prosecute all the violators, the town decided to make these so-called mother-daughter subdivisions legal in some sections.[4]

Returning home is low priced but is not without emotional cost. The situation seems to work best when there is ample space and open communication. Otherwise people become physically and psychologically cramped. One twenty-six-year-old woman complained that her father worried about her coming home late from dates just as he did when she was a teenager. When the arrangement runs smoothly there are many benefits. If young children are involved, they receive the benefits of the extended family—care by both parents and grandparents. And the adults derive benefit from having daily contact with their children and grandchildren.

Although this new living arrangement is adequate for many, for many others it is not. Many incidents of conflict have been reported between the spouse of the child who flew back to the nest and his or her in-laws. If you choose this living arrangement you will have to be prepared to resolve conflict when it arises.

RESOLVE CONFLICTS AS NEEDED

As described in Chapter 9, conflicts arise frequently in both work and personal life. If you do not resolve a conflict that is brewing, it will fester and rise again in perhaps a more destructive form. In personal life, conflict occurs most commonly between people who are emotionally involved with each other. Statistics indicate that you are more likely to be killed or injured by a spouse or family member than by a stranger. Most murders come about as a result of family feuds, not as a result of a mugging or burglary.

Conflicts in social and family life may be triggered by infidelity, table manners, TV preferences, visitation by in-laws, responsibility for household tasks, choice of friends, and so on. Recognizing that some form of conflict is inevitable in marriage, a human relations specialist has formulated some ground rules for resolving marital conflict. The same ground rules would apply to any two people who are emotionally involved. The rules are worth keeping in mind.

1. Good communications go both ways. Many conflicts intensify because the people involved never stop to listen carefully to what the other side is trying to say. After listening to your partner's point of view, express your *feelings* about the issue. Expressing your feelings leads to more understanding than expressing your judgments. It is therefore preferable to say, "I feel left out when you visit your mother" than to say "You're insensitive to my needs; look at the way you visit your mother so regularly."

2. *Restate your partner's point of view.* To help improve understanding, provide mutual feedback. Although you may disagree with your partner, communicate your understanding: "From your point of view it's frivolous of me to spend so much money on bowling. You would prefer that I invest that money in baby furniture."

3. *Define the real problem.* What your partner or you grumble about at first may not be the real issue in the conflict. It will require mutual understanding combined with careful listening and sympathy to uncover the real problem. A man might be verbally attacking a woman's dress when he really means that she has gained more weight than he would like. Or a woman might verbally attack a man's beer drinking when her real complaint is that he should be out in the yard raking leaves instead of sitting inside playing video games.

4. *Stick to the issue.* When two people who are emotionally involved become embroiled in a conflict, there is a natural tendency to bring old wounds into the argument. The two of you might be in conflict over financial matters. One of you might say, "And I remember that weekend you were in Boston. You never called me." A good response here would be, "I'm sorry I did not take the time to call you, but it doesn't have anything to do with our problem today. Let's talk about *that* problem later."

5. *Don't hit below the belt.* Below the belt refers to something that is unfair. Some issues are just plain unfair to bring up in a marital dispute. When you are intimate with another person, you are bound to know one or two vulnerable areas. Here are two below-the-belt comments:

You're lucky I married you. I don't know any other woman among my friends who would have married a man with a prison record.

Don't complain so much about being mistreated. Remember, when I married you you were down on your luck and had no place to live.

Is anyone really as cruel as the above quotes would suggest? Yes, in the heat of a tiff between partners, many cruel, harsh things are said. If two people want to live harmoniously after the conflict, they should avoid below-the-belt comments.

6. *Be prepared to compromise.* For many issues compromise is possible. The compromise you reach should represent a willingness to meet the other person halfway not just a temporary concession. On some issues the only compromise can be letting the other person have his or her way now, and waiting to have your turn later. Among such issues that cannot be split down the middle are whether to have children or not, whether to live in an apartment or a house, whether to go to Miami or Vermont for a second honeymoon, or whether to run a Kosher or non-Kosher household. Several of these issues should be settled before marriage or living together, since no real compromise on the basic issue is possible in these instances. The only solution is to reach some type of agreement:

Okay, you don't want to have children. As a compromise how about having my nephew spend two weeks this summer with us?

Okay, we'll have a non-Kosher household, but we'll dine in a Kosher restaurant twice a week.

7. *Avoid manipulative pressure.* A common way of manipulating your partner is to grant him or her a little favor in order to win the conflict. One partner might buy the other and unexpected present, or prepare a favorite meal. The originator of this list of rules warned, "Marriage partners usually see through manipulative techniques, and end up feeling resentful, especially of those techniques that involve the withholding of love or approval."

8. *Be willing to go the extra mile.* To keep a relationship vibrant, there are times when one side will have to make a major concession to the other. If your relationship is solid, in the long run these extra miles will balance out. A middle-aged woman suggested to her spouse that this year, instead of taking their annual vacation trip, the money be invested in her cosmetic surgery. At first the husband bristled, thinking that she was being too self-centered. After thinking through the problem, the man realized that she had a valid point. He agreed to the surgery and the result was an added closeness between the couple. Such closeness between partners after resolving conflict is a frequent occurrence. As implied in Chapter 9, some conflict (and its resolution) is helpful to human beings.[5]

CHILDREN AS PART OF YOUR LIFE

If you want to enhance your personal life, heed the comments of noted child development expert Urie Bronfenbrenner, "If we'd pay as much attention to families as we pay to firearms and football, this country would be a lot healthier and happier."[6] The term family includes both adults and children. Thus if you pay more attention to your family, you are automatically paying more attention to the children in it.

Obviously, not everyone is prepared to participate in the rewards of parenthood. Some people are unable to bear children because of biological reasons, and the same people might be unsuccessful in trying to adopt a child. Some people are single and believe that being single precludes them from being parents. Some people who are married have careers that do not allow for child rearing. The point is that any of these people can participate in the potential satisfactions of contact with children if they choose. Among the many ways of having meaningful contact with children without being their biological or adoptive parent are:

Volunteering in big brother or big sister programs
Baby-sitting for friends, relatives, and neighbors

Inviting an economically deprived child into your home for the summer (akin to the Fresh Air Fund which sends children from New York City to vacation in smaller towns)

Becoming an athletic coach for a little league team

Aside from benefiting the children, child care is its own reward for the people involved in this type of activity. Anyone can live without meaningful contact with children, just as anyone can live without sex or a hobby. On the other hand, child care is a natural method of enhancing your life.

THE SMOOTH-WORKING, DUAL-CAREER COUPLE

The number of couples in which both partners have full-time jobs of some psychological and economic importance continues to increase. Today over 50 percent of households are two-income families. Two critical factors influencing this steady growth are career aspirations of women and the high cost of living. Housing, in particular, costs more today than in the past. Many families need two incomes in order to live in a one-family, detached house.

It is challenging to run these dual-career households in a way that will enhance the couple's personal life. Ongoing research suggests that many dual-career couples are willing to work hard along the lines suggested below.[7]

Deal with Feelings of Competitiveness

Feelings of competitiveness between husband and wife about each other's career often exist even when both have a modern outlook. Competitive feelings are all the more likely to surface when the husband and wife are engaged in approximately the same kind of work. One young man became infuriated with his wife when she was offered a promotion before he was. They had both entered the same big company at the same time in almost identical jobs. In contrast, the working couple with traditional views is unlikely to have a problem when the husband outdistances the woman in career advancement.

The familiar remedy of discussing problems before they get out of hand is offered again here. One partner might confess to the other, "Everybody is making such a fuss over you since you won that suggestion award. It makes me feel somewhat left out and unimportant." A sympathetic spouse might reply, "I can understand your feelings. But don't take all this fuss too seriously. It doesn't take away from my feelings for you. Besides, two months from now maybe people will be making a fuss over you for something."

Share Big Decisions Equally

A distinguishing characteristic of modern two-income families is that they share equally in making important decisions about the domestic side of life. Under such an arrangement, neither he nor she has exclusive decision-making prerogatives in any particular area. He may make a decision without consulting her over some minor matters (such as the selection of a plant for the living room). She may make the decision the next time a plant is to be selected for inside the house. But on major decisions—such as relocating to another town, starting a family, or investing in the stock market or real estate—husband and wife collaborate.

A delicate problem for many career-oriented working couples is the relocation dilemma.[8] Suppose one partner wants to take a job out of town and the other partner has a difficult-to-replace job? If the couple relocates, one of them usually suffers a career setback. If the couple decides not to relocate, the partner who passed up a good opportunity may brood over it. One woman in a dual-career family explained how she and her husband dealt with this dilemma:

> I had just recently settled into my new job as supervisor when Eric came home with what he considered to be good news. He had been kind of down in the dumps about his job. Unexpectedly, he was made a job offer as a sales rep in the Milwaukee area. He thought it was a great opportunity. I couldn't deny it. After a week of haggling over the problem, we decided that Eric would take the new job. We also decided that the next time we have any problem about whose career comes first, it will be my turn.

In recent years many companies have become more sensitive to the problems of two-income families. Some of them now offer to help the spouse find employment in the firm or in some other location in the local community. A handful of ultramodern couples handle the problem of relocation by having essentially a weekend-and-vacation marriage. Both stay put geographically but visit each other regularly. The prognosis for these marriages is not good. If the physical separation goes on for too long, divorce is almost inevitable. How would you like this arrangement with a spouse that you loved?

Divide Up Household Chores Equitably

Many women who work outside the home rightfully complain that they are responsible for too much of the housework. In the extreme, they function as both career people and full-time homemakers. Under this arrangement, conflict at home is highly probable. The recommended solution is for the working couple to divide household tasks in some equitable manner. Equity could mean that tasks are divided according to preference or the amount of effort required. In one family, the husband might enjoy food shopping while the wife enjoys cleaning. Assignments could be made accordingly. Or yard work might be equated with washing and ironing in terms of the human effort required. Each coupled should negotiate for themselves what constitutes an equitable division of household tasks.

An important underlying principle of sharing household responsibilities is called total task responsibility. Each person has total responsibility for getting something done, rather than merely helping out the partner. In this way each partner can take pride in a job well done. A woman described it in these words:

> What my husband and I enjoy most is the pride that comes from having accomplished a whole thing. If the kitchen looks nice, I can pridefully say, "I did it." Because two people are not meddling in the same chore, there is much less second-guessing about how things should have been done. It's the only sensible way for us. No more being somebody's helper on a simple matter for either Tom or myself.

Take Turns Being Inconvenienced

No one can escape all the potential inconveniences of modern living. Ultimately, you will have your automobile serviced, let the plumber in to repair or replace a leaking pipe, or agonize over a briefcase full of receipts as your tax return is being audited by an Internal Revenue Service examiner. These activities are considered to be inconvenient because they must be performed during normal working hours.

In a very traditional family, the woman assumes the responsibility for managing these inconveniences, even if she, too, has a job outside the home. The underlying assumption may be that her work is less important than his work. For more modern couples, a more equitable solution is to take turns being inconvenienced. If Sue has to go to work late one day to be around for the plumber, Ted can go to work late when the dog has to be taken to the veterinarian. A working couple with children will frequently have to miss work because of a child's illness or accident, parent-teacher conferences, or school plays.

Develop Adequate Support Systems for Child Care

Any working couple with a young child or children will attest to the challenge of adequately balancing work and child demands. Imagine this scenario: Your spouse has already left for work, and you discover that your four-year-old daughter has a fever of 102 degrees F. The child care center will not accept a sick child nor will your neighbor who helps out occasionally. She fears contaminating her children. The logical solution is to stay home from work, but you have a crucial work meeting scheduled for 11 A.M.

One solution to dilemmas of this nature, and less serious problems, is to have a diverse support system. Make arrangements with at least three people, including relatives, who could help you out in an emergency. Retired senior citizens, for example, often welcome the challenge of helping out in an emergency.

Both Be Active Parents

A dual-career family with one or more children can function smoothly only when both parents take an active interest in child rearing. Mother and father have to regard spending extensive amounts of time with their child or children as an appropriate activity for their sex. When both parents work, bringing the child to the dentist is as important for the father as it is for the mother. The following anecdote provides insight into the underlying attitudes about child rearing that help a two-income family to work smoothly:

> Ivan and his wife, Vicki, were conversing with friends at an evening party. One of the women present commented, "I think Ivan must be wonderful, the way he baby-sits for your children. Why this must give you lots of time for yourself. Just the other day I saw Ivan in the supermarket with your children."
>
> Ivan interjected, "Thanks for the nice things you've said about me, but I refuse to be a baby-sitter. Taking care of your children isn't the same as baby-sitting. A baby-sitter is someone who gets paid for taking care of somebody else's child. It's not something you would do if you didn't get paid. Spending time with my children is as natural to me as spending time with Vicki. I'm no more of a baby-sitter than is the children's mother. So although I appreciate your compliment, I don't think I deserve one."

Negotiate Who Pays for What

Two incomes in one family breed many problems: "If one person earns more than the other, does that person pay more expenses?" "Should we pool our money, and treat it as one income?" "Should each person get a special allowance for personal expenses?" Several times when I have introduced this topic in class, a number of students have objected, pointing out that if a couple truly loved each other, dividing their income would not be a problem. Money would not be considered his or hers, but ours.

Unfortunately, the problem of negotiating who pays for what does arise for many two-income families. Many couples find that the additional expenses of a working couple prevent them from getting ahead financially. Taxes are higher; child care expenses are often involved; restaurant meals become more frequent; and a second car is usually a necessity outside of large metropolitan areas.

A division of income that minimizes conflict for many two-paycheck families is to allocate some money for common expenses (such as rent or mortgage payments) and some money for personal expenses. The specific allocation of the latter does not have to be discussed with the partner. For instance, one partner is free to buy a new fishing rod or portable TV with his or her personal money. But an item like new draperies would be a joint expense and a joint decision. Another helpful practice is to have one joint checking account and two personal checking accounts.

The underlying principle here is that the couple should try to negotiate a mutually satisfying division of income. For some unusually close couples there will be no question of "my money" versus "your money," and little discussion will be required. Unless carefully managed, two incomes in one family can create special problems, as illustrated in Exhibit 16–2.

EXHIBIT 16–2   ROSS AND KERRY DIVIDE THE DECISION-MAKING PIE

A dual-career couple, Ross and Kerry believed that households can run smoothly without drawing up formal arrangements of who does what and when. Early in their marriage they learned that such an arrangement created more problems than it solved. Kerry gave this example of one of the problems they faced at the outset:

"We just assumed that because we had decided on a fifty-fifty marriage, things would run smoothly, but they didn't. Just before getting married, we jointly agreed that we needed a new refrigerator. I was hurting for cash because of all the wedding expenses, so Ross agreed to purchase the refrigerator. One day he called me at work from a nearby appliance store. He told me there was a floor sample at a $300 discount, but he didn't want to buy it without first getting my approval. Ross said there were two models left, one coppertone and one avocado.

"I told Ross to do what he thought was best and that he should go ahead and make the decision without me. He came home that night to tell me he decided not to purchase the refrigerator without my seeing it. By the time we both went to see the refrigerator floor samples, they were both gone. We ended up spending at least $325 more for a refrigerator than we needed to because Ross didn't think he should make a decision on his own."

To avoid repetitions of such incidents, Ross and Kerry reached some formal agreements about who would make decisions about what and which decisions should be made jointly. A unique aspect of their agreement was that they would renegotiate their decision-making arrangement each year around the New Year's holiday. The main points of a recent one-year agreement are as follows:

• Ross and Kerry will have an equal vote on all major decisions such as job relocation, whether or not to have a child, whether or not to buy or sell a house, house remodeling, membership in a tennis and swim club, the pursuit of an advanced degree for either person, and whether or not an in-law should live with us. Also, any purchase over $600 calls for a joint decision.

- Ross or Kerry can make any minor decision about the purchase of clothing, home furnishing, or food without consulting the other. Magazine subscriptions, book purchases, car repairs, choice of wine, and so forth fit into this category.
- For this year, Kerry will decide how much money we should save and invest. She will be responsible for all decisions about what food we purchase for the house and in which restaurants we dine.
- However, if either of us violently objects to a decision reached by the other, that objection should be noted and the other person might reconsider. For instance, Ross dislikes Indian food, so when we dine together Kerry should avoid Indian restaurants.

Kerry commented about their experience with this formal arrangement: "At first we were both skeptical that anything so formal and seemingly artificial would work. However, we were pleasantly surprised. We kept to the agreement, and it seemed that fewer things fell between the chairs. Also, it added an element of surprise to our life. For instance, it seemed romantic now that Ross was back selecting a place for us to go on vacation the way he once did when we were single."

Ross and Kerry chose a workable alternative to ambiguity in decision-making authority. If they had not developed a formal method of dividing decision-making responsibilities, the method they had used in the past might have led to conflict in their relationship. It is important on the job as well to formally define who is responsible for making which decisions (with some allowances for flexibility).

KEEPING YOUR RELATIONSHIP ALIVE

About one-half of new marriages result in divorce, and many couples within the other half are less than satisfied with each other. One of the major challenges in life is to keep a relationship alive, well, and vibrant. If people followed some of the basic suggestions provided in books and articles about marriage, their relationship would stand a better chance of remaining a source of satisfaction. (See the suggested additional reading at the end of this chapter.) Here we will look briefly at several possibilities for enhancing life with your partner.

Choose a Partner Carefully

A principal problem in many poor relationships is that the couple used faulty judgment in choosing each other. Of course, it is difficult to be objective when choosing a partner. Your needs at the time may cloud your judgment. Many people have made drastic mistakes in choosing a spouse because they were lonely and depressed when they met the person they married. As one young man said, "I married her on the rebound. I was hurt by my previous girlfriend. My wife came along at the right time. We were married in six months. Three months after the marriage we both knew we had made a big mistake."

The problem of mate selection is indeed complicated. Do you marry for love, companionship, infatuation, or all three? It has been pointed out that the success rate of the arranged marriages still practiced in a few European countries is about as good as that of nonarranged marriages. Since most people have only a limited amount of time to invest in finding the ideal mate, they are content to marry a good fit.

An in-depth study of 300 happy marriages provides a practical clue about mate selection. The most frequently mentioned reason for an enduring and happy marriage was having a generally positive attitude toward each other.[9] If you view your partner as your best friend and like him or her "as a person" you will probably be happy together. As obvious as it sounds, choose only a life partner who you genuinely like. Some people deviate from this guideline by placing too much emphasis on infatuation.

A unique approach to mate selection would be to ask your family and best friends what they thought of your prospects for happiness with your prospective mate. Above all, recognize that when you are contemplating choosing a life partner you are facing one of life's major decisions. Put all of your creative resources into making a sound decision.

Strive for Intimacy, Passion, and Commitment

True love requires intimacy, passion, and commitment, according to psychologist Robert Sternberg.[10] While a relationship can manage to survive with only one or two of these qualities, the fullest love requires all three. Passion is the quickest to develop, and the quickest to fade. Intimacy, a feeling of emotional closeness, develops more slowly. One requirement for intimacy is that the person has established his or her own identity. Commitment develops the most slowly. However, in the current era, commitment is highly sought after by both men and women. Monogamy is becoming the rule rather than the exception for an increasing number of young couples.[11]

Intimacy between partners becomes more important as successful relationships mature. Women usually place a higher value on intimacy. Nevertheless, both partners find it increasingly important to understand each others' wants and needs, to listen to and support each other, and to share values. Although passion peaks in the early phases of a relationship, it still matters to a long-term successful relationship. Happily married men usually regard their wives as physically attractive.

While a strong emotional commitment is essential to a long-term relationship, it is not sufficient. Without passion and intimacy, commitment tends to be hollow.[12]

Maintain Separate Identities

A **nonpossessive relationship** is one in which both people maintain separate identities and strive for personal fulfillment. It does not necessarily mean that both people have sexual relationships outside of marriage, as is often thought. For many couples, the traditional form of marriage is stifling. A married person is often thought of as being part of a team. All social invitations and holiday cards are addressed to the couple. Some people find it frustrating to have their spouse's name frequently associated with their own. Many married people feel compelled to give up a hobby or interest because the partner does not share that interest. Said the disgruntled woman to the marriage counselor, "I was an excellent downhill skier before I met John. I had to give it up because he's afraid to ski."

In a nonpossessive marriage, this woman would not have to give up skiing. Nor would her husband have to give up any of his interests. In any nonpossessive relationship, the couple can take many separate paths and pursue different interests and have friends of their own. Unfortunately, if couples pursue nonpossessive relationships too far, they wind up drifting away from each other. The reason is that happy partners spend considerable time with each other enjoying shared activities. Each couple must find the right balance between maintaining separate identities yet spending sufficient time together to remain close.

Have Communication Sessions

Good communication is vital for creating and maintaining a loving relationship.[13] Therefore, one way to keep a relationship alive is to hold formal communication sessions in which you tell each other almost anything on your mind. The topics can be both positive and negative. One man may want to tell his partner of something she did that he appreciated very much. Or one woman may want to talk about the way he offended her in public. Or the couple may want to discuss concerns about finances, a child, in-law relations, or anything else.

A vital aspect of these sessions is that both facts and feelings are expressed. The statement "I am really afraid we are drifting apart" communicates much more than "You and I haven't been talking too much lately." The role play at the end of this chapter explores the type of communication that can keep a relationship thriving.

Be Open Sensibly

Honest communication is crucial for a good relationship, but be sensible in your openness. Most people are sensitive to criticism and can be easily hurt. Openness is more palatable when what you say allows your partner some alternatives. For instance, Jerry had enough sense to tell his new girlfriend Sheila that he felt uncomfortable dancing—her favorite form of entertainment. Sheila then was aware of the alternatives facing her. She could: (1) drop Jerry for a man who did enjoy dancing, (2) agree to some other mutually satisfying form of entertainment, (3) forget dancing for the present but hope that Jerry would decide to improve his dancing at a later date.

Openness also brings two people closer when feelings are expressed in a constructive rather than destructive way. Bert fell in love with Kathy. When he asked her if she loved him, Kathy replied honestly, "Bert, I consider you a fine person, but I have not fallen in love with you *yet*." Bert could then decide for himself whether or not to continue expressing love to a woman when the feeling was not yet mutual.

Another helpful perspective on openness comes from the study of happily married couples mentioned above. Virtually all of these couples believed that intensely expressed anger can damage the relationship. A sales representative with a thirty-six-year marriage advised, "Discuss your problems in a normal voice. If a voice is raised, stop. Return after a short period of time. Start again. After a period of time both parties will be able to deal with their problems and not say things that they will be sorry about later."[14]

Strive for Novelty in Your Relationship

An unfortunate aspect of many relationships is that they drift toward a routine. A married couple might go to the same place on vacation, meeting the same family and friends for years on end. A man dating a woman might call her every night at the same time. Or a couple's sex life may turn into a routine affair. Many people have suggested that you try pleasant surprises to keep your relationship vibrant and fun. Make up a list of your own, but here are a few ideas to jog your thinking:

Ask her out for dinner on a *Monday* evening.

Write your partner a poem, instead of sending a commercial greeting card.

Record one of your conversations on a tape recorder, then listen to it together to see if you can discover anything about your relationship.

COPING WITH DIVORCE AND SEPARATION

In spite of all the good intentions couples may have when they enter marriage or start living together, almost one half of these partnerships end in divorce or separation. If you want to enhance your personal life then, you may have to develop a strategy for coping with a broken marital relationship. The ideas presented in the previous section should be regarded as methods of preventing a divorce or separation. Here we will summarize a variety of suggestions for coping with such a break. They are based on the general principles of problem solving described in Chapter 3. In general when faced with a problem situation, go through these steps: diagnose the problem, find creative alternatives, weigh alternatives, make the choice, implement the choice, and evaluate the choice. As with any of the following suggestions, it is best to try those that fit your particular circumstance.

1. Be thankful for the good in the relationship. An excellent starting point in recovering from a broken relationship is to take stock of what went right when the two of you were together. Looking for the good in the relationship helps place things in proper perspective. It also helps prevent you from developing the morbid view that your time together was a total waste.

2. Release some of your anger. You will find it is a good time to express anger over a lost relationship when self-confidence begins to come back, nurtured by the support of friends and family. You might try such anger-releasing techniques as yelling about your problem or pounding pillows.

3. Find decent accommodations. One of the most humiliating and depressing aspects of being single again is being forced to move into substandard living quarters. It may prove best for your mental health to give top financial priority to a decent living arrangement.

4. Find new outlets for spare time. Some of the energy you were investing in your partnership can now be invested in spare-time activities, to provide a healthy form of the defense mechanism called compensation or substitution. Ironically, these same spare-time activities often lead to new relationships.

5. Get ample rest and relaxation. A broken relationship is a stressor.

As a result, most people need rest and relaxation to help them overcome the emotional pain associated with the departure of a partner.

6. *Pamper yourself.* Pampering involves finding little ways of doing nice things for yourself. These could take the form of buying yourself a new outfit, taking a weekend vacation, eating a pizza at midnight, or having new seat covers installed in your car.

7. *Use support groups.* A well-researched antidote to a broken relationship can be found in support groups specifically designed to help people cope with recent separation or divorce. Parents without Partners is the best known of these groups.

8. *Seek emotional support from individuals.* Friends and relatives can also be an important source of emotional support to help you cope with postseparation blues. Be careful, however, not to let your divorce or separation dominate conversations with friends to the point of boring them.

9. *Get out and go places.* The oldest suggestion about recovering from a lost relationship is perhaps the most valid—keep active. While you are doing new things, you tend to forget about some of your problems. Also, as you go places and do things, you increase your chances of making new friends. And new friends are the only true antidote to the loneliness of being unattached.

10. *Invite new people into your life.* Try to form new relationships with some of the people you meet. Friends of any type can help compensate for some of the loneliness associated with losing a relationship.

11. *Start dating for fun.* Begin dating just for recreation, thus avoiding emotional entanglements before you are prepared to take on another serious relationship. Once your emotions have settled down, serious dating will probably be fine.

12. *Give expression to your inner self.* Divorce or separation sometimes leads to the positive by-product of feeling free to be yourself again. It works something like this: In some relationships one individual suppresses the other, or that person feels suppressed. Real or imagined, the result is the same. After breaking up, the person who felt suppressed begins to behave in the way he or she would really like to behave—perhaps by being funloving and playful.

13. *Give yourself time to heal.* The greater the hurt, the more time it will take to recover from the broken relationship. Recognizing this fact will help to curb your impatience over disentangling yourself emotionally from your former spouse or partner.

14. *Anticipate a positive outcome.* While you are on the path toward rebuilding your social life, it is crucial to believe that things will get better, that all the emotional energy you have invested into splitting and healing will pay dividends. Self-fulfilling prophecies work to some extent in social relationships. If you believe that you will make a satisfactory recovery from a broken relationship, your chances of doing so will increase. The underlying mechanism seems to be that if you believe in yourself, you exude a level of self-confidence that others find appealing.

SUMMARY

A rewarding and satisfying personal life is an important end in itself. It also can enhance your career or prevent a loss of concentration on the job.

Based on the observations of a group of psychiatrists, ten keys to happiness are: (1) love and friendship; (2) a sense of self-esteem; (3) accomplishment and the ability to enjoy it; (4) appreciation of the joys of day-to-day living; (5) fairness and kindness to others; (6) contributing to the well-being of others; (7) fun in life; (8) coping with anxiety, stress, grief, and disappointment; (10) developing a philosophy or system of belief.

A good social life begins with finding the people you want to date. Such an important activity in life should not be left to chance or fate alone. Instead, use a planned approach that includes exploring many sensible alternatives.

The single lifestyle is on the increase. Its key advantage seems to be freedom and flexibility. Yet to some people, responsibility for the welfare of others is very important. The main drawback of being single is the loneliness that may occur between relationships.

An important way of enhancing your personal life is to find adequate accommodations. A revived trend among young adults, whether married, divorced, or single, is to move back with their parents. For some this is an adequate arrangement; for others it is not.

To keep intimate relationships healthy, you should resolve conflicts as they arise. Suggestions for accomplishing this include: engage in two-way communication; restate your partner's point of view; define the real problem; stick to the issue; don't hit below the belt; be prepared to compromise; avoid manipulative pressure; be willing to go the extra mile.

Meaningful contact with children, whether they be family members or not, can be an important way of enhancing your personal life. Children crave attention and giving it can be a rewarding experience for you.

Dual-career couples are subject to unique pressures. In order to sustain a good relationship, a dual-career couple should consider these approaches; (1) deal with feelings of competitiveness; (2) share important decisions equally; (3) divide household chores equitably; (4) take turns being inconvenienced; (5) develop adequate support systems for child care; (6) both be active parents; (7) negotiate who pays for what.

Keeping a relationship alive and vibrant is a major challenge. Among the strategies proposed to meet this goal are: (1) find your own identity before choosing a partner; (2) choose a partner carefully;

(3) strive for intimacy, passion, and commitment; (4) maintain separate identities; (5) have communication sessions as needed; (6) be open about feelings and criticisms in a sensible manner; (7) strive for novelty in your relationship.

Enhancing your personal life sometimes means that you will have to cope with divorce or separation. A variety of suggestions have been presented to ease the trauma and to facilitate recovery. Included are such tactics as: release some of your anger; find new outlets for your spare time; seek emotional support from others; invite new people into your life; give yourself time to heal; and anticipate a positive outcome.

QUESTIONS AND ACTIVITIES

1. Identify some information in the previous chapters that might help you achieve any of the "ten keys to happiness."
2. Ask an older, happy person what he or she thinks of the validity of the ten keys to happiness.
3. Which two of these ten keys have contributed the most to your happiness so far?
4. What have you found to be the best method of meeting new people of the opposite sex?
5. Why do comedians make so many unflattering jokes about marriage?
6. What do you think are the two most frequent causes of conflict between husbands and wives?
7. How should a working couple handle the problem of not being able to take vacations at the same time?
8. What do you think of the argument that the marital partner who earns the most money should have the most say in making decisions?
9. What can a couple do to prevent divorce and separation?

A HUMAN RELATIONS CASE PROBLEM:
A BAD CASE OF THE BLAHS

At ten o'clock one evening, Dotti's phone range unexpectedly. "Hello, Dotti, this is Beth Michna. I know we haven't talked in months, but I've been thinking about you."

"How nice to hear from you, Beth. What's up?"

"I thought we could talk about that in person. Could we possibly get together for lunch any day next week?"

After exchanging a few neutral comments at the Yellow Rose Cafe the next Tuesday, Beth came directly to the point. "Dotti, I wanted to talk to you about an unusual problem because you were always such a good listener and somebody I could trust. My problem is my marriage. I think I still love George, but our marriage has a bad case of the blahs."

"What do you mean, your marriage has a bad case of the blahs?"

"It's like this, Dotti. George has become such a deadhead. He doesn't want to do anything with me except to go out for dinner once in a while. He spends half the weekend watching TV or fixing his car. We've been married less than a year and we've run out of things to talk about.

"When I try to talk about us, he gets defensive. He tells me that I have no complaints coming. That he's never drunk and he doesn't hit me. It's all so dull. I don't know what to do."

Dotti asked next, "When did you first notice things going downhill?"

"About the second day after the honeymoon. George stopped being so enthusiastic about talking with me."

Questions

1. What advice should Dotti offer Beth? Or should she offer advice?
2. What do you think might be the underlying problem in their marriage?
3. What do you think might be George's viewpoint on this matter?

A HUMAN RELATIONS ROLE PLAY: KEEPING YOUR RELATIONSHIP ALIVE

The role-playing exercise described here will help you experience the type of communication and interaction required for keeping a relationship alive. As with any other role play, visualize yourself in the role briefly described. Try to develop the feel and the flavor of the person depicted.

The man in this relationship is becoming concerned that his wife does not enthusiastically participate in activities involving his family. He prefers that he and his wife spend their Sunday afternoons with his parents and other relatives. He thinks they are all loads of fun and cannot imagine why his wife is beginning to drag her heels about spending time with them. Twice in the last month she has come up with excuses for not going along with him to visit his folks on Sunday.

The woman in this relationship believes she still loves her husband but thinks his preference for Sunday afternoons with his folks is unreasonable. She thinks that it is time for her to pursue her own interests on Sunday afternoon. She plans to confront her husband about the situation this evening.

Two people act out this role play for about fifteen to twenty minutes. Other members of the class can act as observers. Among the observation points will be: (1) How well did the couple get to the key issues? (2) How much feeling was expressed? (3) Do they appear headed toward a resolution of this problem?

REFERENCES

[1] Maury M. Breecher, "C,mon Smile!" *Los Angeles Times,* October 3, 1982.

[2] Ann Elleson, *Human Relations* (Englewood Cliffs, NJ: Prentice-Hall, 1973), p. 211.

[3] Randolph E. Schmid, "The Nation Has Changed a Lot Since 1980," Associated Press story, February 7, 1985.

[4] "Flying Back to the Nest," *Newsweek,* April 7, 1980, p. 86. The trend has accelerated since 1980.

[5] Adapted from Ellenson, *Human Relations,* pp. 258–260.

[6] Susan Byrne, "A Conversation with Urie Bronfenbrenner," *Psychology Today,* May 1977, p. 47.

[7] Research conducted at the University of Rochester, Graduate School of Education and Human Development, 1986.

[8] Eleanor Berman, "Making Two-Career Marriages Work," *Success!,* July 1984, p. 21.

[9] Jeanette Lauer and Robert Lauer, "Marriages Made to Last," *Psychology Today,* June 1985, p. 24.

[10] Daniel Goleman, "Habits of the Heart," *New York Times* reprint, September 28, 1985; "Marriages Made in Heaven Based on Deep Division," *New York Times* reprint, April 6, 1986.

[11] "The Revolution Is Over," *Time,* April 9, 1984, p. 74.

[12] Goleman, "Habits of the Heart."

[13] Virtually every marriage manual reaches the same conclusion. A recent analysis is Leo Buscaglia, "Learning to Love, Falling in Love," *USA Weekend,* February 7–9, 1986, p. 5.

[14] Lauer and Lauer, "Marriages Made to Last," p. 26.

SOME ADDITIONAL READING

DAVIS, KEITH E.   "Near and Dear: Friendship and Love Compared." *Psychology Today,* February 1985, pp. 22–30.

GERSTEL, NAOMI, and HARRIET GROSS.   *Commuter Marriage: A Study of Work and Family.* New York: Guilford Press, 1984.

GILBERT, LUCIA ALBINO.   *Men In Dual-Career Families: Current Realities and Future Prospects.* Hillsdale, NJ: Erlbaum, 1985.

HOOTMAN, MARCIA, and PATT PERKINS.   *How to Forgive Your Ex-Husband (and Get On With Your Life).* New York: Doubleday, 1983.

MORDECAI, CAROLYN.   *The Complete Singles' Guide to Dating and Mating.* New York: Crown Publishers, 1987.

O'CONNOR, DAGMAR.   *How to Make Love to the Same Person for the Rest of Your Life* (*And Still Love It).* New York: Doubleday, 1985.

UTTERBACK, BETTY.   *Suddenly Single: Learning to Start Over Through the Experiences of Others.* New York: Simon & Schuster, 1986.

Glossary

Accident proneness A pattern of behavior indicating that an individual is likely to have an above-average number of accidents because of certain mental and physical characteristics.

Achievement need The need to accomplish something difficult, to win over others.

Action plan A description of the actual steps involved in achieving a goal.

Aggressive Acting in an overbearing, pushy, obnoxious, and sometimes hostile manner.

Anger A feeling of extreme hostility, indignation, or exasperation.

Anxiety Generalized feelings of fear and apprehension that usually result from a real or imagined threat. Feelings of uneasiness and tension usually accompany anxiety.

Assertiveness Expressing feelings openly and acting with an appropriate degree of forthrightness.

Assertiveness training (AT) A self-improvement program based on psychotherapy that teaches people to express their feelings and act with an appropriate degree of openness and assertiveness.

Authority The right to control the actions of others, or control that is approved by the organization or authority.

Bank debit cards A bank card that instantly transfers money from your bank account to the account of a merchant.

Behavior The tangible acts or decisions of people including their actions and words.

Behavior modification (mod) A system or program of motivation that aims to change individual responses by manipulating rewards and punishments.

Behavior shaping   Inducing someone to achieve the desired response by first rewarding any action in the right direction and then rewarding only the closest approximations until finally the desired response is attained.

Behavioral science   Any science concerned with the systematic study of human behavior, such as psychology, sociology, and anthropology.

Bias   A prejudgment toward another person or group based on something other than fact.

Body image   One's perception of one's body.

Brainstorming   A technique by which group members think of multiple solutions to a problem. The basic technique is to encourage uninhibited and spontaneous participation by group members, thus encouraging creativity.

Broken record technique   An assertive skill of calmly repeating over and over again your position without showing signs of anger or irritation.

Budget   A plan for spending money to improve your chances of using your money wisely and not spending more than your net income.

Burnout   A condition of emotional exhaustion and cynicism toward work in response to long-standing job stressors.

Business manners   Polite social behavior especially appropriate to work settings.

Career   A lifelong series of positions that forms some kind of coherent pattern. People usually invest emotional energy in their careers.

Career counselor   A specialist whose professional role is to provide counseling and guidance to individuals about their careers. Career counselors often work in educational settings, but others offer their services to the public for a fee.

Career path   A sequence of positions necessary to achieve a goal.

Career pathing   A process of laying out in advance the track that must be followed to reach a certain high-level position.

Chain of command   The official statement in an organization of who reports to whom.

Charisma   A leadership characteristic of charm and personal magnetism.

Chronological résumé   A job résumé that presents work experience, education, and interests along with accomplishments in reverse chronological order.

Communication   The sending and receiving of messages.

Compulsiveness   A tendency to pay careful attention to detail and to be neat.

Computer stress   A strong negative reaction to being forced to spend many more hours working at a computer than one desires.

Concentrate on one bill at a time   A technique of debt reduction by which you pay off your smallest debt with a variable payment and then concentrate successively on your next smallest debts.

Conflict   The opposition of persons, forces, or motives, that give rise to some tension, anxiety, or frustration.

Confrontation   Bringing forth a controversial topic or contradictory material in which another party is personally involved. To say, "You are not pulling your weight" will initiate a confrontation.

Coping   To contend with something or someone on even terms or with some success, such as coping with financial problems or aggressive people.

Creative-style résumé   A job résumé put together in an unusual format, such as in orchid color or accompanied by a videocassette, in order to attract favorable attention.

Creativity   The ability to develop good ideas that can be put into action.

Data   Facts, information, statistics, or the like either gathered fresh or based on historical information.

Decision   A choice among alternatives, or the passing of judgment on an issue under consideration.

Decision making   Selecting one alternative from the various alternatives or courses of action that can be pursued.

Dialogue   A conversation between two or more people in which the people react to each other's statements and thoughts. It is the opposite of a monologue.

Disarm the opposition   A method of conflict resolution in which you disarm the criticizer by agreeing with his or her valid criticism of you.

Dollar-cost averaging   An investment technique in which you purchase the same amount of money in a stock or mutual fund at regular intervals over a long period of time. You thereby average out high and low prices.

Effectiveness   Accomplishing important results while maintaining high quality.

Emotion   A complex state of feeling involving conscious experience and internal and external responses. Emotions include hate, anger, fear, love, and joy.

Energy cycle   The idea that your fund of energy runs in a predictable phase. At the top of the cycle you have a great deal of energy, and you have very little energy at the bottom.

Enterprise   A company organized for business purposes; a firm.

Environment   The aggregate of things surrounding a person, particularly those that exert an influence on the person.

Etiquette   A special code of behavior required in certain situations.

Eustress   A positive stress that elevates performance.

Expectancy theory of motivation   An explanation of motivation stating that people will be motivated if they believe that their effort will lead to a desired outcome.

Expectation   A subjective estimate a person makes that a particular behavior will satisfy a particular need. One might have the expectation that a career as a computer specialist will satisfy his or her need for job security.

External locus of control   A belief that external forces control one's fate.

Feedback   Information that tells you how well you have performed. Also, knowledge of results about your behavior that helps you judge the appropriateness of your responses and to make corrections where indicated.

Feelings   An emotional state or disposition, such as the feeling of happiness or sadness. Feelings are closely related to attitudes.

Fight or flight response   The body's battle against a stressor that helps one deal with emergencies.

Fogging   The technique of accepting manipulative criticism by calmly acknowledging that the criticism contains an element of truth.

Foresight   In leadership, a positive idea about where the leader is going and what to do about it.

Framework   A basic system or design for understanding something. A framework serves as a basic outline or model.

Frustration   State of dissatisfaction arising from the thwarting or blocking of a need, wish, or desire.

Functional résumé   A job résumé that organizes your skills and accomplishments into the functions or tasks that support the job you are seeking.

Gentle confrontation   A method of resolving conflict in which the person with a gripe expresses it openly but tactfully and without threats of retaliation.

Goal   An event, circumstance, object, condition, or purpose for which a person strives. Also, a conscious intention to do something.

Grazing   Eating meals on the run in order to make good use of time ordinarily spent sitting down for meals.

Group norms   The unwritten set of expectations for group members—what people ought to do.

Grudge   Unresolved or unexpressed anger felt against someone who we believe has wronged us.

Hands-on experience   Direct, practical experience in performing a task or skill. The expression seems to have derived from the hands-on experience of physicians in taking care of patients.

Human behavior   Any actions or activities engaged in by people, including both external (such as movement) and internal activities (such as thinking and feeling).

Human relations   The art of using systematic knowledge about human behavior to improve personal and job effectiveness.

Insight   A depth of understanding that requires considerable intuition and common sense.

Internal locus of control   A belief that one is the primary cause of events happening to oneself.

Interpersonal   Anything relating to the interactions between and among people.

Intimacy   A feeling of emotional closeness.

Intuition   Direct perception of truth or fact that seems to be independent of any reasoning process. Also, a keen and quick insight that can be helpful in solving complex problems.

IRA (individual retirement account)   A plan with tax advantages that supplements other retirement plans such as Social Security and employer benefit programs.

Job objective   The position one is applying for now or intends to hold in the future.

Job performance   The output of a job activity, or how well an employee does in meeting the demands of the job.

Job satisfaction   The amount of pleasure or contentment associated with a job. In contrast, **job motivation** refers to the effort directed toward achieving job goals.

Keogh Plan   A tax-deductible retirement plan for individuals who are self-employed or who earn part of their income from self-employment.

Leader   A person who exerts influence over others to achieve certain objectives.

Leadership   The process of influencing others to achieve certain objectives.

Leadership effectiveness   The extent to which the leader helps the group accomplish its objectives.

Leading task   An easy, warm-up activity that helps you get started on a project that you might otherwise procrastinate about doing.

Life-change units   Numerical values measuring the impact of specific changes on people.

Lifestyle   A person's typical approach to living, including moral attitudes, clothing preferences, and ways of spending money.

Liquid assets   Cash or valuables that can be converted into cash relatively quickly.

Maslow's need hierarchy   A widely accepted theory of motivation emphasizing that people strive to fulfill needs. These needs are arranged in a hierarchy of importance—physiological, safety, belongingness, esteem, and self-actualization. People tend to strive for need satisfaction at one level only after satisfaction has been achieved at the previous one.

Meditation   Putting oneself in a state of deep rest through conscious effort in order to reduce tension and feel well rested.

Medium   In communication, the mode in which the message is sent, such as writing or speaking.

Mental health   The general well-being of a person's emotional makeup. If you are tense, troubled, and unable to handle your problems you are said to be in poor mental health.

Mentor   Bosses who take subordinates under their wings and guide, teach and coach them.

Modeling   A form of learning in which a person learns a complex skill by watching another person or group of persons perform that skill. Also called leaning by limitation.

Motivation   An inner state of arousal directed toward a goal. Work motivation is motivation directed toward organizational objectives. Motivation is also an activity of managers designed to increase employee effort.

Need   A deficit within an individual that creates a craving for its satisfaction.

Negative inquiry   The active encouragement of criticism in order to use helpful information or exhaust manipulative criticism.

Negotiation   Dealing or bargaining with another individual, often with the interest of resolving conflict.

Net income   Income after certain standard deductions are made such as taxes, retirement fund payments, and medical and dental insurance.

Networking   Developing a wide range of personal contacts who can directly or indirectly help you in your career.

Nonpossessive relationship   A relationship in which both people maintain separate identities and strive for personal fulfillment.

Nonprogrammed decision   A decision for which alternative solutions have not been prepared in advance.

Nonverbal communication   Sending messages other than by direct use of words such as in writing and speaking. Also referred to as body language and silent messages.

Nonverbal feedback   Nonverbal communication used by the receiver in response to a message that suggests how well the message is being received. For example, the receiver might move closer to you if you are sending a message of interest to that person.

Office politics   Any method of gaining advantage that is not strictly related to merit in a job environment. Examples include laughing at your boss's jokes or going out of your way to compliment an important executive.

Oral communication   Any message or sending a message by speaking, singing, laughing, whispering, and so forth.

Participative leader   One who involves group members in decision making.

Passive (or nonassertive)   Behavior in which people let things happen to them without letting their feelings be known.

Perfectionism   A passion for extremely high standards along with a displeasure at achieving anything less. A perfectionist has compulsive tendencies.

Performance standard   A company statement of what constitutes acceptable performance.

Personal annual report   A yearly summary of your assets and liabilities.

Personal growth group   Small training groups similar in design and intent to encounter groups with an emphasis on personal growth. People usually attend growth groups to learn more about themselves and to get in touch with their feelings.

Personal productivity   One's level of efficiency and effectiveness.

Positive mental attitude   A strong belief that things will work out in your favor.

Positive reinforcement   Receiving a reward for making a particular response, such as getting approval from a boss for being prompt.

Power need   A strong need to control other people and resources and to seek fame.

Proactive/Reactive   Planning for events versus responding to events after they take place.

Problem   A gap between what exists and what you want to exist.

Programmed decision   A decision in which the alternative solutions are known in advance.

Private brainstorming   A modification of brainstorming conducted by yourself, rather than in a group setting.

Procrastination   Delaying action for no good reason at all.

Psychology   The study of mental processes and the behavior of human and animal organisms. Or, simply, the study of behavior.

Psychotherapy   A specialized discussion method for helping people deal with emotional problems.

Quality control   Checking to determine if the quality of a product or service is as high as planned.

Recognition   Explicitly noticing something of value that an individual has attained, such as handing out a trophy for good athletic performance.

Recognition need   The need to be noticed by others, usually for a worthwhile accomplishment.

Reference check   Calling or writing a previous employer of a job applicant to learn about his or her strengths and weaknesses.

Relaxation response   A bodily reaction in which you experience a slower respiration and heart rate, lowered blood pressure, and lowered metabolism.

Resource   Something of value held by an individual or an organization, including money, material, and time.

Rigid mental set   A fixed way of looking at things.

Role   Behavior expected of an individual occupying a given position within a group. It is part of a nutritionist's role, for example, to offer advice about eating the proper foods.

Role confusion   Being uncertain about what role you are carrying out.

Role underload   The experience of having too little to do in your job, often creating stress.

Schmoozing   Informal socializing on the job including small talk and telephone conversations.

Self   The total being of the individual, or one's interests, welfare, or advantage.

Self-acceptance   The attitude that what you do and what you are is favorable. Similar to self-approval or tolerance for both your strengths and weaknesses.

Self-actualization   Making maximum use of one's potential.

Self-concept   What you think of you and who you think you are.

Self-confidence   A belief in your own capabilities.

Self disclosure   The process of revealing yourself to others.

Self-employment   Earning, or attempting to earn, income through a business you establish or services you provide to the public.

Self-esteem   A sense of being worthwhile, similar to self-respect.

Self-understanding   The extent to which you have knowledge about yourself, particularly with respect to your mental and emotional aspects. Also, insight into oneself.

Sensitivity   Taking people's needs and feelings into account when dealing with them.

Sexism   A set of beliefs indicating that males and females should occupy distinctly different roles. The belief results in some forms of discrimination against members of each sex, such as not hiring a man for a secretarial position or a woman as a construction supervisor.

Sexual harassment   Any unwanted sexual advances toward another individual including demands for sexual favors, touching, or spoken comments.

Shy   To be hesitant about or have difficulty in expressing feelings, attitudes, and opinions, especially to strangers.

Skill   A learned, specific ability such as riding a bicycle, or using a specific computer program.

Social support   Friendly, approachable, trustworthy, cooperative, and warm attitude of the social network to which a person belongs.

Sponsor   A higher-ranking individual who is favorably impressed with you and therefore recommends you for promotion and choice assignments.

Stress   An internal reaction to any force that threatens to disturb a person's equilibrium.

Stress interview   A deliberate method of placing a job applicant under considerable pressure and then observing his or her reactions.

Stressor   A force that creates stress such as heavy work demands or aggravation.

Style   A person's body language rather than the content of his or her message. Also, a person's characteristic approach to handling situations.

Swim against the tide   A career-advancement tactic in which you take an unconventional path to career success.

Swiss-cheese method   A method of fighting procrastination whereby you "eat holes" in a large task until it is completed. You thus work on the task a little bit at a time.

Synergy   The action of two or more people to achieve an effect that none of the people could achieve individually. The whole is greater than the sum of the parts.

Target position   The ultimate goal you are seeking in your career path.

Target résumé   A job résumé focusing on a specific job target, or position that presents only information about you that supports the target.

Team player   A group member who freely cooperates with others and is more concerned about group success than personal success.

Technical competence

Tension   Mental or emotional strain; a feeling of internal uneasiness that is usually associated with stress or an unsatisfied need.

Type A behavior   A pattern of being aggressively involved in a chronic, incessant struggle to achieve more in less and less time. A Type A personality exhibits Type A behavior.

Unsolicited letter campaign   A job search method in which the job seeker sends letters to prospective employers without knowing if a job opening exists.

Visualization   As a stress-management technique, picturing yourself doing something you would like to do. In general, a method of imagining yourself behaving in a particular way in order to achieve that behavior.

Work habits   A person's characteristic approach to work, including such things as organization, handling of paper work, and the setting of priorities.

Indexes

NAME INDEX

446

SUBJECT INDEX